Law and Religion in the Early Modern Period
Recht und Religion in der Frühen Neuzeit

Law and Religion in the Early Modern Period
Recht und Religion in der Frühen Neuzeit

VOL. 5

Tarald Rasmussen, Jørn Øyrehagen Sunde (Eds.)

Protestant Legacies in Nordic Law

The Early Modern Period

BRILL | SCHÖNINGH

Cover illustration:
King Gustav Vasa of Sweden with a ceremonial sword, symbolizing the king's responsibility to defend the Law of God (Lex Dei) and the Swedish Law (Lex Svedsiae). The picture is painted in a law codex at the National Library of Sweden. Photograph: Hans Lindahl

Bibliographic information published by the Deutsche Nationalbibliothek

The Deutsche Nationalbibliothek lists this publication in the Deutsche Nationalbibliografie; detailed bibliographic data available online: http://dnb.d-nb.de

www.schoeningh.de

Cover design: Nora Krull, Hamburg
Production: Brill Deutschland GmbH, Paderborn

ISSN 2629-6926
ISBN 978-3-506-79074-3 (hardback)
ISBN 978-3-657-79074-6 (e-book)

Contents

Introduction

The Nordic has become a *topos*. The Nordic model[1] and Nordic exceptionalism[2] are popular notions and research topics.[3] However, the idea of the Nordic countries Iceland, Norway, Denmark, Sweden and Finland as different is a rather old one. For example, in his influential *The Spirit of the Laws* from 1748, Charles Montesquieu differentiates between the north and south as a part of his climate theory, and claims that the cold climate in the north favoured a higher moral standard:

> You will find in the northern climates peoples who have few vices, enough virtues, and much sincerity and frankness. As you move toward the countries of the south, you will believe you have moved away from morality itself: the liveliest passions will increase crime; each will seek to take from others all the advantages that can favor these same passions. In temperate countries, you will see peoples whose manners, and even their vices and virtues are inconstant; the climate is not sufficiently settled to fix them.[4]

More important is that Montesquieu's idea of freedom in the north was especially developed by Paul Henri Mallet,[5] which in turn influenced how Nordic intellectuals, for instance Tyge Rothe, viewed the Nordic. The ideas of Nordic exceptionalism do not, however, appear to gain a broader popular interest in the Nordic countries before the second half of the nineteenth century, embedded in the Scandinavianism movement. For example, the students in Lund in southern Sweden wrote to their fellow students in Oslo in Norway in 1869,

1 See for instance https://www.investopedia.com/articles/investing/100714/nordic-model-pros-and-cons.asp accessed 19 October 2021 and https://www.lo.no/language/english/english-news/the-nordic-model-for-dummies/ accessed 19 October 2021.

2 See for instance; R. Hirsch, "The Nordic counternarrative: Democracy, human development, and judicial review", *International Journal of Constitutional Law*, Vol. 9 no. 2 2011: 449–469.

3 See for instance https://worldhappiness.report/ed/2020/the-nordic-exceptionalism-what-explains-why-the-nordic-countries-are-constantly-among-the-happiest-in-the-world/ accessed 19 October 2021, https://nordics.info/themes/the-nordic-model/ accessed 19 October 2021, and https://www.sv.uio.no/iss/english/research/research-areas/the-nordic-model/ accessed 19 October 2021. See also *Institutional Change in the Public Sphere: Views on the Nordic Model*, F. Engelstad, H. Larsen, J. Rogstad (eds.), Berlin: 2017, and J. Delhey, K. Newton, "Predicting Cross-National Levels of Social Trust: Global Pattern or Nordic Exceptionalism?" *European Sociological Review*, Vol. 21, no. 4 2005: 311–327.

4 C. Montesquieu, *The Spirit of the Laws*, A. M. Cohler, B. C. Miller, H. S. Stone (eds.) Cambridge 1989: 234.

5 H. A. Barton, "The Discovery of Norway Abroad, 1760–1905", *Scandinavian Studies*, Vol. 27 no. 1 2007: 27 (25–40).

underlining that the purpose of higher education was to sow the seeds for a common Nordic culture, seeds that are found in all in the Nordic countries.[6] The Scandinavianism movement soon adopted different types of institutional structures. Among the least successful we find the Scandinavian church meetings from 1857 to 1861,[7] while amongst the most successful we find the Nordic Meeting of Lawyers from 1872 until the present.[8]

The idea of the Nordic as a unity with internal similarities and external differences can be tested by applying a cultural model developed by Geert Hofstede.[9] This model measures the feeling of power distance,[10] individualism versus collectivism,[11] masculinity versus femininity,[12] uncertainty avoidance,[13]

6 *Morgenbladet* 29 July 1869; (…) i samma mån skola och de frön till en werkligt gemensam nordisk kultur, hvilka Nordens folk under alla egendomligheterna bära hos sig, alltmer kallas till if och skjuta brodd."

7 D. Torkildsen, "Lutherdom og nasjonal identitet i Norden", *Teologisk tidsskrift*, 6 (2017): 46–48 (42–54).

8 J. Ø. Sunde, "The History of Nordic Legal Culture and Court Culture: The Story of What Should not Have Been, but Still Came to Be", L. Evro, P. Letto-Vanamo, A. Nylund (eds.): *Rethinking Nordic Courts*, Springer, 2021: 62–64.

9 This is also done in Sunde (2021): 50–51 (47–69).

10 "People in societies exhibiting a large degree of Power Distance accept a hierarchical order in which everybody has a place and which needs no further justification. In societies with low Power Distance, people strive to equalise the distribution of power and demand justification for inequalities of power"; https://hi.hofstede-insights.com/national-culture accessed 20 October 2021.

11 "The high side of this dimension, called Individualism, can be defined as a preference for a loosely-knit social framework in which individuals are expected to take care of only themselves and their immediate families. Its opposite, Collectivism, represents a preference for a tightly-knit framework in society in which individuals can expect their relatives or members of a particular ingroup to look after them in exchange for unquestioning loyalty"; https://hi.hofstede-insights.com/national-culture accessed 20 October 2021.

12 "The Masculinity side of this dimension represents a preference in society for achievement, heroism, assertiveness, and material rewards for success. Society at large is more competitive. Its opposite, Femininity, stands for a preference for cooperation, modesty, caring for the weak and quality of life. Society at large is more consensus-oriented"; https://hi.hofstede-insights.com/national-culture accessed 20 October 2021.

13 "The Uncertainty Avoidance dimension expresses the degree to which the members of a society feel uncomfortable with uncertainty and ambiguity. (…) Countries exhibiting strong UAI maintain rigid codes of belief and behaviour, and are intolerant of unorthodox behaviour and ideas. Weak UAI societies maintain a more relaxed attitude in which practice counts more than principles"; https://hi.hofstede-insights.com/national-culture accessed 20 October 2021.

long-term versus short-term orientation,[14] and indulgence versus restraint.[15] According to this model, the Nordic countries are characterised – in short and with some variations – by a mentality of equality, collectivism, cooperation, stability, strong social norms and a balance between an orientation towards the past and the future.[16] If we compare with the Baltic states Estonia, Latvia and Lithuania – an area in Europe that can be considered almost semi-Nordic – we find that they score similarly to the Nordic countries, but there they are more focused on the future and have much weaker social norms.[17] If we instead compare with north-western Europe, which historically has been economically and culturally close to the Nordic countries, we find that there is less of a desire to cooperate on stability and more of a focus on the future rather than the past in the United Kingdom, France, Belgium, the Netherlands and Germany than in the Nordic countries.[18] If we then lastly compare with the Mediterranean countries, we find that any similarities with France, Portugal, Spain and Italy are coincidental in an otherwise pattern of differences.[19]

As we have seen, the Scandinavian church meetings from 1856 to 1861 and the Nordic Meeting of Lawyers from 1872 were early attempts to institutionalise Nordic cooperation based on a notion of Nordic exceptionalism. The peculiarities of the Nordic Reformation and the Nordic Protestant Churches have contributed to this notion. When exploring this phenomenon from a legal point of departure, Heikki Pihlajamäki, Jaakko Husa and Kimmo Nuotio

14 "Every society has to maintain some links with its own past while dealing with the challenges of the present and the future. (…) Societies who score low on this dimension, for example, prefer to maintain time-honoured traditions and norms while viewing societal change with suspicion. Those with a culture which scores high, on the other hand, take a more pragmatic approach: they encourage thrift and efforts in modern education as a way to prepare for the future", https://hi.hofstede-insights.com/national-culture accessed 20 October 2021.

15 "Indulgence stands for a society that allows relatively free gratification of basic and natural human drives related to enjoying life and having fun. Restraint stands for a society that suppresses gratification of needs and regulates it by means of strict social norms"; https://hi.hofstede-insights.com/national-culture accessed 20 October 2021.

16 https://www.hofstede-insights.com/country-comparison/denmark,finland,norway,sweden/ and https://www.hofstede-insights.com/country-comparison/iceland/ accessed 20 October 2021.

17 https://www.hofstede-insights.com/country-comparison/estonia,latvia,lithuania/ accessed 20 October 2021.

18 https://www.hofstede-insights.com/country-comparison/belgium,germany,the-netherlands,the-uk/ accessed 19 October 2021.

19 https://www.hofstede-insights.com/country-comparison/france,italy,portugal,spain/ accessed 19 October 2021.

conclude that "Lutheran influence is relevant for the Nordic legal mentality in general." They continue:

> We do not claim that the Nordic countries were the only geographical area where this secularisation of religious ethics took place, but this aspect of Lutheranism has flourished and is important even today in the Nordic legal and social life.[20]

Even if Pihlajamäki, Husa and Nuotio give some examples of Lutheran influence on the development of secular law in the Nordic countries, their mission is one of comparative law and not the relationship between law and religion in the Nordic countries, and hence they do not explore this theme in more depth. That is instead the point of departure for the *Protestant Legacies in Nordic Law* (ProNoLa) project:

> ProNoLa aims to provide a nuanced and critical genealogy of the negotiations of law and religion in the northern parts of Europe from the Reformation and up to the present. The research efforts will focus on the particular constellations between law and religion in the West-Nordic realm (Denmark and Norway), the East-Nordic realm (Sweden and Finland), and the German realm (the mixed case), in order to analyse the use of theological norms and standards as a framework for a general understanding of law as secular.[21]

The project was funded by HERA (Humanities in the European Research Area), with Lisbet Christoffersen (Roskilde and Copenhagen) as project leader. The first seminar in the project, on Confessionalization and Institutionalization, covered the period from the early sixteenth to the late eighteenth centuries, with the aim of exploring the relationship between Lutheranism and law in this formative period for the modern Nordic states.[22] The obvious point of departure is the Reformation in Germany. In his chapter, Henning Bühmann explores the disputations at the Wittenberg Theological Faculty 1511–1522. The open and critical debate these disputations initiated can be seen as the very framework of the Reformation. It is hence of great interest that legal arguments were frequently used in them. However, Bühmann also finds a change in the character of these legal arguments from canon law to divine law, as expounded

20 J. Husa, K. Nuotio, H. Pihlajamäki, "Nordic Law – Between Tradition and Dynamism", *Nordic Law – Between Tradition and Dynamism*, J. Husa, K. Nuotio, H. Pihlajamäki (eds), Antwerpen 2007: 24 (1–39).

21 https://teol.ku.dk/pronola/about/ accessed 21 October 2021.

22 Another volume deals with recent developments: Slotte, Pamela; Gregersen, Niels Henrik & Årsheim, Helge: *Internationalization and Re-Confessionalization. Law and Religion in the Nordic Realm 1945–2017*. Odense 2022.

in Scripture. But just as important as the character of the legal arguments was the combination of the religious reform and social justice they were tied to. This led to the demand for man-made law to improve the situation of the unfortunates in society, with theology not as the source of law but as an input in the legislative process. This can be seen as the "seculiarsation of religious ethics" that Pihlijamäki, Husa and Nuotio speak of as a fundamental trace of Nordic law even today, in their eyes underpinning the Nordic welfare state.

Wim Decock's chapter shows how the development towards a focus on law and social justice within the Reformed Church offered Catholic *teólogos-juristas* a challenge they responded to by putting more attention on the socio-economic aspects and participation in the administration of justice and charity. The drive towards an order of theology as an input in a legislative process run by secular authorities was hence strengthened through scholarly efforts in the remaining Catholic parts of Europe as in the newly reformed parts. Decock also discusses this as secularisation, and stresses that it neither implies "the loss of religious faith", nor "a diminished role of the Christian belief as a source of inspiration for legislation and governance". Instead, Decock refers to Harold Berman's view that it can be better seen as a "transfer of jurisdictional power from ecclesiastical institutions to secular authorities in the sixteenth century."

Decock's chapter reminds us of the complex effects of historical events and how ideas take different forms as they travel from one context to another. This is also an underlying theme in Mathias Schmoeckel's chapter. The main protagonist in his text is Johannes Bugenhagen, one of the theologians in the circle around Martin Luther. He was first a key person in establishing the Reformation in the southern part of the Danish-Norwegian realm, the duchy of Schleswig-Holstein. Later, in 1537, he designed the Church ordinance for Denmark, also applied in Norway. By studying Bugenhagen's contribution to the Danish-Norwegian Reformation, Schmoeckel can document how the same man with the same ideas exercised different influence in different parts of the same realm depending on the context. In doing this, Schmoeckel turns the Danish-Norwegian realm into a laboratory for studying the hypothesis that "[i]t might be possible that the Reformation influenced the European territories in different ways."

Tarald Rasmussen's chapter deals with the specific profile of the Danish Reformation and Bugenhagen's Church ordinance for Denmark, compared to the Swedish ordinance from 1571, in the context of the quite different reformation process in Sweden. The comparative approach has a focus on two specific issues: the relationship of the King to the ecclesiastical hierarchy and the way of defining and regulating the office of the Superintendent/Bishop. A detailed analysis of these issues is also relevant for identifying more fundamental differences between the Reformation in two realms otherwise dominated by the same kind of confessional culture.

Johan Bastubacka's text brings us to the eastern regions of the kingdom of Sweden around 1640, at that time recently added to the realm as new territories. Integrating the population of these regions – with another language and writing system, other ecclesiastical structures, another law and another administrative practice – into the realm was an important challenge for the emerging absolute monarch. Bastubacka investigates this little known part of Swedish history by using a 1643 report from Bishop Bjugge from Kexholm in the periphery of the Swedish realm as a key source.

One reason why the Reformation had a different outcome in the Danish-Norwegian realm than in other parts of Europe is the lack of a solid learned law tradition. We have seen how in his chapter Bühmann explores the legal arguments in the disputations in Wittenberg 1511–1522, and how Decock examines the work by Catholic *teólogos-juristas*. Even if there were individuals working in this learned tradition in the Nordic countries, for example Niels Hemmingsen in Denmark, Gjeble Pederssøn in Norway and Olaus Petri in Sweden, there was no broad and continuous tradition. This is part of the context that Schmoeckel deals with, and it is the theme for Kjell Åke Modéer's chapter. In short, the Nordic countries used the sixteenth century to shake off the Middle Ages, and in the seventeenth century started to establish a learnèd tradition, closely linked to a growth in administration that in the eighteenth century would become the bureaucracy, the code of the modern Nordic state. Part of the Reformation-initiated intellectual renewal was the role Mosaic law played in updating Swedish law in the seventeenth century. This is also a core example of how the – at this time – underdeveloped legal tradition acquired a much needed dynamic through theology.

Kristian Mejrup's chapter deals with the intertwinement of religion and law in the radical reform processes taking place in Denmark in the 1730s. Celebrating 200 years of Lutheran Reformation in Denmark in 1736 was accompanied on the one hand by new royal decrees aimed at strengthening individual Protestant piety in the population, and, on the other hand, by efforts to promote legal studies and enforce new and modern standards of legal education for civil servants in Denmark. The outcome was a significant and quite original combination of traditional religion and enlightenment.

Jørn Øyrehagen Sunde Tarald Rasmussen

The Use of Legal Concepts and the Definitions of Law Used in the Disputation Theses Discussed at the Wittenberg Theological Faculty 1511–1522

Henning Bühmann

Any exploration of the influence of Lutheran theology and academic culture on the development of law and its understanding requires us to return to the very beginnings of Lutheranism. The Reformation movement started in 1517 as "a partial revolt in the sector of university theology [...]."[1] As its vehicle, the Wittenberg movement around Martin Luther sought to develop a new form of theology. Adopting a collective approach to this task, Luther and his collaborators developed their innovative theology through group discussion.[2]

1 *"Die lutherische Reformation war, aufs Ganze der europäischen Gesellschaft gesehen, in ihrer allerersten Phase, die 1516/17 sichtbar wird, eine ganz partielle Revolte in einem einzigen wichtigen Lebenssektor, nämlich im Bereich der Universitätstheologie"* (Kurt Victor Selge. "Das Autoritätengefüge der westlichen Christenheit im Lutherkonflikt 1517 bis 1521." *HZ* 223 [1976]: 591–618, 593). I was able to present initial ideas for this article at the panel "Religious Colloquies in the 1520s and 1530s" held at the International Congress for Luther Research in Wittenberg in Summer 2017, thanks to a grant from the HERA (Humanities in the European Research Area)-funded project "Protestant Legacies in Nordic Law". I would like to thank Professor Gordon Jensen (Lutheran Theological Seminary Saskatoon) and Professor Cameron MacKenzie (Concordia Theological Seminary Fort Wayne) for their helpful comments. I would also like to extend my thanks to the Deutsche Forschungsgemeinschaft (DFG) for its support in funding the project "The Early Wittenberg Theses: Theses and Disputations in Wittenberg 1516 to 1523". During the period covered by the project, I was able to expand the article substantially, deepening my understanding of the issues involved. Professor Ulrich Bubenheimer (Reutlingen) read the script for my talk at the Rosendahl Conference and provided many new insights, which I tried to incorporate in this essay. Dr. Rick Serina jr. (Ringwood, NJ) also read an earlier draft. I would also like to thank Ariel Royer (Göttingen) and Alyssa Lehr Evans (Princeton) for correcting early drafts of the text. Dr. Harald Bollbuck (Göttingen) and Michael Dormandy (Cambridge) checked the Latin quotations and their translations. Andrew Smith (Berlin) thoroughly revised and checked the final manuscript; John Anthony (Trondheim) performed proof reading. My forthcoming *Habilitationsschrift "Die frühen Wittenberger Thesen: Studien zum Wittenberger Disputationswesen und seiner Überlieferung"* will incorporate a German language version of this article.

2 Cf. Jens Martin Kruse. *Universitätstheologie und Kirchenreform: Die Anfänge der Reformation in Wittenberg 1516–1522*. Mainz: von Zabern 2002, 391–396; Ulrich Bubenheimer labels it "experimental theology", cf. Ulrich Bubenheimer. "Andreas Karlstadts und Martin Luthers frühe Reformationsdiplomatie. Thesenanschläge des Jahres 1517, Luthers 'Asterisci' gegen Johannes Eck und Wittenberger antirömische Polemik während des Augsburger Reichstages." *Blätter für Pfälzische Kirchengeschichte und religiöse Volkskunde* 85 (2018): 265–302,301 f.

 | DOI:10.30965/9783657790746_002

The popular dissemination of the results of this academic debate and the wide public acclaim with which it was met transformed what began as an obscure academic undertaking into a mass movement, which would eventually transform the religious and political landscape of Latin Europe almost beyond recognition.[3] The revolutionary nature of the new Wittenberg theology meant that it soon had implications for the legal order of first the Church, then the State, and finally society at large. Affecting not just the regulation of various public corporations, Luther's theology went to the root of doctrines of law, the relationship between law and the divine origin of justice, and the fundamental theory and practice of jurisprudence.

The radically innovative impact of the Wittenberg academic debate in transforming not only academic theology, but the world around it, makes its study a matter of pressing historical concern. Important and previously neglected sources for these discussions are provided by the disputation theses used as a central part of academic training at the Wittenberg Theological Faculty during the early phase of the Reformation. The preservation of over 80 sets of theses allows a comprehensive insight not only into the formal nature of sixteenth century academic training, but also into the new theology to which it gave rise.[4] Whilst legal matters never dominated the principally theological discourse in Wittenberg, we shall see that from their inception, Luther's proposals for religious reform had implications both for the legal constitution of Church and State and academic jurisprudence.

This article seeks to explore how law and jurisprudence were treated in the disputation theses presented and debated at Wittenberg Theological Faculty between 1511 and 1522. To this end, it seeks to analyse the ways in and purposes to which legal terminology was deployed in the disputations and the assumptions on which they rested. How did the authors of these disputation theses define 'law' and how did these definitions change during the period under investigation?

3 Cf. Thomas Kaufmann. *Erlöste und Verdammte. Eine Geschichte der Reformation.* 2nd ed. Munich: Beck, 2017, passim.

4 At present, the Wittenberg theses have not been collected. For Luther's theses, cf. Reinhard Schwarz, "Disputationen." In *Luther-Handbuch*, ed. Albrecht Beutel. Tübingen: Mohr Siebeck 2005, 328–340; several of Melanchthon's theses are printed in Philipp Melanchthon. *Melanchthons Werke in Auswahl, vol. 1. Reformatorische Schriften*, ed. Robert Stupperich. Gütersloh: Bertelsmann, 1951; for Karlstadt's disputations cf. Hermann Barge. *Andreas Bodenstein von Karlstadt, vol. 1. Karlstadt und die Anfänge der Reformation.* Leipzig: Brandstetter 1905, 472–497; several other sets of theses edited by Theodor Kolde. "Wittenberger Disputationsthesen aus den Jahren 1516 bis 1522." *ZKG* 11 (1890), 448–471.

This analysis will proceed in five steps. Firstly, it will introduce the role assumed by disputations in academic discourses in traditional university instruction. This will be followed by a chronological reconstruction of the way in which legal issues were addressed in disputation theses in Wittenberg over four periods:[5] 1516 to 1518 (the development of a new theology); 1519 to 1520 (the impact of the papal attempt to suppress the Reformation on the Reformers' view of law); 1521 to 1522 (the development and implementation of a package of social and ecclesiastical reforms); and the period after 1522 during which the Wittenberg Reformers took a range of decisions which set in train the development towards a state church. This final section will trace how the failure of the Wittenberg circle to re-establish the life of the Church on the foundation of evangelical principles forced Luther and Melanchthon to reconsider their ecclesiology after 1522, and how this resulted in a concept of ecclesiastical government in which the Church was subject to the rule of princes and magistrates as its supreme governors. It will also include an examination of the function performed by disputations in legitimising the Magisterial Reformation and the reforms of cities and territories which it entailed. The conclusion will summarise the role played by disputations in the development of the early Lutheran Reformation, as well as the interaction of the Wittenberg Reformers with issues of law.

1. Disputations in Wittenberg

The ongoing debate as to whether Luther did in fact nail his *95 Theses Against Indulgences* to the doors of All Saints' Church Wittenberg[6] is a continuing reminder of the role and significance which disputations assumed in the formulation and development of Reformation theology.[7] In the 1520s, printed collections of disputation theses from Wittenberg achieved widespread dissemination, presenting the results of the discussions held in Wittenberg to the European Republic of Letters.[8] The centrality of disputations as a vehicle

5 This periodisation follows Kruse, *Universitätstheologie*, 28 f.

6 Cf. Joachim Ott and Martin Treu, eds. *Luthers Thesenanschlag: Fakt oder Fiktion*. Leipzig: Evangelische Verlagsanstalt, 2008.

7 This has been demonstrated by Kruse, *Universitätstheologie*, esp. 394.

8 *Insignium theologorum Domini Martini lutheri, domini Andree Carolstadii, Philippi Melanthonis et aliorum, conclusiones varie, per divine gratie defensione ac commendatione: contra scolasticos & pelagianos: disputate in preclara academia Wittenbergensi* ... Leiden: Jan Seversz, 1521. I would like to thank Dr Alejandro Zorzin (Göttingen) for providing me with a digitalisation of this text from the Waldensian library in Torre Pellice. *Insignium theologorum*

for the progress of the Reformation discourse is explained by reference to the medieval university context and the vital role which disputations assumed in it.[9] That disputations were an everyday part of university life is shown by a study of the statutes of the theological faculty in Wittenberg. Students were already familiar with the practice of disputation from their studies of the *artes liberales* and were required to participate in weekly circular disputations during their academic theological training. Every examination for a degree culminated in a graduation disputation and doctoral candidates were required to pass two such disputations. For their part, professors were required to hold regular public disputations, which performed a central representative function in advertising the work of the faculty.[10]

Socialised in the complex process of argumentation required by the practice of disputation, by the time they had come to study theology, students had internalised the complex rules[11] according to which disputations were 'performed' and the various highly-formalised roles assigned to their participants.[12] In the

---

Domini Martini Lutheri, domini Andree Barolostadii, Philippi melanthonis et aliorum conclusiones varie, pro divinae gratiae defensione ac commendatione, contra scolasticos et pelagianos disputate in praeclara academia.Wittembergensi ... Paris: Pierre Vidoue, 1521?. *Christianissimi Wittenbergensis Gymnasii multarum Disputationum paradoxa & plane enigmata in Papistica illa mendaciis Confusissima ecclesia*. Basel: Adam Petri, 1521. *Lutheri, Melanch., Carolostadii etc. propositiones Wittembergae viva voce tractatae, in hocque pleraeque aeditae ab auctoribus, ut vel nos absentes cum ipsis agamus, vel certe ut veritatis, & seductionum admoneatur boni* ... Basel: Adam Petri, 1522. *Proposiciones a Marti. Luthero subinde disputatae* ... Wittenberg: Joseph Klug 1530.

9 For the Wittenberg disputation culture, cf. Henning Bühmann. "The Wittenberg Disputation Culture and Luther's and Eck's Debate in Leipzig." In *Luther at Leipzig: Martin Luther, the Leipzig Debate and the Sixteenth Century Reformations*, ed. Mickey L. Mattox / Jonathan Mumme / Richard J. Serrina jun. Leiden et al.: Brill, 2019: 61–92.

10 For the different kinds of disputation specified by the statutes of Wittenberg Theological Faculty, cf. Paul Drews. *Disputationen Dr. Martin Luthers in den Jahren 1535–1545 an der Universität Wittenberg gehalten.* Göttingen: Vandenhoeck und Ruprecht, 1895, VII–XXV. Professor Bubenheimer pointed out to me that the participation of Wittenberg professors in disputations held outside Wittenberg also served a representative function. One example is the participation of Karlstadt in a disputation held in Halberstadt in 1509; cf. Gustav Bauch, "Andreas Carlstadt als Scholastiker." *ZKG* 18 (1898): 37–57, 50.

11 An excellent summary of these rules is provided in Anselm Schubert. "Libertas Disputandi. Luther und die Leipziger Disputation als akademisches Streitgespräch." *ZThK* 105 (2008): 411–442, 414–419. For a practical discussion, cf. Schubert's reconstruction of the Leipzig debate, ibid., 419–442.

12 Despite finds of exercise material for the instruction of disputations, almost no research has been conducted into the ways in which disputation techniques were taught to students, cf. Jan-Hendrik de Boer. "Disputation, quaestio disputata." In *Universitäre Gelehrtenkultur vom 13.–16. Jahrhundert: Ein interdisziplinäres Quellen- und Methodenhandbuch*, ed. Jan-Hendryk de Boer, Marian Füssel, and Maximilian Schuh. Stuttgart: Franz Steiner

early sixteenth century, disputations were conducted on the basis of a set of theses.[13] Faced by the attacks of one or several opponents, a single participant was cast in the role of the '*respondens*,' and tasked with defending a set of theses, usually composed by the presiding professor as *magister* or *praeses*, who was then required to determine the result of the disputation, summarising the positive and negative points made in the discussion.[14] This arrangement ensured that arguments became more complex, as respondents were only permitted to answer the arguments of their adversaries.[15]

The shared culture of disputation, common to the Faculty of Arts and the higher faculties of Theology, Law and Medicine,[16] was indicative of a universal belief in, and search for, an indivisible and attainable 'Truth'. The consensus was that the veneration of received authorities combined with the correct application of the rules of scholastic dialectic within a highly-formalised academic discourse would act as a fail-safe guide to this Truth.[17] This was thought to be as true for Scripture and the Church Fathers as for the codes of civil and canon law. It was in this vein that Frederick the Wise, Prince-Elector of Saxony, had established Wittenberg University: to become a beacon of truth to guide the ships of both Church and State within his territory.[18]

The trans-disciplinary belief in the attainability of universal truth made for a high degree of interdisciplinary consultation. Put simply, if a Theologian assumed that his legal colleagues were capable of unearthing real truth, he

---

Verlag, 2018, 223. Ulrich Bubenheimer has found at least one manuscript which sheds light on this training (private communication with the author).

13 Cf. de Boer, "Disputation," 227 f.; de Boer's essay gives a good a general overview. For further literature, cf. Marion Gindhart, Hanspeter Marti, and Robert Seidel, eds. *Frühneuzeitliche Disputationen: Polyvalente Produktionsapparate gelehrten Wissens*, Cologne: Böhlau, 2016; Alex J. Novikoff. *The Medieval Culture of Disputation: Pedagogy, Practice and Performance*. Philadelphia: University of Pennsylvania Press, 2013.

14 Cf. Ulrich Bubenheimer. *Thomas Müntzer und Wittenberg*. Mühlhausen: Thomas Müntzer-Gesellschaft e. V., 2014, 20 f. Concerning the authorship of sets of theses cf. Drews, *Disputationen*, XVI.

15 Cf. Schubert, "Libertas Disputandi," 417, de Boer, "Disputation," 222 f.

16 On the traditional university system, cf. Herbert Grundmann. *Vom Ursprung der Universität im Mittelalter*. 2nd ed. Darmstadt: Wissenschaftliche Buchgesellschaft, 1960.

17 Anselm Schubert calls disputations a "*nach strengen Regeln funktionierendes logisches Verfahren zur Wahrheitsfindung*" (Schubert, "Libertas Disputandi," 413); for the concept of universal Truth cf. Ernst Wolf. "Zur wissenschaftsgeschichtlichen Bedeutung der Disputationen an der Wittenberger Universität im 16. Jahrhundert." In *Peregrinatio, vol. 2. Studien zur reformatorischen Theologie, zum Kirchenrecht und zur Sozialethik*, by ibid. Munich: Chr. Kaiser, 1965, 48–50.

18 Cf. Natalie Krentz. *Ritualwandel und Deutungshoheit: Die frühe Reformation in der Residenzstadt Wittenberg (1500–1533)*. Tübingen: Mohr Siebeck, 2014, 103–124.

considered himself well-advised to listen to them. This is borne out by evidence from Wittenberg showing close and interested contacts between staff at the Faculties of Law and Theology. This situation was reinforced by the disciplinary intersection of canon law within the otherwise separate faculties,[19] and also explains the common practice of theologians studying for a law degree. Whilst Luther had quit his legal studies before entering the Augustinian monastery at Erfurt, his colleague Andreas Bodenstein von Karlstadt held a doctorate in both civil and canon law.[20]

The confluence of interest between the legal and theological faculties explains the participation of the staff from each faculty in the disputations of the other. One example is provided by an entry in the Dean's Book of the Faculty of Law. In December 1511, Hieronymus Schurff, Professor of Law at Wittenberg, convened a disputation for a Bachelor's degree in civil and canon law which saw the attendance of professors of theology such as Petrus Lupin, Johann Dölsch, and Karlstadt, but not Luther.[21] The subject of this disputation is of particular interest:

> *"Sicut solus conatus regulariter, quamvis careat effectu, de iure puniendus est, ita sola voluntas et firmum propositum contritorum confitendi suo sacerdoti tempore ab ecclesia instituto absque actuali confessione sufficiunt regulariter ad consequendas indulgentias, a summo pontifice vel ab inferiori vere contritis et confessis concessas."*[22]

A sentence drawn from the study of civil law was presented as a guiding principle for a theological question: the question of forgiveness of sin and the remission of the penalties incurred. This disputation thesis is a good example of the common approach maintained at this time between theology and law and the overlapping interests of the two disciplines. Whilst the question of forgiveness was at root theological, in the case of indulgences it also became a question for canon lawyers. Thus, it becomes clear that a general discussion of indulgences

---

19 Cf. Walter Friedensburg. *Geschichte der Universität Wittenberg*. Halle (Saale): Niemeyer, 1917, 57–62.

20 Cf. Ulrich Bubenheimer. *Consonantia theologiae. Andreas Bodenstein von Karlstadt als Theologe und Jurist zwischen Scholastik und Reformation*. Tübingen: Mohr, 1977, 48–51. For Karlstadt's hermeneutics, which were heavily shaped by legal thought, cf. ibid., 281–287.

21 Cf. Bauch, "Carlstadt," 50 f.; Bubenheimer, *Consonantia*, 14 f.

22 "Just as an attempt alone, even if it remains without effect, is rightly to be punished by law, so intention alone and a firm commitment on the part of penitents to confess to their priest at the time set by the church, even if an actual confession did not take place, rightly suffices to achieve the indulgences, which are conceded by the Supreme Pontiff or by a minor [prelate] to those who are truly contrite and confessing"; quoted in Bauch, "Carlstadt," 51.

was underway in Wittenberg before Luther posted or otherwise issued his 95 theses.[23] As we shall see in the next section, the precise definition of the effects of indulgences was still controversial. This uncertainty meant that Luther's attack, not on the existence, but on the abuse of indulgences launched in the autumn of 1517 had a much greater impact than either he or others could ever have imagined.

2. The Development of Wittenberg University Theology 1516–1518 and its Legal Dimensions

Luther took his theological doctorate in 1512, a year after the first Wittenberg disputation on indulgences held at the Faculty of Law. Close examination of his subsequent teaching shows his adoption around 1515 of a new theology. Lecturing on Paul's Letter to the Romans, he displayed a revised understanding of human righteousness and divine justice. Moving away from the traditional focus on human responsibility and Man's capacity to earn grace through good works, he stressed instead the imputation of unearned merit on the basis of divine grace.[24]

2.1 *Disputations in Wittenberg 1516 and 1517*

Luther introduced his theology to his colleagues in autumn 1516 within the scope of the graduation disputation of his student Bartholomäus Bernhardi. During the disputation, Luther cast doubt on the traditional attribution to Augustine of the treatise *De vera et falsa poenitentia*.[25] Indeed, it was this disputation which persuaded Karlstadt first to make a closer study of at Augustine's teaching and then adopt Luther's theological position.[26] The disputation did

23 A further disputation on indulgences was held on All Saints' Day 1516, in which Luther criticised the monopoly held by the clergy of All Saints' Church, on hearing the confessions tied to the indulgences issued for visiting the collection of relics in Wittenberg. Upon hearing his theses, Karlstadt reprimanded Luther and threatened him with an accusation of heresy; cf. Bubenheimer, "Reformationsdiplomatie," 269 f.; Bubenheimer, *Consonantia*, 122–124.

24 Cf. Kruse, *Universitätstheologie*, 53–71.

25 On the disputation in September 1516, cf. Matthias Mikoteit. "Autoritätenverwendung in Bartholomäus Bernhardis Disputation der 'Quaestio de viribus hominis sine gratia'". In *Reformatorische Theologie und Autoritäten: Studien zur Genese des Schriftprinzips beim jungen Luther*. Tübingen: Mohr Siebeck, 2015, 22.

26 For the impact of Augustine on Karlstadt's thought, cf. Stefania Salvadori. "Der Augustin-Kommentar des Andreas Bodenstein von Karlstadt zwischen der Stilisierung einer Bekehrungsgeschichte und der (Wieder-)Entdeckung der biblisch-patristischen

not take any aspect of canon law as its immediate focus. Nevertheless, Luther knew that the pseudo-Augustinian *De vera et falsa poenitentia* constituted a major source for the *Decretum Gratiani*, which in turn had acted as the main source for canon law. As such, his attack had fundamental implications for the authority of canon law.[27]

This disregard for canon law shows the close links between theology and jurisprudence posited in the discussion; it also suggests the implications any campaign to reform Church doctrine might have on this jurisprudence. This consideration also applied to a set of 152 theses which Karlstadt posted on the doors of the churches in Wittenberg in April 1517,[28] and which served as an invitation to a disputation. Of especial importance was his seventh thesis: "*Sententia beati Augustini in moralibus nulli cedit<.> – co'ntra' can'onistas'.*"[29] As part of their programme, Karlstadt and the Wittenberg theologians attacked all received authorities whose teachings diverged from their understanding of Augustine's doctrine of sin and grace. As Ulrich Bubenheimer has demonstrated, this did not immediately lead Karlstadt to change his understanding and use of canon law concepts and his acceptance of papal authority. In a set of disputation theses from 1518, he deployed several arguments drawn from authorities on Roman and canon law to argue that jurisprudence was a better guide to theological reasoning than the traditional reliance on Aristotelian philosophy.[30]

2.2 *The Legal Implications of Luther's 95 Theses Against Indulgences*

The decisive step in the development of Wittenberg theology was the publication of Luther's *95 Theses* on indulgences in the autumn of 1517. Although at root a matter of theology, indulgences also touched on issues of canon law. Issued on the legal authority of a bishop or (in case of full indulgences) the Pope, they were originally only intended to grant freedom from works of penance imposed on the repentant sinner. The medieval Church viewed this solely as a matter of ecclesiastical jurisdiction, exercised on the basis of the Petrine

---

Quellen." *Blätter für Pfälzische Kirchengeschichte und religiöse Volkskunde* 85 (2018): 241–264.

27 Cf. Kruse, *Universitätstheologie*, 82; Mikoteit, "Autoritätenverwendung," 22.

28 In March 1517, Luther noted approvingly that Karlstadt was preparing an attack against scholastic theologians, whom Luther denounced as 'sophists', and against lawyers; cf. Bubenheimer, "Reformationsdiplomatie," 267 f.

29 "Sentences of the blessed Augustine concerning moral questions cede to no one. Against the Canonists"; Andreas Bodenstein von Karlstadt. "Centum Quinquagintaunum Conlusiones de natura, lege et gratia (1517, 26. April)." In *Kritische Gesamtausgabe der Schriften und Briefe Andreas Bodenstein von Karlstadts*, ed. Thomas Kaufmann, Harald Bollbuck et al., vol. 1,1. Gütersloh: Gütersloher Verlagshaus, 499.

30 Cf. Bubenheimer, *Consonantia*, 217–225.

authority to bind and loose (Matt 16:19). Theologians and lawyers alike regarded it as a privilege of ecclesiastical office holders, especially the Pope, to alleviate or even to remit works of satisfaction necessary to obtain forgiveness of sins. The papal dispensation (itself a legal act) intervened in the sacramental act of forgiving sin, thereby clouding the boundary between law and theology.[31]

During the course of the Middle Ages, the reach of indulgences had been extended from the sphere of earthly penance to that of purgatory; by the sixteenth century an indulgence could even be acquired by proxy on behalf of the deceased. The thirteenth century saw Albertus Magnus, Bonaventure and Thomas Aquinas discuss the ability of the Church on earth to influence the fate of souls in purgatory; these tentative discussions were first expressed as doctrine (in a papal bull) as late as 1476.[32] This extension of papal jurisdiction operated on the basis of the doctrine of the treasury of merit (*thesaurus ecclesiae*), the excess of virtue generated by Christ and the saints, which the episcopy could impute to the faithful in order to expiate divine anger.[33]

In spite of their centrality to Church teaching and practice, the concepts underpinning indulgences suffered from a paucity of definition. A matter of particular controversy was the question as to what exactly was pardoned by indulgences, and how their issue benefitted souls in purgatory.[34] Several

31 The argument of Cardinal Caietan's treatise *De indulgentiis*, explaining the theology of indulgences through an examination of papal enunciations, demonstrates the close connection between early modern law and theology in the early 16th century, cf. Bernhard Alfred M. Felmberg. *Die Ablasstheologie des Kartinal Cajetan (1469–1534)*. Leiden, Boston, and Cologne: Brill, 1998, 101–107. On the theology of medieval indulgencies cf. Arnold Angenendt. *Geschichte der Religiosität im Mittelalter.* Darmstadt: Wissenschaftliche Buchgesellschaft, 1997, 652–657; Bernd Moeller, "Die letzten Ablaßkampagnen: Luthers Widerspruch gegen den Ablaß in seinem geschichtlichen Zusammenhang." In *Die Reformation und das Mittelalter. Kirchenhistorische Aufsätze*, by Bernd Moeller. Göttingen: Vandenhoeck & Ruprecht, 1991, 53–72; Martin Heckel. *Martin Luthers Reformation und das Recht: Die Entwicklung der Theologie Luthers und ihre Auswirkung auf das Recht unter den Rahmenbedingungen der Reichsreform und der Territorialstaatsbildung im Kampf mit Rom und den Schwärmern.* Tübingen: Mohr Siebeck, 2016, 92–95; Robert W. Shaffern. "The Medieval Theology of Indulgences." In *Promissory Notes on the Treasure of Merit: Indulgences in Late Medieval Europe*, ed. Robert N. Swanson. Leiden and Boston: Brill, 2006, 11–36.

32 Cf. Sixtus IV. "Bulle 'Salvator noster' zugunsten der Kirche des hl. Petrus zu Saintes, 3. Aug. 1476." In *Kompendium der Glaubensbekenntnisse und kirchlichen Lehrentscheidungen*, ed. Heinrich Denzinger and Peter Hünermann. Freiburg et al.: Herder, 43 2010, no. 1398: 441 f.; on the origins of this practice and scholastic discussions of it cf. Robert W. Shaffern. "Learned Discussions of Indulgences for the Dead in Middle Ages." Church History 61 No. 4 (1992): 267–381.

33 Cf. Felmberg, *Ablasstheologie*, 114 f., 161–165.

34 Cf. Nikolaus Paulus. *Geschichte des Ablasses im Mittelalter, vol. 3. Geschichte des Ablasses am Ausgange des Mittelalters*. Paderborn: Schöningh, 1923, 92–116. One especially difficult

positions existed which even sought to limit the influence of indulgences to the remission of penalties, and rejected the possibility of issuing indulgences to the dead. Despite this ambiguity, most canonists and theologians argued that the issue of a papal letter of indulgence on earth did in fact influence the fate of souls in purgatory.[35]

As a legal institution, indulgences provided a link between the canonical jurisdiction of the Pope and the judgement of God in the afterlife, which in this way, was influenced by the decisions of the Catholic Church on earth.[36] Nevertheless, the lack of clarity in Church doctrine on indulgences combined with their widespread propagation constituted an open flank for critics like Luther, who were able to use it as a gateway for more thorough-going attacks on issues of fundamental doctrine. This situation was not only recognised by Luther, but also by his later adversary Cardinal Caietan, who sought to fill the gap in Church teaching with his treatise *De indulgentiis* from December 1517.[37] For his part, in launching his campaign, Luther was forced to consider areas of canon law which hitherto had not been the focus of his academic studies.

Luther dealt with the limitations of canon law early on in his *95 Theses*, from theses 5 to 13.[38] Thesis five declared: "*Papa non vult nec potest ullas penas remittere preter eas, quas arbitrio vel suo vel canonum imposuit.*"[39] In the eighth thesis Luther maintained: "*Canones penitentiales solum viventibus sunt impositi nihilque morituris secundum eosdem debet imponi.*"[40] In Luther's view, only the living were subject to the authority of canon law and the power of the Pope.[41] This subject is addressed again in thesis 13: "*Morituri per mortem omnia solvunt*

---

question was whether indulgences constituted an act of jurisdiction or rather intercession on behalf of the dead, cf. Shaffern, "Learned Discussions," 368–374; for discussions by canon lawyers cf. ibid., 374 f.

35 Cf. Christopher Voigt-Goy, "Luther und das Kanonische Recht in den 'Resolutiones disputationum de indulgentiarum virtute'." In *Reformatorische Theologie und Autoritäten. Studien zur Genese des Schriftprinzips beim jungen Luther*, ed. Volker Leppin. Tübingen: Mohr Siebeck, 2015, 89–92.

36 Whilst many scholastic theologians hesitated to regard the souls in Purgatory as subject to papal jurisdiction, several theologians emphasised the legal quality of papal actions, cf. Felmberg, *Ablasstheologie*, 116 f.

37 Cf. ibid., 11–13.

38 Luther, Martin. "Disputatio pro declaratione virtutis indulgentiarum. 1517." In *D. Martin Luthers Werke. Kritische Gesammtausgabe, vol. 1*, ed. Karl Knaake. Weimar: Böhlau, 233.18–234.2.

39 "The Pope cannot and does not want to remit any penalties, except those which he imposed either by his own will or the canons"; ibid., 233, 18 f.

40 "Penitential canons are only applied to the living; no part of them should be imposed on the dead", ibid., 233, 25 f.

41 Cf. Felmberg, *Ablasstheologie*, 281–284.

et legibus canonum mortui iam sunt, habentes iure earum relaxationem."[42] As such, Luther maintained that the dead were no longer subject to earthly penalties for sins committed during their lifetime, which had been remitted through death.[43]

Sets of theses were often accompanied by so-called *resolutiones*, which explained the arguments in favour of a certain thesis. Luther's *Resolutiones on the Theses on Indulgence* (published in 1518) also used canonical sources and authorities which supported his own interpretation of canon law.[44] In his *resolutio* to thesis 8, he argued:

> "*De solo enim verbo Christi dictum est: Inaeternum, domine, permanet verbum tuum, in saeculum saeculi veritas tua. Et iusticia eius manet in saeculum saeculi. Verbum autem et iusticia hominum manet ad tempus duntaxat.*"[45]

Luther sought to demonstrate that eternity can only be governed by God. The validity of human decrees, to which canon law belonged, were restricted to earthly existence and had no remit in the afterlife.[46] Luther argued that only Christ and not the Pope could grant remission from the burden of sin itself, as he asserted in the *resolutio* to his seventh thesis. Luther turned his ire less on the Pope (who at this point he still believed to be preaching the Gospel) than over-zealous canon lawyers, who, in Luther's view, sought to inflate the powers of the Pope and place him over the Word of Christ:

> "*Nec Iuristae eiusdem carnificinae segnes sunt authores, qui, dum nimio studio extollunt potestatem Papae, plus foecerunt aestimari et mirari potestatem Papae quam verbum Christi honorari fide, Cum docendi sint homines, ut non in potestatem Papae, sed in verbum Christi Papae promittentis confidere discant, Si modo velint esse pacati in conscientiis suis. Non enim quia Papa dat, aliquid habes, sed si credideris te accipere, habes: tantum habes, quantum credis propter promissionem Christi.*"[47]

---

42 "Dying persons are entirely absolved by their death and are already dead to canon law, because they have been freed from these [laws] by justice." Luther, "Disputatio pro declaratione," 231.1 f.

43 The expression '*relaxatio*' had been in use since the 11th century to describe the effect of indulgences, cf. Shaffern, "Medieval Theology," 12.

44 Cf. Voigt-Goy, "Luther," 87–95. For the text, cf. Luther Martin. "Resolutiones disputationum de indulgentiarum virtute. 1518." In *WA 1*, 522–628.

45 "It is said of the Word, that is Christ, alone: Your word lasts in eternity and your truth will abide forever and ever. And his justice will remain forever and ever. But the word and justice of men remain only for a time"; Resolutiones disputationum de indulgentiarum virtute. 1518. In WA 1, 545.21–24; cf. Felmberg, *Ablasstheologie*, 286–288.

46 Cf. ibid., 296 f.

47 "And are not some idle lawyers authors of the same tortures? While they work too hard to extol the power of the Pope, they cause the power of the Pope to be valued and admired

This text provides a clear perspective on Luther's theology, which was critical of both Church practice and significant tendencies within canon law studies. For Luther, papal authority was clearly subordinate to the Word of God; only Christ could grant forgiveness and deliverance from purgatory.[48] Nevertheless, at this stage, Luther did not cast any doubt on the general authority of either canon law or papal jurisdiction;[49] he sought only to limit their reach to this world.

Although the theology and jurisprudence of indulgences remained a contested issue, it must be noted that Luther adopted an extreme position within this debate. He refuted any link between the decrees of the earthly Church and the fate of souls after death. Moreover, his attack on papal authority constituted a strong criticism of the constitution of the Western Church. This was immediately clear to his contemporaries. A professor of law from Wittenberg asked Luther in 1517 whether in writing his *95 Theses* he was seeking conflict with the Pope.[50]

2.3 *The Heidelberg Disputation of 1518 and Luther's Doctrine of Law and Gospel*

When writing of *lex* at this stage in his work, Luther usually intended to differentiate between Law and Gospel in a theological sense and not to refer to the rules governing church or community life.[51] In the spring of 1518, Luther took part in a provincial chapter of his order in Heidelberg at which he was invited to present his new theology within the scope of the academic disputation that such meetings often included. Unlike the 95 theses, the 28 theological and 12 philosophical theses which he presented to his brethren were intended to act as an introduction to his general theological programme, culminating in his

even more than Christ's word is honoured by faith, although the people are to be taught that they should learn not to trust in the power of the Pope, but in the word of Christ, which is proclaimed by the Pope, if somehow they want peace in their consciences. You do not have anything because the Pope grants it, but if you believe that you have received it, you have it: you have as much as you believe because of the promise of Christ" (Luther, "Resolutiones," 543.3–9).

48 At this juncture, Luther regarded Purgatory as a place where departed souls underwent a process of sanctification and moral improvement. This process could not be shortened by interference from this world, cf. Felmberg, *Ablasstheologie*, 237–248.

49 Cf. Heckel, *Martin Luthers Reformation*, 96.

50 Cf. Selge. "Autoritätengefüge," 611 f.

51 The same is true for Karlstadt. In a commentary on Augustine's *De spiritu et littera*, composed predominantly in the second half of 1518, he described the function of God's Law in Augustinian terms as a means to lead sinners to repentance, cf. Salvadori, "Augustinkommentar," 253–257.

theology of the cross of Christ and an attack on the use of Aristotle in theological education.[52] In thesis one on theology, Luther highlighted the distinction between Law and Gospel and refuted any notion of human ability to please God through observance of His divine law: "*Lex Dei, saluberrima vitae doctrina, non potest hominem ad iusticiam promovere, sed magis obest.*"[53]

This argument shows that '*lex*' in this case does not mean a legal code regulating social interactions, but the (unfulfillable) ethical demands placed on human action by God. Luther and his colleagues concentrated their deliberations on this theological understanding of divine law. Within the Wittenberg framework, God understands that man is incapable of satisfying his Law; only those justified by the imputed merits of Christ obtained through faith in the Gospel can escape guilt and punishment.[54] As Bucer's account shows, this theological understanding of 'law' was the main point that Luther's new adherents (mostly young theologians from southern Germany) took with them from the Heidelberg disputation.[55] For the Wittenberg theologians and their supporters, it was more important to understand the dichotomy of Law and Gospel in its theological sense than to criticise the technicalities and impact of canon law. In his early disputations, Luther upheld the legitimacy of canon law and the legal institutions of the Church, such as the Papacy. Nevertheless, taken as a whole, his programme contained the potential to undermine the position and influence of canon law by subordinating it to the authority of the Word of God.[56]

3. Growing Conflict Between Wittenberg and the Church (1519–1520)

Originally seeking to work with the established Church in its reform, the conclusions reached by the Wittenberg Reformers slowly but steadily moved them

52 On the Heidelberg disputation cf. Kruse, *Universitätstheologie*, 131–139.

53 "The Law of God, the healthiest doctrine of life, cannot bring man to righteousness but is rather an obstacle to it" (Thesis 1, Martin Luther. "Disputatio Heidelbergae habita." In *WA 1*, 353.13 f.).

54 For Luther's understanding of law, cf. Johannes Heckel. *Lex charitatis: Eine juristische Untersuchung über das Recht in der Theologie Martin Luthers*. Cologne and Vienna: Böhlau, ^{2}1973, 21–26.

55 Cf. Kaufmann, "Bucers Bericht von der Leipziger Disputation." *ARG* 82 (1991): 147–170, 159–161; ibid., *Erlöste*, 119.

56 Cf. Volker Leppin. "Die Genese des reformatorischen Schriftprinzips: Beobachtungen zu Luthers Auseinandersetzung mit Johannes Eck bis zur Leipziger Disputation." In *Reformatorische Theologie und Autoritäten. Studien zur Genese des Schriftprinzips beim jungen Luther*, ed. Volker Leppin. Tübingen: Mohr Siebeck, 2015, 98–119.

away from the path of orthodoxy and into a position of outright opposition to Rome. Luther may well have found vocal support amongst the humanist establishment and a growing public, but he also found himself subject to heresy proceedings. In the words of Diarmaid MacCulloch, what had started as an argument in a "side alley of medieval soteriology – indulgences"[57] descended into a far-reaching ecclesiastical and political conflict, eventually resulting in Luther's excommunication and his famous answer at the Diet of Worms in 1521.[58]

3.1 *The Leipzig Debate and Wittenberg's Rejection of Papal Authority (1519)*

The intransigent and authoritarian reaction from the Church hierarchy forced Luther and his collaborators to address questions of theological and ecclesiastical authority to which they had previously accorded no priority. One of the important stages on the route leading to this destination presented itself at Leipzig during a disputation held in June 1519 with Johannes Eck, a doctor of theology from Ingolstadt. This had been preceded by an academic controversy starting in the spring of 1518, during which Eck accused Luther of denying papal authority. The matter was to be resolved in a disputation between the leading lights of the Wittenberg movement – Luther and Karlstadt – and Eck, held before the Duke of Saxony.[59]

Eck's attack required the Wittenberg Reformers to clarify their theological position towards both the Pope and wider questions of theological authority. Before the debate, Luther had already come to the conclusion that the office of Pope was instituted on human authority alone and not by God.[60] At Leipzig, Eck forced him to acknowledge that his theology bore close resemblance to the teachings of Jan Hus, condemned as heretical by the Council of Constance,

---

57 Diarmaid MacCulloch. *Reformation: Europe's House Divided 1490–1700*. London: Penguin, 2003, 126. I owe thanks to Andrew Smith for pointing me to this quotation.

58 Cf. Selge, "Autoritätengefüge," passim.

59 Cf. Schubert, "Libertas Disputandi," 419–442; for the conflict between Luther and Eck prior to the Leipzig Debate cf. Bubenheimer, "Reformationsdiplomatie," 284–295; Kurt-Victor Selge. "Der Weg zur Leipziger Disputation zwischen Luther und Eck im Jahre 1519." In *Bleibendes im Wandel der Kirchengeschichte: Kirchenhistorische Studien*, ed. Bernd Moeller and Gerhard Ruhbach. Tübingen: Mohr Siebeck, 1973, 169–210; Thomas Kaufmann. *Die Mitte der Reformation: Eine Studie zu Buchdruck und Publizistik im deutschen Sprachgebiet, zu ihren Akteuren und deren Strategien, Inszenierungs- und Ausdrucksformen*, Tübingen: Mohr Siebeck, 2019, 486–512.

60 Luther privately entertained the opinion that the Pope could be the Antichrist as early as March 1518, cf. Martin Brecht. *Martin Luther, vol. 1. Sein Weg zur Reformation*. Stuttgart: Calwer Verlag, 1981, 292 f.

and to admit publicly that the fallibility of ecumenical councils in doctrinal matters was a necessary corollary of his new theology.[61] The controversy and disputation with Johann Eck forced Luther to address the question of the legitimacy of the ecclesiastical authorities. Manoeuvred onto this terrain by the attacks of his opponent, he began to articulate serious doubts about the role and legitimacy of the Bishop of Rome.[62] Luther's new position was reinforced by the greater emphasis which he now placed on the authority of Scripture as the sole arbiter of theological inquiry.[63]

3.2 *Melanchthon's Baccalaureate Theses from 1519: Sola Scriptura and Natural Law*

The result of this process of clarification was made public in another important disputation held in the September of the same year, at which Philipp Melanchthon, tutor for Greek at the Faculty of Arts since 1518, defended a set of theses for his Baccalaureate in theology. These theses later became famous as the first clear statement of the principle 'by Scripture alone'.[64] The position of *sola scriptura* becomes especially apparent in Theses 16–18:

> "16. *Catholicum praeter articulos, quorum testis est scriptura, non est necesse, alios credere.*
> 17. *Conciliorum auctoritas est infra scripturae auctoritatem.*
> 18. *Ergo citra haeresis crimen est non credere caracterem, transsubstantiationem et similia.*"[65]

61 Cf. Kruse, *Universitätstheologie*, 205–219; Brecht, *Luther*, vol. 1, 304–306. Luther's new insights can be regarded as the fruit of a process of clarification that had already started in the controversies of 1518 and 1519. Luther had entertained the notion of the fallibility of ecumenical councils in practical issues (but not issues of faith) in his controversy with Sylvester Prierias in 1518, cf. Christopher Spehr. *Luther und das Konzil: Zur Entwicklung eines zentralen Themas in der Reformationszeit*. Tübingen: Mohr Siebeck, 2010, 60–65. Whilst he still considered Hus as a heretic in 1518, he regarded his attacks on the Church as a stimulus for Church reform. In his preparation for the Leipzig debate, he quoted Hus with approval; cf. Thomas Kaufmann. *Der Anfang der Reformation: Studien zur Kontextualität der Theologie, Publizistik und Inszenierung Luthers und der reformatorischen Bewegung*. 2nd ed. Tübingen: Mohr Siebeck 2018, 35–38.

62 Cf. Thomas Kaufmann. *Geschichte der Reformation in Deutschland*. Berlin: Suhrkamp, 2016, 254.

63 On the controversy prior to Leipzig, cf. Kruse, *Universitätstheologie*, 153–172 and 186–219; on the debate itself, cf. Schubert, "Libertas disputandi," 433; on the theological consequences cf. Volker Leppin, "Die Genese," 129–134.

64 Cf. Kruse, *Universitätstheologie*, 227 f.

65 "(16.) It is not necessary to believe other articles to be Catholic, apart from those, whose testimony is Scripture. (17.) The authority of Councils is subordinate to the authority of Scripture. (18.) Therefore, it is [possible] without crime of heresy, not to believe in

Bringing Luther's arguments in Leipzig to their logical conclusion, Melanchthon underscored the status of Scripture as the sole source of theological authority, a position with key implications for jurisprudence.[66] Apart from this basic innovation, analysis of Melanchthon's theses provides other insights into the conception of law holding sway in the Wittenberg circle, as can be seen in his third and fourth thesis:

> "3. *Cum divina tum naturalis lex statuit deum propter sese diligendum esse.*
> 4. *Quod eum non possimus, lex in causa est, ut serviliter metuamus deum."*[67]

Following Luther, Melanchthon stressed man's inability to fulfil the demands of divine law and that this failure reveals the very purpose of divine law itself: to demonstrate this inability to sinful man and to point to the need to trust fully in divine mercy for his salvation. Yet another point is important: although primarily interested in expounding on divine law, Melanchthon went on to differentiate between divine law and natural law. His concept of natural law is referenced again in thesis 22: "*Leges naturae habitus sunt concreati animae.*"[68]

The idea of natural law enjoyed widespread acceptance in scholastic theology. Understood as a common code of morality, originally authored by God, it was written into the fabric of the human heart, and thus accessible to human reason. In this way, scholastic theologians distinguished it from the divine law revealed in Scripture and all forms of man-made law.[69] Although the Wittenberg circle accepted this concept of natural law and its differentiation from other sources of law,[70] they accorded greater priority to Augustine's teaching on the fragility of human reason and understanding. As such, sin often served to lead man astray from the path of compliance with both natural as well as divine law. Thesis three of Melanchthon's Baccalaureate disputation asserted man's inability to fulfil the prime precept of natural law: to love God.[71]

---

the character [indelebilis of baptism], transubstantiation and similar things" (Philipp Melanchthon. "Bakkalaureatsthesen." In *MWA* 1, 24 f.).

66 Cf. Leppin, "Die Genese," 139.

67 "(3.) Divine as well as natural law states that God must be loved for himself. (4.) Because we cannot do this, the law causes us to fear God like slaves" (Melanchthon, "Bakkalaureatsthesen," 24).

68 "Natural laws are the [divinely] co-created *habitus* of the soul" (ibid., 25).

69 Cf. Merio Scattola. *Das Naturrecht vor dem Naturrecht. Zur Geschichte des "ius naturae" im 16. Jahrhundert.* Tübingen: Niemeyer, 1999, 29–35.

70 For Karlstadt cf. Bubenheimer, *Consonantia*, 168 n. 29, and 188 n. 4b; for Luther's concept of natural law cf. Heckel, *Martin Luthers Reformation*, 423–447.

71 Cf. Hermann Pfister. *Die Entwicklung der Theologie Melanchthons unter dem Einfluß der Auseinandersetzung mit Schwarmgeistern und Wiedertäufern.* Freiburg: Dt. Pax-Christi-Bewegung 1968, 17–30.

Developing a specific concept of natural law in a treatise on rhetoric from 1518 – which exhibits the clear influence of Cicero – Melanchthon defined natural law as a set of socially accepted moral precepts. At this stage, he believed that these concepts were embodied in the maxims of Roman law.[72] In his Baccalaureate theses, presented in 1519, Melanchthon strengthened the relationship between divine law and natural law, which he also established as a divine institution. Just as with the revealed Law of God, mankind was shown to be incapable of following natural law, the sole purpose of which for Melanchthon, was to lead sinners to repentance and trust in God's mercy. In the ensuing years, Melanchthon further emphasised this function of divine law, presenting natural law as merely a distorted version of the Ten Commandments.[73] This changed after 1521, when Melanchthon established the political function of natural law as a divinely instituted mechanism of secular government. His new teachings on natural law, which shall be discussed in the fifth section, were to prove highly influential in early modern discourse on the subject.[74]

3.3 *Divine Law vs. Canon Law (1519/20)*

At this point (1519/20), the question of natural law assumed a subordinate position in the discussion of legal topics at Wittenberg. Far greater importance was attached to the other concept which Melanchthon examined in his Baccalaureate theses: that of divine law. What exactly was commanded by God? Moreover, what did these commandments mean for laws shaped by man, especially in the Church? How and to what extent did traditional Church doctrine and practice contradict the Word of God? One illustration of the significance of divine law to the Wittenberg scholars is provided by Luther's set of disputation theses *De lege et fide*, probably debated in 1519.[75] Luther was again mainly concerned with establishing the distinction between Law and Gospel. The purpose of divine law, he argued, was to reveal sin. In addition to this theological function, Luther differentiated between divine and man-made law, with the former working as a corrective to the latter. Examining the Sermon on the Mount, Luther contended that:

---

72 Cf. Adolf Sperl. *Melanchthon zwischen Humanismus und Reformation: Eine Untersuchung über den Wandel des Traditionsverständnisses bei Melanchthon und die damit zusammenhängenden Grundfragen seiner Theologie*. Munich: Kaiser, 1959, 32–36.

73 Cf. Clemens Bauer. "Die Naturrechtslehre des jüngeren Melanchthon." In *Festschrift für Gerhard Ritter zu seinem 60. Geburtstag*, ed. Richard Nürnberger. Tübingen: Mohr, 1950, 244–255.

74 Cf. Scattola, *Naturrecht*, esp. 35–55.

75 Martin Luther. "Disputatio de lege et fide. 1519." In *WA 6*, 23 f.

> *"5. Errat item, qui inter legem Divinam et Humanam non discernit.*
> *6. Vim vi repellere lege humana constat.*
> *7. Divina lex imperat, et pallium cedendum esse tollenti tunicam."*[76]

Luther used this distinction between man-made and divine law to criticise the claim to jurisdiction by canon law and the Papacy in areas which constituted the proper dominion of Scripture. According to Luther, every man-made law should follow divine law and was unjust, if it did not: "*Lex humana, non consentiens divinae, iniusta est.*"[77]

This position clarified the implicit criticism of man-made law contained in the Wittenberg disputations from 1517 and 1518. Luther and his colleagues went further, however, rejecting the validity of human traditions which did not follow the precepts contained in the Word of God. This criticism was articulated by representatives of the Wittenberg circle in their function as the *opponentes* in a disputation conducted at a regional chapter of the Saxon province of the Franciscan order convened in Wittenberg in the autumn of 1519.[78] A protocol of this disputation, preserved in a Dutch printing from around 1520[79] shows how the Wittenberg circle launched a fundamental attack on the theological foundations of the Franciscan order, and its mandate as "*ecclesiae suae militantis militiam* [...]."[80] Melanchthon made clear that it was the intention of the Wittenberg Reformers to evaluate the claims of the Franciscans against Biblical precepts.[81] Arguing that all Christians belonged to the Church militant by virtue of their baptism,[82] he contended that a man-made vow establishing a sub-grouping within the Church, which could be dissolved by the ecclesiastical authorities, could not be viewed as an institution of divine law. According to Melanchthon, no human institution was able to issue a dispensation which circumvented the demands of divine law or had the power to dissolve a

---

76 "(5) He makes the same error, who does not distinguish divine from human law. / (6) Human law demands to repel force by force. / (7) Divine law commands you to give away your cloak to him who takes away your shirt" (ibid., 24.8–10).

77 "Human law, inconsistent with divine law, is unjust" (ibid., 24.12; thesis 8).

78 Cf. Gerhard Hammer. "Militia Franciscana seu militia Christi. Das neugefundene Protokoll einer Disputation der sächsischen Franziskaner mit Vertretern der Wittenberger theologischen Fakultät am 3. und 4. Oktober 1519." Part 1: *ARG* 69 (1978): 51–81; part 2: *ARG* 70 (1979): 59–105; Kruse, *Universitätstheologie*, 232–236.

79 Martin Luther. "Franziskanerdisputation." In *WA* 59, 606–697. I owe thanks to Ulrich Bubenheimer for pointing me to the legal discourse in this disputation.

80 "[...] a [special] militia of His Church Militant" (ibid., 678.7).

81 "*Potius ergo talis religio et ceterae reliciendae sunt et ambulandum in praeceptis dei, cum nihil nisi simulachrum aliquod faciant et idolum*" (ibid., 680.18–20).

82 Ibid., 680. 3 f.

vow, which was binding in the eyes of God.[83] Moreover, he contended that Franciscan independence from episcopal jurisdiction and the local congregation was a clear infringement of Biblical practice, which stipulated nothing beyond the structures of parish and diocese.[84]

Basing his own attack on the supremacy of Scripture, Luther made the controversial point that neither the Church Fathers nor Church teaching could be taken as a source of divine law; rather it was imperative that all tradition be evaluated against the teachings of the Bible and the Word of Christ.[85] In a calculated provocation, Luther contended that the Franciscan vows of poverty, chastity and obedience in no way established their superiority over the laity, whose daily work actually represented to some a more perfect way of life than the demands of a monastic existence.[86] Finishing with a further barb, he maintained that it was not heretical to doubt the divine origin of the mission of Francis of Assisi:

> "[…]; *sed haec religio non constat iure divino, quia a summo pontifice comfirmata et a sancto Francisco fundata sive erecta. Sed Franciscus homo erat et non deus; igitur et humanum eius institutum est. Sapere enim contra humanum institutum neminem facit haereticum.*"[87]

Karlstadt denied the Christian character of the Franciscan Order, which in his view followed the example of Francis, rather than Christ.[88] Arguing from an Old Testament perspective, he focused on the demands of Deut 15:4, and claimed that its strictures against begging also applied to Christian society: "*Mendicitas talis etiam iure divino prohibita est. Nam in veteri testamento erat*

83 "[…] *'vota' vestra non sunt* [*vota*]. […] *De vestris autem 'votis' dispensatur per homines; igitur non sunt vota, et multominus divinitus instituta, cum homini super ius divinum nulla sit dispensatio*" (ibid., 680.30 f.; 33–36).

84 Ibid., 681.1–7.

85 "*Doctores enim legem dei non constituunt; quotquot enim fuere, homines fuere. Et ideo dicit Augustinus hominum dogmata sive verba ad Christi et bibliae verba conferenda, atque per illa approbari debere*" (ibid., 685.8 f.).

86 "*Laici quidem in suis laboribus ad prolis et suam necessitatem levandam sub praeceptis viventes perfectiores sunt nobis religiosis hanc necessitudinem non habentibus*" (ibid., 685.32–34).

87 "[…] this religious order does not exist by divine right. This is because it is confirmed by the Supreme Pontiff and founded or built by St. Francis. But Francis was a man and not God. Therefore, his institution is man-made. To doubt a human institution makes no one a heretic" (ibid., 686.33–36).

88 "*Christiani ergo non estis, quia aliam a Christo et perfectiorem* (*sancti Francisci videlicet*) *vitam geritis*" (ibid., 688.9 f.).

omnino prohibita [...]."[89] As such, the purportedly virtuous life of the mendicant order was in fact, sinful.[90] Answering the Franciscan response – a repetition of the argument of Bernard of Clairvaux that Christ himself had lived on charity[91] – Karlstadt proclaimed: *"Igitur labore a nobis victus quaerendus esset, et non otio. Aut quae causa vobis est in otio vitam expendere?"*[92]

Taken together, these arguments amounted to nothing less than a call for the dissolution of the mendicant orders.[93] Rejecting their 'calling' to celibacy, monastic vows and begging as unbiblical, the special status accorded to the monastic vocation was depicted as an infringement of divine law. Karlstadt's attack on accepting alms typified the new approach taken in Wittenberg, which now established Scripture as the touchstone for and supreme rule of all Christian life.

The question as to the legitimacy of the Pope and his position at the apex of the Church hierarchy was of paramount importance for the legal order of the Church. Although Luther and Karlstadt by now both rejected papal authority, closer examination of their argumentation reveals subtle differences. Karlstadt was very reluctant to entertain the notion of a Church without a Pope until Rome threatened Luther and his followers with excommunication at the end of 1520. Once he realised the degree of papal intransigence faced by the Wittenberg circle, writing in "*De pontificum decretis*"[94] from 1522, Karlstadt rounded on the very existence of the office of the Pope and Church councils, denying them any authority, whether earthly or divine. Karlstadt substantiated this attack with examples of heretical pronouncements made by a number of councils. For him, this revealed not only their fallibility, but their entirely man-made nature. Karlstadt's first thesis opens with an example of an erroneous decision taken by a council, the synod of Meaux in 845, which denied the validity of forced marriages. This contradicted a judgment ascribed to Jerome affirming the validity of such unions, which was subsequently incorporated in the *Decretum Gratiani*, thereby revealing a clash of authorities and underlining Karlstadt's case.

89 "Such a mendicant lifestyle is even prohibited by divine law. Because it was totally forbidden in the Old Testament" (ibid., 689.12 f.).

90 Ibid., 689.19 f.

91 Ibid., 689.24–27.

92 "Therefore, sustenance has to be sought by our labour and not by leisure. Or for what reason do you spend your life in leisure?" (ibid., 689, 31–33).

93 Cf. Bubenheimer, "Reformationsdiplomatie," 268.

94 *Lutheri, Melanch., Carolostadii.* Basel, 1522, D V r f.; edited in Bubenheimer, *Consonantia*, 290 f.

Working with the argument of the canon lawyer Panormitanus (Nikolaus de Turdeschi 1386–1445), who used the faulty decision of the synod of Meaux to conclude that a general council could err in certain cases,[95] Karlstadt contended that a synod which requires the belief of heretical doctrine excommunicates itself (thesis 2). Applying this argument to the Papacy, Karlstadt argued that its decretals had been heretical since the thirteenth century (thesis 3); and as such, this Pope was excommunicated *latae sententiae*. In consequence, the Papacy was unable to excommunicate someone else (thesis 4). Karlstadt concluded with the assertion of the invalidity of papal decretals, one of the main sources of canon law:

> "7. *Ergo ipso iure excommunicatus est, qui spiritalia negotia humanis traditionibus metitur.*
> 8. *Etiam si legem dei resipiant.*
> 9. *Igitur tollendae sunt pontificiae decretales.*"[96]

By differentiating between divine and man-made law, Karlstadt had established a guiding principle against which to evaluate papal laws. In this analysis, he cast papal decretals as mere 'human traditions' that contradict divine law as revealed in Scripture. In expecting his flock to follow his own man-made decrees, the Pope had effectively relinquished all authority. In effect, Karlstadt sought to use the principles of canon law to invalidate papal authority itself, thereby rendering ineffective the excommunication spoken on the Wittenberg theologians. Despite this revolutionary claim, Karlstadt still found himself arguing within the confines of canon law. As Ulrich Bubenheimer has shown, this position is indicative of the strong and continuing hold over him exercised by his legal training.[97]

Luther's pronouncement on the Pope issued in a set of theses "*De non vindicando*" from 1520, was no less stark:

> "*Pontifices, neglecta evangelii praedicatione, ad ceremoniarum cultum sive quarumcunque rerum administrationem conversi a Samuele cum Saulo Iudaeorum*

95 Cf. ibid., 96–109; Spehr, Luther, 60–65.

96 "(7) Therefore, he is by his own law excommunicated, who evaluates spiritual business by human traditions, (8) even if they [the human traditions H.B.] have the flavour of divine law. (9) Thus papal decretals have to be abolished" (*Lutheri, Melanch., Carolostadii ...* Basel, 1522, D V r f.). In the interest of clarity, in subsequent quotations from 16th century thesis collections, I have expanded ligatures and abbreviations without noting this. I have normalised the orthography slightly. Roman numerals have been replaced by arabic numbers.

97 Cf. Bubenheimer, *Consonantia*, 171–175.

> *rege audire merentur 'Quoniam abiecisti Sermones domini, abiecit te deus ne sis rex'.*"[98]

Despite joining Karlstadt in issuing a divine judgement on the Pope as the Antichrist, Luther was not arguing as a canon lawyer, but instead assumed the mantle of a prophet. Nevertheless, analysis of the eighth and eleventh theses of this disputation reveals that Luther followed Karlstadt in his reasoning:

> "8. *Suas traditiones aeque cum divina lege nitentes observari non Christi et Apostolorum, sed Satanae et Antichristorum vices gerere apertis scripturarum testimoniis convincuntur.*
> [...]
> 11. *Inobedentiae crimen non incurrunt, qui hominum traditiones contra legem Dei non ducunt audiendas.*"[99]

The differences in the arguments advanced by the two Reformers were probably rooted, at least in part, in hermeneutical divergence. Nevertheless, we should not overemphasise the significance of differing positions within the Wittenberg circle, which can be explained by reference to its culture of discussion. Its members regularly circulated their ideas, asking for feedback on experimental positions whilst remaining united in their campaign against a common enemy.[100] All rejected the claims of canon law over Scripture, together with any notion that man could legislate against the revealed Word of God. The public burning of the papal bull *Exsurge domine* (threatening Luther with excommunication) and the *Corpus Iuris canonici*, at a public event staged in

98 "The Popes, who after neglecting to preach the Gospel have turned to the ceremonial cult or the administration of all kinds of things, deserve to hear from the prophet Samuel with Saul, the king of the Jews: Since you have rejected the oracles of the Lord, God has rejected you, that you may no [longer] be king" (Martin Luther. "Disputatio de non vindicando &c. habita. 1520." In *WA* 6, 575.13–16).

99 "(8) All those who are striving to observe their traditions equally with divine law do not hold the places of Christ and the Apostles but of Satan and the Antichrists and are refuted by the obvious testimonies of the Scriptures. [...] (11) It is entirely right to ignore human tradition when it contradicts the law of God [verbatim: those, who do not consider human traditions to be heard against the Law of God, do not commit the crime of disobedience]" (ibid., 575.20–22.27 f.). For the differences in the positions of Karlstadt and Luther in this matter, cf. Bubenheimer, *Consonantia*, 169 f.

100 For the experimental characteristics of Wittenberg theological discourse, cf. Bubenheimer, "Reformationsdiplomatie." 301 f. I would like to thank Professor Bubenheimer for several enlightening discussions on this point.

December 1520, was a symbolic action expressing a unity of purpose in rejecting the authority of the Papacy and canon law.[101]

3.4 *Reform Proposals for Sacramental Theology and Church Practice (1520)*

The disputations held in Wittenberg during this early period of the Reformation did not just focus on articulating the Lutheran rejection of papal authority and the traditional system of canon law. Luther also used them as a vehicle with which to develop and expound his views on a range of subjects including his new understanding of the Sacraments, through which he sought to establish divine truth over the mere doctrines of men. The findings of these undertakings were recorded in a number of published treatises. Luther announced his new understanding of the Sacraments (worked out in several disputations) in *De captivitate babylonica ecclesiae*, published in 1520.[102] All these theses were issued with the aim of demonstrating beyond doubt the separate and superior nature of Scripture over man-made traditions, and establishing this differentiation as the conceptual bedrock on which to proceed with the programme of Church reform which the Wittenberg circle envisaged.

During these years, the Reforming drive to recast the fabric of the Church's constitution and liturgical order produced an increasingly detailed and coherent programme of ecclesiastical and social reform, which Luther spelled out in his treatise *To the Christian Nobility of the German Nation*.[103] The broadening of the discussion which this involved was also reflected in the disputations held at Wittenberg University. A printed collection of sets of theses published in Leiden in 1521 contains an anonymous set of *Twelve Conclusions about the Law Thou Shalt Not Steal*.[104] Comparing this set of theses to Karlstadt's works from 1518 to 1520, Ulrich Bubenheimer convincingly attributed them to Karlstadt, dating them to the last months of the year 1520.[105] The first conclusion of this set of theses maintains that the literal fulfilment of the Commandment not to

101 Cf. Anselm Schubert. "Das Lachen der Ketzer: Zur Selbstinszenierung der frühen Reformation." *ZThK* 108 (2011), 405–430.

102 Cf. Oswald Bayer. *Promissio: Geschichte der reformatorischen Wende in Luthers Theologie*. Göttingen: Vandenhoeck & Ruprecht, 1971, 162 f. I should like to thank Professor Bayer for pointing me to this important finding from his habilitation thesis.

103 Cf. Kaufmann, *Geschichte*, 271–274; Kruse, *Universitätstheologie*, 253–255.

104 Cf. [Andreas Bodenstein von Karlstadt]. "12 Conclusiones: De legis non furtum facies impletione et testamentorum legatione [1520, Ende?]." In Karlstadt. *Kritische Gesamtausgabe der Schriften und Briefe Andreas Bodenstein von Karlstadts*, vol. 3, ed. by Thomas Kaufmann. Gütersloh: Gütersloher, Verlagshaus 2020, 553 f.

105 Cf. Ulrich Bubenheimer, "Einleitung [12 Conclusiones]." In Karlstadt, *Kritische Gesamtausgabe*, vol. 3, 550–552. I would like to thank Professor Bubenheimer for showing

steal "does not make someone righteous in the eyes of God but [only] in the eyes of men."[106] Its main function was to reveal human sinfulness.

At root of the new theology therefore was an innovative understanding of the function of law. Rather than acting as a guide on the quest for moral perfection, Luther and his colleagues saw that all law had been instituted by God as an unfulfillable set of precepts. The purpose was to establish His moral requirements and convince mankind of its inability to satisfy them, and its inherent need for God's forgiveness. Law and Gospel existed therefore as a dichotomy and not as two equal parts of salvation history. In this way, Karlstadt believed in the fundamental inability of mankind to comply with the Commandment against theft in such a way as to please God: "*Lex ista/ sicut et alie divine/ impossibile nobis precipit.*"[107] Merely abstaining from stealing – which in keeping with Roman law, Karlstadt understood as the use of someone else's property against the will of the owner[108] – did not mean that a person had fulfilled the Will of God. For Karlstadt, the injunction also mandated a more active and thorough-going altruism in ensuring that no one wanted for anything at any time and not just in times of grave need: "*Hanc regulam an imitentur/ qui fratri non nisi in extrema necessitate/ succurendum fore censent/ ipsi videant.*"[109]

Whilst stressing the impossibility of complying with the Commandment not to steal, Karlstadt nevertheless considered it to be normative for Church practice and criticised the practice of limiting charity to posthumous bequests. He reserved special censure for the practice of grants for Mass stipends and private altars. Karlstadt not only found no Biblical basis for such practices, he condemned them as wasteful and in effect an act of theft: "[...] *qui neglectis sanctis vivis egentibus/ tandem morituri/ nescio quas memorias aut que altaria/ etcetera id genus a deo minime precepta/ sua (ut aiunt) ultima voluntate fundare volunt.*"[110] In condemning bequests for masses and altars, Karlstadt

me a preliminary version of his edition of Karlstadt's *conclusiones* and discussing its legal implications with me.

106 "[...] *iustos non coram deo [22] sed coram hominibus facit*"; [Karlstadt], "12 Conclusiones," 553. 3 f.

107 "For us it is impossible to fulfil this law, like other divine divine laws", thesis 3, [Karlstadt], "12 Conclusiones," 553. 6.

108 Cf. ibid., n. 4 (to thesis 2) and Bubenheimer, "Einleitung," 551.

109 "Those should check if they follow this rule, who consider that they will not come to aid to [their] brother, unless in instances of extreme necessity" (thesis 6 [Karlstadt], "12 Conclusiones," 553, 11 f.); cf. Bubenheimer, "Einleitung," 551 f.

110 "[...], who, while they neglect the needs of the living saints, establish, when they are in the process of dying, in their (as they say) last will, I do not know how many memorial or altar foundations and other [foundations] of this kind, which are [not] in the least way commanded by God" (thesis 8, [Karlstadt], "12 Conclusiones," 553. 15–17). Karlstadt

was essentially calling for a major reform of Church finance, which largely depended on this practice.[111] He also viewed the accumulation of benefices as theft:

> *"Videbunt et isti quo pacto sibi amicos de iniquitatis mammona fecerint/ qui tot ecclesiastica possederunt beneficia/ unde quinque/ octo/ decem vel pluribus/ qui alias* ***egere coacti*** *sunt/* ***provideri*** *potuissent."*[112]

In this thesis, Karlstadt – himself the holder of a considerable benefice – turned against the Church hierarchy, which he accused of theft by amassing monies which otherwise could go to the poor (Luke 16:9). In this way, he deployed a range of Biblical precepts to articulate his criticism of Church abuses and propose specific reforms. Not restricting himself to the Church, Karlstadt also saw the need and opportunity to recast society along Biblical lines, by launching an attack on a range of parasitic practices such as gambling, which he argued, deprived the poor of their money, and thus contravened God's will: "*Omnis ludus/ ex cupiditate ortum habens/ est contra charitatem.*"[113] In itself nothing new,[114] this concern with social norms showed the full scope of Karlstadt's ambitions. His zeal not only to relieve, but prevent poverty also provides a foretaste of his later interest in secular social policy.[115]

Many of the demands that Karlstadt articulated in this set of theses were also voiced in Luther's treatise *On the German Nobility*; this agreement demonstrates the common goals of the Wittenberg circle.[116] In a relatively short space

---

and the other Reformers wanted to divert the monies accumulated for foundations, Mass stipends, altars and curacies into a common chest for poor relief, cf. Bubenheimer, "Bodenstein," 69.

111 Indeed, his application of the Commandment not to steal to this common practice represented Karlstadt's main innovation in this set of theses cf. Bubenheimer, "Einleitung," 552.

112 "Even these people, who by that treaty made themselves friends with the mammon of unrighteousness and who possessed so many ecclesiastical benefices, will see that they could have provided for up to five, eight, ten or more, who were forced, to [depend on] others to [sustain] their need" (thesis 10, [Karlstadt], "12 Conclusiones," 3, 554. 1–3). Some mistakes in the edition of this particular thesis were corrected to accord with the original printings. Any words changed have been indicated in bold.

113 "Every game, which has its origin in greed, is against brotherly love" (ibid., thesis 12); cf. Bubenheimer, "Einleitung," 552.

114 Cf. ibid.

115 Cf. ibid; Bubenheimer, "Bodenstein," passim. For Karlstadt's concept of an integrated religious and social Reformation in Wittenberg, cf. the following section of this article.

116 Luther also wanted to prevent people from becoming beggars, cf. Thomas Kaufmann. *An den christlichen Adel deutscher Nation von des christlichen Standes Besserung*. Tübingen: Mohr Siebeck, 2014, 384–391. Joining Karlstadt in arguing for a reform of Mass stipends and altar foundations (cf. ibid., 391–395), Luther regarded the accumulation of several

of time, the circle had moved from theological protest to the presentation of a coherent and increasingly comprehensive programme of reform, encompassing both the structure and practice of the Church as well as aspects of wider society.[117] Elements of the programme were even incorporated in the reform of municipal poor relief in Wittenberg.[118] Nevertheless, the largely unchanged liturgical and institutional life of the Church in Wittenberg did not yet fully reflect the full scope of the theoretical challenge which the Wittenberg theologians mounted against the authority of Rome. The Elector Frederick's vast collection of relics even remained on public display as late as 1521.[119] Only after Luther's appearance at the Diet of Worms and his subsequent exile at Wartburg Castle did his collaborators turn their attention to the practical implementation of their theologising. In the words of Thomas Kaufmann, this point marked the "transition from Word to action."[120]

4. From Criticism to Change: the Wittenberg Movement (1521–1522)

The theoretical debates of the early Reformation were succeeded by a period of intense action following Luther's appearance at the Diet of Worms. The year 1521 saw the birth of what was later to become known as the 'Wittenberg movement'. Beginning in the summer of 1521 with a debate on several important areas of reform, action followed in the autumn of that same year, as discussion on the nature of evangelical worship was translated into a reform of the Mass and further practical changes in the worship of the Wittenberg community. The first public evangelical Communion was celebrated on Christmas day 1521. These changes were formalised in a town constitution promulgated in early 1522, which in addition to prohibiting the use of images in church worship, included a number of social reforms. Worried in early 1522, by the radical nature of the changes and the popular disturbances, which he feared that the reforms would provoke, the Prince-Elector decided to intervene. Luther officially returned to Wittenberg in March 1522 and came out in support of Frederick's more conservative position, calling for a slower pace of reform.[121]

benefices as the result of greed and argued for the limitation of this practice, cf. ibid., 395 f.

117 Cf. Kruse, *Universitätstheologie*, 243–256.

118 Cf. ibid., 273–277.

119 Cf. Krentz, *Ritual und Deutungshoheit*, 263–268.

120 "*Übergang vom Wort zur Tat*" (Kaufmann, *Geschichte*, 382).

121 Cf. Kruse, *Universitätstheologie*, 279–389; Ulrich Bubenheimer. "Scandalum et Ius divinum: Theologische und rechtstheologische Probleme der ersten reformatorischen Innovationen

This revealed a split in the circle of Wittenberg theologians over differences of hermeneutics and the pace of change.

4.1 *The Rejection of Celibacy and the Discussion on the Validity of Monastic Vows (1521)*

One of the first areas of practical reform on which the Wittenberg movement focused was the issue of clerical marriage, a measure which Luther had long advocated and which was now put into practice. By 1521, a number of Reform-minded priests in Saxony and Thuringia had married, including Bartholomäus Bernhardi, Luther's former student, who informed his old teacher of this development in May 1521. Such marriages were concluded in clear violation of canon law and carried penalties. As a result, several married priests were arraigned and imprisoned. A process was opened against Bernhardi, but the Elector's protection meant that he suffered no consequences.[122]

Returning to Wittenberg from a brief visit to Denmark in June 1521, where he had served as an advisor to the Danish King Christian II,[123] Karlstadt started a public defence of clerical marriage.[124] This defence included his seven theses *De coelibatu*, which provided the basis for the arguments of his book *Supra Coelibatu*.[125] Of especial relevance are theses one, two, and seven:

> "1. *Sicut viduas reiicimus iuniores, sic monachos et iuvenes presbyteros coelibes.*
> 2. *Non sunt ad sacros ordines ii vocandi, qui coniugia nescierunt.*
> [...]
> 7. *Deberent Episcopi sacerdotes concubinarios ad contractum matrimonii cogere.*"[126]

---

in Wittenberg 1521 / 22." *Zeitschrift der Savigny-Stiftung für Rechtsgeschichte / Kanonistische Abteilung* 90 (1973): 263–342; Ulrich Bubenheimer. "Luthers Stellung zum Aufruhr in Wittenberg 1520–1522 und die Wurzeln des landesherrlichen Kirchenregiments." *Zeitschrift der Savigny-Stiftung für Rechtsgeschichte / Kanonistische Abteilung* 71 (1985): 147–214.

122 Cf. Ulrich Bubenheimer. "Streit um das Bischofsamt in der Wittenberger Reformation 1521 / 22: von der Auseinandersetzung mit den Bischöfen um die Priesterehen und den Ablaß in Halle zum Modell des evangelischen Gemeindebischofs; Teil 1." *Zeitschrift der Savigny-Stiftung für Rechtsgeschichte / Kanonistische Abteilung* 73 (1987): 155–209, 170–190.

123 Hermann Barge suggests Karlstadt had a strong influence on the reform of the Danish Church implemented at this time, which raised the age limit for taking monastic vows to 25 years. The text of this law also contained provisions that priests should marry and probably reflects the influence or input of Karlstadt, who was known to argue that 1 Tim 3 was applicable in this context, cf. Barge, *Karlstadt*, vol. 1, 257–259; Bubenheimer, *Consonantia*, 237 n. 180. On Karlstadt's stay in Denmark, cf. Barge, *Karlstadt*, vol. 1, 467–471.

124 Bubenheimer, *Consonantia*, 237–243.

125 Cf. Barge, *Karlstadt*, vol. 1, 475.

126 "(1) As with young widows [who Paul decreed should re-marry, H. B.], we reject that young monks and priests [be] celibate (better: choose a life of celibacy). (2) Those should not be

Basing his arguments on 1Tim 5, in which Paul urges young widows to remarry, Karlstadt argued that not only should the young not be urged to lead a celibate life, but that the unmarried should not be ordained. In his disputation theses *De coelibatu presbyterorum*, he contended that Paul's requirement expressed in 1Tim 3, that a bishop should have only one wife, was also binding for priests, who must therefore marry.[127] He added several admonitions against celibacy and urged regional bishops to force priests living with a concubine to marry. This is typical of Karlstadt's hermeneutics. Ulrich Bubenheimer has described Karlstadt's argumentation as the "Biblicism of a lawyer".[128] Although he sought to replace canon law with Scripture as the basis for a new evangelical church order, his methodology and approach to Biblical exegesis remained that of a canon lawyer. His description of Scripture as a code of law formed his argumentative terminology; he now used 'divine law' and 'Biblical law' as interchangeable terms.[129]

Karlstadt's statements on clerical celibacy were only one contribution to a wider discussion on Church organisation and a projected evangelical church order. One of the most enlightening sources for this discussion are Luther's *Themata de Votis*, composed whilst in the Wartburg and sent to Wittenberg in September 1521. Addressing the legitimacy and binding nature of monastic vows to chastity, he did not reject the practice of taking vows, but argued that those taken without the full understanding of God's grace were not binding. In this way, he transcended Karlstadt's legalism, arriving at a less inflexible position through a pastoral approach.[130]

In spite of hermeneutical differences within the Wittenberg circle, the fruits of its discussions were soon disseminated and provided the legitimation for priests, monks and nuns to marry. Ulrich Bubenheimer has kindly drawn my attention to a handwritten manuscript copy of Karlstadt's seven theses *De coelibatu*, copied by the Württemberg Reformer Johann Mantel,[131] to which

---

called to holy orders, who do not know marriage. [...] (7) The bishops must force priests living with concubines to enter a contract of marriage" (*Lutheri, Melanch., Carolostadii ...* Basel, 1522, D VI r).

127 Edited in Barge, *Karlstadt*, vol. 1, 476–478, cf. especially theses 40–42, in ibid. 478.

128 "[*J*]*uristischer Biblizismus*" (Bubenheimer, *Consonantia*, 244).

129 This interpretation follows Bubenheimer's summary of Karlstadt's legal thought; cf. ibid., 241–245.

130 Cf. Bubenheimer, "Scandalum," 328 f.

131 *AD LIBRVM EXIMII MAGISTRI NOSTRI MAGISTRI AMBROSII CATHARINI DEFENSORIS SILVESTRI PRIERATIS ACERRIMI Responsio Martini Lutherí.* VVITTEMBERGAE MENSE Aprili. [...], Landeskirchliche Zentralbibliothek Stuttgart, Bestand Alte Pfarramtsbibliothek Weinsberg: A 4901 85 (deposited at Landeskirchliche Zentralbibliothek Stuttgart). The manuscript was originally found by Professor

Mantel added the comment: "this well pleases us, Grethle, because Christ is risen."[132] This shows how the discussions in Wittenberg were disseminated to other regions of the Holy Roman Empire. Mantel himself later took Karlstadt's advice and married the former Beguine Margarethe.[133]

4.2 *The Reform of Communion Liturgy* (1521/1522)

Whilst the constraints of space preclude a comprehensive discussion of the Wittenberg reform of doctrine and Church practice, a short examination of the Reformers' debate on the reform of communion will shed light on the conflict of hermeneutics that broke out amongst them.[134] Discussion centred on the legitimacy of private masses and the introduction of communion in both kinds. Those pressing for abolition of the former and introduction of the latter declared that Biblical law commanded such a change. A set of theses *De scandalo et missa*[135] presented arguments for reform of the Mass, arguing for abolition of all practices not consistent with the Word of God and as such, blasphemous. This contradicted Luther's later injunction that scandalisation of a weak conscience did not constitute the need to act: "*Nec scandali respectus est habendus in dispensandis humanis traditionibus, si cum iure divino observari non possint.*"[136]

The main argument advanced in favour of reforming the Mass was that private masses and communion under one kind countered the mandate of

---

Martin Brecht in Weinsberg in the early 1980s. Mantel was an Augustinian and former lecturer in Wittenberg, for his biography cf. Bossert, "Mantel, Johann." In Albert Hauck, ed. *Realencyklopädie für protestantische Theologie und Kirche*, vol. 24. Leipzig: J. C. Hinrichsche Buchhandlung, ^{3}1913, 59–64. Armin Kohnle and Beate Kusche, eds. *Professorenbuch der Theologischen Fakultät der Universität Wittenberg 1502 bis 1815/17*. Leipzig: Evangelische Verlagsanstalt, 2017, 139 f.

132 This reads in a mixture of German and Latin "*placet nobis Grethle, q<uia> christ ist erstanden*"; cf. *AD LIBRVM EXIMII …*

133 Cf. Gustav Bossert. "D. Joh. Mantels Lebensende und der Eheprozeß des Michael Back und seiner Gattin." *ARG* 12 (1915): 161–204, 162–164. I would like to thank the staff of the central library of the Evangelical Church in Württemberg for providing me with a scan of the manuscript.

134 Cf. Bubenheimer, "Scandalum," 315–331.

135 Author and date are disputed; a marginal comment in one copy of the thesis collection attributes the disputation to Karlstadt and sets the date of publication to September 1521. Barge accepts Karlstadt as the author but argues for a later date; cf. Barge, *Karlstadt*, vol. 1, 491. In 1973, Bubenheimer originally argued for Melanchthon's authorship and a later date of publication; cf. Bubenheimer, "Scandalum," 336–338. Bubenheimer has told me that he now believes Karlstadt to be the author of this set of theses.

136 "There should be no respect to scandal [i.e. we should not care if it causes a scandal] to dispense with (better: to abolish) human traditions, if they cannot be observed according to divine law" (*Lutheri, Melanch., Karolostadii.* Basel, 1522, G VII v).

Scripture. This was a standard line of argument in the Wittenberg movement: human law must be brought into line with divine law as revealed in Scripture.[137] Although at this point still ready to defer to pastoral concerns regarding the weak in faith, Karlstadt (and to a lesser extent Melanchthon) sought to avoid any violation of divine law by acting quickly to reform the liturgy of communion. Luther, on the other hand, now preferred to avoid scandalising the conscience of the weak, who were not yet ready to take the chalice at communion. He wanted to prepare the ground for reform through sermons and teaching.[138] This difference replicated the positions adopted by Luther and Karlstadt in the discussion on celibacy and monastic vows.

4.3 *Recreating the Jubilee: Karlstadt's Agenda for Old Testament Social Reform (1520–1522)*

Debates on legal issues in the early Reformation focused mainly on such matters of canon law as the constitution of the Church, liturgical practice and the administration of the Sacraments. Acts of charity and their secular administration were clearly commanded by Scripture and therefore also fell under the reforming purview.[139] Possibly moved to write by the ongoing debate in Wittenberg on new legislation regulating poor relief, eventually introduced at the beginning of 1521,[140] Karlstadt published a treatise in August 1520 dealing with the Old Testament concept of the jubilee year.[141] The idea re-surfaced during discussions held in late 1521 relating to the introduction of a municipal constitution for Wittenberg. A printed collection of Wittenberg disputation theses, published in Basel in 1522, included a set of anonymous contributions arguing for social reforms to be implemented on the basis of Biblical principles. These theses discussed the applicability of the jubilee year to sixteenth century society.[142]

---

137 Cf. Bubenheimer, "Scandalum," 286–291, 310; for Karlstadt's theology of law cf. Bubenheimer, *Consonantia*, 246–250.

138 Cf. Wilhelm H. Neuser. *Die Abendmahlslehre Melanchthons in ihrer geschichtlichen Entwicklung (1519–1530)*. Neukirchen-Vluyn: Verlag der Buchhandlung des Erziehungsvereins, 1968, 127–160; Wolfgang Simon. *Die Messopfertheologie Martin Luthers: Voraussetzung, Genese, Gestalt und Rezeption*. Tübingen: Mohr Siebeck 2002, 419–513.

139 Cf. Carter Lindberg. "'There Should Be No Beggars Among Christians': Karlstadt, Luther and the Origins of Protestant Poor Relief." *Church History* 46 (1977): 313–334.

140 Cf. ibid., 326–329. The present author finds little to support Lindberg's assertion that Karlstadt's interest in this subject was merely academic, cf. ibid., 324.

141 Cf. Martin Brecht. "Der Kanon der Heiligen Schrift." In *Querdenker der Reformation: Andreas Bodenstein von Karlstadt und seine frühen Wirkung*, ed. Ulrich Bubenheimer and Stefan Oehmig. Würzburg: Religion und Kultur-Verlag, 2001, 147 f.

142 *Lutheri, Melanch., Karolostadii*. Basel, 1522, F VIII v.

Deut 15:1–18, the text which the Wittenberg theologians had used in their disputation with the Franciscans some years previously, decreed that debts should be remitted and Hebrew slaves freed every seven years. Papal decrees had used this institution as a proof text for the theology of indulgences, spiritualising the remission of debts as liberation from the penalty for sin. Indeed, special indulgences were tied to holy years proclaimed by the Pope.[143] The discourse on the jubilee in Wittenberg took the social provisions of this Mosaic institution in much more literal terms. The anonymous author of the aforementioned set of theses concluded that the command of Deut 15:1–18 still applied to Christians albeit as a general principle not bound to certain years:

> "2. *Fidelis tamen in domo CHRISTI, Iubilei tum literam tum spiritum custodit.*
> 3. *Item annum remissionis Christiani debent observare, quamquam non sit illis septimus sed continuus.*
> 4. *Debemus itaque mutuum dare fratri egenti, neque usuram, neque sortem petentes.*
> 5. *Remissionis enim anni ius postulat, ut non solum servum fratrem emancipes, verumetiam viaticum addas."*[144]

As such, Christians were obliged to give to the needy and forbidden from lending for interest; they were also to set their 'servants' free. The problem in interpreting the demand made by the anonymous theses is the lack of clarity in the sixteenth century understanding of who counted as a servant.

The new emphasis placed on the inseparable nature of secular and Church law was given expression in the town constitution promulgated by Wittenberg council in early 1522. Establishing communion in both kinds and prohibiting worship with images, it combined these religious measures with the establishment of a common treasury from which poor relief was to be funded and poor artisans could borrow in times of hardship. Such loans did not incur interest and could even be remitted if the borrower was unable to repay them.[145]

Karlstadt responded to this development with a treatise (the combination of two sermons) in which he welcomed the new town constitution and

---

143 Cf. Shaffern, "Medieval Theology," 26 f.

144 "(2) But the believer in the house of CHRIST must keep the jubilee in letter as well as in spirit. (3) Furthermore, Christians must keep the year of remission, although for those it is not the seventh [year], but always. (4) Thus, we must mutually give to the needy brother, whilst seeking neither interest nor goods. (5) For the law of the year of remission demands, that you not only free [your] servant brother, but you should also add something [for him] to eat on the way" (*Lutheri, Melanch. Karolostadii* … Basel, 1522, F VIII v).

145 Cf. Anonymous. "Ordnung der Stadt Wittenberg." In *Flugschriften der frühen Reformationsbewegung (1518–1524)*, vol. 2, ed. Adolf Laube, Sigrid Looß, and Annerose Schneider. Vaduz: Topos Verlag, 1983, 1033.

demanded its complete enforcement.[146] *Von abtuhung der Bylder Vnd das keyn Betdler vnther den Christen seyn soll* demonstrates that the fight against religious images and his advocacy of social reform were intertwined components of his theology.[147] In his first sermon, Karlstadt had based his arguments on Exodus and Deuteronomy, contending that although a Christian community should not tolerate the use of graven images, their removal remained a matter for the town magistrate and not popular outcry.[148] The focus of the second sermon on the social reforms and its extensive examination of the jubilee year points to Karlstadt as the author of the set of theses on the jubilee year, the disputation of which probably provided the backdrop for the establishment of the town order.[149]

Karlstadt's treatise *Von abtuhung der Bylder Vnd das keyn Betdler vnther den Christen seyn soll* includes extensive quotations from the Old Testament; he viewed the concept of the jubilee year as binding for Christians. In keeping with the position that he had advocated in the disputation attributed to him by Bubenheimer, Karlstadt did not advocate the institution of the Old Testament seven-year cycle, but a distillation of its essence into a general principle. As such, he argued that Christians had a duty of charity which was to be performed without expectation of return.[150] Interestingly, as the anonymous author of the theses on the jubilee, Karlstadt did not entirely prohibit the practice of loaning money, and believed that solvent debtors should be obliged to repay their loans (Theses 6–9).[151] In his sermon, Karlstadt also demanded the liberation of unfree people, yet did not reflect on the contemporary nature and status of serfdom. He made fleeting reference to the moral obligation of the Wittenberg citizenry to make gifts of money to departing servants, whilst writing at length on the responsibility of abbots and abbesses to emancipate their charges.[152] As such, he sought to establish the principle rather than the practice of the jubilee year; the injunction of 'Biblical law' to free slaves and clear debts was still applied to the changed social context, but in an adapted form. He

146 Andreas [Bodenstein von] Karlstadt. *Von Abtuhung der Bilder: Und das keyn Bedtler unther den Christen seyn sollen 1522 und die Wittenberger Beutelordnung*, ed. Hans Lietzmann. Bonn: A. Marcus und E. Weber's Verlag, 1911.

147 Cf. Ulrich Bubenheimer. "Andreas Bodenstein von Karlstadt und die Reform von Gottesdienst und Leben." In *Martin Luther: Zeuge des Glaubens in Kirche und Gesellschaft*, ed. Evangelisches Bildungswerk Berlin. Abteilung kirchliche Erwachsenenbildung. Berlin: [self published, 1983], 65–79.

148 Cf. Karlstadt, *Abtuhung*, 4–22.

149 Cf. Bubenheimer, "Scandalum," 333 f.

150 Cf. Karlstadt, *Abtuhung*, 25 f.

151 *Lutheri, Melanch. Karolostadii ...* (Basel, 1522), F VIII v.

152 Cf. Karlstadt, *Abtuhung*, 26 f. (servants and maids), 27 f., and 29 f. (monks and nuns).

was clear, however, that the Bible contained a mandate for the contemporary magistrate:

> "9. *Magistratuum quoque est creditoribus conniventibus debitores ex avaricia solutionem differentes iure gladii compellere.*
> 10. *Sicut enim vindicta ad ius gladii pertinet, ita et rerum divisio."*[153]

Secular government not only had the right to act (cf. Rom 13) in order to achieve an equitable distribution of resources, but the responsibility to do so in order to achieve justice on earth. The mixing of the fields of theology and politics in this treatise reveals Karlstadt's understanding of law. Karlstadt never advocated a root-and-branch reform of the institutions of secular law, and never sought to treat the civil law of the Pentateuch as a matter for pure emulation.[154] He did wish, however, to make the corpus of early modern civil law more reflective of God's revealed priorities. Banishing images from churches and ensuring social justice were not separate issues, but two different aspects of an indivisible legal competence.[155] Moses legislated for both, so could Wittenberg town council.

4.4 *A Parting of Ways: Hermeneutical Differences within the Wittenberg Camp*

Despite the painstaking fashion in which Karlstadt argued his case, his theses still remained socially explosive. One controversial topic was the remission of debts. Academic discussions on debt in sixteenth century Europe did not usually make recourse to the Old Testament concept of the jubilee year but rather stressed the importance of repaying borrowed money. The preferred option in cases of insolvency was deferral of payment rather than debt relief.[156] The

153 "(9) It is also [the business of] the magistrates by law of the sword to force debtors, who put off the redemption to lenient creditors for [reasons of] avarice, [to pay back their debts]. (10) Because as punishments belong to the law of the sword, so also [does] the division of goods" (*Lutheri, Melanch. Karolostadii* … [Basel, 1532], F VIII v).

154 Cf. Bubenheimer, *Consonantia*, 246–250.

155 The idea of establishing Wittenberg as a sacred community came from Karlstadt and represented one of his leading concerns; cf. Stefan Oehmig. "'Christlicher Bürger' – 'christliche Stadt'? Zu Andreas Bodensteins von Karlstadts Vorstellungen von einem christlichen Gemeinwesen und den Tugenden seiner Bürger." In *Querdenker der Reformation: Andreas Bodenstein von Karlstadt und seine frühen Wirkung*, ed. Ulrich Bubenheimer and Stefan Oehmig. Würzburg: Religion und Kultur-Verlag, 2001, 151–185.

156 This approach is stressed by Wim Decock in his analysis of the teaching of the school of Salamanca in 16th and 17th century Spain on debt relief, cf. Wim Decock. "Law, Religion, and Debt Relief: Balancing above the 'Abyss of Despair' in Early Modern Canon Law and Theology. *American Journal of Legal History* 57.2 (2017): 125–141. I would like to thank Professor Decock for providing me with a preprint of this article.

idea of the jubilee was even more radical when applied to the emancipation of those in a situation of legally restricted freedom. What would happen, if these provisions were applied not just to monks, nuns, manservants and maids, but to the serfs?[157] Luther recognised the dangers of the unrestricted application of Mosaic Law to the social institutions of early modern rural society and in 1525 accused Karlstadt of judaising. Indeed, in a treatise written in 1524, Karlstadt interpreted the command to honour the Sabbath as mandating not just the decision to rest from all labour, but an injunction to landowners not to prevent their labourers from doing so.[158] This demonstrates Karlstadt's continuing interest in the contemporary applicability of Biblical law and his desire to implement the social provisions of the Pentateuch.

Luther was also interested in using the concept of the jubilee year as a template for social legislation. Unlike Karlstadt however, he did not view the jubilee as a divine commandment[159] – a subtle, yet important difference.[160] Luther saw that responsibility for the administration of social affairs lay with the secular authorities, who although directly responsible to God, were themselves not bound by the precepts of Mosaic Law. Karlstadt regarded these laws as universally binding, although he did not call for a literal restoration of the

157 Bubenheimer contends that Karlstadt's arguments in favour of the jubilee year also represented a covert attack on the institution of serfdom, cf. Bubenheimer, "Bodenstein," 71. The nervous state of secular government became apparent when in 1523 Johann Mantel –– who approved of Karlstadt's position on celibacy –– used the idea of the jubilee year to call for social reforms in Württemberg. He was imprisoned by the Habsburg government for two years, cf. Martin Brecht and Hermann Ehmer. *Südwestdeutsche Reformationsgeschichte. Zur Einführung der Reformation im Herzogtum Württemberg 1534*. Stuttgart: Calver Verlag, 1984: 91; Bossert, "Mantel," 60–62. I owe thanks to Professor Bubenheimer, who directed me to Mantel's social criticism.

158 On Luther's criticism of judaising, cf. Thomas Kaufmann. *Luthers Juden*. 3rd ed. Stuttgart: Reclam 2017, 88 f. For Karlstadt's treatise on the Sabbath cf. Volkmar Joestel. "Andreas Bodenstein von Karlstadt's Schrift *Von dem Sabbat und gebotenen Feiertagen* im Spiegel der sozialen Bewegung in Ostthüringen (1522–1524)." In *Querdenker der Reformation: Andreas Bodenstein von Karlstadt und seine frühen Wirkung*, ed. Ulrich Bubenheimer and Stefan Oehmig. Würzburg: Religion und Kultur-Verlag 2001, 211–227. In this treatise, Karlstadt also criticised the abuse of the pulpit by some priests to demand that their parishioners repay debts; cf. ibid., 221–224. The question as to how far Luther's growing distance from his earlier philosemitic position was influenced by his fear of judaising '*Schwärmer*' like Karlstadt has been addressed by Volkmar Joestel in a talk at the International Luther Congress 2017.

159 Cf. Martin Luther. "Wider die himmlischen Propheten, von den Bildern und Sakrament. 1525." In *WA* 18, 81.20–26. This point was raised by Volkmar Joestel at the International Luther Congress 2017.

160 For Luther's general position on the jubilee, cf. Heckel, *Lex charitatis*, 170. Melanchthon also referred to the jubilee year in his lectures from 1522, cf. Kruse, *Universitätstheologie*, 368 n. 529.

seven-year cycle.[161] This hermeneutical parting of the ways in reaction to the failure of the Wittenberg movement led to division amongst the Reformers and the intervention of the secular powers in their programme of Church reform. Luther and Melanchthon sought sanctuary from increasingly radical elements in the Wittenberg movement in an alliance with the magistrate. Karlstadt, on the other hand, left academia for a country parsonage, from where he hoped to mobilise the common man as a new factor in Church reform.[162]

5. The Road to the State Church (1522 and after)

Close study of the Wittenberg disputations reveals a change in the understanding of law on the part of the Wittenberg Reformers after 1522. Having established the first evangelical municipal constitution, the protagonists of the Wittenberg movement were now caught between the competing pressures of the opposition of the political authorities on the one hand (supported by Luther) and pressure from the more radical elements of the lower orders of the town population on the other. This situation caused a split. Whilst a minority in the Wittenberg circle around Karlstadt sought to strengthen the influence of the wider community, the majority decided to work within the existing political structures of the early modern territories and autonomous cities. Former radicals such as Melanchthon joined Luther in taking steps to slow the pace of reform and implement it, wherever possible, in close collaboration with the secular authorities,[163] thus paving the way for the construction of a state church.[164]

This process left its mark in the disputations conducted in the 1520s. Firstly, the authority of secular government was strengthened within Protestant doctrine, as can be shown by a disputation presided over by Melanchthon in June 1522. This disputation formulated essential elements of the magisterial Reformation, expressing the Lutheran principles of the relationship between Church and State, and the doctrine of the three estates. Secondly, a new genus of disputation was developed in the Swiss cantons and German Imperial cities; the so-called political disputation. No longer held in an academic context,

161 Apart from his emphasis on the importance of Biblical law, this position can be explained by his view that grace enabled the Christian to follow the Law, cf. Heckel, *Martin Luthers Reformation*, 387 f.

162 Cf. Kaufmann, *Erlöste und Verdammte*, 166–169.

163 In this process, magisterial Reformers consciously exploited the disorder allegedly caused by the Wittenberg movement to call for a more orderly method of establishing a reformed community, cf. Krentz, *Ritualwandel*, 215–242; Kaufmann, *Geschichte*, 385–392.

164 Cf. Bubenheimer, "Luthers Stellung," 211–214.

they were employed by municipal governments to institute and legitimise the nascent Protestant church. Within this context, disputations acquired a function within the process of establishing law itself.

5.1 *Melanchthon's Theological Justification of the Magisterial Reformation (1522)*

Melanchthon's perception of the Reform process changed in 1522. Feeling the burden of official disapproval and facing the threat of popular unrest, he abandoned his close alliance with Karlstadt and revised his stance regarding the pressing need to reform both the Mass and the practice of worship with images. Opting for a more cautious approach, he came to an agreement with Wittenberg council and representatives of the university, concluded in February 1522.[165] As such, Luther's announcement, made upon his return to Wittenberg, that many of the reforms would be rescinded (including the reinstatement of images) represented less of a decision than public confirmation of a change in policy already underway. Despite this new course, developments in early 1522 testified to the existence of greater levels of disagreement between the Reformers than the thesis collections of 1520 to 1522 would indicate.[166] Karlstadt, who remained steadfast in his demands for radical reform, was established as a scapegoat for the unrest supposed to have been provoked by the radicalism of the Wittenberg movement.[167]

Whilst Karlstadt himself remained consistent in his demands to recast Church and society in accordance with Biblical law, Melanchthon distanced himself from a reform based on narrow Biblicism, arguing in favour of a strict separation between *temporalia* and *spiritualia*. Seeking to avoid placing too great an emphasis on Old Testament law, he worked out his own version of the 'doctrine of the two kingdoms' to provide a contemporary legitimation for secular government. Set out in a circular disputation from June 1522, he adopted arguments made by Luther in his *Invocavit* sermons from the spring of 1522.[168] The importance of these new disputation theses was highlighted by

165 For Melanchthon's change of mind, cf. several statements on the Mass and images in Nikolaus Müller (ed.). *Die Wittenberger Bewegung 1521 und 1522: Die Vorgänge in und um Wittenberg während Luthers Wartburgaufenthalt. Briefe, Akten und dergleichen und Personalien*. Leipzig: Heinsius, 1911, 85; on the dating and character of these sentences, cf. Bubenheimer, "Scandalum," 292–295, on the negations with the Prince-Elector cf. Krentz, *Ritualwandel*, 209 f.

166 Cf. Kruse, *Universitätstheologie*, 287–293.

167 Cf. Krentz, *Ritualwandel*, 236–241.

168 Cf. Bubenheimer, "Luthers Stellung," 202–210.

their double publication in both an independent print run[169] and a new edition of the *Loci communes*.[170]

Melanchthon started with a definition of the two authorities (the spiritual and corporeal) to which the individual is subject, with especial reference to the worldly, corporeal regime:

> "1. *Duplex est regimen, spirituale et corporale.*
> 2. *Corporale regimen de externo rerum usu constituit.*
> 3. *Estque civilis administratio, qua cohercetur corpus, res dividuntur, vis prohibitur.*"[171]

He differentiated between a corporeal regime, covering the government of natural man, which was capable only of effecting an inferior form of "*iustitia carnis*"[172] and a spiritual regime, ruling over the souls of men to bring salvation and justice by the Word of God. This 'spiritual justice' – of which a sinner could only partake through the process of justification and which brought eternal life – was in no way comparable to natural 'carnal justice' (theses 27 and 28).[173] The 'corporeal regime' covered only natural things, and was governed by reason. Melanchthon's definition of the divine institution of the corporeal regime was very similar to that presented by Luther in his doctrine of the two kingdoms. Melanchthon's theses also constitute an early example of the doctrine of the three estates, which provided the foundation for Lutheran ethics. The influence of this doctrine on Melanchthon's thinking can be seen in the emphasis which he placed on the origin of temporal power, which he located within the patriarchal reign of the household: "*Proinde iure divino commissum est parentibus, ut familiam corporaliter regant.*"[174] This constituted the basis for authority within the worldly sphere:

---

169 Edited in Philipp Melanchthon. "Themata ad sextam feriam discutienda. 1522." In *MWA 1*, 168–170.

170 For the date ibid., 168. On the contents of this change for Melanchthon cf. Paul Schwarzenau, *Der Wandel im theologischen Ansatz bei Melanchthon 1525–1535*, Gütersloh: Bertelsmann 1956, 15–17.

171 "(1) There is a twofold mode of government, of spiritual things and of corporeal things. (2) The corporeal mode of government establishes the use of external things. (3) It consists of civil administration, by which the body is tamed, things are divided, violence is prohibited" (Melanchthon. "Themata ad sextam feriam," 168.1–5).

172 "[C]arnal justice" (Thesis 9, ibid., 169.1).

173 "(27) Nam iustitia spiritus est vita aeterna, verbum enim vita est. Iohan. 1. / 28. Quid autem vitae aeternae cum iustitiis carnis, quae circa res usu pereuntes versatur?" (ibid.: 170. 4–7)

174 "Therefore, by divine right it is commissioned to the parents that they corporeally reign over their family" (thesis 6, ibid., 168.11 f.).

> "10. *Parentum loco sunt, quibus illi vicem suam committunt, ut paedagogi, magistratus in urbibus, principes, ad quos consensu civium defertur imperium.*
> 11. *Hoc est quod Paulus Ro. 13. potestatem ordinatione dei vocat.*"[175]

Melanchthon opened his argument with reference to the origins of corporeal government, which he saw as rooted in Adam's rule over Eve as described in Gen 2.[176] As such, the household provided the foundation of the entire secular political order. Although designed to be wielded by the *pater familias*, this power could be delegated to schoolteachers and secular government, the latter of which was sanctioned by divine command in Rom 13. Despite carrying certain democratic undertones, the significance for Melanchthon of the doctrine of the consensus of the governed should not be exaggerated. Melanchthon's approach remained firmly rooted in existing concepts of power and authority. Within this structure, he accorded an autonomous role to the Church, the household and worldly government, all three of which enjoyed divine sanction and which were all subordinate to, yet maintained separately from spiritual justice.

Melanchthon displayed greater interest in and placed greater emphasis on natural law in his later works, adjusting his previous position and now viewing natural law as a set of universally agreed principles instituted by God to govern the corporeal realm and binding not only for secular government but also the agents of education, employers, and the household. Although Melanchthon had never recommended that secular rulers rely completely on Biblical law, writing in his *Loci communes* (1521), he had recommended and hoped that the princes take the judicial law of the Pentateuch into account within their own legislative practice.[177] Moving away from his previous reliance on Mosaic Law, which he no longer saw as binding contemporary civil government,[178] Melanchthon now found value not only in Roman law – which he considered

175 "(10) [Taking] the place of parents are those, to whom they entrust their place, such as teachers, magistrates in the towns, princes, to whom by the consensus of the governed the power to rule is delegated. (11) This is, what Paul in Romans 13 calls power by the ordinance of God" (ibid.: 169.3–8). Luther first proposed the idea of legitimising government on the basis of parental authority in his *Sermon about Good Works* from 1520; cf. Brecht, *Luther*, vol. 1, 350.

176 Thesis 4, Melanchthon, "Themata ad sextam feriam," 168.6–8.

177 Cf. Philipp Melanchthon. *Loci communes 1521. Lateinisch und deutsch*. Gütersloh: Gütersloher Verlagshaus Mohn, 1993, 305 (7.44).

178 Cf. Guido Kisch. *Melanchthons Recht- und Soziallehre*. Berlin: De Gruyter, 1967, 102–115; Pfister, *Entwicklung*, 75 f.

as far superior to the Germanic common law tradition[179] – but also canon law, which he was now able to appreciate both as a template for contemporary legislation and an instrument for the instruction of the laity in matters of Faith. This was already apparent in his disputation from 1522:

> "22. *Ecclesiasticae traditiones civiles leges sunt et paedagogia quaedam, nihil ad regimen spirituale pertinens.*
> 23. *Loquor autem de iis traditionibus, in quibus nihil contra scripturam decretum est.*"[180]

The Melanchthon of 1521 who brooked no delay in the reform of the Mass had by now adopted a more relaxed attitude. This Melanchthon viewed liturgical forms as part of man-made law and not a vehicle of spiritual justice. As such, their reform could legitimately be driven by reference to reason and he saw no impediment to the retention of images in Church worship. He also had no problem with continuing to withhold the cup from the laity, at least for a time. These things were not necessary for salvation. The only limitations to his new-found latitude related to practices which he regarded as clearly violating the teachings of Scripture.[181] This position was far removed from that of Karlstadt and enabled the retention of canon law within Protestant university education and Church government.[182]

Melanchthon's position on the status of the liturgy and the jurisdiction of civil law in Church affairs reinforced the direction of travel towards a settlement in which princes were established as the supreme governors of the Church in their territory. Karlstadt took a different view in his pronouncements from 1521

179 Cf. Isabelle Deflers. *Lex und Ordo: eine rechtshistorische Untersuchung der Rechtsauffassung Melanchthons*. Berlin: Duncker und Humblot, 2005, 139–146; Kisch, *Melanchthons Recht- und Soziallehre*, 116–130.

180 "(22) Ecclesiastical traditions are civil laws and [in a] certain [way] pedagogical [institutions]; they do not in any way impinge upon spiritual justice. (23) But I speak about such traditions, in which nothing against Scripture is decreed" (Melanchthon, "Themata ad sextam feriam," 169. 31–35). For Melanchthon's growing appreciation of church traditions cf. Sperl, *Melanchthon*, 148–154.

181 He defended Luther's reversal of the reforms in a letter to Johann Hess in Breslau, cf. Barge, *Karlstadt*, vol. 1, 451.

182 For the survival of canon law in the German Lutheran churches cf. Johannes Heckel, "Das Decretum Gratiani und das deutsche evangelische Kirchenrecht." In *Das blinde, undeutliche Wort 'Kirche'*, by Johannes Heckel. Cologne and Graz: Böhlau, 1964, 1–49. For Melanchthon's role ibid., 28–30; another major advocate of canon law within Wittenberg university was the professor of law Hieronymus Schurff cf. Wiebke Schaich-Klose. *D. Hieronymus Schürpf: Leben und Werk des Wittenberger Reformationsjuristen 1481–1554*. Trogen, Switzerland: Buchdruckerei Fritz Meili, 1967, 53–60.

and 1522, advocating a concept of theocratic government by the magistrate. Conceiving for this office a new role as the executor of God's will, he argued that the magistrate should be guided in his task by a limited form of minimalist Biblicism. For his part, Melanchthon saw that whilst the secular authorities should enforce the precepts of God's Word, they should legislate (also in Church matters) on the basis of reason, and not some form of narrow Biblicism. Melanchthon's view accorded secular governments a certain degree of flexibility, even concerning the constitution and liturgy of the Church, which thesis 22 referred to as the subject of civil legislation.[183] Luther and Melanchthon's new attitude towards the scope and function of secular government was reinforced by their reaction to the Peasants' war, and exhibited a new-found willingness to work with the existing authorities.[184]

The originally radical Melanchthon eventually reconciled with the conservative Luther and set about formalising certain Lutheran concepts such as the political implications of the separation of the two kingdoms. The outcome of this process was a theological justification for an evangelical state church. In taking this path, Melanchthon was able to provide a Lutheran justification for the existing political order whilst retaining the influence of traditional philosophy (he relied heavily on Cicero) and Roman law in theological training.[185] Moreover, by aligning the new movement with political realities and preserving the influence of traditional philosophy and law in its doctrine, he made Lutheranism an acceptable and practicable doctrine for the new ruler-friendly Church settlement.

5.2 *From Academia to the Public Sphere: the Development of Political Disputations (1523–1536)*

Very few disputation theses from Wittenberg Theological Faculty exist for the years after 1522. Formal graduations were suspended for several years and the medieval form of disputation fell on hard times within the new academic culture.[186] Despite the decline of this venerable institution in Wittenberg, it was taken up with gusto by the Swiss Reformer Huldrych Zwingli in Zurich. In 1523,

183 Cf. Sperl, *Melanchthon*, 148 f.

184 For Melanchthon's leading role in the visitations in Saxony after 1527 cf. Wilhelm Maurer. *Der junge Melanchthon zwischen Humanismus und Reformation, vol. 2. Der Theologe*. Göttingen: Vandenhoeck & Ruprecht, 1969, 470–481. For Luther's position on the ecclesiastical responsibility of secular government cf. Heckel, *Martin Luthers Reformation*, 584–638.

185 On the importance of Melanchthon's change of mind in 1522, cf. Sperl, *Melanchthon*, 146–154; Pfister, *Entwicklung*, 66–77.

186 Cf. Wolf, "Bedeutung," 43 f.

Zwingli mounted two defences of his theology against Catholic opponents. These disputations, based on sets of theses composed by the Swiss Reformer, were attended by the assembled citizenry of Zurich and its magistrate. The magistrate not only required attendance by all the city's priests, but adjudicated on the outcome. In January 1523, the magistrate decided that Zwingli's theology was true, and in October adopted his cautious approach to Church reform against both Catholic resistance and radical demands from the nascent left-wing of the Reformation.[187]

As Volker Leppin has shown, Zwingli's transfer of the academic disputation to the political sphere represents the logical conclusion to the history of disputations in the early Reformation period. Since the Leipzig debate of 1519, disputations had acquired a wider audience which far exceeded their original academic context. They were now used by the Wittenberg movement to propagate reform. As the driving force in bringing them to Zurich, Zwingli took the next logical step, transforming them into an instrument with which to legitimise religious change within a city.[188] The 33 political disputations organised or at least proposed in several towns and cities in the Swiss Confederation and the Holy Roman Empire between 1523 and 1536 bear testimony to the success of his approach.[189] The vast majority of these disputations were called by municipal magistrates to heal the religious divide within their own particular jurisdiction.[190] This aim marks them out from academic disputations. Held in churches and not universities, they were conducted in the vernacular;[191] the result was usually adjudicated not by academic or Church authorities, but by

---

187 Cf. Bernd Moeller, *Zwinglis Disputationen: Studien zur Kirchengründung in den Städten der frühen Reformation*. Göttingen: Vandenhoeck & Ruprecht, ²2011, 13–52; Kaufmann, *Mitte*, 531–545.

188 Cf. Volker Leppin. "Disputationen als Medium der Theologie und Kirchenreform: Zur Transformation eines akademischen Mediums." In *Transformationen: Studien zu den Wandlungsprozessen in Theologie und Frömmigkeit zwischen Spätmittelalter und Reformation*, by Volker Leppin. Tübingen: Mohr Siebeck, 2015: 419–428.

189 Cf. Moeller. *Zwinglis Disputationen*, 57–176.

190 Cf. ibid., 193–196. There are two exceptions in 1526: Firstly, a disputation in Baden (Aargau) was organised by the non-Protestant cantons to contain the influence of the Zurich Reformation on their own areas. Secondly, the territorial Reformation in Hesse was preceded by a synod in Homberg at which a political disputation was held. As a result, the synod concluded that it was necessary to issue a Protestant church order for the principality. Despite this finding, Luther's opposition to the proposed *Reformatio Ecclesiarum Hassiae* meant that it was never enacted; cf. ibid.: 104–117; Johannes Schilling: *Klöster und Mönche in der hessischen Reformation*. Gütersloh: Gütersloher Verlagshaus, 1997, 186–204.

191 Cf. Moeller. *Zwinglis Disputationen*, 185 f. This development was preceded by Luther's decision to address the audience of the Leipzig disputation in German, cf. Schubert. "Libertas Disputandi," 437 f., and 441 f.

the magistrate.[192] This development grew out of the doctrine of the priesthood of all believers, which established orthodox magistrates as a better judge of Truth than heterodox clergymen and university professors.[193]

The character of these disputations also differed from their early Wittenberg counterparts. Not open-ended and eschewing discussion, they were performed less as a search for the Truth than as set pieces with the intention of legitimising the final introduction of a pre-determined policy of Church reform.[194] Persuasion and propaganda were combined with social discipline. The combination of deliberation and order was specifically suited to achieving the stated ideal of establishing the city as a sacred community of citizens.[195] Nevertheless, as the chosen instrument with which to legitimise evangelical preaching and Church order, disputations performed a similar function to reform by princely imposition, adapted to assuage the more independent sensibilities of the citizens of self-governing communes.[196] Political disputations thus performed a specific function in sanctioning political decisions pertaining to Church government and doctrine.[197] They became part of the process which amalgamated civil law with religious principles to produce confessionally-homogenous cities.[198] Starting as an instrument through which to deliberate on, demand and propagate change during the early Reformation, disputations thus developed into the preferred instrument with which secular authorities sought to initiate and legitimise legal changes within a community.[199]

192 Cf. Gottfried Seebaß. *Geschichte des Christentums III: Spätmittelalter – Reformation – Konfesionalisierung*. Stuttgart: W. Kohlhammer, 2006: 165.

193 Cf. Kaufmann, *Mitte*, 531 f., esp. n. 310. Protestant *Flugschriften* also presented discussions between laymen and theologians as disputations, providing another example for the dissolution of traditional academic forms; cf. ibid., 538–540 (ch. III, 2.4); Susanne Schuster: *Dialogflugschriften der frühen Reformationszeit. Literarische Fortführung der Disputation und Resonanzräume reformatorischen Denkens*. Göttingen: Vandenhoeck und Ruprecht, 2019.

194 Cf. Bernd Moeller. *Reichsstadt und Reformation: Neue Ausgabe*. Tübingen: Mohr Siebeck, 2011, 177 f.

195 Cf. ibid., passim.

196 For the Reformation of the Princes cf. Kaufmann, *Geschichte*, 504 f.

197 For northern Germany cf. Otto Scheib. "Die Religionsgespräche in Norddeutschland in der Neuzeit und ihre Entwicklung." *Jahrbuch der Gesellschaft für niedersächsische Kirchengeschichte* 75 (1977): 39–88, 50–64, and 84–88.

198 Cf. Wolfgang Reinhard. "Was ist katholische Konfessionalisierung?" In *Die katholische Konfessionalisierung: wissenschaftliches Symposion der Gesellschaft zur Herausgabe des Corpus Catholicorum und des Vereins für Reformationsgeschichte 1993*, ed. Wolfgang Reinhard and Heinz Schilling. Gütersloh: Gütersloher Verlagshaus, 1995, 419–452.

199 Cf. Leppin, "Disputationen," 428.

Whilst these political disputations differed strongly from their academic forerunners, they also exhibited a number of similarities in terms of both form and their attitude towards authority. The Wittenberg model of academic disputation served as the inspiration for political disputations, and Wittenberg theologians sometimes even tried to initiate political disputations in other cities.[200] The form taken by the political disputation prepared by Johann Hess in Breslau in 1524 bore a striking resemblance to an academic event.[201] Indeed, it is possible that he based the disputation on two collections of Wittenberg theses, one published in Basel in 1522, and a manuscript of 23 further sets of handwritten theses, composed around 1524.[202] Moreover, Hess' introduction to the set of theses providing the basis for the political disputation closely resembles Luther's introduction to a set of theses used in an academic debate held in 1518.[203]

200 One example is a set of 16 theses focusing on grace and free will, which Luther's former colleague Nikolaus von Amsdorf had planned to defend against the preachers of Magdeburg cathedral. Although the disputation did not take place, Amsdorf's theses were incorporated in later collections of Wittenberg theses, cf. *Propositiones a Marti. Luthero*. Wittenberg, 1530, D VIII v–E v; for the context cf. Hans Stille. *Nikolaus von Amsdorf: Sein Leben bis zu seiner Einweisung als Bischof in Naumburg.* (*1483–1545*). Zeulenroda: Sporn 1937, 63 f. When the former Augustinian Henry of Zutphen was called to a provincial synod, he sent his Archbishop a set of theses which he had defended during an Augustinian chapter in Grimma in 1522 and possibly also within the scope of his graduation as *baccalaureus biblicus* in Wittenberg in 1521; cf. Otto Clemen, "Miscellen zur Reformationsgeschichte." *Theologische Studien und Kritiken* 74 (1901): 126–140, 130 f.

201 Cf. Moeller, *Zwinglis Disputationen*, 165–170; Otto Scheib, "Die Breslauer Disputation von 1524 als Beispiel eines frühreformatorischen Religionsgespräches eines Doktors der Theologie." In *Festschrift für Bernhard Stasiewski: Beiträge zur ostdeutschen und osteuropäischen Kirchengeschichte*, ed. Gabriel Adriány and Joseph Gottschalk. Cologne and Wien, 1975: 98–106.

202 Hess' copy of the Basel printed collection and the manuscript collection of disputation theses are now to be found in the volume Ms. theol. lat. oct. 91 at Berlin *Staatsbibliothek*, for a description, cf. Beate Braun-Niehr. *Die theologischen Handschriften in octavo der Staatsbibliothek zu Berlin Preußischer Kulturbesitz*. Wiesbaden: Harrassowitz, 2007, 159–164. Ulrich Bubenheimer made some corrections to Niehr's description of it in Karlstadt, *Kritische Gesamtausgabe*, vol. 1.1, 485–487; the manuscript collection is edited in Kolde, "Disputationsthesen," passim.

203 Cf. "D. Iohannes Hessus, Christianae Theologiae Professor, Canonisus (sic!) et Parochus Vratislauensis de Subiectis Axiomatis pro veritate inquirenda et timidis conscientiis consolandis disseret. M. D. XXIIII." In Johann Erhard Kapp. *M. Johann Erhard Kappens, Kleine Nachlese einiger, größten Theils noch ungedruckter, und sonderlich zur Erläuterung Der (sic!) Reformations-Geschichte nützlicher Urkunden. Anderer Theil.* Leipzig: Braun, 1727, 606–610. The original set of theses: Martin Luther. "Pro veritate inquirenda et timorentis conscientiis consolanda. 1518". In *WA 1*, 630–633.

5.3 *Academic Disputations after 1530*

The development of the confessional state also influenced the nature of academic disputations. Revived as an instrument for formal academic training and discourse by the university reform of the 1530s, disputations returned with a different character and purpose. Despite gaining significance as the preferred means through which to articulate a Lutheran condemnation of Catholic teachings and Protestant heresies,[204] they lost the experimental quality which had characterised their role as part of an open-ended search for the Truth.[205] With the institutional and doctrinal confines of the nascent confessional state firmly established, disputations were now intended to flesh out the details of this given settlement and not extend or otherwise alter it. The successors to Luther and Melanchthon were vigilant in preserving their theological independence against government intrusion,[206] yet remained conscious of their responsibility as theologians to maintain the welfare of the local church within the existing political settlement. The triumph of the Lutheran state church was taken as an axiom not to be questioned.[207]

6. Conclusion

This article has attempted to reconstruct the ways and ends to which the Wittenberg circle used legal arguments, and the basic definition of law that underpinned their efforts. In analysing sets of theses, composed as the basis for academic discussion, it was able to demonstrate a vigorous interaction on the part of the Wittenberg theologians with several concepts of law and a range of legal arguments. These arguments were presented and discussed within a climate of open inquiry, involving the development of an 'experimental theology'[208] that sought to develop the resulting new insights into coherent structures of doctrine and Church practice. Using this sophisticated form of intellectual inquiry, the Wittenberg circle developed its own understanding of law and applied its findings to their project of religious reform.

---

204 Cf. the collection of Luther's later disputations in Drews, *Disputationen*, passim.

205 A similiar conclusion in Kaumfann, *Mitte*, 531–545.

206 Cf. Kenneth G. Appold. *Orthodoxie als Konsensbildung: Das theologische Disputationswesen an der Universität Wittenberg 1570–1710*. Tübingen: Mohr Siebeck, 2004, 312–317.

207 Even Jakob Martini (1570–1649), a strong proponent of the doctrine of the priesthood of all believers and Church autonomy, did not question the legitimacy of the government of the Church by the political authorities, cf. ibid., 278–280.

208 Cf. Bubenheimer, "Reformationsdiplomatie," 301 f.

This discussion was shown to have unfolded in four distinct phases. The Wittenberg circle was initially reluctant to abandon canon law and indeed used it to mount a sustained critique of a certain brand of jurisprudence, expressed in the theology of indulgences. At this early stage of the Reformation, Luther had yet to reject papal authority and still viewed the Papacy as an instrument of the Gospel. He did argue, however, that the reach of papal authority and canon law was restricted to the government of the earthly Church. Despite retaining these elements of medieval ecclesiology, the innovative potential of the nascent Wittenberg theology was apparent even at this early stage.

A second phase followed Luther's return to Wittenberg from the Leipzig disputation. Melanchthon sought to establish Scripture as the sole basis for theological discussion and the touchstone of all debate. The arguments presented in the disputations conducted on the subject of papal authority and the authority of canon law pointed to the necessity of establishing the transient and non-binding nature of man-made jurisprudence and its inferiority to the precepts of divine law, as expounded in Scripture. By the time of Luther's excommunication, the Wittenberg circle had fleshed out a coherent programme of ecclesiastical reform, as well as generating a number of proposals for the reform of welfare legislation.

After the Diet of Worms, the focus of the Wittenberg circle shifted from theological enquiry to matters of practical reform: the Reformers addressed questions of Church practice, calling for quick changes. In effect, academic disputations were now used both to advocate further steps of reform as well as to review the process of their implementation. The result of this reform discourse was a fundamental change in the ecclesiastical landscape of Wittenberg. The vision of the Reformers, especially Karlstadt, was of a root-and-branch Reformation of the town of Wittenberg, combining religious reform with social justice.

This period saw the development of hermeneutical differences between the Reformers. Whilst Karlstadt still argued like a lawyer who now wanted to apply 'Biblical law' to every area of Church and society, Luther emphasised the need for a cautious approach so as to accommodate the conscience of the weak in faith, who were not yet ready for overly drastic change. He proposed slowing the process of reform and placing a stronger emphasis on preaching and education before implementing further change. Melanchthon, who in 1521 was sometimes even more radical than Karlstadt, became increasingly moderate and finally adopted Luther's position.

Luther's return to Wittenberg in 1522 coincided with the increasing weight of opinion swinging behind moves to establish a Lutheran state church. In Melanchthon's new approach to law and government, reason was still able to govern the world of the outer man. This was applied not only to secular law, but also the constitution of the Church, which Melanchthon now viewed as falling under the purview of civil law.

During the 1520s, the focus of disputations changed. Political disputations, which superseded academic disputations for a time, became a means by which the political authorities sought to initiate and legitimise the formation of confessional polities. Translated from their original university context to the public sphere, disputations were transformed from an instrument with which to articulate a new understanding of theology, to a component in the law-making process. Whilst the practice of disputation certainly returned to academia in the 1530s, the rise of the confessional state had changed its function. Although Lutheran theologians in Wittenberg and elsewhere maintained their liberty to discuss theological issues, they did not question the unity of State, Church and society.

The analysis of the types of questions discussed in Wittenberg during the crucial years of the early Reformation has revealed how the interaction of theology and jurisprudence in the Wittenberg disputations provided the intellectual framework for the development of Lutheran legal and ethical thought. As other chapters in this volume will show, the discussions held in Wittenberg from 1517 to 1522 did not simply prepare the groundwork for concepts which would later become central to Lutheran legal and ethical thought. They also have a long-term significance which far outstrips their relevance to the early Reformation. In asking whether Biblical precedents were directly applicable to the legislative process of Lutheran states, Karlstadt unwittingly fired the starting gun on a debate that would come to exercise future generations of jurists up to the eighteenth century, for example, in their discussions on the applicability of Mosaic Law to the death penalty for certain offences.[209] Moreover, the establishment by Melanchthon (and to a certain extent, Luther) of a Protestant legal theory on the basis of natural law opened a debate on the place of natural law in jurisprudence which continues to this day.[210]

209 For Scandinavia cf. Heikki Pihlajamäki. "Scandinavian Law in the Early Modern Period." In *The Oxford Handbook of European Legal History*, ed. Heikki Pihjalamäki, Markus D. Dubber, and Mark Godfrey. Oxford: Oxford University Press, 2018, 817, 823 f., 826 f.

210 Cf. Scattola, *Naturrecht*, 52–55, 205–215; Heckel, *Martin Luthers Reformation*, 448–457.

Bibliography

1. *Early Modern Prints*

Christianissimi Wittenbergensis gymnasii, multarum disputationum paradoxa & plane enigmata in Papistica illa mendaciis confusissima: Ecclesia: vulgaria uero uerae Christi Ecclesiae pronunciata. Atque ex his lector iudicabis, quid agatur in vere Christiana schola quamque haeretica sit Lutecia, & omnes filiae eius. Auctores sunt Martinus Luther, Andreas Carolostadius, Philippus Melanchthon &c. Basel: Adam Petri, 1521, recorded at VD 16 C 2306 with a copy to be found at Basel University Library FM1 XI 9.7 (digitalised: https://www.e-rara.ch/bau_1/content/pageview/70970 accessed August 25, 2022).

Insignium Theologorum Domini Martini Lutheri, domini Andree Barolostadii, Philippi melanthonis & aliorum, conclusiones varie, pro diuinae gratie defensione ac commendatione, contra scolasticos & pelagianos: disputate in praeclara academia Wittembergensi. Lege lector & afficieris, versa facie catalogum inuenies. Paris: Pierre Vidoue, 1521?, recorded in Josef Benzing and Helmut Claus. *Lutherbibliographie: Verzeichnis der gedruckten Schriften Martin Luthers bis zu dessen Tod*, 2 volumes. Baden-Baden: Koerner, 1989–94, I: 86 with an exemplar at Wolfenbüttel, Herzog August Bibliothek Li 5530 (38,662) (digitalised: http://diglib.hab.de/drucke/li-5530-38b-662s/start.htm accessed on August 25, 2018).

Insignium theologorum Domini Martini lutheri, domini Andree Carolostadii, Philippi Melanthonis et aliorum, conclusiones varie, pro divine gratie defensione ac commendatione: contra scholasticos & pelagianos: disputate in preclara academia Wittenbergensi. Lege Lector & afficieris, versa facie catalogum invenies. Leiden: Jan Seversz, 1521, a record is provided in Benzing and Claus, *Lutherbibliographie*, II: 85 an copy is held at Torre Pellice Bibliotheca della Fondazione Centro culturale valdese A. III. 12.64 (digitalised: http://diglib.hab.de/drucke/ed000744/start.htm accessed on August 25, 2022).

Lutheri, Melanch., Carolostadii &c. Propositiones Wittembergae viva voce tractatae in hocque pleraeque aeditae ab auctoribus, ut vel nos absentes cum ipsis agamus vel certe ut veritatis, et seductionem admoneatur boni. Basel: Adam Petri, 1522, recorded at VD 16 L 7642, a copy is held at Bavarian State Library Munich Polem 3020.13 (digitalised: http://daten.digitale-sammlungen.de/0003/bsb00036294/images/index.html?fip=193.174.98.30&id=00036294&seite=1 accessed August 25, 2022).

M. Johann Erhard Kappens, des grossen Fürsten Collegii zu Leipzig Collegialen und z. Z. Praepositi, wie auch der Philosophischen Facultät daselbst Assessorn Kleine Nachlese einiger, größten Theils noch ungedruckter, Und sonderlich zur Erläuterung Der Reformations-Geschichte nützlicher Urkunden, Anderer Theil (Leipzig: Braun, 1727), recorded in VD 18: 90272552, with a copy to be found at Halle University

Library Jc 3065 (2) (digitalised: http://digitale.bibliothek.uni-halle.de/urn/urn:nbn:de:gbv:3:11-516338 accessed on August 25, 2022).

Proposiciones a Marti. Luthero subinde disputatae. Wittenberg: Joseph Klug 1530, recorded at VD 16 ZV 10025, with a copy to be found at Austrian National Library Vienna, Sammlung von Handschriften und alten Drucken (ALT), Prunksaal Josefsplatz: 79.X.61 (digitalised: http://digital.onb.ac.at/OnbViewer/viewer.faces?doc=ABO_%2BZ181743907 accessed October 18, 2018).

2. *Manuscript Sources*

Karlstadt, Andreas Bodenstein von. "De coelibatu (seven theses)." In *AD LIBRVM EXIMII MAGISTRI NOSTRI MAGISTRI AMBROSII CATHARINI DEFENSORIS SILVESTRI PRIERATIS ACERRIMI Responsio Martini Lutherí. VVITTEMBERGAE MENSE Aprili.* [...], Landeskirchliche Zentralbibliothek Stuttgart, Bestand Alte Pfarramtsbibliothek Weinsberg: A 4901 85 (deposited at Landeskirchliche Zentralbibliothek Stuttgart). Manuscript by Johann Mantel.

Lutheri, Melanch., Carolostadii &c. Propositiones. Basel: Adam Petri, 1522, and a copy originally in the possession of Johann Hess (Breslau), to be found at Berlin Staatsbibliothek Ms. theol. lat. oct. 91 (digitalised: https://digital.staatsbibliothek-berlin.de/werkansicht?PPN=PPN718087968&PHYSID=PHYS_0001&DMDID= accessed on August 25, 2022), also including a manuscript containing 23 sets of theses by Luther, Melanchthon, Karlstadt et al. (to be found at ibid., 56r–77r) and other manuscripts.

3. *Published Literature*

Angenendt, Arnold. *Geschichte der Religiosität im Mittelalter.* Darmstadt: Wissenschaftliche Buchgesellschaft, 1997.

Anonymous. "Ordnung der Stadt Wittenberg." In *Flugschriften der frühen Reformationsbewegung (1518–1524)*, vol. 2. Vaduz: Topos Verlag, 1983: 1033–1037.

Appold, Kenneth G. *Orthodoxie als Konsensbildung: Das theologische Disputationswesen an der Universität Wittenberg 1570–1710.* Tübingen: Mohr Siebeck, 2004.

Barge, Hermann. *Andreas Bodenstein von Karlstadt, vol. 1. Karlstadt und die Anfänge der Reformation.* Leipzig: Brandstetter, 1905.

Bauch, Gustav. "Andreas Carlstadt als Scholastiker." *ZKG* 18 (1898): 37–57.

Bauer, Clemens. "Die Naturrechtslehre des jüngeren Melanchthon." In *Festschrift für Gerhard Ritter zu seinem 60. Geburtstag*, ed. Richard Nürnberger. Tübingen: Mohr, 1950: 244–255.

Bayer, Oswald. *Martin Luthers Theologie: Eine Vergegenwärtigung.* Tübingen: Mohr Siebeck, 2003.

Bayer, Oswald. *Promissio: Geschichte der reformatorischen Wende in Luthers Theologie*, Göttingen: Vandenhoeck & Ruprecht, 1971.

Benzing, Josef and Helmut Claus. *Lutherbibliographie: Verzeichnis der gedruckten Schriften Martin Luthers bis zu dessen Tod*, 2 vols. Baden-Baden: Koerner, 1989–94.

Bossert, Gustav. "D. Joh. Mantels Lebensende und der Eheprozeß des Michael Back und seiner Gattin." *ARG* 12 (1915): 161–204.

Bossert, Gustav. "Mantel, Johann." In *Realencyklopädie für protestantische Theologie und Kirche*, vol. 24. Leipzig: J. C. Hinrichsche Buchhandlung ^{3}1913: 59–64.

Braun-Niehr, Beate. *Die theologischen Handschriften in octavo der Staatsbibliothek zu Berlin Preußischer Kulturbesitz*. Wiesbaden: Harrassowitz, 2007.

Brecht, Martin. "Der Kanon der Heiligen Schrift." In *Querdenker der Reformation: Andreas Bodenstein von Karlstadt und seine frühen Wirkung*, ed. Ulrich Bubenheimer and Stefan Oehmig. Würzburg: Religion und Kultur-Verlag 2001: 135–150.

Brecht, Martin. *Martin Luther, vol. 1. Sein Weg zur Reformation*, Stuttgart: Calwer Verlag, 1981.

Brecht, Martin and Hermann Ehmer. *Südwestdeutsche Reformationsgeschichte. Zur Einführung der Reformation im Herzogtum Württemberg 1534*. Stuttgart: Calwer Verlag, 1984.

Bubenheimer, Ulrich. "Andreas Bodenstein von Karlstadt und die Reform von Gottesdienst und Leben." In *Martin Luther: Zeuge des Glaubens in Kirche und Gesellschaft*. Ed. Evangelisches Bildungswerk Berlin. Abteilung kirchliche Erwachsenenbildung. Berlin: [Self-published, 1983]: 65–79.

Bubenheimer, Ulrich. "Andreas Karlstadts und Martin Luthers frühe Reformationsdiplomatie: Thesenanschläge des Jahres 1517, Luthers 'Asterisci' gegen Johannes Eck und Wittenberger antirömische Polemik während des Augsburger Reichstages." *Blätter für Pfälzische Kirchengeschichte und religiöse Volkskunde* 85 (2018): 265–302.

Bubenheimer, Ulrich. *Consonantia Theologiae et Iurisprudentiae: Andreas Bodenstein von Karlstadt als Theologe und Jurist zwischen Scholastik und Reformation*. Tübingen: Mohr, 1977.

Bubenheimer, Ulrich. "Einleitung [12 Conclusiones: De legis non furtum facies impletione et testamentorum legatione, altarium et missarum fundatione]." Wittenberg, [1520, Ende?]." In Karlstadt. *Kritische Gesamtausgabe*, vol. 3, Gütersloh: Gütersloher Verlagshaus, 2020: 550–552.

Bubenheimer, Ulrich. "Luthers Stellung zum Aufruhr in Wittenberg 1520–1522 und die Wurzeln des landesherrlichen Kirchenregiments." *Zeitschrift der Savigny-Stiftung für Rechtsgeschichte / Kanonistische Abteilung* 71 (1985): 147–214.

Bubenheimer, Ulrich. "Scandalum et Ius divinum. Theologische und rechtstheologische Probleme Probleme der ersten reformatorischen Innovationen in Wittenberg 1521 / 22." *Zeitschrift der Savigny-Stiftung für Rechtsgeschichte / Kanonistische Abteilung* 90 (1973): 263–342.

Bubenheimer, Ulrich. "Streit um das Bischofsamt in der Wittenberger Reformation 1521 / 22: von der Auseinandersetzung mit den Bischöfen um die Priesterehen und den Ablaß in Halle zum Modell des evangelischen Gemeindebischofs; Teil 1." *Zeitschrift der Savigny-Stiftung für Rechtsgeschichte / Kanonistische Abteilung* 73 (1987): 155–209.

Bubenheimer, Ulrich. *Thomas Müntzer und Wittenberg*. Mühlhausen: Thomas Müntzer-Gesellschaft e. V., 2014.

Bubenheimer, Ulrich and Stefan Oehmig, ed. *Querdenker der Reformation: Andreas Bodenstein von Karlstadt und seine frühen Wirkung*. Würzburg: Religion und Kultur-Verlag, 2001.

Bühmann, Henning. "The Wittenberg Disputation Culture and Luther's and Eck's Debate in Leipzig." In *Luther at Leipzig: Martin Luther, the Leipzig Debate and the Sixteenth Century Reformations*, ed. Mickey L. Mattox, Jonathan Mumme, and Richard J. Serrina jun. Leiden et al.: Brill, 2019: 61–92.

Clemen, Otto. "Miscellen zur Reformationsgeschichte." *Theologische Studien und Kritiken: Beiträge zur Theologie und Religionswissenschaft* 74 (1901): 126–140.

De Boer, Jan Hendryk. "Disputation, quaestio disputata." In *Universitäre Gelehrtenkultur vom 13.–16. Jahrhundert: Ein interdisziplinäres Quellen- und Methodenhandbuch*, ed. Jan-Hendryk de Boer, Marian Füssel, and Maximilian Schuh. Stuttgart: Franz Steiner Verlag, 2018: 221–254.

Decock, Wim. "Law, Religion, and Debt Relief: Balancing above the 'Abyss of Despair' in Early Modern Canon Law and Theology." *American Journal of Legal History* 57.2 (2017): 125–141.

Deflers, Isabelle. *Lex und Ordo: eine rechtshistorische Untersuchung der Rechtsauffassung Melanchthons*. Berlin: Duncker und Humblot, 2005.

Denzinger, Heinrich and Peter Hünermann, eds. *Kompendium der Glaubensbekenntnisse und kirchlichen Lehrentscheidungen*. Freiburg et al.: Herder, ^{43}2010.

Drews, Paul. *Disputationen Dr. Martin Luthers in den Jahren 1535–1545 an der Universität Wittenberg gehalten*. Göttingen: Vandenhoeck und Ruprecht, 1895.

Felmberg, Bernhard Alfred M. *Die Ablasstheologie des Kartinal Cajetan (1469–1534)*. Leiden, Boston, and Cologne: Brill, 1998.

Friedensburg, Walter. *Geschichte der Universität Wittenberg*. Halle: Niemeyer, 1917.

Gindhart, Marion, Hanspeter Marti, and Robert Seidel, eds. *Frühneuzeitliche Disputationen: Polyvalente Produktionsapparate gelehrten Wissens*. Cologne: Böhlau, 2016.

Grundmann, Herbert. *Vom Ursprung der Universität im Mittelalter*. 2nd ed. Darmstadt: Wissenschaftliche Buchgesellschaft 1960.

Hammer, Gerhard. "Militia Franciscana seu militia Christi. Das neugefundene Protokoll einer Disputation der sächsischen Franziskaner mit Vertretern der Wittenberger theologischen Fakultät am 3. und 4. Oktober 1519." Part 1: *ARG* 69 (1978): 51–81; part 2: *ARG* 70 (1979): 59–105.

Heckel, Johannes. Das Decretum Gratiani und das deutsche evangelische Kirchenrecht. In *Das blinde, undeutliche Wort 'Kirche': Gesammelte Aufsätze*, by Johannes Heckel. Cologne and Graz: Böhlau, 1964: 1–49.

Heckel, Johannes. *Lex charitatis: Eine juristische Untersuchung über das Recht in der Theologie Martin Luthers*, Cologne and Vienna: Böhlau, ^{2}1973.

Heckel, Martin. *Martin Luthers Reformation und das Recht: Die Entwicklung der Theologie Luthers und ihre Auswirkung auf das Recht unter den Rahmenbedingungen der Reichsreform und der Territorialstaatsbildung im Kampf mit Rom und den Schwärmern*. Tübingen: Mohr Siebeck, 2016.

Joestel, Volkmar. "Andreas Bodenstein von Karlstadt's Schrift *Von dem Sabbat und gebotenen Feiertagen* im Spiegel der sozialen Bewegung in Ostthüringen (1522–1524)." In *Querdenker der Reformation: Andreas Bodenstein von Karlstadt und seine frühen Wirkung*, ed. Ulrich Bubenheimer and Stefan Oehmig. Würzburg: Religion und Kultur-Verlag, 2001: 211–227.

Karlstadt, Andreas Bodenstein von. "Centum Quinquagintaunum Conlusiones de natura, lege et gratia (1517, 26. April)." In *Kritische Gesamtausgabe der Schriften und Briefe Andreas Bodenstein von Karlstadts*, vol. 1,1, ed. Thomas Kaufmann, Harald Bollbuck et al. Gütersloh: Gütersloher Verlagshaus: 485–514.

[Karlstadt, Andreas Bodenstein von]. " 12 Conclusiones: De legis non furtum facies impletione et testamentorum legatione, altarium et missarum fundatione. Wittenberg, [1520, Ende?]." In Karlstadt. *Kritische Gesamtausgabe*, vol. 3: 553 f.

Karlstadt, Andreas Bodenstein von. *Kritische Gesamtausgabe der Schriften und Briefe Andreas Bodenstein von Karlstadts*, vol. 1.1, ed. Thomas Kaufmann, Harald Bollbuck et al. Gütersloh: Gütersloher Verlagshaus, 2017.

Karlstadt, Andreas Bodenstein von. *Kritische Gesamtausgabe der Schriften und Briefe Andreas Bodenstein von Karlstadts*, vol. 3, ed. Thomas Kaufmann. Gütersloh: Gütersloher Verlagshaus, 2020.

Karlstadt, Andreas [Bodenstein von]. *Von Abtuhung der Bilder: Und das keyn Bedtler unther den Christen seyn sollen 1522 und die Wittenberger Beutelordnung*, ed. Hans Lietzmann. Bonn: A. Marcus und E. Weber's Verlag, 1911.

Kaufmann, Thomas. *An den christlichen Adel deutscher Nation von des christlichen Standes Besserung*. Tübingen: Mohr Siebeck, 2014.

Kaufmann, Thomas. *Der Anfang der Reformation: Studien zur Kontextualität der Theologie, Publizistik und Inszenierung Luthers und der reformatorischen Bewegung*. 2nd ed. Tübingen: Mohr Siebeck, 2018.

Kaufmann, Thomas. *Die Mitte der Reformation: Eine Studie zu Buchdruck und Publizistik im deutschen Sprachgebiet, zu ihren Akteuren und deren Strategien, Inszenierungs- und Ausdrucksformen*. Tübingen: Mohr Siebeck, 2019.

Kaufmann, Thomas. *Erlöste und Verdammte. Eine Geschichte der Reformation*. 2nd ed. Munich: Beck, 2017.

Kaufmann, Thomas. *Geschichte der Reformation in Deutschland.* Berlin: Suhrkamp, 2016.

Kaufmann, Thomas. *Luthers Juden*. 3rd ed. Stuttgart: Reclam, 2017.

Kisch, Guido. *Melanchthons Recht- und Soziallehre*. Berlin: De Gruyter, 1967.

Kohnle, Armin and Beate Kusche, eds. *Professorenbuch der Theologischen Fakultät der Universität Wittenberg 1502 bis 1815/17*. Leipzig: Evangelische Verlagsanstalt, 2017.

Kolde, Theodor. "Wittenberger Disputationsthesen aus den Jahren 1516 bis 1522." *ZKG* 11 (1890): 448–471.

Krentz, Natalie. *Ritualwandel und Deutungshoheit: Die frühe Reformation in der Residenzstadt Wittenberg (1500–1533)*. Tübingen: Mohr Siebeck, 2014.

Kruse, Jens Martin: *Universitätstheologie und Kirchenreform. Die Anfänge der Reformation in Wittenberg 1516–1522*. Mainz: von Zabern, 2002.

Laube, Adolf, Sigrid Looß, and Annerose Schneider, eds., *Flugschriften der frühen Reformationsbewegung*, 2 volumes. Vaduz: Topos Verlag 1983.

Leppin, Volker. "Die Genese des reformatorischen Schriftprinzips: Beobachtungen zu Luthers Auseinandersetzung mit Johannes Eck bis zur Leipziger Disputation." In *Reformatorische Theologie und Autoritäten. Studien zur Genese des Schriftprinzips beim jungen Luther*, ed. Volker Leppin. Tübingen: Mohr Siebeck, 2015: 97–139.

Leppin, Volker. "Disputationen als Medium der Theologie und Kirchenreform: Zur Transformation eines akademischen Mediums." In *Transformationen: Studien zu den Wandlungsprozessen in Theologie und Frömmigkeit zwischen Spätmittelalter und Reformation*. Tübingen: Mohr Siebeck, 2015: 419–428.

Leppin, Volker, ed. *Reformatorische Theologie und Autoritäten. Studien zur Genese des Schriftprinzips beim jungen Luther*. Tübingen: Mohr Siebeck, 2015.

Lindberg, Carter: "'There Should Be No Beggars Among Christians': Karlstadt, Luther and the Origins of Protestant Poor Relief." *Church History* 46 (1977): 313–334.

Luther, Martin. "Disputatio de lege et fide. 1519." In *WA 6*: 23 f.

Luther, Martin. "Disputatio de non vindicando &c. habita." 1520. In *WA 6:* 574 f.

Luther, Martin. "Disputatio Heidelbergae habita. 1518." In *WA 1*: 350–374.

Luther, Martin. "Disputatio pro declaratione virtutis indulgentiarum. 1517." In *WA 1*: 229–238 (=*95 Theses*).

Luther, Martin. "Franziskanerdisputation" In *WA 59*: 606–697.

Luther Martin. "Resolutiones disputationum de indulgentiarum virtute. 1518." In *WA 1*: 522–628.

Luther, Martin. *D. Martin Luthers Werke. Kritische Gesammtausgabe*, vol. 1, ed. Karl Knaake. Weimar: Böhlau 1883 (=*WA 1*).

Luther, Martin. *D. Martin Luthers Werke. Kritische Gesammtausgabe*, vol. 6, ed. Karl Knaake. Weimar: Böhlau, 1888 (=*WA 6*).

Luther, Martin. *D. Martin Luthers Werke. Kritische Gesamtausgabe*, vol. 59. Nachträge. Weimar: Böhlau, 1983 (=*WA 59*).

MacCulloch, Diarmaid. *Reformation: Europe's House Divided 1490–1700*. London: Penguin 2003.

Markschies, Christoph. *Kaiserzeitliche christliche Theologie und ihre Institutionen: Prolegomena zu einer Geschichte der antiken christlichen Theologie*. Tübingen: Mohr Siebeck, 2007.

Maurer, Wilhelm. *Der junge Melanchthon zwischen Humanismus und Reformation. Vol. 2. Der Theologe*. Göttingen: Vandenhoeck & Ruprecht, 1969.

Melanchthon, Philipp. *Loci communes 1521. Lateinisch und deutsch*. Gütersloh: Gütersloher Verlagshaus Mohn, 1993.

Melanchthon, Philipp. "Melanchthons Baccalaureatsthesen. 1519." In *MWA 1*: 23–25.

Melanchthon Philipp. *Melanchthons Werke in Auswahl, vol. 1. Reformatorische Schriften*, ed. Robert Stupperich. Gütersloh: Bertelsmann, 1951 (= *MWA 1*).

Melanchthon, Philipp. "Themata ad sextam feriam discutienda. 1522." In *MWA 1*: 168–170.

Mikoteit, Matthias. "Autoritätenverwendung in Bartholomäus Bernhardis Disputation der 'Quaestio de viribus hominis sine gratia'." In *Reformatorische Theologie und Autoritäten. Studien zur Genese des Schriftprinzips beim jungen Luther*, ed. Volker Leppin. Tübingen: Mohr Siebeck, 2015: 19–38.

Moeller, Bernd. "Die letzten Ablaßkampagnen. Luthers Widerspruch gegen den Ablaß in seinem geschichtlichen Zusammenhang." In *Die Reformation und das Mittelalter. Kirchenhistorische Aufsätze*, by Bernd Moeller. Göttingen: Vandenhoeck & Ruprecht 1991: 53–72.

Moeller, Bernd. *Reichsstadt und Reformation: Neue Ausgabe*. Tübingen: Mohr Siebeck, 2011.

Moeller, Bernd. *Zwinglis Disputationen: Studien zur Kirchengründung in den Städten der frühen Reformation*. Göttingen: Vandenhoeck & Ruprecht, ²2011.

Müller, Nikolaus. *Die Wittenberger Bewegung 1521 und 1522: Die Vorgänge in und um Wittenberg während Luthers Wartburgaufenthalt. Briefe, Akten und dergleichen und Personalien*. Leipzig: Heinsius, 1911.

Neuser, Wilhelm H. *Die Abendmahlslehre Melanchthons in ihrer geschichtlichen Entwicklung (1519–1530)*. Neukirchen-Vluyn: Verlag der Buchhandlung des Erziehungsvereins, 1968: 127–160.

Novikoff, Alex J. *The Medieval Culture of Disputation: Pedagogy, Practice and Performance*. Philadelphia: University of Pennsylvania Press, 2013.

Oehmig, Stefan. "'Christlicher Bürger' – 'christliche Stadt'? Zu Andreas Bodensteins von Karlstadts Vorstellungen von einem christlichen Gemeinwesen und den Tugenden seiner Bürger." In *Querdenker der Reformation: Andreas Bodenstein von Karlstadt und seine frühe Wirkung*, ed. Ulrich Bubenheimer and Stefan Oehmig. Würzburg: Religion und Kultur-Verlag, 2001: 151–185.

Ott, Joachim and Martin Treu, eds. *Luthers Thesenanschlag: Fakt oder Fiktion*. Leipzig: Evangelische Verlagsanstalt, 2008.

Paulus, Nikolaus. *Geschichte des Ablasses im Mittelalter, vol. 3. Geschichte des Ablasses am Ausgange des Mittelalters*. Paderborn: Schöningh, 1923.

Pfister, Hermann: *Die Entwicklung der Theologie Melanchthons unter dem Einfluß der Auseinandersetzung mit Schwarmgeistern und Wiedertäufern*, Freiburg: Dt. Pax-Christi-Bewegung, 1968.

Pihlajamäki, Heikki. "Scandinavian Law in the Early Modern Period." In *The Oxford Handbook of European Legal History*, ed. Heikki Pihjalamäki, Markus D. Dubber, and Mark Godfrey. Oxford: Oxford University Press, 2018: 806–829.

Reinhard, Wolfgang. "Was ist katholische Konfessionalisierung?" In *Die katholische Konfessionalisierung: wissenschaftliches Symposion der Gesellschaft zur Herausgabe des Corpus Catholicorum und des Vereins für Reformationsgeschichte 1993*, ed. Wolfgang Reinhard and Heinz Schilling. Gütersloh: Gütersloher Verlagshaus 1995: 419–452.

Salvadori, Stefania. "Der Augustin-Kommentar des Andreas Bodenstein von Karlstadt zwischen der Stilisierung einer Bekehrungsgeschichte und der (Wieder-)Entdeckung der biblisch-patristischen Quellen." *Blätter für Pfälzische Kirchengeschichte und religiöse Volkskunde* 85 (2018): 241–264.

Scattola, Merio. *Das Naturrecht vor dem Naturrecht. Zur Geschichte des "ius naturae" im 16. Jahrhundert*. Tübingen: Niemeyer, 1999.

Schaich-Klose, Wiebke. *D. Hieronymus Schürpf: Leben und Werk des Wittenberger Reformationsjuristen 1481–1554*. Trogen, Switzerland: Buchdruckerei Fritz Meili, 1967.

Scheib, Otto. "Die Breslauer Disputation von 1524 als Beispiel eines frühreformatorischen Religionsgespräches eines Doktors der Theologie." In *Festschrift für Bernhard Stasiewski: Beiträge zur ostdeutschen und osteuropäischen Kirchengeschichte*, ed. Gabriel Adriány and Joseph Gottschalk. Cologne, and Vienna: Böhlau, 1975: 98–106.

Scheib, Otto. "Die Religionsgespräche in Norddeutschland in der Neuzeit und ihre Entwicklung." *Jahrbuch der Gesellschaft für Niedersächsische Kirchengeschichte* 75 (1977): 39–88.

Schilling, Johannes: *Klöster und Mönche in der hessischen Reformation*. Gütersloh: Gütersloher Verlagshaus, 1997.

Schubert, Anselm. "Das Lachen der Ketzer: Zur Selbstinszenierung der frühen Reformation." *ZThK* 108 (2011): 405–430.

Schubert, Anselm. "Libertas Disputandi. Luther und die Leipziger Disputation als akademisches Streitgespräch." *ZThK* 105 (2008): 411–442.

Schuster, Susanne: *Dialogflugschriften der frühen Reformationszeit: Literarische Fortführungen der Disputation und Resonanzräume reformatorischen Denkens.* Göttingen: Vandenhoeck & Ruprecht, 2019.

Schwarz, Reinhard. "Disputationen." In *Luther-Handbuch*, ed. Albrecht Beutel. Tübingen: Mohr Siebeck, 2005: 328–340.

Schwarzenau, Paul. *Der Wandel im theologischen Ansatz bei Melanchthon 1525–1535.* Gütersloh: Bertelsmann, 1956.

Seebaß, Gottfried. *Geschichte des Christentums III: Spätmittelalter – Reformation – Konfesionalisierung*. Stuttgart: W. Kohlhammer, 2006.

Selge, Kurt Victor. "Das Autoritätengefüge der westlichen Christenheit im Lutherkonflikt 1517 bis 1521." *HZ* 223 (1976): 591–618.

Selge, Kurt Victor. "Der Weg zur Leipziger Disputation zwischen Luther und Eck im Jahre 1519." In *Bleibendes im Wandel der Kirchengeschichte: Kirchenhistorische Studien*, ed. Bernd Moeller and Gerhard Ruhbach. Tübingen: Mohr Siebeck, 1973: 169–210.

Shaffern, Robert W. "Learned Discussions of Indulgences for the Dead in Middle Ages." *Church History* 61 No. 4 (1992): 267–381.

Simon, Wolfgang. *Die Messopfertheologie Martin Luthers: Voraussetzung, Genese, Gestalt und Rezeption.* Tübingen: Mohr Siebeck, 2002.

Sixtus IV. "Bulle 'Salvator noster' zugunsten der Kirche des hl. Petrus zu Saintes, 3. Aug. 1476." In *Kompendium der Glaubensbekenntnisse und kirchlichen Lehrentscheidungen*, ed. Heinrich Denzinger and Peter Hünermann. Freiburg et al.: Herder [43]2010, no. 1398: 441 f.

Spehr, Christopher. *Luther und das Konzil: Zur Entwicklung eines zentralen Themas in der Reformationszeit.* Tübingen: Mohr Siebeck, 2010.

Sperl, Adolf: *Melanchthon zwischen Humanismus und Reformation: Eine Untersuchung über den Wandel des Traditionsverständnisses bei Melanchthon und die damit zusammenhängenden Grundfragen seiner Theologie*, Munich: Kaiser, 1959.

Stille, Hans: *Nikolaus von Amsdorf: Sein Leben bis zu seiner Einweisung als Bischof in Naumburg. (1483–1545).* Zeulenroda: Sporn, 1937.

Voigt-Goy, Christopher. "Luther und das Kanonische Recht in den 'Resolutiones disputationum de indulgentiarum virtute'." In *Reformatorische Theologie und Autoritäten. Studien zur Genese des Schriftprinzips beim jungen Luther*, ed. Volker Leppin. Tübingen: Mohr Siebeck 2015: 87–95.

Wolf, Ernst. "Zur wissenschaftsgeschichtlichen Bedeutung der Disputationen an der Wittenberger Universität im 16. Jahrhundert." In *Peregrinatio, vol. 2. Studien zur reformatorischen Theologie, zum Kirchenrecht und zur Sozialethik*, by Ernst Wolf. Munich: Chr. Kaiser, 1965: 38–51.

Salamanca Meets Secularism

Clerics' Role in the Administration of Justice and Charity

Wim Decock

1. "Secularization" and the "School of Salamanca"

The secularization of the Christian West is hardly conceivable without the Protestant Reformation. It entailed a major shift in power from ecclesiastical to secular authorities. This contribution investigates the reaction by Catholic *teólogos-juristas* to the shift in administrative power from the Church to the temporal authorities witnessed in the early modern period – a shift accelerated by the "secularizing" forces inherent in the theology of the Lutheran Reformation.[1] Against the threat of these "secularizing" forces, Catholic theologians such as Tomás de Mercado (1520–1575) and Domingo de Soto (1495–1560) stressed the role that clergymen had to play in guaranteeing the socio-economic order by actively participating in the administration of justice and charity. Against Luther's basic instincts, they maintained that the Church was truly competent in regulating the market and organizing poor relief. They considered clergymen as "fathers of the republic" and stressed that the canon law was not just an "ecclesiastical law", merely dealing with matters of internal Church administration. In their view, canon law and moral theology must provide a normative order capable of dealing with all sorts of issues, including social welfare and the regulation of the marketplace.

As will be further explained in this section, "secularization" is not understood here as the loss of religious faith. Neither does it imply a diminished role of the Christian belief as a source of inspiration for legislation and governance. Following Harold Berman, "secularization" is employed as a concept designating the transfer of jurisdictional power from ecclesiastical institutions to secular authorities in the sixteenth century.[2] While Luther preached that Christian magistrates rather than clerics should administer justice and charity – however much those magistrates were supposed to take into account the advice of

1 On the link between Lutheranism and secularization, see Mathias Schmoeckel. *Das Recht der Reformation: Die epistemologische Revolution der Wissenschaft und die Spaltung der Rechtsordnung in der Frühen Neuzeit.* Tübingen: Mohr, 2014, 297.

2 Harold J. Berman. *Law and Revolution: The Formation of the Western Legal Tradition.* Cambridge Mass.: Harvard UP, 1983, 29.

 | DOI:10.30965/9783657790746_003

theologians – the Catholic Church fought back to maintain its direct control over secular affairs. The Church continued to strive for a close institutional collaboration between spiritual and temporal forces in governing the world.

This article will feature two case studies illustrating Catholic resistance against the secularizing tendencies inherent in Lutheran doctrine. The main example will be taken from Tomás de Mercado's *Suma de tratos y contratos*, a treatise on trade, contracts and the regulation of the market. An additional, shorter example of Catholic theologians' reaction against the threat of secularization will be drawn from Domingo de Soto's *Deliberatio in causa pauperum*, a treatise on poor relief and migration. Little is known about Mercado's life, except that he entered the Dominican order and contributed to the spreading of the teachings of the University of Salamanca in New Spain (Mexico).[3] Mercado made one of the clearest arguments in favor of the sustained collaboration, on an equal basis, between spiritual and secular authorities in the administration of justice. He emphasized the juridical character of conscience and the judicial role of confessors. Soto entered the Dominican order in 1524, obtaining his doctorate in theology in Salamanca in 1532 from the hands of Francisco de Vitoria (1483/1492–1546).[4] Alongside Vitoria he became one of the iconic figures of the Thomistic revival movement at the University of Salamanca. His work, too, reveals Catholic theologians' opposition to the secularist approach to government following from Luther's theology. Mercado and Soto strongly advocated the view that clerics must continue to play a major role in the government of temporal affairs.

Mercado and Soto were Dominican friars belonging to the so-called "School of Salamanca."[5] The School of Salamanca designates scholars influenced by the renaissance of scholastic theology at the University of Salamanca in the sixteenth century. They reacted to the challenges posed by the Reformation, the discovery and colonization of the New World, the increasing power of imperial states and the emergence of global trade networks by reinforcing the medieval synthesis between law and theology. Theologians such as Francisco de Vitoria, who is regarded as the founder of the school, stayed in the Dominican convent

3 Manuel J. Lagares Calvo. "Seis incógnitas y algunas respuestas sobre la vida de Fray Tomás de Mercado." *Iberian Journal of the History of Economic Thought* 3 (2016): 68–77; Thomas Duve. "Von der Europäischen Rechtsgeschichte zu einer Rechtsgeschichte Europas in globalhistorischer Perspektive." *Rechtsgeschichte – Legal History* 20 (2012): 18–71 (36–37).

4 Wim Decock. "Domingo de Soto, De iustitia et iure." In *The Formation and Transmission of Western Legal Culture: 150 Books that Made the Law in the Age of Printing*, eds. Serge Dauchy et al. Berlin: Springer, 2016, 94.

5 The term became common after the publication of Majorie A. Hutchinson's *The School of Salamanca. Readings in Spanish Monetary Theory, 1544–1605*. Oxford: OUP, 1952.

of San Estebán in Salamanca and taught at the University of Salamanca. He rapidly acquired reference status among Catholic theologians and lawyers across Europe and the world, contributing to the notion that Salamanca created a school, even including scholars who did not specifically enroll as students at the University of Salamanca.[6]

There is a tremendous amount of specialized literature on the phenomenon of "secularization" written by sociologists at least since the time of Max Weber.[7] In a rather pragmatic fashion, this article starts from the definition of secularization as the shift from spiritual authorities' jurisdictional power over temporal affairs to the autonomization of secular leadership in regulating things of this world. Following Karel Dobbelaere, a sociologist of religion, we hold that secularization essentially involves the loss of institutionalized religious authorities' control over the economy, the family, the law, etc.[8] It is not primarily about the loss of faith. Especially from a juridical point of view, secularization is about the shift of jurisdictional power from religious to secular authorities. From a historical point of view, Luther played a paramount role in this process. He rejected the privileged status of clerics, opposed their role in the administration of justice and charity, and undermined the jurisdictional power wielded by the Church. Luther denounced the Church as an institution of power, preached the closing of ecclesiastical courts, and announced freedom of the laity from clerical hegemony. "Luther emphasized that formal legal authority lay with the state, not with the Church, with the magistrate, not with the cleric," as John Witte Jr. aptly summarized this shift.[9]

Even if secularization in the sixteenth century implied a transfer of jurisdictional power from the spiritual to the temporal authorities, it certainly did not entail a loss of religion. As a matter of fact, even in the modern period, the radicalization of the secularization process did not necessarily lead to the demise of the Christian faith. As Dobbelaere has rightly observed with regards even to the modern period, secularists have been definitely anti-clerical, but not necessarily anti-religious.[10] This observation holds certainly true in

---

6 Juan Belda Plans. *La escuela de Salamanca y la renovación de la teología en el siglo XVI*. Madrid: BAC Maior, 2000; James Gordley. *The Jurists: A Critical History*. Oxford: OUP, 2013, 82–110.

7 Karel Dobbelaere. "The Meaning and Scope of Secularization." In *The Oxford Handbook of the Sociology of Religion*, ed. Peter B. Clarke. Oxford: OUP, 2009, 599–615.

8 Dobbelaere, "The Meaning and Scope of Secularization," 600.

9 John Witte Jr. *Law and Protestantism: The Legal Teachings of the Lutheran Reformation*. Cambridge: CUP, 2002, 8.

10 Dobbelaere, "The Meaning and Scope of Secularization," 602.

a sixteenth-century context.[11] Luther's followers opposed the involvement of clerics in the administration of worldly affairs, but they obviously did not oppose the Christian faith. Moreover, Luther's "castigation of Catholic clerics gave way to cultivation of Protestant magistrates as fathers of the community called to govern on God's behalf."[12] As a consequence, the decline in administrative power of the Church in the wake of the Lutheran Reformation was accompanied by "a process of spiritualization of secular law" in those territories that adopted the Lutheran faith.[13] Law and religion continued to "intertwine"[14] in Lutheran territories. Lutherans stressed the religious roots of legal norms, urging the magistrate to draw inspiration from the Gospel in laying down laws. As a result, Lutheran theologians continued to counsel political leaders, or, for that matter, write about contract law.[15] Christian normativity remained part of the "common unconscious," also in countries that adopted Lutheranism in the sixteenth century, as Lisbet Christoffersen has aptly observed with regards to Denmark.[16] Only much later, "when secularism itself became secularized" and "God was no longer thought to be hidden in the secular world," did secularization start to refer not only to the emancipation of secular rule from ecclesiastical hegemony, but also to the loss of faith itself.[17]

2. Conscience and the Church's Jurisdictional Power Over Souls

Until its legal power was challenged by the Reformers, the Church was unanimously recognized as exercising true jurisdictional power.[18] Since the thirteenth

11 Christoph Strohm. "Die produktive Kraft konfessioneller Konkurrenz für die Rechtsentwicklung." In *Reformation und Recht. Ein Beitrag zur Kontroverse um die Kulturwirkungen der Reformation*, ed. Christoph Strohm. Tübingen: Mohr Siebeck, 2017, 170.

12 Witte, *Law and Protestantism*, 2002, 3.

13 Harold J. Berman. *Law and Revolution II: The Impact of the Protestant Reformations on the Western Legal Tradition*. Cambridge Mass.: Harvard UP, 2003, 197.

14 Lisbet Christoffersen. "Intertwinement: A New Concept for Understanding Religion-Law Relations." *Nordic Journal of Religion and Society* 19 (2006): 107–126.

15 Paolo Astorri. *Lutheran Theology and Contract Law in Early Modern Germany (ca. 1520–1720)*. (Law and Religion in the Early Modern Period, 1), Leiden/Paderborn, Brill/Schöningh 2019.

16 Christoffersen, "Intertwinement: A New Concept for Understanding Religion-Law Relations," 112.

17 Harold J. Berman. *The Interaction of Spiritual and Secular Law: The Sixteenth-Century and Today*. Fulton Lectures, 1997, https://chicagounbound.uchicago.edu/cgi/viewcontent.cgi?article=1008&context=fulton_lectures, 9.

18 Richard H. Helmholz. *The Spirit of Classical Canon Law*. Athens and London: The University of Georgia Press, 1996, 116–144.

century, this power to administrate justice was exercised in tribunals of the Church, also called "officialities."[19] It was not limited to matters that could be considered as purely spiritual or ecclesiastical, such as benefices for the clergy. It extended to cases involving marriage, the family, child benefits, contractual affairs, trade and crimes. In many regions across Christian Europe, lawyers had to swear an oath before the ecclesiastical tribunal before they could practice their trade before any other tribunal. Litigation about marriage, in particular, became one of the principal affairs dealt with by ecclesiastical courts.[20] In the course of the sixteenth century, the law of marriage was nationalized and the administration of justice in marital affairs was shifted towards courts controlled by the secular authorities, especially in Protestant lands.[21] A recently studied example is the impact of the Scottish Reformation on marriage litigation in Scotland.[22] Following the Reformation crisis in 1559–1560, the officialities were suppressed and jurisdiction about marriage was transferred to the Commissaries of Edinburgh, who became exclusively competent in all lawsuits concerning marriage. The Commissaries were directly appointed by Mary Stewart, Queen of Scots, the temporal authority in Scotland. Despite the transfer in jurisdictional power from the Church to the temporal authorities, the substantive law applied in the new courts remained heavily indebted to pre-Reformation canon law on marriage, even if it was often disguised as customary law or daily "practick" of Scotland.[23]

For present purposes, it is important to realize that the jurisdictional power of the church was not only exercised in the ecclesiastical tribunals. It also extended to the individual's soul.[24] Within the Church's jurisdiction a further division emerged between the so-called external ecclesiastical jurisdiction and the sacramental jurisdiction of the interior or the soul (*forum internum*),

19 Véronique Beaulande-Barraud and Martine Charageat (eds.). *Les officialités dans l'Europe médiévale et moderne. Des tribunaux pour une société chrétienne*. Turnhout: Brepols, 2014; Wilfried Hartmann and Kenneth Pennington (eds.). *The History of Courts and Procedure in Medieval Canon Law*. Washington DC: Catholic University of America Press, 2016.

20 e.g. Charles Donahue Jr. *Law, Marriage, and Society in the Later Middle Ages: Arguments about Marriage in Five Courts*. Cambridge: CUP, 2008.

21 Laurent Waelkens. *Amne adverso: Roman Legal Heritage in European Culture*. Leuven: Leuven UP, 2015, 235.

22 Thomas Green. "The Sources of Early Scots Consistorial Law. Reflections on Law, Authority and Jurisdiction during the Scottish Reformation." In *Law and Authority in British Legal History, 1200–1900*, ed. Mark Godfrey. Cambridge: CUP, 2016, 120–139.

23 Green, "The Sources of Early Scots Law," 136.

24 The next paragraphs are slightly adapted from Wim Decock. "Collaborative Legal Pluralism. Confessors as Law Enforcers in Mercado's Advice on Economic Governance (1571)." *Rechtsgeschichte – Legal History* 25 (2017): 103–114 (107–110).

also called the court of conscience (*forum conscientiae*).[25] In other words, for theologians such as Mercado, the question of the moral bindingness of the *tasa del trigo* did not only concern the enforcement of royal legislation in the civil or ecclesiastical courts, but also in the court of conscience. The Catholic understanding of conscience as a juridical space may come as a surprise to the modern reader, but for centuries it was the immediate background for clerics' direct engagement with legal doctrine.[26] The legal character of conscience in the late medieval and early modern Catholic world has nevertheless escaped the average modern observer, even if specialists have continuously warned against anachronistic readings of early modern theological texts.[27]

The modern, subjectivist understanding of conscience is due to Protestant reformers such as Martin Luther in the first place. Luther abhorred the view that salvation could be depended on following laws in conscience. He separated the realm of conscience from the realm of law, rejecting clerics' jurisdictional competence over the soul.[28] It is small wonder, then, that Luther's understanding of conscience was attacked during the Council of Trent (1545–1563). The Fathers of the Council strongly affirmed the juridical conception of conscience, insisting on the judicial character of the confessor's role in the sacrament of penance.[29] The penitent resembled a defendant in the jurisdictional space named "the confessional" or "sacred tribunal of penance."

Martin Luther's shielding of individual conscience against outside regulation by clerics was rightly seen by Catholics such as Mercado as a fundamental threat to their jurisdictional power. The main objective of early modern Catholic theologians was to oppose that "secularizing" tendency inherent in Lutheran theological doctrine. They insisted that conscience falls under the jurisdiction of a confessor competent to determine what laws bind the

25 Paolo Prodi. "Il giuramento e il tribunale della coscienza: dal pluralismo degli ordinamenti giuridici al dualismo tra coscienza e diritto positivo." In *Cristianesimo e potere*, ed. Paolo Prodi. Bologna: Il Mulino, 163–178 (167–169).

26 Wim Decock. *Theologians and Contract Law: The Moral Transformation of the Ius commune (c. 1500–1650)*. Leiden/Boston: Brill/Nijhoff, 2013, 69–86.

27 Adriano Prosperi. "Die Beichte und das Gericht des Gewissens." In *Das Konzil von Trient und die Moderne*, eds. Paolo Prodi and Wolfgang Reinhard. Berlin: Duncker & Humblot, 2001, 175–197.

28 Harald Maihold. "'Himmel und Erde.' Die Abgrenzung von forum internum und forum externum in der Frühen Neuzeit." In *Das Gewissen in den Rechtslehren der protestantischen und katholischen Reformationen*, eds. Michael Germann and Wim Decock. Leipzig: Evangelische Verlagsanstalt, 2017, 51–71.

29 John O'Malley. *Trent: What Happened at the Council*. Cambridge Mass.: Harvard UP, 2013, 153.

individual.[30] Mercado's emphasis on the moral bindingness of the *tasa del trigo* taps into that context. It was formulated in his *Suma* less than a decade after the conclusion of the Council of Trent. "It is such a well-established truth that preceptive [imperial and civil] laws, which are the rules of our operations, are binding the subjects [in conscience]," Mercado explained,[31] "that it is almost a matter of faith, as the Catholic Church establishes and teaches in the Council of Constance, sessions 8 and 15 against Wycliff, and Pope Leo X in his condemnation of Luther (who said the opposite), article 20, and the Council of Trent." Contrary to Luther, the Catholic theologians saw conscience primarily as the locus for the internalization of human laws, not as a bulwark of resistance against them.[32]

3. Mercado and the Regulation of the Grain Market[33]

Although the sixteenth century is generally remembered as Spain's golden age, the economy was plagued by low agricultural productivity, high inflation and lack of innovation, driving a lot of people, including noblemen, into poverty. To protect Spanish consumers against rising prices, a maximum price for grain, the so-called *tasa del trigo*, was adopted by successive rulers from the early 1500s onwards. The immediate background of Tomás de Mercado's treatment of the regulation of the grain market in his *Suma de tratos y contratos* was a new decree on the *tasa del trigo* issued by King Philip II in March 1558, which was eventually included in book 5, title 25 of the *Nueva Recopilación* (1567), the most important contemporary collection of Spanish law. As a result of King Philip II's legislative initiative, the maximum price for grain became permanent. This policy alleviated consumers, but aggravated the fate of poor farmers.[34] It also triggered questions about the bindingness of the maximum grain

30 Antonio González Polvillo. *El gobierno de los otros. Confesión y control de la conciencia en la España moderna*. Sevilla: Universidad, 2010, 251–255.

31 Cited in Decock, "Collaborative Legal Pluralism," 108.

32 Frank Grunert, "Äußere Norm und inneres Gewissen. Das Gewissen in den Naturrechtslehren von Samuel Pufendorf und Christian Thomasius." In *Das Gewissen in den Rechtslehren*, eds. Germann and Decock, 277.

33 The following paragraphs are slightly adapted from Decock, "Collaborative Legal Pluralism", 104–106.

34 Abelardo Del Vigo Gutiérrez. *Economía y ética en el siglo XVI. Estudio comparativo entro los Padres de la Reforma y la Teología española*. Madrid: Biblioteca de Autores Cristianos, 2006, 183.

price in conscience.[35] As a matter fact, the decree on the *tasa del trigo* provided that the *tasa del trigo* was binding on pain of eternal damnation of the soul.[36]

Since the regulation referred to the moral obligation to respect the maximum grain price, it is not surprising to find that theologians discussed it. However, the reflections of theologians on the bindingness of grain prices are part of a much larger conversation on the morality of the market in the history of Christian moral theology. The Spanish scholastic theologians, in particular, are well-known for having responded to some of the most pressing social, political and economic needs of their time.[37] Drawing upon medieval scholastic economics, but adapting it to the new times, they refined the normative, contractual framework to deal with challenges such as the rise of global trade and international financial networks.[38] The issue of price regulation, in particular, attracted attention from dozens of theologians, as meticulous research by Abelardo Del Vigo Gutiérrez has revealed.[39] They universally agreed that specific circumstances can allow the prince to establish a legal price of certain goods, binding on pain of sin, for the sake of the public good.[40] However, they disagreed about the desirability of price-fixing and the severity of the obligation in conscience.

Mercado belonged to a group of theologians who emphasized the extreme severity of the bindingness in conscience of the *tasa del trigo*. In fact, he published a second edition of his *Suma de tratos y contratos* in 1571 containing an extended treatment of the regulation of the grain market precisely to insist on this point.[41] Following traditional Thomistic legal philosophy, Mercado insisted that human laws are always binding in conscience as long as they are just and

35 Francisco Gómez Camacho. *Economía y filosofía moral: la formación del pensamiento económico europeo en la Escolástica española*. Madrid: Síntesis, 1998, 187–205.

36 Nueva Recopilación, ed. Madrid: Zuñiga, 1745, online available on Google Books, vol. 1, lib. 5, tit. 25, l. 4, nr. 7, p. 832, see also James Casey. *Early Modern Spain: A Social History*. London: Routledge, 1999, 57.

37 Thomas Duve. "Salamanca in Amerika." *Zeitschrift der Savigny-Stiftung für Rechtsgeschichte: Germanistische Abteilung* 132 (2015): 116–151 (123–137).

38 Paolo Prodi. *Settimo non rubare. Furto e mercato nella storia dell'Occidente*. Bologna: Il Mulino, 2009; Wim Decock, "In Defense of Commercial Capitalism: Lessius, Partnerships and the contractus trinus." In *Companies and Company Law in Late Medieval and Early Modern Europe*, eds. Bram Van Hofstraeten and Wim Decock. Leuven: Peeters, 2016, 55–90.

39 Abelardo Del Vigo Gutiérrez. "Las tasas y las Pragmáticas reales en los moralistas españoles del Siglo de Oro." *Burgense* 22 (1981): 427–470.

40 James Gordley. *The Philosophical Origins of Modern Contract Doctrine*. Oxford: Clarendon, 1991, 98.

41 The Seville 1571-edition edited by Nicolás Sánchez-Albornoz in 1977 is available online at http://www.cervantesvirtual.com/nd/ark:/59851/bmc1c1t9 (unpaginated).

necessary for the public good. Hence, even the slightest deviation from the maximum grain price entailed a sin, imperiling the salvation of the sinner's soul. Conversely, if the prince realized that the regulation of the market was necessary to safeguard the tranquility and the peace of the kingdom, but he failed to act, he committed a sin. As God's vicar on earth, the prince must act in the interest of the common good. Mercado advocated strong government control over the market, backed up by clerical enforcement in "the court of conscience" – a notion that we will revert to later. Mercado shared the view of Domingo de Soto that, in an ideal world, all prices should be fixed by the authorities for the sake of the public good.[42]

Mercado was suspicious of individuals' tendency to seek their own advantage while neglecting the interests of their neighbor. In this regard, he was indebted to the rather pessimistic view of man that was also typical of Saint Augustine and further spread by Martin Luther. Incidentally, a big contrast can be observed between Mercado's protectionist and anti-liberal instincts, on the one hand, and the liberal, profit-endorsing attitude adopted by contemporary theologians such as Saravia de la Calle and successive generations of Jesuit moral theologians such as Luis de Molina, Leonardus Lessius and Juan de Lugo, on the other.[43] For example, Luis de Molina doubted the effectiveness of market regulation, fearing negative side-effects such as favoritism and corruption, although he still maintained that citizens were obliged to respect the *tasa del trigo* because they owed obedience to the ruler.

4. Mercado on Clerics' Role as Law Enforcers[44]

Confronted with the Lutheran attack on clerics' role in administering justice, Catholic theologians recalled secular authorities that the jurisdictional power of the Church was largely to their benefit. They stressed the synergetic relationship between ecclesiastical and temporal power. The existence of a jurisdictional space of conscience, guarded by clerics, allowed for the

42 Oreste Popescu. *Studies in the History of Latin American Economic Thought*. New York: Routledge, 1997, 39–40.

43 Michael Thomas D'Emic. *Justice in the Marketplace in Early Modern Spain. Saravia, Villalón and the Religious Origins of Economic Analysis*. Lanham, MD: Lexington Books, 2014; Murray N. Rothbard. *An Austrian Perspective on the History of Economic Thought*. Auburn: Ludwig von Mises Institute, 2006 (reprint of the Edward Elgar edition, 1995), vol. 1, 97–133.

44 The following paragraphs are borrowed from sections in Decock, "Collaborative Legal Pluralism," 107–110. References to the primary sources are included in that article.

effective enforcement of the laws enacted by temporal authorities. The confessor's role as a judge in the forum of conscience was considered as a crucial policy instrument to guarantee the stability of the Christian political order.[45] Mercado admonished that a well-ordered republic rests on both good laws and wise judges to enforce those laws, mentioning civil laws and civil courts, on the one hand, and divine laws and conscience, on the other. In this manner, Mercado recalled the fact that conscience should be considered as a tribunal in the proper sense of the word. "The confessor is to Christianity what a prince is to a city," Mercado explained,[46] "it is his task to make sure that all live in order and that the law is being observed and executed. He collaborates with the penitents to make sure that they observe the law which they proclaimed at the moment of baptism since confessors are judges of conscience." Mercado's admonishments were not just pious hopes or lofty sermons. On account of their jurisdictional power, clerics could effectively sanction wicked behavior. "The confessor compells and forces with his power," Mercado explained, "just like a true judge."

In Mercado's eyes, ecclesiastical jurisdiction had been given by Christ to the Church not only for spiritual reasons, but also to support secular rulers. Christ knew that human authorities alone would never be able to guarantee peace and order. People had to believe that violating the law would not only lead to punishment on earth, but also in heaven. "One of the great tasks of the confessor," Mercado explicated,[47] "is to make the penitent understand how important it is for salvation that subjects obey their princes." Confessors were necessary for the wellbeing of the republic since they guaranteed a higher form of loyalty and obedience of Christian citizens towards their prince. Through their judicial power in the court of conscience, confessors could compel penitents to observe not only the divine law revealed in the Gospel but also the civil laws issued by the prince. Confessors were seminal in ensuring justice, order and a peaceful political life. According to Mercado, they fostered a culture of reconciliation, even helping creditors to collect debts that could no longer be recovered through the external court for lack of proof. "Fathers-confessors," Mercado concluded, "are very much fathers of the republic (*padres confesores muy padres de la república*)."[48]

The notion that confessors are not just "fathers-priests" but also "fathers of the republic" sums up the convergence of political and religious interests

45 Prosperi, "Die Beichte und das Gericht des Gewissens," 186.
46 Cited in Decock, "Collaborative Legal Pluralism," 109.
47 Cited in Decock, "Collaborative Legal Pluralism," 109.
48 Cited in Decock, "Collaborative Legal Pluralism," 110.

strived for by Mercado and other theologians of the School of Salamanca in the face of the Lutheran threat of secularization. For the sake of "the peace and the tranquility of the republic," they argued that crime and sin are inseparable, thus contributing to the internalization of positive law. Mercado's plea in favor of mutual jurisdictional collaboration between spiritual and temporal authorities was not new, but rather a strong re-affirmation of traditional Catholic theology of law and politics.[49] Like much of early modern scholastic political doctrine, especially as developed in Salamanca, it was aimed at the restoration of the medieval dream of a Christian commonwealth.[50] In the spirit of the Council of Trent, Mercado re-affirmed the basic principle of Thomistic political theology that just laws, issued for the sake of the common good, are binding in conscience. Fearing the disruptive potential of Martin Luther's idea of evangelical liberty, he considered the view that civil laws are not binding in conscience as heretical.

5. Soto and the Rise of Public Poverty Relief[51]

Another attempt to restore, or rather, protect the medieval dream of the Christian commonwealth is offered by Domingo de Soto. Soto is not only remembered as one of the great theologians at the University of Salamanca and as the confessor to Emperor Charles V. In this context, it is also worthwhile mentioning that, as the prior of the Dominican Convent of San Estebán, he had been in charge of organizing poor relief in Salamanca on several occasions.[52] In his *Deliberation on the Cause of the Poor* (1545), Soto attacked statutory regulations on poverty relief in cities such as Zamora, Valladolid and Salamanca. Those regulations shifted the power to administer charity from religious orders and ecclesiastical institutions to public authorities. This was a phenomenon

49 Orazio Condorelli. "Le origini teologico-canonistiche della teoria delle leges mere poenales (secoli XIII–XVI)." In *Der Einfluss der Kanonistik auf die europäische Rechtskultur*, vol. 3: *Straf- und Strafprozessrecht*, eds. Mathias Schmoeckel, Orazio Condorelli and Franck Roumy. Köln: Böhlau, 2012, 55–98 (56).

50 Massimo Meccarelli. "Das Problem der Rechtsmodernisierung durch die Theologen der Spätscholastik." In *Rechtsgeschichte heute. Religion und Politik in der Geschichte des Rechts*, eds. Nils Jansen and Peter Oestmann. Tübingen: Mohr Siebeck, 2014, 119–130 (130).

51 The following paragraphs rely on Wim Decock. "Social Crisis and Rule of Law. Domingo de Soto on the Rights of the Deserving Poor." *Rivista internazionale di diritto comune* 28 (2017), forthcoming.

52 Edouard Fernandez-Bollo. "Le contexte historique et philosophique de la controverse." In *Domingo de Soto: La cause des pauvres*, introd., trad. Edouard Fernandez-Bollo, Paris: Dalloz, 2013, p. 96.

widely observed across Europe from the early sixteenth century onwards that received special impetus by the Lutheran Reformers.[53] For example, following the advice of Martin Luther, the city of Wittenberg radically changed its approach to poor relief in 1521–1522, granting municipal authorities control over the administration of charity.[54] In Zürich, the Swiss reformer Ulrich Zwingli (1484–1531) overhauled the traditional organization of poor relief in 1525, forbidding all mendicancy.[55] In Denmark, ecclesiastical poor relief was nationalized.[56]

The abolition of religious orders in Protestant regions facilitated the transfer of poor relief from ecclesiastical institutions to secular authorities.[57] Yet, Catholic cities, too, changed their approach to poor relief in the early sixteenth century. This can be witnessed in the Spanish Netherlands, where the Flemish city of Ypres became one of the pioneers in reorganizing the administration of charity in 1525.[58] An intellectual justification for these new policies was offered in 1526 by Juan Luis Vives (1493–1540), a Spanish migrant of Jewish descent in Bruges and a humanist scholar highly critical of ecclesiastical authority. In his work *On Assistance to the Poor* he denounced clerical abuse in the administration of charity and argued in favor of public control over poverty relief.[59] Vives wanted public servants to exercise strict control over who was really poor or not. Only the real poor were entitled to receive assistance by the city. Fearing fraud on the part of the candidates, Vives wanted medical doctors to examine the sick poor to check whether they were not lying about their health condition. In Vives's view there was no such a thing as a "right to laziness." Observing

53 Waelkens, *Amne adverso*, 391.

54 J. Friedrich Battenberg. "Obrigkeitliche Sozialpolitik und Gesetzgebung. Einige Gedanken zu mittelrheinischen Bettel- und Almosenordnungen des 16. Jahrhunderts." *Zeitschrift für Historische Forschung* 18 (1991): 33–70 (57).

55 Richard Tawney. *Religion and the Rise of Capitalism*, Harmondsworth: Penguin Books, 1977 [1926], p. 123.

56 See the contributions in *Den nordiske protestantisme og velfaerdsstaten*, ed. Tim Knudsen, Arhus: Arhus Universitetsforlag, 2000.

57 For an overview of the changes in social legislation and policy in different European areas in the early modern period, see the two-volume work edited by Theodor Strohm and Michael Klein. *Die Entstehung einer sozialen Ordnung Europas*. Heidelberg: Winter, 2004.

58 Paul Bonenfant. "Les origines et le caractère de la réforme de la bienfaisance publique aux Pays-Bas sous le règne de Charles-Quint." *Revue belge de Philologie et d'Histoire* 5 (1926): 887–904 (891); Wim P. Blockmans and Walter Prevenier. "Poverty in Flanders and Brabant from the Fourteenth to the Mid-Sixteenth Century: Sources and Problems." *Acta Historiae Neerlandicae* 10 (1978): 20–57.

59 Gilbert Tournoy. "Towards the Roots of Social Welfare. Joan Lluís Vives's *De subventione pauperum*." *City* 8 (2004): 266–273.

that textile industry in Bruges was flourishing, he deplored that the bosses could not find enough people who were willing to work.

Following the examples of German and Flemish cities, the estates of Madrid, Salamanca, Valladolid and Zamora started submitting petitions to Charles V from the 1520s onwards to ask for the implementation of similar measures in Spain. In 1540, the imperial council gave in and prepared an instruction on begging, vagrancy and poverty relief for the cities that was officially published in 1544. It stipulated that poor relief must be organized by public authorities, subjecting the right to beg to strict conditions. Every city must appoint a public servant who carefully examines beggars and vagabonds and makes a distinction between the true and the false poor. Recognition as a deserving poor was made conditional upon control and public examination of one's state of necessity. The rightful poor must acquire a licence, an administrative document, to be able to receive public assistance. Moreover, the license was only granted if the poor man first subjected himself to the sacrament of confession. The unlawful poor were forced to work or punished. Each city must provide for its own public poor relief system, so that the poor do not migrate to other cities. Except in the cases of famine or pest, even the legitimate poor were obliged to stay in their original place of living.

6. Poverty, Almsgiving and the Economy of Salvation[60]

Domingo de Soto was skeptical about the new, public approach to poverty relief that emerged in the first half of the sixteenth century. Against the secularizing tendencies inherent in the new approach to the administration of charity, he defended the traditional way of coping with poverty. That traditional approach appealed to the practice of private charity, viz. almsgiving, and to the institutional assistance provided by the Church to alleviate the plight of the poor.[61] It was an approach rooted in a static worldview centered around the idea that the rich and poor were "bound together in a symbiotic relationship of mutual necessity,"[62] fixed for eternity according to a divinely ordered plan. While the poor needed material support from the rich to safeguard their bodily existence, the rich needed the help of the poor to gain salvation of their souls. By

60 The following paragraphs are adapted from sections in Decock, "Social Crisis and Rule of Law. Domingo de Soto on the Rights of the Deserving Poor," Rivista Internazionale di Diritto Comune, 28 (2017), 159–178.

61 Marco H. D. van Leeuwen. "Logic of Charity. Poor Relief in Preindustrial Europe." *Journal of Inderdisciplinary History* 24 (1994): 589–614.

62 Diana Wood. *Medieval Economic Thought*. Cambridge: CUP, 2002, 42–43.

giving alms, the rich could "build a treasury in heaven" and redeem their sins.[63] Drawing on Prov 10:2, the Judeo-Christian tradition developed the notion that giving alms accumulated one's treasury in heaven. Gary A. Anderson has argued that this was not just a metaphor. In the Judeo-Christian tradition, charitable deeds have been literally considered as storable commodities, however alien that may be to a Protestant mindset.[64] An authoritative Biblical text adduced for this proposition was the story of Nebuchadnezzar's terrifying nightmare about the demise of his kingdom and Prophet Daniel's reassuring words that he could avert evil by being generous to the poor (Dan 4:24). "In a world in which sins were understood as financial debts," Anderson explains, "it made sense to fund a "treasury in heaven" in order to bring one's penance to conclusion."[65]

In Soto's view, doubting the necessity of private charity and other good works for the redemption of sins – as Martin Luther did in *The Freedom of a Christian* – was heretical. It came down to questioning divine providence and the economy of salvation. Moreover, he insisted that Church leaders, not urban institutions or secular authorities, needed to take special care of the poor, since God was the advocate and father of miserable persons. Both the responsibility for the miserable persons and the jurisdictional power to deal with cases involving them lay with spiritual authorities such as bishops and abbots.[66] Soto cited provisions from the medieval canon law to bolster this claim, especially from the *Liber extra* and the Constitutions of Pope Clemens V. It would largely exceed the boundaries of this paper to provide a fully-fledged analysis of Soto's fascinating engagement with the theoretical and practical aspects of poverty relief.[67] Suffice it to say that Soto built on his knowledge of the Bible, the medieval *ius commune* and natural law to rebuke the new statutory provisions on dealing with the poor. The guardian of the old worldview, Soto resented the legislative initiatives in the Spanish Netherlands and Germany, because they

63 Gary A. Anderson. *Sin: A History*. New Haven, Yale: UP, 2009, 135–151.

64 Gary A. Anderson. *Charity: The Place of the Poor in the Biblical Tradition*. New Haven, Yale: UP, 2013, 113–148.

65 Gary A. Anderson. "Heavenly Treasure. A Review of the Ransom of the Soul." *First Things*, 2015, https://www.firstthings.com/article/2015/05/heavenly-treasure.

66 Richard H. Helmholz. *The Spirit of Classical Canon Law*. 116–144; Thomas Duve. *Sonderrecht in der Frühen Neuzeit. Studien zum ius singulare und den privilegia miserabilium personarum, senum und indorum in Alter und Neuer Welt*, Frankfurt am Main: Klostermann, 2008.

67 Good introductions are Camacho, *Economía y filosofía moral*, 109–140; Annabel S. Brett. *Changes of State: Nature and the Limits of the City in Early Modern Natural Law*. Princeton: Princeton UP, 2011, 11–36; Edouard Fernandez-Bollo. "Introduction: Philosophie, droit et pauvreté." In *Domingo de Soto: La cause des pauvres*, introd., trad. Edouard Fernandez-Bollo, Paris: Dalloz, 2013, 5–18.

were symptomatic of a profound shift in the understanding of the relationship between spiritual and secular rule in a Christian commonwealth that was fostered by the Lutheran Reformation.

7. Concluding Remarks: Clerics as Fathers of the Republic

The secularization of the Christian West is hardly conceivable without the Protestant Reformation. It entailed a major shift in power from ecclesiastical to secular authorities. As Richard Tawney once put it,[68] "authority, expelled from the altar, found a new and securer home upon the throne." Moreover, the Lutheran denunciation of the Church as a hegemonic institution of power was accompanied by a critique on theology as an overarching science. This created space for the autonomous development of other disciplines and authorities.[69] An emancipation of secular authorities and secular scholars from ecclesiastical institutional power took place, regardless of how strong the religious convictions of those authorities and scholars remained. The contrast with the experience in the early modern Catholic world is obvious. As Francisco de Vitoria claimed in the opening sentence of his *Lecture on civil power*, "the office and calling of a theologian are so wide, that no argument or controversy on any subject can be considered foreign to his profession."[70] At Salamanca, hundreds of voluminous treatises were written in which Catholic theologians and canon lawyers reinforced the medieval symbiosis of law and Christian morality. While Luther and his followers believed that it was not the true mission of the Church to develop legal doctrines, Catholic theologians in the early modern period went to great lengths to achieve just that: they wrote sophisticated treatises on contracts, property, restitution, criminal law, social policy, etc.

Tomás de Mercado's *Suma de tratos y contratos* and Domingo de Soto's *Deliberatio in causa pauperum* are examples of the Catholic resistance against both Lutheranism and secularization in the early modern period. Following other Catholic theologians and jurists, they resisted the emancipation of the administration of justice and charity from ecclesiastical authority and theological thinking. Mercado and Soto sensed the secularist threat inherent in Lutheran theology and reclaimed spiritual authorities' role in the administration of worldly affairs. Against Luther's basic instincts, they maintained that the Church was truly competent in regulating the market and organizing poor

68 Tawney, *Religion and the Rise of Capitalism*, 110.

69 Schmoeckel, *Das Recht der Reformation*, 297.

70 Decock, *Theologians and Contract Law*, 43.

relief. Incidentally, this proves Christoph Strohm's point that developments in the early modern Catholic world are no less interesting for legal historians than those in the Protestant lands, even if, relatively speaking, they have received far less attention.[71]

Fears of the destabilizing, "secularizing" effects on political order ensuing from Luther's theology were a substantial part of Catholic critique from the earliest days of the Reformation. A letter by Pope Adrian VI from 1522 to Cardinal Francesco Chieregati clearly echoes that threat.[72] Adrian of Utrecht (1459–1523) became famous as the first pope from the Low Countries (1522–1523), but he started his career as a tutor of the future emperor Charles V and a professor of theology at the University of Louvain. His *Miscellaneous Questions* (1515) were a constant reference point in the work of Domingo de Soto and other theologians of the School of Salamanca, making his views on Luther as a contemporary observer all the more interesting. Adrian VI's letter to Cardinal Chieregati, his representative at the Reichstag of Nuremberg, was written just two years after the publication of Luther's *On the Freedom of a Christian* (1520). It contained instructions on how to address the German princes gathered at the Reichtstag of Nuremberg. Pope Adrian VI wanted to make them aware of the political danger looming in accepting the tenets of the Lutheran faith. "They have to be aware of what the Lutherans are striving for under the guise of evangelical liberty," Adrian warned Chieregati,[73] "namely to abolish all power of superior authorities."

In their reaction against rising secularism, Catholics were driven by a nostalgic desire to restore the great age of Pope Innocent III (1198–1216), "when the Church controlled the formal process of political, juridical, commercial, and social intercourse."[74] Major Jesuit theologians steeped in the tradition of Salamanca such as Leonardus Lessius revisited the conclusions of the Third Lateran Council (1215) concerning the administrative power of the Church, including the jurisdictional power of its judges.[75] They stressed that the canon law was not just an "ecclesiastical law" or "Kirchenrecht," merely dealing

71 Strohm, "Die produktive Kraft konfessioneller Konkurrenz für die Rechtsentwicklung," 170.

72 This paragraph is adapted from Wim Decock, "Adrian of Utrecht (1459–1523) at the Crossroads of Law and Morality: Conscience, Equity and the Legal Nature of Early Modern Practical Theology." *Tijdschrift voor Rechtsgeschiedenis* 81 (2013): 573–593.

73 Decock, "Adrian of Utrecht (1459–1523) at the Crossroads of Law and Morality," 583.

74 Bryan Wilson. *Contemporary Transformations of Religion*. Oxford: OUP, 1976, 9–10.

75 Leonardus Lessius (using the pseudonym William Singleton). *Discussio decreti magni concilii Lateranensis et quarundam rationum annexarum de potestate Ecclesiae in temporalibus*. Mainz, 1613, 37.

with the internal organization of the church, but rather a universal law dealing with all possible temporal and spiritual affairs, touching all citizens.[76] They warned that the spiritual "fathers," the clerics, were not just preachers, but administrators essential to the well-being of the political community. Secular princes could only do without support of the clergy at the cost of losing influence. A prosperous reign presupposed collaboration with the Holy See.[77] Alluding to the metaphor of the Christian magistrate as the "father of the republic," widespread among Lutheran Reformers,[78] Catholics insisted, instead, that clerics were "very much fathers of the republic."

Bibliography

Primary Sources

Lessius, Leonardus (using the pseudonym William Singleton) (1613). *Discussio decreti magni concilii Lateranensis et quarundam rationum annexarum de potestate Ecclesiae in temporalibus.* Mainz.

1745. *Nueva Recopilación*, ed. Madrid: Zuñiga. Online available on Google Books.

Mercado, Tomás de (1977). *Suma de tratos y contratos.* The Seville 1571 edition edited by Nicolás Sánchez-Albornoz in 1977 is available online at http://www.cervantesvirtual.com/nd/ark:/59851/bmc1c1t9 (unpaginated).

Soto, Domingo de (1547). *In causa pauperum deliberatio*, Venice, online available on Google Books.

Secondary Sources

Anderson, Gary A. (2009). *Sin: A History.* New Haven, Yale: University Press.

Anderson, Gary A. (2013). *Charity: The Place of the Poor in the Biblical Tradition.* New Haven, Yale: University Press.

Anderson, Gary A. (2015). "Heavenly Treasure. A Review of the Ransom of the Soul." *First Things*, 2015, https://www.firstthings.com/article/2015/05/heavenly-treasure.

Astorri, Paolo (2018). *Lutheran Theology and Contract Law in Early Modern Germany (ca. 1520–1720).* (Law and Religion in the Early Modern Period, 1), Leiden/Paderborn, Brill/Schöningh, 2019.

Battenberg, J. Friedrich (1991). "Obrigkeitliche Sozialpolitik und Gesetzgebung. Einige Gedanken zu mittelrheinischen Bettel- und Almosenordnungen des 16. Jahrhunderts." *Zeitschrift für Historische Forschung* 18, 33–70.

76 Dag Michalsen. *Rett en internasjonal historie.* Oslo: Pax, 2011, 178.

77 Lessius, *Discussio decreti magni concilii Lateranensis*, 135.

78 Witte, *Law and Protestantism*, 9.

Beaulande-Barraud, Véronique, and Charageat, Martine eds. (2014). *Les officialités dans l'Europe médiévale et moderne. Des tribunaux pour une société chrétienne.* Turnhout: Brepols.

Berman, Harold J. (1983). *Law and Revolution: The Formation of the Western Legal Tradition.* Cambridge Mass.: Harvard University Press.

Berman, Harold J. (2003). *Law and Revolution II: The Impact of the Protestant Reformations on the Western Legal Tradition.* Cambridge Mass.: Harvard University Press.

Berman, Harold J. (1997). "The Interaction of Spiritual and Secular Law: The Sixteenth-Century and Today." *Fulton Lectures*, 1–12. https://chicagounbound.uchicago.edu/cgi/viewcontent.cgi?article=1008&context=fulton_lectures.

Blockmans, Wim P., and Walter Prevenier (1978). "Poverty in Flanders and Brabant from the Fourteenth to the Mid-Sixteenth Century: Sources and Problems." *Acta Historiae Neerlandicae* 10, 20–57.

Bonenfant, Paul (1926). "Les origines et le caractère de la réforme de la bienfaisance publique aux Pays-Bas sous le règne de Charles-Quint." *Revue belge de Philologie et d'Histoire* 5, 887–904.

Brett, Annabel S. (2011). *Changes of State: Nature and the Limits of the City in Early Modern Natural Law.* Princeton: Princeton University Press.

Calvo, Manuel J. Lagares (2016). "Seis incógnitas y algunas respuestas sobre la vida de Fray Tomás de Mercado." *Iberian Journal of the History of Economic Thought* 3, 68–77.

Casey, James (1999). *Early Modern Spain: A Social History.* London: Routledge.

Christoffersen, Lisbet (2006). "Intertwinement: A New Concept for Understanding Religion-Law Relations." *Nordic Journal of Religion and Society* 19.2, 107–126.

Condorelli, Orazio (2012). "Le origini teologico-canonistiche della teoria delle leges mere poenales (secoli XIII–XVI)." Mathias Schmoeckel, Orazio Condorelli and Franck Roumy, eds. *Der Einfluss der Kanonistik auf die europäische Rechtskultur*, vol. 3: *Straf- und Strafprozessrecht.* Köln: Böhlau, 55–98.

Decock, Wim (2013). "Adrian of Utrecht (1459–1523) at the Crossroads of Law and Morality: Conscience, Equity and the Legal Nature of Early Modern Practical Theology." *Tijdschrift voor Rechtsgeschiedenis* 81, 573–593.

Decock, Wim (2017). "Collaborative Legal Pluralism. Confessors as Law Enforcers in Mercado's Advice on Economic Governance (1571)." *Rechtsgeschichte – Legal History* 25, 103–114.

Decock, Wim (2016). "Domingo de Soto, De iustitia et iure." Serge Dauchy et al., eds. *The Formation and Transmission of Western Legal Culture: 150 Books that Made the Law in the Age of Printing.* Berlin: Springer, 94–96.

Decock, Wim (2016). "In Defense of Commercial Capitalism: Lessius, Partnerships and the contractus trinus." Bram Van Hofstraeten and Wim Decock, eds. *Companies and Company Law in Late Medieval and Early Modern Europe.* Leuven: Peeters, 55–90.

Decock, Wim (2017). "Social Crisis and Rule of Law. Domingo de Soto on the Rights of the Deserving Poor." *Rivista internazionale di diritto comune* 28, (2017), 159–178.

Decock, Wim (2013). *Theologians and Contract Law: The Moral Transformation of the Ius commune (c. 1500–1650)*. Leiden/Boston: Brill/Nijhoff.

D'Emic, Michael Thomas (2014). *Justice in the Marketplace in Early Modern Spain. Saravia, Villalón and the Religious Origins of Economic Analysis*. Lanham, MD: Lexington Books.

Dobbelaere, Karel (2009). "The Meaning and Scope of Secularization." Peter B. Clarke, ed. *The Oxford Handbook of the Sociology of Religion*. Oxford: Oxford University Press, 599–615.

Donahue, Charles Jr. (2008). *Law, Marriage, and Society in the Later Middle Ages: Arguments about Marriage in Five Courts*. Cambridge: Cambridge University Press.

Duve, Thomas (2008). *Sonderrecht in der Frühen Neuzeit. Studien zum ius singulare und den privilegia miserabilium personarum, senum und indorum in Alter und Neuer Welt*, Frankfurt am Main: Klostermann.

Duve, Thomas (2015). "Salamanca in Amerika." *Zeitschrift der Savigny-Stiftung für Rechtsgeschichte: Germanistische Abteilung* 132, 116–151.

Duve, Thomas (2012). "Von der Europäischen Rechtsgeschichte zu einer Rechtsgeschichte Europas in globalhistorischer Perspektive." *Rechtsgeschichte – Legal History* 20, 18–71.

Fernandez-Bollo, Edouard (2013). "Introduction: Philosophie, droit et pauvreté." Edouard Fernandez-Bollo, introd., trad. *Domingo de Soto: La cause des pauvres*. Paris: Dalloz, 5–18.

Fernandez-Bollo, Edouard (2013). "Le contexte historique et philosophique de la controverse." Edouard Fernandez-Bollo, introd., trad. *Domingo de Soto: La cause des pauvres*, Paris: Dalloz.

Gómez Camacho, Francisco (1998). *Economía y filosofía moral: la formación del pensamiento económico europeo en la Escolástica española*. Madrid: Síntesis.

González Polvillo, Antonio (2010). *El gobierno de los otros. Confesión y control de la conciencia en la España moderna*. Sevilla: Universidad.

Gordley, James (2013). *The Jurists: A Critical History*. Oxford: Oxford University Press.

Gordley, James (1991). *The Philosophical Origins of Modern Contract Doctrine*. Oxford: Clarendon.

Green, Thomas (2016). "The Sources of Early Scots Consistorial Law. Reflections on Law, Authority and Jurisdiction during the Scottish Reformation." Mark Godfrey, ed. *Law and Authority in British Legal History, 1200–1900*. Cambridge: Cambridge University Press, 120–139.

Grunert, Frank (2017). "Äußere Norm und inneres Gewissen. Das Gewissen in den Naturrechtslehren von Samuel Pufendorf und Christian Thomasius." Michael

Germann and Wim Decock, eds. *Das Gewissen in den Rechtslehren der protestantischen und katholischen Reformationen*. Leipzig: Evangelische Verlagsanstalt, 297–312.

Hartmann, Wilfried, and Pennington, Kenneth, eds. (2016). *The History of Courts and Procedure in Medieval Canon Law*. Washington DC: Catholic University of America Press.

Helmholz, Richard H. (1996). *The Spirit of Classical Canon Law*. Athens and London: The University of Georgia Press.

Hutchinson, Majorie A. (1952). *The School of Salamanca. Readings in Spanish Monetary Theory, 1544–1605*. Oxford: Oxford University Press.

Knudsen, Tim, ed. (2000). *Den nordiske protestantisme og velfærdsstaten*. Arhus: Arhus Universitetsforlag.

Leeuwen, Marco H.D van (1994). "Logic of Charity. Poor Relief in Preindustrial Europe." *Journal of Inderdisciplinary History* 24, 589–614.

Maihold, Harald (2017). "'Himmel und Erde.' Die Abgrenzung von forum internum und forum externum in der Frühen Neuzeit." Michael Germann and Wim Decock, eds. *Das Gewissen in den Rechtslehren*. Leipzig: Evangelische Verlagsanstalt, 51–71.

Meccarelli, Massimo (2014). "Das Problem der Rechtsmodernisierung durch die Theologen der Spätscholastik." Nils Jansen and Peter Oestmann, eds. *Rechtsgeschichte heute. Religion und Politik in der Geschichte des Rechts*. Tübingen: Mohr Siebeck, 119–130.

Michalsen, Dag (2011). *Rett en internasjonal historie*. Oslo: Pax.

O'Malley, John (2013). *Trent: What Happened at the Council*. Cambridge Mass.: Harvard University Press.

Plans, Juan Belda (2000). *La escuela de Salamanca y la renovación de la teología en el siglo XVI*. Madrid: BAC Maior.

Popescu, Oreste (1997). *Studies in the History of Latin American Economic Thought*. New York: Routledge.

Prodi, Paolo (2012). "Il giuramento e il tribunale della coscienza: dal pluralismo degli ordinamenti giuridici al dualismo tra coscienza e diritto positivo." Paolo Prodi, ed. *Cristianesimo e potere*. Bologna: Il Mulino, 163–178.

Prodi, Paolo (2009). *Settimo non rubare. Furto e mercato nella storia dell'Occidente*. Bologna: Il Mulino.

Prosperi, Adriano (2001). "Die Beichte und das Gericht des Gewissens." Paolo Prodi and Wolfgang Reinhard, eds. *Das Konzil von Trient und die Moderne*. Berlin: Duncker & Humblot, 175–197.

Rothbard, Murray N. (2006). *An Austrian Perspective on the History of Economic Thought*. Auburn: Ludwig von Mises Institute (reprint of the Edward Elgar edition, 1995), vol. 1, 97–133.

Schmoeckel, Mathias (2014). *Das Recht der Reformation: Die epistemologische Revolution der Wissenschaft und die Spaltung der Rechtsordnung in der Frühen Neuzeit*. Tübingen: Mohr.

Strohm, Theodor, and Klein, Michael, eds. (2004). *Die Entstehung einer sozialen Ordnung Europas*. Heidelberg: Winter.

Strohm, Christoph (2017). "Die produktive Kraft konfessioneller Konkurrenz für die Rechtsentwicklung." Christoph Strohm, ed. *Reformation und Recht. Ein Beitrag zur Kontroverse um die Kulturwirkungen der Reformation*. Tübingen: Mohr Siebeck.

Tawney, Richard (1977). *Religion and the Rise of Capitalism*. Harmondsworth: Penguin Books, [1926].

Tournoy, Gilbert (2004). "Towards the Roots of Social Welfare. Joan Lluís Vives's *De subventione pauperum*." *City* 8, 266–273.

Vigo Gutiérrez, Abelardo Del (2006). *Economía y ética en el siglo XVI. Estudio comparativo entro los Padres de la Reforma y la Teología española*. Madrid: Biblioteca de Autores Cristianos.

Vigo Gutiérrez, Abelardo Del (1981). "Las tasas y las Pragmáticas reales en los moralistas españoles del Siglo de Oro." *Burgense* 22, 427–470.

Waelkens, Laurent (2015). *Amne adverso: Roman Legal Heritage in European Culture*. Leuven: Leuven University Press.

Wilson, Bryan (1976). *Contemporary Transformations of Religion*. Oxford: Oxford University Press.

Witte, John Jr. (2002). *Law and Protestantism: The Legal Teachings of the Lutheran Reformation*. Cambridge: Cambridge University Press.

Wood, Diana (2002). *Medieval Economic Thought*. Cambridge: Cambridge University Press.

The King as the Warrant of Faith

Bugenhagen's Danish Church Ordinances (1537/9) and their Effects on Schleswig-Holstein, Denmark, and Norway

Mathias Schmoeckel

1. Introduction

Since the nineteenth century historians and others, Max Weber for example, have tried to define "the" necessary or typical effect of Protestant Reformation. Effects on politics, economics and culture have been traced back to the Reformation. In law we cannot deny that Luther's "Zwei-Regimenter-Lehre"[1] ("Two-Regiments theory") liberated secular administration from ecclesiastical supremacy. But did this lead to the establishment of political regimes with typical characteristics? The large discussion on "confessionalism" still held to the conviction that a confession had certain consequences for the territories in which it was established. But historians like Robert von Friedeburg have shown in recent years that Lutheranism, for instance, could lead to quite divergent approaches towards the state.[2] The usual reaction to this provocation has been to ask for further differentiation between the protagonists of Reformations, more concentration on formative ideas or even on decades alone, but this differentiation would still lead to one determining the dominant effect of the Reformation in the context.[3] It could well be that there is no necessary or even typical effect at all, that the Reformation could differ in its effects with respect to the country in question, its traditions and political problems of the moment. It might be possible that the Reformation influenced the European territories in different ways.

---

1 Cf. Martin Heckel. *Martin Luthers Reformation und das Recht.* Tübingen: Mohr Siebeck, 2016, 584ss.

2 Robert von Friedeburg. "Das Gewissen in den Rechtslehren der protestantischen und katholischen Reformationen/Conscience in the Legal Teachings of the Protestant and Catholic Reformations." In *Leucorea-Studien zur Geschichte der Reformation und der Lutherischen Orthodoxie*, 31. ed. W. Decock/ M. Germann. Leipzig: Evangelische Verlangsanstalt, 2017, 287–296.

3 The development of this discussion is described by Chang Soo Park. "Luthertum und Obrigkeit im Alten Reich in der Frühen Neuzeit: Dargestellt am Beispiel von Tilemann Heshusius (1527–1588)." In *Historische Forschungen* No. 109 (2016): 15–29.

 | DOI:10.30965/9783657790746_004

Indeed, the 500th jubilée of Luther's critique of the indulgencies and the beginning of the Protestant Reformation had different reactions in the European countries. In France the date passed almost unnoticed, in Germany it ended the "Protestant Decade" starting with Calvin's 500th birthday in 2006 and in Norway the old union of State and Church finally came to an end on January 1, 2017, when the Norwegian church acquired the status of an autonomous legal entity distinct from the Norwegian state.[4] This difference in reactions might mirror the differences in how the Protestant Reformation took place initially and to which degree it has helped to shape the countries over the past centuries.

For these reasons it is important to compare the reactions to the Protestant Reformation. Could it be that even a single church ordinance could exert different influences in the countries of its enactment? I will concentrate in this paper on Johannes Bugenhagen's church ordinance of 1537 for Christian III. It was enacted for his three territories Denmark, Norway and Schleswig Holstein. But was this Bugenhagen's achievement alone? For the sake of comparison, however, I will start with a preliminary remark on Zwingli's Reformation in Zurich from 1522 until 1525, which is perhaps the first example of a Protestant government (II.1). It will help to distinguish the particularities of Bugenhagen and to determine features in common. I will concentrate on Bugenhagen's theology next (II.2). As an example of his first experiences with ordinances, I will refer to the Reformation in Hamburg from 1526 until 1529 (II.3).

After this imagined trip from Zurich via Wittenberg to Hamburg, I will describe the evolution of Lutheranism in the realms of the Danish kings.[5] As Luther's Reformation spread from south to north, I will start with the duchies of Schleswig and Holstein (III.1), where the establishment of the Reformation was completed before the same monarch could settle it in Denmark (III.2). Although the same ordinance was also enacted for Norway, its effect there was quite different. It is necessary, therefore, to have a final look at the consequences of the 1537 ordinance for Norway. In this case again we have to understand how the Protestant Reformation was introduced and how this changed the structures of the realm (IV.1). Afterwards, by comparing the effect which the 1537 ordinance had on Norway in the long run (IV.2) we will understand how this ordinance helped to create special characteristics in Norway (IV.3).

4 Cf. https://www.regjeringen.no/no/aktuelt/farvel-til-statskirken--fortsatt-folkekirke/id2525748/, last accessed 15 Aug. 2017.

5 It is impossible to consult all the existing literature on the subject, cf. Erik Gøbel/Knut Sprauten. *Kommenteret bibliografi til dansk-norsk historie 1536–1814 især vedrørende centraladministrationen*. Copenhagen/Oslo: Rigsarkivet, 1997, particularly as not all of the books and journals can be sent to Bonn.

After a period during which I focused on possible links between two dogmatic sciences, theology and jurisprudence[6], I am more interested here in the historical particularities during the introduction of the Protestant Reformation, how it was installed and began to change lives, and which effect it had in the long run for the administration of the central seat of power.

On the whole I assume that the same ordinance could have had quite different effects. The way the Reformation was introduced and the way it was administered influenced the perception people had of it tremendously. These experiences initiated new traditions in each country and traces of their effects are found even centuries afterwards.

2. Models for the Reformation of the Law: From Zurich to Hamburg

2.1 *Zwingli in Zurich*

While Martin Luther immediately became the spokesman for the Reformation, the electorate of Saxony did not instantly become the model of a Protestant territory. Even though he protected Luther and his university, the Elector personally clung on to the old faith and the innovations developed slowly until the 1530.[7] To change the perspective, we will therefore start with Zurich where Huldrych Zwingli (1484–1531) established the new faith between 1522 and 1525. In 1519 he became the priest for the population ("Leutpriester") in the convent of the minster of Zurich. He influenced Zurich as a preacher and never held another official rank. While he might have been influenced in many ways by Luther, some of his ideas preceded those of Luther. It is hard to determine who influenced the other and it might have been rather a mutual give-and-take relationship.[8] We should not forget that many of the topics had been developed before as others in Zurich were also in touch with Wittenberg, such as the printer Christoph Froschauer (approx. 1490–1564) who edited works of Luther and Zwingli.[9]

---

6 A first summary was presented in Mathias Schmoeckel. *Das Recht der Reformation.* Tübingen: Mohr Siebeck, 2015.

7 Ingetraut Ludolphy: "Friedrich der Weise." *Theologische Realenzyklopädie,* Vol. 11 (1983): 666–669.

8 Ulrich Gäbler. *Huldrych Zwingli: Eine Einführung in sein Leben und sein Werk.* Munich: C.H. Beck, 1983, 53; Gottfried Wilhelm Locher. "Huldrych Zwingli." In *Die Reformationszeit I.: Gestalten der Kirchengeschichte 5,* ed. Martin Greschat. Stuttgart: Kohlhammer, 1988, 188.

9 Paul Leemann-van Elck. "Froschauer, Christoph der Ältere." *Neue Deutsche Biographie* 5 (1961): 664–665.

On the first Sunday of Lent, March 9, 1522, the famous "eating of the sausages" celebrated the infringement of the Lenten fast. Evidently Froschauer followed Luther's argumentation that good works do not ameliorate man, but faith alone can lead to his salvation. Froschauer had to appear in court, and Zwingli wrote a tract for his defence. Now the magistrate of Zurich had to decide if their priest could still be regarded as appropriate for his office. Even though this question implied a purely theological decision on the question of faith, the magistrate was prepared to rule over and resolve this matter. A public disputation was arranged on January 29 1523, and Zwingli presented his 67 theses in which he summarised his theological convictions. In the end Zwingli remained in office, abolished the Latin mass in 1525 and married. In the following year he published his major work, the "Commentarius de vera et falsa religione". At this time the magistrate enacted new ordinances which established Zwingli's Protestant ideas on church and state. Only in a few rare cases was the Protestant Reformation introduced in such a peaceful, uneventful way.

Zwingli agreed with Luther that not good works but faith leads to salvation. Following old norms like Lentern Fast could not ameliorate men, particularly if they were only complying with external pressure and not driven by inner conviction.[10] In following his faith, every Christian should be essentially free to follow the rules he could accept.[11] Man could only hope to be saved by divine mercy alone.[12] No earthly power, not even the Pope, could influence Christ's free decision.[13] Government and laws in themselves could not be regarded as instruments of divine ire. This statement on Christian liberty was, unfortunately, just as misleading as Luther's tract, which inspired the Peasants' War in 1525.[14]

But already in his tract on fasting, Zwingli was convinced that a Christian government could enact laws to encourage virtues.[15] In his work on "divine and human justice", written in 1523, Zwingli developed a new perspective.[16] He

10 Huldrych Zwingli. "Von Erkiesen und Freiheit der Speisen." In *Huldreich Zwinglis sämtliche Werke vol. 1: Corpus Reformatorum 88*, ed. Emil Egil. Berlin: Schwetschke, 1905, 111.

11 Zwingli, "Von Erkiesen und Freiheit," 106.

12 Zwingli, "Von Erkiesen und Freiheit," 95, 104.

13 Huldrych Zwingli. "Aktenstücke zur ersten Zürcher Disputation: I, Die 67 Artikel Zwinglis." In *Huldreich Zwinglis sämtliche Werke. vol. 1: Corpus Reformatorum No. 88, 17*: "Das Christus ein einiger ewiger obrester priester ist; daruß ermessen würt, daß, die sich obrest priester ußgeben hand, der eer und gewalt Christi widerstreben, ja verschupfen."

14 Martin Haas. *Huldrych Zwingli und seine Zeit, Leben und Werk des Zürcher Reformators.* Zurich: Theologischer Verlag, 1969, 122–125.

15 Zwingli, "Von Erkiesen und Freiheit," 135.

16 Haas, *Huldrich Zwingli und seine Zeit*, 126–128.

distinguished between a human and a divine justice. Divine justice, on the one hand, aimed for the soul, the inner core of man. God wanted men to act according to the principle of charity: to pardon offences, not to quarrel with others, not to give in to anger, not to commit adultery or slander, to be charitable, love one's enemy and refrain from coveting another man's wife or goods[17], where the model of the Ten Commandments is clearly visible in these rules. Earthly justice, on the other hand, aimed at outward appearance.[18] Such norms as the prohibition to take the goods of others could overlap occasionally with divine justice, as this coincided with the interdiction to covet another's property. But men would decide on this according to what they could see, whereas God could see into the inner core of man and would know who was just or guilty. Nonetheless, human justice was still necessary.[19] Human disobedience had to be punished. Man had to be told what he was to do. Instead of just punishing offenders like animals, men had to take recourse in the courts and through legal procedure and thus obtain valid sentences. In this respect, human judges acted as ministers of God.[20] Even though human law could never be perfect, it was nonetheless necessary even after Christ had come to abolish and renew the ancient law.[21]

The magistracy had to observe the development of society and punish misdemeanours, and had to inspire society in how to live more in accordance with the precepts of divine justice.[22] The government did not only have to use the sword to punish offenders, it also had to teach its citizens how to fulfil their duties.[23] Whilst a government might be highly defective, it was still a necessity for the amelioration of society. Everybody therefore had to strive to fulfil the precepts of human justice and behave obediently.[24] Thus human law could help to point to and understand God's will. Therefore, everybody should learn

17 Huldrych Zwingli. "Von götlicher und menschlicher gerechtigheit, wie die zemen schind und standind." In *Huldreich Zwinglis sämtliche Werke. vol. 1: Corpus Reformatorum No. 88.* Berlin: Schwetschke, 1905, 479–482.
18 Zwingli, "Von götlicher und menschlicher gerechtigheit," 484.
19 Zwingli, "Von götlicher und menschlicher gerechtigheit," 486.
20 Zwingli, "Von götlicher und menschlicher gerechtigheit," 488.
21 Zwingli, "Von götlicher und menschlicher gerechtigheit," 496.
22 Zwingli, "Von götlicher und menschlicher gerechtigheit," 503–504, 520.
23 Zwingli, "Von götlicher und menschlicher gerechtigheit," 507.
24 Zwingli, "Von götlicher und menschlicher gerechtigheit," 497.

the (human) law,[25] as long as it was still valid and had not become obsolete in the course of time.[26]

Together with Luther, Zwingli was convinced that only the truly pious would act instinctively according to God's law and therefore would not need human enactments. But this did not lead him to despise the law. There was never such a sharp distinction between law and gospel in Zurich as in Wittenberg. Divine law was part of the eternal divine will,[27] and human law could help to detect elements of divine justice. The gospel could be seen as the promise, the law as the commanding word of God which man had to learn.[28] God's laws were written into the hearts of mankind, whereas human laws had to be published to inform the people.[29] This could even help to grant some security to mankind.[30]

In this perspective, the magistracy was not only important when it came to punishing criminals, but also in terms of enacting suitable ordinances which would help to inform the people about God's instructions for mankind. Human justice was useful and important for making the members of society better people. In spite of all human weaknesses, the office of the magistrate of Zurich retained its authority as long as it fulfilled these duties. The use of the sword and the law proved that the officials of Zurich were prepared to obey God's will.

In sum, Zwingli strengthened the "Obrigkeit", a word which does not differentiate between the Aristotelian forms of politics. No matter who has the power, this magistrate has been installed by God himself. He has to fulfil God's will, and as long as this obedience to God's orders marks the government, it derives its legitimisation immediately from God. This requires that the leading theologians cooperate with the magistracy.

The new function of the government to ensure the salvation of their citizens led to more political power. When independent ecclesiastical institutions were abolished, this liberated the territories from their bishops. In the end,

25 Huldrych Zwingli. "Eine kurze christliche Einleitung [17.11.1523]." In *Huldreich Zwinglis sämtliche Werke vol. 2: Corpus Reformatorum, No. 89*. ed. Emil Eger, Leipzig: Heinsius, 1908, 647.

26 Zwingli, "Eine kurze christliche Einleitung," 649; Berndt Hamm. *Zwinglis Reformation der Freiheit*. Neukirchen-Vluyn: Neukirchener Verlag, 1988, 84.

27 Huldrych Zwingli. "De vera et falsa religione commentarius, [März 1525]." In *Huldreich Zwinglis sämtliche Werke vol. 3: Corpus Reformatorum, 90*. Leipzig: Heinsius, 1914, 628–911, 707; Hamm, *Zwinglis Reformation der Freiheit*, 84–85.

28 Gottfried Wilhelm Locher. *Die Zwinglische Reformation im Rahmen der europäischen Kirchengeschichte*. Göttingen: Vandenhoeck & Ruprecht, 1979, 214.

29 Zwingli, "De vera et falsa religione commentarius," 707.

30 Hamm, *Zwinglis Reformation der Freiheit*, 83.

whatever it took to save the people would be a lawful action on the part of the magistracy.

A new edition of the ordinances put together by the mayor and the city council in the two centuries following the Reformation shows how the magistracy responded to Zwingli's teaching.[31] Two packed volumes display the great number of about 242 ordinances which can still be found today. They regulate Protestant marriages and baptism and install a new marriage court. They prohibit luxury, expletives, public games, beggars, pictures of saints, traditional customs for fasting and masses. Even in the seventeenth century, we can find enactments on such broader subjects as regulations on pastors, synods and the "Großes Mandat" of 1609/1619, instead of such specialized regulations that aimed to establish a more general description of public order.[32]

But there was no attempt to alter the government of the city by its mayor and the "Great Council" or the "upper 200" ("unser Gnedig Herren Burgermeister klein und groß Rath der Statt Zürich"). There can be no doubt that the magistracy followed Zwingli's theory and took over control of ecclesiastical matters. But just as the Reformation had been achieved in Zurich in a very uneventful way, it continued to have hardly any substantive changes within the Zurich constitution.

2.2 *Bugenhagen in Wittenberg*

Johannes Bugenhagen (1485–1558) came from Pomerania and therefore is also known as "Doktor Pomeranus". He studied *artes* in Greifswald, but probably neither theology nor law.[33] He was appointed as the rector of a school near Treptow in 1504 and was even appointed as notary public by the authority of the Pope.[34] In 1509 he was ordained as a priest, but it was not until 1521 that he travelled to Wittenberg to study theology with Luther. Already in 1523 the authorities of Wittenberg decided to appoint him as the new pastor of the town. His attempts to install Lutheran Reformation in Wittenberg and a first letter to the citizens of Hamburg in 1526 earned him an invitation to Braunschweig in 1528, where he was asked to establish a new Protestant order. After his first success with an ecclesiastical ordinance, many more were requested from him.

---

31 Emidio Campi/Philipp Wälchli (eds.). *Zürcher Kirchenordnungen 1520–1675*, Vol. 1. Zurich: Theologischer Verlag, 2011.

32 Campi/Wälchli (eds.). *Zürcher Kirchenordnungen*, Vol. 2, 482 n. 193: "zů abstellung aller unmaß und lychtfertigkeit/gůte wohlmeinlche Ordnung angesehen/ und mengklichen zů einem bůßertigen chrisenlichen Gottsförchigen/ehrbaren läben und wandel vermannet".

33 Hans-Günter Leder. *Johannes Bugenhagen Pomeranus – vom Reformer zum Reformator*. Frankfurt am Main: Peter Lang, 2002, 47, 77, 79.

34 Karl August Traugott Vogt. *Johannes Bugenhagen Pomeranus*. Elberfeld: Friderichs, 1867, 7.

These enactments literally introduced Protestantism in Germany's north and Scandinavia.[35]

Bugenhagen followed the lines drawn by Luther, which separates him from Zwingli and Melanchthon. Luther's position with respect to law and government had been rather negative until the mid 1520s. Following his attack on indulgencies, he argued against any role for penitence and insisted on the exclusive power of salvation for the faith granted by Christ (*sola fide – solus Christus*). Consequently, all law became part of externalities that had nothing to do with faith and therefore could not have any influence on salvation. Obeying the law was not an ethical accomplishment, but obedience fuelled by fear. Only the Gospel and faith could lead to anything good. Gospel and law were more and more separated.[36]

Subsequently, the ruler only had to provide for security and peace in his country.[37] As the contents of the law could not lead to moral improvement, the function of his reign was limited to giving room for faith in the private sphere. When it came to society, the Prince had to use the sword in order to deter criminals. In this perspective, the ruler could be compared to a stork standing in a pond: Eating all croaking frogs, the stork would immediately end all uproar and commotion in the lake. The state therefore only had to secure silence,[38] the quality of the Prince depended on his merciless use of the sword alone. Law and the state only had to fight evil. In this perspective, both became first steps towards hell and doom,[39] as particularly Cranach illustrated in his famous picture.[40]

For this reason, the law could only list all possible prohibitions (*usus civilis*) and thereby show that man cannot know and obey all laws (*usus theologicus*). Thus man learns about his immanent condemnation.[41] This assertion

---

35 Hans-Günter Leder. *Johannes Bugenhagen Pomeranus – nachgelassene Studien zur Biographie*. Frankfurt am Main: Peter Lang, 2008, 709–711.

36 John Witte jr. *Law and Protestantism: The Legal Teaching of Luther's Reformation.* Cambridge: Cambridge University Press, 2002, 104.

37 Witte jr. *Law and Protestantism: The Legal Teaching of Luthers Reformation*, 109–111.

38 Martin Luther. "Von weltlicher Uberkeytt wie weyt man yhr gehorsam schuldig sey." (1523) In *Martin Luthers Werke. Kritische Gesamtausgabe. vol. 11: Predigten und Schriften 1523*, ed. Heidelberger Akademie der Wissenschaften. Weimar: Universitätsverlag Winter, 1900, 245–280 268; cf. Schmoeckel. *Das Recht der Reformation*, 150; Harro Höpfl. "Luther and Calvin on Secular Authority." In *Cambridge Texts in the History of Political Thought.* Cambridge: Cambridge University Press, 1991.

39 Zur Rolle des Staates nach dieser Dichotomie, die zur heute gelehrten Zweireiche-Lehre führte vgl. v.a. Johannes Heckel. *Lex charitatis*. 2. ed. Cologne/Vienna: Böhlau Verlag, 1973, sowie Heckel, *Martin Luthers Reformation und das Recht.*

40 Christoph Weimer. *Luther, Cranach und die Bilder, Gesetz und Evangelium – Schlüssel zum reformatorischen Bildgebrauch*, Stuttgart: Calwer, 1999, 3.

41 Witte jr. *Law and Protestantism: The Legal Teaching of Luthers Reformation*, 102–105.

was possible without any reference to the quality of the law and rule: Any law would lead to doom and salvation, and lawyers, who were people focused on the law, necessarily were bad Christians, as Luther's famous words suggested.[42]

The perspective of the theologians of Wittenberg changed when in 1521/22 they became responsible themselves for a new ordinance for Wittenberg when it had to implement the reforms. This attempt, however, was not approved by the Elector. The ordinance for the "common money box" (*Gemeiner Kasten*) for the city of Leisnig, which received even Luther's approbation in his preface, followed in 1523.[43] In 1525, Luther and his collaborators learnt about the contempt the peasants showed for the law and government, which they claimed to have learnt from Luther himself. Luther clearly condemned the violence of the peasants,[44] but left it to others to legitimise a certain respect for law and magistracy in their new theology.

Mainly Philipp Melanchthon and Johannes Bugenhagen undertook this task.[45] Whereas Melanchthon turned to Aristotle and developed new schemes for the law, Bugenhagen followed Luther more precisely. According to Luther's principles of *sola fide* and *sola gratia*, he could not attribute any importance to penitence.[46] Obeying the law and fasting had become externalities without any effect on faith or salvation.[47] For Bugenhagen, counting on the law, either human or even divine, seemed to be a fatal error in 1524.[48] Nothing good could follow from obedience to the law. In his first reaction to the Peasant's War, however, in his sermon from April 29, 1525, he emphasised the importance of peace and respect for the law.[49] Apparently, Bugenhagen's opinion slowly changed.[50] According to his new perception, the law could assume a role for the inner

---

42 Witte jr. *Law and Protestantism: The Legal Teaching of Luthers Reformation*, 119–121.

43 Hans Lietzmann (ed.). *Die Wittenberger und Leisniger Kastenordnung: 1522, 1523*. Bonn: Nabu Press 1907.

44 Michael Basse. "Luthers Kreuzestheologie und ihre Rezeption in der Evangelischen Theologie des 20. Jahrhunderts." In *Glaube und Lernen* 27 (2012): 33–44.

45 Mathias Schmoeckel. "Eine neue Konzeption des Rechts durch die Reformation." In *Reformation. Impulsgeber für die Moderne?*, eds. Andreas Lindemann/Christian Ammer. Leipzig: Evangelische Verlangsanstalt, 2017, 41–68.

46 Anneliese Bieber. *Johannes Bugenhagen zwischen Reform und Reformation. Die Entwicklung seiner frühen Theologie anhand des Matthäuskommentars und der Passions- und Auferstehungsharmonie*. Göttingen: Vandenhoeck & Ruprecht, 1992, 261, 299–301.

47 Bieber, *Johannes Bugenhagen zwischen Reform und Reformation*, 164–165.

48 *Johannes Bugenhagen: Werke*. Göttingen: 2013, 740, 742.

49 Johannes Bugenhagen. *Ungedruckte Predigten Johann Bugenhagens aus den Jahren 1524 bis 1529*. Leipzig: Heinsius, 1910, 202–206.

50 Ralf Kötter. *Johannes Bugenhagens Rechtfertigungslehre und der römische Katholizismus: Studien zum Sendbrief an die Hamburger (1525)*. Göttingen: Vandenhoeck & Ruprecht, 1994, 38.

soul of man and thus was no longer an externality alone.[51] This dual nature of the law helped him to stay faithful to Luther's principle of *sola fide*.[52] But the norms of the Gospel and human laws had to be taught so that man could learn how to behave. All human endeavours remained fruitless, of course, without God's free gift of redemption. But this education helped to argue for the doom of those who still did not want to comply.

In 1526 Bugenhagen started to teach the correct way of installing a new Protestant order. His "letter to the people of Hamburg" explained to them how to practise the Protestant faith.[53] He still clung faithfully to Luther's theory:[54] It was still Christ alone, the Saviour, who could redeem a soul; the use of the rosary would have no effect. For this reason, his followers were called "Christians", not "Rosarians".[55] Only divine mercy could save a man as human powers were not sufficient in this respect.[56] The faith was a free gift of God.[57] Only the true Christian could discover sin and hate his own errors.[58]

Now Bugenhagen called it a misunderstanding to presume that Lutherans would reject all good works. They could be used to dominate the body and its pretentions. Fasting, work, prayer and vigils could help one to understand what charity demanded of men,[59] but they could be accepted as good works only in

51 Kötter. *Johannes Bugenhagens Rechtfertigungslehre und der römische Katholizismus Studien zum Sendbrief an die Hamburger* (1525), 157–159.

52 Hans Hermann Holfelder. *Solus Christus, Die Ausbildung von Bugenhagens Rechtfertigungslehre in der Paulusauslegung* (1524/25) *und ihre Bedeutung für die theologische Argumentation im Sendbrief "Von dem christlichen Glauben"* (1526)*: Eine Untersuchung zur Genese von Bugenhagens Theologie*. Tübingen: Mohr Siebeck, 1981, 100–101.

53 Bugenhagen: *Von dem christlichen Glauben und rechten guten Werken weder den falschen Glauben und erdichtete gute Werke, dazu, wie man's soll anrichten mit guten Predigern, daß solche Glaube und Werke gepredigt werden, an die ehrenreiche Stadt Hamburg*, zit. nach: Vogt. *Johannes Bugenhagen Pomeranus* (S. 101–267). For the beginnings of Protestantism in the German cities of the North cf. Bernhard Lohse. "Humanismus und Reformation in norddeutschen Städten in den 20er und frühen 30er Jahren des 16. Jahrhunderts." In *Die dänische Reformation vor ihrem internationalen Hintergrund*, eds. L. Grane/K. Hørby. Göttingen: Vandenhoeck & Ruprecht, 1990, 11–27, particularly 17–16 for Hamburg.

54 Olli-Pekka Vainio. *Justification and Participation in Christ. The Development of the Lutheran Doctrine of Justification from Luther to the Formula of Concord* (1580). Leiden/Boston: Brill, 2008, 54; Kötter. *Johannes Bugenhagens Rechtfertigungslehre und der römische Katholizismus Studien zum Sendbrief an die Hamburger* (1525), 46.

55 Johannes Bugenhagen. *Johannes Bugenhagen, Pomeranus: Leben und ausgewählte Schriften*. Elberfeld: Friderichs 1867, 108–109.

56 Bugenhagen. *Johannes Bugenhagen, Pomeranus: Leben und ausgewählte Schriften*, 113–115.

57 Bugenhagen. *Johannes Bugenhagen, Pomeranus: Leben und ausgewählte Schriften*, 125–126.

58 Bugenhagen. *Johannes Bugenhagen, Pomeranus: Leben und ausgewählte Schriften*, 136, 141.

59 Tim Lorentzen. *Johannes Bugenhagen als Reformator der öffentlichen Fürsorge*. Tübingen: Mohr Siebeck, 2008, 135–136.

an appropriate situation.[60] Corporal exercises would make it easier to eradicate the "inner Adam" and to concentrate on the works of charity. Teaching the people, punishment and solace were not only externalities, but could help to show people the right way.[61] They could help a man to find the right decisions through his free will. Of course, only free decisions, not enforced by fear or guilt, could redeem a soul in the Last Judgment. Inspiration from the faith could help in providing hope for the redemption,[62] as God had promised his assistance.[63]

This was not a question of reason, as children sometimes could perceive the father more easily.[64] But education and practice could help to concentrate on the questions of the soul and to live in accordance with these provisions. The Ten Commandments, the Gospel, and the existence of the Judgment had to be taught, particularly the law of charity towards the other.[65] Thus everybody should learn the order of his community. The freedom of the Christian would not imply that law could no longer hold any function. Government was still necessary to establish order and peace. House fathers, just like bishops of their home, would teach their families the Gospel and the provisions of good order.[66] Pastors would lead their parishes to a correct understanding of the Gospel and the necessity of peace and security.[67]

For Bugenhagen, faith and good works belong together, as the true Christian acts according to the provisions of the Gospel.[68] The Holy Spirit would help to comply with God's law and thus would lead to faith.[69] This new esteem for

60 Lorentzen. *Johannes Bugenhagen als Reformator der öffentlichen Fürsorge*, 140.

61 Bugenhagen. *Johannes Bugenhagen, Pomeranus: Leben und ausgewählte Schriften*, 166–168.

62 Bugenhagen. *Johannes Bugenhagen, Pomeranus: Leben und ausgewählte Schriften*, 149–151.

63 Lorentzen. *Johannes Bugenhagen als Reformator der öffentlichen Fürsorge*, 138.

64 Bugenhagen. *Johannes Bugenhagen, Pomeranus: Leben und ausgewählte Schriften*, 198–200, 207.

65 Bugenhagen. *Johannes Bugenhagen, Pomeranus: Leben und ausgewählte Schriften*, 237–239.

66 Bugenhagen. *Johannes Bugenhagen, Pomeranus: Leben und ausgewählte Schriften*, 266.

67 Luise Schorn-Schütter. *Perspectum: Ausgewählte Aufsätze zur Frühen Neuzeit und Historiographiegeschichte anlässlich ihres 65. Geburtstages*. Munich: Oldenbourg Verlag, 2014, 275.

68 Kötter. *Johannes Bugenhagens Rechtfertigungslehre und der römische Katholizismus Studien zum Sendbrief an die Hamburger* (1525), 250.

69 Bugenhagen, cited: in Anneliese Sprengler-Ruppenthal. "Bugenhagen und das protestantische Kirchenrecht." *Zeitschrift für Rechtsgeschichte: Kanonistische Abteilung* 57 (1971), 196–233, 202 "Vere Christianus non indiget praeceptis morum. Fidei enim spiritus ducit eum ad omnia quae deus vult et fraterna exigit charitas".

normativity might have been a reaction to Thomas Müntzer,[70] but he did not contradict Luther. As God's words and norms were inscribed in man's heart and could be regarded as manifest,[71] no human activity was needed for salvation. But a sermon could spread the divine words and thus would help to understand God's will. In this respect it was necessary to ascertain that the true theory was taught and that the practice of the sacraments followed the commandments of the Gospel. Good administration and efficient control, therefore, came into focus. Bugenhagen might have learned from Melanchthon about the importance of education,[72] but he did not adopt Melanchthon's new theories on the use of the law. He concentrated on teaching and learning instead, which became more and more the common characteristics of the Protestant government.[73]

Nonetheless, Bugenhagen provided a new argument for the necessity of government, which was not all about security and peace. The government now had to ascertain the correctness of education and practice as well. Luther published his tract on schools already in 1524,[74] and started a movement for better education.[75] He consequently developed a plan for schools on different levels for the education of young people.[76] But he saw many more fields in which the correctness of theological knowledge and practice had to be ascertained by officials. The parish priest, the magistrates and all others up to the King

70 Kötter. *Johannes Bugenhagens Rechtfertigungslehre und der römische Katholizismus Studien zum Sendbrief an die Hamburger* (1525), 245–247.

71 Otto Vogt. *Dr. Johannes Bugenhagens Briefwechsel*, Hildesheim: Georg Olms, 1966, 58, 12: Cf. letter to Nicolaus Gerbel, dated 4.11.1525: *manifesta verba Christi;* August 1523 to the University of Wittenberg: *verba manifesta*.

72 Jens Olesen. "Staat und Stadt – über die Rolle der Landesväter und Behörden im Denken und Handeln Johannes Bugenhagens." In *Johannes Bugenhagen (1485–1555): Der Bischof der Reformation*. eds. Irmfried Garbe/Heinrich Kröger. Leipzig: Evangelische Verlagsanstalt, 2007, 93–110, 95.

73 Cf. already James M. Kittelson. "Learning and Education: Phase Two of the Reformation." In *Die dänische Reformation vor ihrem internationalen Hintergrund*, eds. Leif Grane/ Kai Hørby. Göttingen: Vandenhoeck & Ruprecht, 1990, 149–163, but not reserved for the Second Reformation.

74 Martin Luther. "An die Ratsherren aller Städte deutschen Landes, dass sie christliche Schulen aufrichten und halten sollen." In *Dr. Martin Luthers Werke, Kritische Gesamtausgabe*, No. 15, Weimar: Böhlau, 47.

75 Heinz Scheible. *Melanchthon: Vermittler der Reformation: Eine Biographie*. Munich: C.H. Beck, 2016, 52, 559.

76 For the dominance of teaching the youth in the work of Bugenhagen cf. Walter Ziegler. "Braunschweig-Lüneburg- Hildesheim." In *Die Territorien des Reichs im Zeitalter der Reformation und Konfessionalisierung: Land und Konfession 1500–1650, Volume 3: Der Nordwesten: Katholisches Leben und Kirchenreform im Zeitalter der Glaubensspaltung, 51*, eds. A. Schindling/ W. Ziegler. Münster: Aschendorff, 1991, 8–43.

had to provide for a society living in accordance with Christian discipline.[77] In Bugenhagen's perspective, Church law was a service for realising divine order.[78] Discipline had to be ascertained in the secular and ecclesiastical matters of parishes. This had to be adapted in the marriages and families, but also in the poor houses. In all places, people should learn how to behave according to God's will.[79] As a last resort, the ruler had been installed as the *defensor fidei*.[80] We find these ideas repeated in the ecclesiastical ordinances of Brunswick in 1528,[81] Hamburg 1529,[82] Lübeck 1531,[83] and Pomerania 1535.

These not only implied establishing new schools and universities, but also new provisions for the different sources of income and expenses of the territory with one single administration of the "common money box" (Gemeiner Kasten).[84] Replacing the diversity of historical foundations, benefices and endowments, all money now had to be collected directly by the local administration in order to provide a common standard of education, administration and poor relief. This was a major achievement for a regular school education for all boys, scholarships for poor families and other social accomplishments.[85]

For Brunswick and Hamburg, Bugenhagen argued for the necessity of obedience with regard to the "Obrigkeit". This term indistinctly refers to the

---

77 Olesen. "Staat und Stadt – über die Rolle der Landesväter und Behörden im Denken und Handeln Johannes Bugenhagens," 100.

78 Sprengler-Ruppentha. "Bugenhagen und das protestantische Kirchenrecht", 207.

79 Kötter. *Johannes Bugenhagens Rechtfertigungslehre und der römische Katholizismus Studien zum Sendbrief an die Hamburger (1525)*, 199.

80 Olesen. "Staat und Stadt – über die Rolle der Landesväter und Behörden im Denken und Handeln Johannes Bugenhagens," 100, 106.

81 Cf. Aemilius Ludwig Richter. *Die evangelischen Kirchenordnungen des sechzehnten Jahrhunderts. Bd. 1: Vom Anfange der Reformation bis zur Begründung der Consistorial-Verfassung im Jahr 1542*. Weimar: Verlag des Landes-Industriecomptoirs, 1846, 107.

82 Johannes Bugenhagen. *Der ehrbaren Stadt Hamburg christliche Ordnung 1529*. reprint Hamburg: Wittig, 1976, 3.

83 For the classification of the church ordinance Bugenhagens, cf. Heiner Lück. "Prudentia legislatorial: Regelungssystematik und Regelungstechnik in den Kirchenordnungen Johannes Bugenhagens." In *Johannes Bugenhagen (1485–1558): Der Bischof der Reformation*, eds. I. Garbe/H. Kröger. Leipzig: Evangelische Verlagsanstalt, 2007, 171–189.

84 For the relevenance of the finances and the educational system in the ordinance of Hamburg cf. Traugott Koch. "'Der Ehrbaren Stadt Hamburg Christliche Ordnung' durch Johannes Bugenhagen (1529)." In *500 Jahre Theologie in Hamburg. Hamburg als Zentrum christlicher Theologie und Kultur zwischen Tradition und Zukunft: Arbeiten zur Kirchengeschichte, 95*), ed. J. A. Steiger. Berlin/New York: deGruyter, 2005, 1–15, 6, 8.

85 Kaarlo Arffman. "The Lutheran Reform of Poor Relief: A Historical and Legal Viewpoint." In *Lutheran Reformation and the Law*, ed. Virpi Mäkinen. Leiden/ Boston: Brill, 2006, 205–230.

people who govern the territory, regardless of their ranks and titles, and the Aristotelian form of government. Bugenhagen's new theory applied to towns and dukedoms alike in the empire, and even to sovereign kings. A Christian had to accept his leaders indiscriminately. All Christian governments had to punish evil and protect lawful people.

Although Bugenhagen's church ordinances differ to some extent[86] as he seemed to learn from experiences, they all tried in a rather abstract way to determine a just balance between control and liberty in religious matters. Any government and law were necessary means to assure structures that guaranteed the existence of the church and the correct faith. Bugenhagen's theory comprises the following characteristics of his new government:

- The secular government is head of the (visible) church as well. This considerable gain in political power comes together with an increase in duties and their degree of severity.
- Pastors have to be controlled, perhaps even appointed and paid by the public. The visible church and their representative slowly become civil servants.
- Knowledge has to be spread so that the public can learn God's own will and the laws of the government. Church and school serve each other reciprocally: knowledge is the condition for sermoners and the correct faith dictates what the necessary knowledge consists of.
- The new tasks of the government imply the necessity for further financial means. The common treasury chest was a useful invention to collect all incomes in order to be able to pay for the new institutions. At least this helped to direct the money in a more organised way.
- The Protestant government of Bugenhagen is a secular nation, but has a theological or soteriological task: it establishes peace, security and education as preconditions for each individual to achieve their salvation.

But fundamentally, four elements belong together and characterise Bugenhagen's theory:

1. The magistracy has to ensure that the correct doctrine is taught. It is necessary that the sermon teaches the right understanding of the Gospel.
2. The correct application of the sacraments has to be ascertained. In order to ensure the appropriate form of service and liturgy, the wording and

86 For the other church ordinances of Bugenhagen cf. Sprengler-Ruppenthal. "Bugenhagen und das protestantische Kirchenrecht," 203–204. I just want to mention those for Pomerania 1534, Braunschweig-Wolfenbüttel 1543, and Hildesheim 1544; derivative forms can be found in Osnabrück 1543, Minden 1530, Herford 1534, Göttingen 1531, and Wittenberg 1533.

perhaps even the music of the chants have to be published and made available to the public.

3. The public has to be taught to read the Gospel and the laws. The government therefore has to establish a structure of education for everybody and for the more gifted pupils.
4. The charity of the community is proven by its poor relief. The "common money box" demonstrates the legitimisation of its magistracy.

These four elements correspond: The urge for correct teaching leads to accepting the role of the government. The magistracy installs the pastors who demonstrate that the state obeys God's orders. This is proven by the establishment of effective forms of care for the poor.

2.3 *The Reformation of Hamburg*

One of Bugenhagen's first targets was the reformation of Hamburg, a merchant city like Zurich. His 1526 directive was addressed to Hamburg and he personally intervened in 1529. There was little struggle to introduce the Protestant Reformation in Hamburg because the city suffered from different notorious prelates. Formally, Hamburg belonged to the archdiocese of Bremen. The archbishop of the time, Prince Christoph von Braunschweig-Wolfenbüttel (1487–1559, archbishop since 1511), was nicknamed "the squanderer" (der Verschwender). Other members of the cathedral chapters gave further reason to criticise the church in its existent form.[87]

But it was not until April 1528 that the final decision on religion could be reached. A theological discussion took place in the presence of members of the city council who had to declare the winner. When the Protestant side was proclaimed victorious, Roman-Catholic masses were forbidden and priests and monks had to leave the town.

Bugenhagen was now invited to come to Hamburg. Thanks to his theological influence and his reconciliation between the parties,[88] Hamburg was given a new law regulating the administration of the city, the "Langer Rezess" (long charter) of February 1529. "Rezess" had been the traditional source of the city's

---

87 Wolf-Dieter Hauschildt. "Die Reformation in Hamburg, Lübeck und Eutin." In *Schleswig-Holsteinische Kirchengeschichte, No. 3: Reformation.* Neumünster: Matthiesen, 1982, 185–239, 186; for the function of the cathedral chapter, cf. Sybille Weber. *Die Stellung Hamburgs in der Verfassung des Alten Deutschen Reichs.* Diss.jur. Bonn/Munich: Hut, 2005/2007, 174. A classical very detailed study on this subject is Kurt Beckey. *Die Reformation in Hamburg.* Hamburg: Boysen Verlag, 1929.

88 Hans Wenn. "Johannes Bugenhagens Hamburger Ordenige. Beiträge zu ihrer Entstehung und Überlieferung." In *Johannes Bugenhagen: Der Ehrbaren Stadt Hamburg Christliche Ordnung 1529.* Hamburg: Wittig, 1976, 286.

major laws,[89] and in its art. 59, the Reformation was installed as the city's new religion.[90] It commanded that Hamburg's inhabitants should sing and preach according to Bugenhagen's teaching.[91]

Bearing this in mind, Bugenhagen drafted a new church ordinance which was enacted on 15 May 1529. It started with a regulation of the schools. Unlike other territories, Hamburg had already had some important schools since the Middle Ages, but now others were founded, for example the famous "Johanneum", on 24 May 1529. Another part of the ordinance was dedicated to the pastors and parishes. The different ceremonies for the liturgy were explained afterwards. The ordinance concluded with provisions for the care of the poor. On the whole, this church ordinance was particularly short with only short sections referring to local particularities.[92]

But there was more to the "Lange Recess", which earned its name well with its 132 articles. The Protestant Reformation changed some major structures of the city administration. The city took over the administration of the churches within the city from the cathedral chapter. Pastors should now be elected by their parishes. Services were to be given in Low-German (*plattdeutsch*) and had to follow the text of the Gospel strictly. Monasteries and other ecclesiastical institutions were opened to the public and the treasures of the church had to be rendered to the city.

The first consequence was that the mayor and the church council of Hamburg acquired ecclesiastical superiority over the city and the superiority of the archbishop of Bremen was rescinded. With regard to secular superiors, the Reformation brought Hamburg closer to Denmark. As the Emperor had become the leader of the Roman-Catholic faction, Hamburg was even compelled to seek an alliance with the princes united in the league of Schmalkalden. The equidistance of the city between the two realms helped to develop their independence.[93] It should therefore come as no surprise that the question of Hamburg's position within the empire and its independence became a major issue over the next centuries.

---

89 For the development of this peculiar Hanseatic term, cf. Thomas Behrmann. "Der lange Weg zum Reze." In *Frühmittelalterliche Studien* 36 (2002), eds. Wolfram von Drews/ Bruno Quast, 433–467.

90 Hauschildt. "Die Reformation in Hamburg, Lübeck und Eutin," 196.

91 Wenn, "Johannes Bugenhagens Hamburger Ordenige. Beiträge zu ihrer Entstehung und Überlieferung," 286 on Bugenhagen's influence on the Recess.

92 Wenn, "Johannes Bugenhagens Hamburger Ordenige. Beiträge zu ihrer Entstehung und Überlieferung," 135, 297.

93 Weber, *Die Stellung Hamburgs in der Verfassung des Alten Deutschen Reichs*, 38–39.

Within the city, the citizens demanded to take part in decision-making and succeeded in having more and more participation in the writing of legislation.[94] In 1528, citizens were already formulating clear demands referring to particular politicians and questions of the future structure.[95] Art. 1 of the "Langer Rezess" proclaimed a special liberty for the mayor, the members of the city council and for every citizen and inhabitant of Hamburg: no one could be forced from their home and their city with the exception of criminal cases that laid down capital punishment.[96]. This betrayed the principle character of this charter as it contained privileges for the inhabitants of Hamburg. This special provision, which is close to the English concept of "Habeas-Corpus" particularly gave some immunity against criminal prosecution. It is in this light that the following provisions for criminal procedures in Hamburg should be seen. But of course, provisions for last wills (c.26s) were necessary in this time when there was much confusion around this subject. At this early time in history, the articles on the security of successions and of property (art.38) had a hint of human rights provisions.[97] Finally, the "Langer Rezess" declared that all future legislation had to be passed by the "verordneten Bürger", the city council. On the whole, this charter enhanced the political participation of the citizens and inhabitants and increased their security against criminal prosecution.

The development in Hamburg differed somewhat from Zurich as the establishment of Protestantism had more enemies in Hamburg than in Zurich and it took longer. But it took less time to establish it than it did to organise the law suit at the Imperial Chamber court, where its decision in 1533 in favour of the old faith came too late.[98] The new laws in Hamburg had long-lasting influ-

94 Tilman Repgen. "Art. Hamburg." In *Handwörterbuch zur Deutschen Rechtsgeschichte*, Vol. 2, 2nd ed. Berlin: E. Schmidt, 2012, 684–690, 686.

95 Postulate der Bürger von 1528, the 26th August, in: Supplementband zu dem neuen Abdrucke der Grundgesetze der Hamburgischen Verfassung und dessen Nachtrage mit einer Anlage die Verhandlungen über die Verfassung der freien Hansestadt Bremen betreffend, Supplement, Hamburg 1825, 38.

96 Rezess von 1529, in: Supplementband zu dem neuen Abdrucke der Grundgesetze der Hamburgischen Verfassung, 47.

97 Rezess von 1529, in: Supplementband zu dem neuen Abdrucke der Grundgesetze der Hamburgischen Verfassung, art. 38, 66: "Ein E. Rath will Niemand in seinem rechtmäßigen Besitz in seiner Freiheit und in seinem Eigenthum verkürzen, sondern einem Jeden im geruhigen Besitz, nach bewiesener rechtmäßigen Besitzergreifung, dem Inhalte und den Worten der Siegel und Briefe oder des Beweises gemäß, beschirmen, also daß ein Jeder den ruhigen Besitz, nach gebührlicher und treuer Ergreifung, in Gemäßheit unseres Stadtbuchs G. 4ten Art., genießen möge."

98 For this lawsuit, cf. Weber, *Die Stellung Hamburgs in der Verfassung des Alten Deutschen Reichs*, 177.

ence.[99] Both cities acquired their autonomy over religious matters, but where the effect of Lutheranism on legislation was stronger in Hamburg. Whilst the Zurich constitution remained almost untouched, the new charter for Hamburg used the occasion to promote the secular autonomy of both the city and its citizens. When it came to secular supremacy, just as Hamburg sought its independence from Holstein and the kings of Denmark, who still counted Hamburg as well as Altona among their possessions, the Emperor tried to establish his dominion over Hamburg. Unlike Zurich, again, the magistracy of Hamburg could not immediately establish their rule as a free and independent imperial city. And yet their enactments demonstrated their struggles to directly provide the fundamentals for a life in the true religion. Based on Luther's liberty for Christians, the inhabitants of Hamburg had all the institutions and laws necessary to live their lives in accordance with Luther's teaching. This encouraged the city to highlight the numerous liberties granted to the inhabitants of Hamburg. Unlike Zwingli, Bugenhagen did not recognise a divine origin in the magistracy, but based on his ordinances the administration became more actively involved in the salvation of its subjects.

When it came to the cities along the Rhine, as well as Lübeck, Nuremberg and others, the first Reformation was certainly spread in and among the cities. Initially, the Reformation was not just a matter for Protestant princes but was spread to a large degree by the cities and commerce. Merchants and former students from Wittenberg communicated the new ideas, which were readily accepted.

3. From Hamburg to Bergen: the Reign of Christian III

3.1 *Schleswig Holstein*

3.1.1 A Peaceful Conquest

The Lutheran Reformation spread from the south to the north. Progressing from the cities and merchant routes it reached Holstein first, but a little later Haderslev (German: Hadersleben) in the north of Schleswig also became a centre of the new faith.[100] But this natural development was much fostered by the princes in the north. King Christian II (1481–1559) of Denmark, Norway and Sweden might have been in favour of Luther as early as in 1521, but this feeble

99 Wenn, "Johannes Bugenhagens Hamburger Ordenige. Beiträge zu ihrer Entstehung und Überlieferung," 276.

100 Walter Göbell. "Die Anfänge der Reformation in Dänemark und in den Herzogtümern Schleswig und Holstein unter Herzog und König Friedrich I." In *Schleswig-Holsteinische Kirchengeschichte, vol. 3: Reformation*, ed. Walter Göbell. Neumünster: Wachholtz, 1982, 9–34, 42.

influence was eradicated in 1523, when Gustav Ericsson of the house of Vasa expelled Christian II from Sweden, which eventually caused him to leave all his realms. Free from political obligations, the former King visited Wittenberg together with his wife, a sister of Emperor Charles I, and both clearly adopted the new religion.[101]

Contrary to his brother and predecessor, Frederik I of Denmark and Norway was not prepared to accept the Reformation as the official religion in his territories. Only occasionally did he grant privileges to Lutherans.[102] But nevertheless he married his daughter Dorothea in 1526 to Albrecht, Duke of Prussia, formally the last Grandmaster of the Teutonic Order, who in becoming Protestant had secularised his territory. In the same year, Frederic openly violated the fasting rules.[103] This revealed that he was open to the changes Protestantism introduced. For this reason, the Church officials accepted his reign as the lesser evil, but had to acknowledge their feeble influence as well. Furthermore, Lutheranism was used by his opponents as a threat to deny his authority, as they hinted at the possibility of reinstalling Christian II.[104]

His son and presumptive heir, Christian (1503–1559), was installed as the ruling Duke of Schleswig and Holstein in 1523 with Haderslev as his principle residence. A very pious man, he had become an ardent Lutheran at the imperial diet in 1521. He had close relations to his brother-in-law Albrecht of Prussia and to Philipp of Hesse.[105] In 1460, through the electoral constitution of Christian I, the duchies of Schleswig and Holstein had obtained their fundamental privilege never to be separated again. Although Schleswig belonged to Denmark and Holstein to the Empire, Schleswig was especially mixed with Germans and Danes and the privilege particularly helped the nobility to acquire possessions

101 Cf. Göbell, "Die Anfänge der Reformation in Dänemark und in den Herzogtümern Schleswig und Holstein unter Herzog und König Friedrich I." 12; Johannes Oskar Andersen. *Overfor kirkebruddet: den første Lutherske bevægelse og Christiern II's Forhold dertil.* Copenhagen: Universitetsbogtrykkeriet, 1917.

102 Walter Göbell. "Das Vordringen der Reformation in Dänemark und in den Herzogtümern unter der Regierung Friedrichs I. 1523–1533." In *Schleswig-Holsteinische Kirchengeschichte, vol. 3: Reformation.* Neumünster: Wachholtz, 1982, 35–113, 35, 47 concerning tolerance of Lutherans in the duchies.

103 Martin Schwarz Lausten. "Weltliche Obrigkeit und Kirche bei König Christian III. von Dänemark (1536–1559). Hintergründe und Folgen." In *Die dänische Reformation vor ihrem internationalen Hintergrund. The Danish Reformation against its International Background,* eds. idem/ K. Hørby. Göttingen: Vandenhoeck & Ruprecht, 1990, 91–107, 95.

104 Martin Schwarz Lausten. "The early Reformation in Denmark and Norway 1520–1559." In *The Scandinavian Reformation,* ed. O. P. Grell. Cambridge: Cambridge University Press, 1995, 12–41, 14.

105 Martin Schwarz Lausten. "König und Kirche. Über das Verhältnis der westlichen Obrigkeit zur Kirche bei Johannes Bugenhagen und König Christian III. von Dänemark." In *Johannes Bugenhagen – Gestalt und Wirkung.* Berlin: Evangelische Verlagsanstalt, 1984, 144–167, 148.

in both territories. More and more, these initially rather different territories started to develop a new homogenous territory of their own. The stronger the estates became, the more cautiously the Duke had to act.

As Duke of Schleswig and Holstein, Christian therefore acted with utmost caution and tact. He did not directly oppose the Bishop of Schleswig and Lübeck, Balthasar Rantzau (1536–1547), as some members of the old nobility remained Roman-Catholics. Instead, he sought to collaborate with the estates in his duchies rather than offend them. How difficult the affairs were is demonstrated by the composition of the assembly (*Landtag/herendag*) of Rendsburg in 1540, where Count Johann Rantzau represented the Protestant side, while his brother Kay Rantzau was the spokesman for the Catholic opposition. Therefore, the Reformation progressed slowly in small steps. When a special tax had to be collected for the Danish King in 1528, it was easy to secularise the first monasteries and other ecclesiastical institutions in order to accumulate the enormous amount of money,[106] such as the Cistercian Rüdekloster in Flensburg, the future ground for Glücksburg Castle.

Rather then having legislation that introduced the Confessio Augustana of 1530, the Duke acted in smaller steps. In 1528, all priests had to personally give him an oath of fidelity. As a reward, all the old positions and titles, such as *Bishops* or *Praepositi* (*Pröbste*), were maintained. The "Articles of Hadersleben" ("Articuli pro pastoribus ruralibus") of 1528 established a model for Lutheran parish government.[107] Drawn up by locals, these provisions are one of the oldest examples of a legislative competence in cases of necessity for Protestant Princes.[108]. They emphasised the task of pastors to teach the people, decreed the correct chants and times for services – given in the Danish language – and made marriage obligatory for pastors. To control the clergy not only visitation according to the Saxon models was introduced and the *Praepositi* (*Pröbste*) controlled the lower clergy, but pastors were also obliged to preach loyalty to the Prince. The "Confessio Hafniensis", presented in 1530 in Copenhagen,

---

106 Schwarz Lausten, "The early Reformation," 13.

107 Göbell, "Das Vordringen der Reformation in Dänemark und in den Herzogtümern unter der Regierung Friedrichs I. 1523–1533," 61, 63–65 with a German translation; a Danish edition in Max W. Olsen. *Den danske Kirkeordinants af 1539 og andre Aktstykker vedrørende den lutherske Kirkereformations Inaførelse i Danmark.* Copenhagen: Akademisk Forlag, 1936, 23–32.

108 Göbell, "Das Vordringen der Reformation in Dänemark und in den Herzogtümern unter der Regierung Friedrichs I. 1523–1533," 61.

finally introduced Protestant Theology in the duchies.[109] By the early 1530s, the Protestant Reformation had definitely been introduced.[110]

We can distinguish at least three characteristics of this development.[111]

1. The system of visitations was installed according to the Saxon model. The Duke gained control over the clergy and had the right and duty to control their administration. From now on, the pastors received their letter of appointment from the Duke.
2. The clergy even had to swear to the Duke that they would act faithfully in their office, follow the Lutheran doctrine and exercise moral conduct.
3. Furthermore, they had to take an oath of allegiance but no longer to the correct confession, but directly to the Duke.[112] Thus, the Reformation helped to introduce new common political structures for the duchies. Reciprocally, church and Duke strengthened the rule of the other.[113]

3.1.2 Later Developments

When Christian moved his focus to Denmark, the development in the duchies slowed down. A convocation of the clergy, a local council, was not put into practice.[114] Even after the defeat of his adversaries in Denmark and the enactment of his church ordinance of 1537, the new King felt bound by the estates, especially the knights of Schleswig and Holstein, as his faithful allies. Neither the power nor the policy of the Duke ever resembled the actions of King Christian III in Denmark.[115] He never doubted the privileges of the nobility in the duchies, which he revoked to some extent in Denmark. Even the Roman-Catholic bishop of Schleswig was respected until his death in 1544, when he was succeeded by a minor brother of the King.[116] Lübeck had a Roman-Catholic bishop

109 Göbell, "Das Vordringen der Reformation in Dänemark und in den Herzogtümern unter der Regierung Friedrichs I. 1523–1533," 75.

110 Cf. Ulrich Lange. "Stände, Landesherr und Große Politik." In *Geschichte Schleswig-Holsteins: Von den Anfängen bis zur Gegenwart, 2nd ed.*, ed. idem. Neumünster: C.H. Beck, 2003, 153–190, 167; Wolfgang Seegrün. "Schleswig-Holstein." In *Die Territorien des Reichs im Zeitalter der Reformation und Konfessionalisierung. Land und Konfession 1500–1650, vol. 2: Der Nordosten – Katholisches Leben und Kirchenreform im Zeitalter der Glaubensspaltung No. 50*, eds. A. Schindling/W. Ziegler. Münster: Aschendorff, 1990, 152.

111 Cf. Schwarz Lausten, "König und Kirche," 46.

112 Lange, "Stände, Landesherr und Große Politik," 167.

113 Schwarz Lausten, "König und Kirche," 148.

114 Cf. Walter Göbell (ed.). *Die Schleswig-Holsteinische Kirchenordnung von 1542*. Neumünster: Wachholtz Verlag, 1986, 17.

115 Erich Hoffmann. "Der Sieg der Reformation in den Herzogtümern Schleswig und Holstein." In *Schleswig-Holsteinische Kirchengeschichte, Volume 3: Reformation*. Neumünster: Wachholtz Verlag, 1982, 145–183, 146–147.

116 Lange, "Stände, Landesherr und Große Politik," 172.

until 1559. As long as both confessions had strong supporters in the nobility of the duchies, he acted in small, rather uncontroversial steps. Even in 1533 he still promised not to diminish the status or property of the two bishops.[117] But slowly, even the bishops. like the Bishop of Lübeck, agreed to take the oath for the Duke-King.[118]

Although the Danish church ordinance of 1537 was also theoretically enacted for the duchies, there was no specific provision for these territories. Bugenhagen himself complained that the duchies, which he called the "Holstenlande", needed further regulations.[119] In 1542, a new ordinance was enacted, which followed the Danish church ordinance of 1537,[120] but which tried to implement the new structures with regard to the particularities of the region.[121] This new law was the last step in a slow process of negotiation within the duchies. The decisive steps were taken not by the monarch, but by the assemblies of the estates (*Landtage*). For this reason, the Protestant Reformation was rather the result of a free adoption of the new faith by the people of Schleswig and Holstein. But on the whole there can be no doubt that the ideas of the 1537 ordinance were crucial for the later development in the duchies.[122] The new ordinance remained valid until 1867, which is evidence of the long-lasting effect of this law.

Whereas the King had abolished bishops in Denmark, in 1541 he offered Bugenhagen the bishopric of Schleswig.[123] Evidently, Lübeck and Schleswig had more continuity compared to Denmark. This indicates that even the ecclesiastical administration of Schleswig and Holstein differed from the Danish model to some extent, although it stayed faithful to the convictions of Bugenhagen. The church of the duchies, the new *Landeskirche*, never merged with the Danish Church. Unlike Denmark, the church ordinance of Schleswig-Holstein remained in force until 1868.

---

117 Göbell, "Das Vordringen der Reformation in Dänemark und in den Herzogtümern unter der Regierung Friedrichs I. 1523–1533," 149, 151.

118 Göbell, "Das Vordringen der Reformation in Dänemark und in den Herzogtümern unter der Regierung Friedrichs I. 1523–1533," 51.

119 Hoffmann, "Der Sieg der Reformation, in den Herzogtümern Schleswig und Holstein," 144.

120 E.G. it mirrowed the "two ordinances", of God and by the king (see below n. 151): cf. Göbell, "Das Vordringen der Reformation in Dänemark und in den Herzogtümern unter der Regierung Friedrichs I. 1523–1533," 23.

121 Seegrün, "Schleswig-Holstein," 154 for the "Kerke Ordeninge" of 1542.

122 Göbell, "Das Vordringen der Reformation in Dänemark und in den Herzogtümern unter der Regierung Friedrichs I. 1523–1533," 160.

123 Göbell, "Das Vordringen der Reformation in Dänemark und in den Herzogtümern unter der Regierung Friedrichs I. 1523–1533," 156.

For the administration of his new possessions, the Duke needed new central institutions. For his private affairs, the office of a *Kammersekretär* (secretary of the chancery) was installed. All the revenues were directed to the new *Rentkammer* as the central office for all financial matters, which mirrored the *Gemeine Kasten* in the parishes. A Rentmeister presided over this office. More and more learnèd officers were needed to govern the duchies in an effective way. These steps have already been described as the beginnings of the modern state.[124] The independence of the duchies was expressed by the continued use of the German Chancery (*Tyske Kancelli*) in Copenhagen as opposed to the *Dankse Kancelli.*

The church ordinance helped to separate the duchies from Denmark. New schools, as in Haderslev,[125] not only spread knowledge, but also strengthened the cohesion of the duchies with German culture. This is even more true as Holstein profited from the existing schooling structures in Lübeck and Hamburg, whereas only Schleswig needed a higher "Latin school" of its own.[126] The ordinance of 1542 strengthened public education, but this was an education once again provided in German. Another effect of the new confession affected the language of the duchies. The church ordinance for Schleswig-Holstein was of course rendered in a Low-German translation. But it was precisely the influence of Saxony, Martin Luther's Bible-translation and other Wittenberg professors, that led to High-German becoming more and more frequent in the administration of the duchies. The Elector of Saxony was frequently asked and referred to as an authority on Reformation matters.[127] Another reason was the decreasing political influence of Lübeck and the Hansa League. High German became the language of the educated and the families involved in the administration of the duchies.

The Reformation in Schleswig-Holstein united the Duke and the Prince of Denmark, but from the house of Oldenburg, with his new subjects in the new faith. The Reformation profited from the new pious monarch, but this was never seen as an octroy or the work of the Prince alone. Instead, it was the result of an intense cooperation between the estates (*Landtage*) and the court. As the estates had cooperated when the Reformation was introduced, it was easy to envisage this project as the will of the people. Moreover, the leading role of the estates had been confirmed during the introduction of the Reformation.

124 Lange, "Stände, Landesherr und Große Politik," 179.
125 Schwarz Lausten, "The early Reformation," 15.
126 Göbell, *Die Schleswig-Holsteinische Kirchenordnung von 1542*, XVI.
127 Göbell, *Die Schleswig-Holsteinische Kirchenordnung von 1542*, 9.

Whereas the Reformation in Zurich and Hamburg liberated the cities from ecclesiastic power, the case was more complicated in the duchies. Politically, already before the Reformation, the Duke – particularly as King of Denmark – had dominance over the governance of Schleswig. Matters were more complicated in Lübeck, where the bishop received his regalia from the Emperor, even when the bishopric had become Lutheran.[128] And yet the church ordinance of 1542 helped to develop structures that slowly established a particular church of this realm (*Landeskirche*).[129] These features distinguished the duchies from the Empire as well as from Denmark and emphasised its autonomy. Due to the family connections of the Duke, however, the rulers of Denmark and the Empire were much closer to each other than in the case of Hamburg or Zurich. But at last the situation of the Duke of Schleswig and Holstein resembled more and more the position of the highest princes of the Empire. Although he did not have the prerogative to elect the Emperor, this shortcoming was made up for by his royal lineage and his chances to inherit the throne of Denmark and Norway. It did not take long to develop the ambition to become the leading protestant monarch of Europe.[130]

3.2 *Reformation in Denmark*

3.2.1 The Feud of the Counts

In Denmark, the first traces of Protestantism can be detected in Jutland and Malmø during the mid-1520s,[131] from where it spread to Copenhagen. Hans Tausen (approx. 1494–1561), who had studied in Wittenberg, introduced Lutheranism in Viborg in 1527. He was accused, but Frederick I took him under

---

128 Hauschildt. "Die Reformation in Hamburg, Lübeck und Eutin," 216–218.

129 Göbell, "Das Vordringen der Reformation in Dänemark und in den Herzogtümern unter der Regierung Friedrichs I. 1523–1533," 172 on this debate.

130 Jens Ejnar Olesen. "Dänemark, Norwegen und Island." In *Dänemark, Norwegen und Schweden im Zeitalter der Reformation und Konfessionalisierung. Nordische Königreiche und Konfession 1500 bis 1660: Katholisches Leben und Kirchenreform im Zeitalter der Glaubensspaltung No. 62*, eds. Matthias Asche/Anton Schindling. Münster: Aschendorff, 2003, 27–106.

131 Olesen, "Dänemark, Norwegen und Island," 50–51; Ole Peter Grell. "The Emergence of Two Cities: The Reformation in Malmø and Cogenhagen." In *Die dänische Reformation vor ihrem internationalen Hintergrund*, eds. L. Grane/ K. Hørby. Göttingen: Vandenhoeck & Ruprecht, 1990, 129–145; for the Humanist background cf. Kai Hørby. "Humanist Profiles in the Danish Reform Movement." In *Teaching the People – The education of the Clergy and the Instruction of the People in the Danish Reformation Church: Die dänische Reformation vor ihrem internationalen Hintergrund*, eds. L. Grane/ K. Hørby: Göttingen: Vandenhoeck & Ruprecht, 1990, 28–38; Schwarz Lausten, "The early Reformation," 23.

his protection, saving him from condemnation.[132] After Frederick's death, however, some followers of the old Church initiated a conflict which came to be known as the "feud of the counts" (*Grevens fejde*).[133] First the Council of State (*Rigsråd*) refused to offer the crown to a Lutheran, then the Prince rejected the proposal from a Lutheran majority of the Council with backing from Lübeck. When most of the territory had been taken by the opponents, the State Council finally voted on 4 July 1534 for Christian as their new King. Christian III was proclaimed, although he refused to confirm the hereditary rights of the estates. His electoral capitulation (Handfeste or "Versicherungsbrief") did not repeat the usual privileges.

Christian III had to impose his rule by means of the army and navy. His policy, therefore, was less benevolent and consensual compared to the duchies. In 1536 he conquered Copenhagen. With the approval of Luther, the remaining three Roman-Catholic bishops were deposed and imprisoned. The members of the State council now were asked to consent to a threefold plan: 1) to exclude all bishops and archbishops from the government, 2) to be ready for a future general council of Christianity, and 3) to abstain from all measures against Lutheranism.[134] Having obtained their consent, the rest of the bishops were imprisoned and removed. With the accusation of a *crimen laesae maiestatis* they had to face a severe law suit. The confiscation of church property in Denmark and Norway gave the King the means to defeat his remaining adversaries and to build up a new powerful government. He used his contacts in Germany to obtain the presence of Luther, Melanchthon or Bugenhagen in Copenhagen.[135]

A new bill, the "Recessen om reformationen", enacted by the estates on 30 October 30 1536, can be regarded as a new constitution for his territories.[136] Because of their evil deeds, the bishoprics were abolished and bishops could no longer be members of the State Council. Their possessions were seized for the crown respectively for the use of the King and for the common good. The

132 Schwarz Lausten, "Weltliche Obrigkeit und Kirche," 95; Dietrich Schäfer. G*eschichte von Dänemark, vol. 4*. Gotha: F. Perthes, 1893, 128–130.

133 Hoffmann, "Der Sieg der Reformation," 130–137; Lange, "Stände, Landesherr und Große Politik," 168.

134 Schwarz Lausten, "Weltliche Obrigkeit und Kirche," 96.

135 Martin Schwarz Lausten. "Kirchenordnungen in Dänemark-Norwegen in der Reformationszeit." In *Ordnungen für die Kirche – Wirkungen auf die Welt: Spätmittelalter, Humanismus, Reformation No. 84*, eds. S. Arend/ G. Dörner. Tübingen: Mohr Siebeck, 2015, 275–290, 280–281.

136 Schwarz Lausten, "The early Reformation," 31; edited in Olsen, *Den danske Kirkeordinants af 1539 og andre Aktstykker vedrørende den lutherske Kirkereformations Inaførelse i Danmark*, 154.

state now became responsible for care of the poor. Superattendents instead of bishops should teach and preach the word of God and ensure that the people followed the correct faith. To emphasise how they differed from Catholic bishops, Bugenhagen introduced the seven superintendents into their new office, which excluded their apostolic succession in the Roman-Catholic tradition as well as the traditional archbishopric of Lund in Scania. The existing patronage rights were respected as well as – for the moment at least – monasteries. In some respects, therefore, the Danish church ordinance had some specific elements compared to Bugenhagen's other work.[137]

But there were problems on the protestant side as well. For the first time, Luther and his followers had to decide how to install a King. Bugenhagen decided to coronate the King and his wife, Dorothea of Saxe-Lauenburg (1511–1571), which took place on 12 August 1537,[138] four weeks after the ordination of the superintendents. It was reputed that Luther reacted furiously, particularly as Bugenhagen used the medieval ceremony of coronation as his model.[139] The questions of whether Protestants could accept bishops and how to ordain them were still unresolved by Luther. For the ordination of pastors it was made clear that this did not create a special status for priests. For Denmark's new superintendents Bugenhagen used a special form of ordination. Did Bugenhagen's ceremony and unction, therefore, make the new King a member of the clergy? Bugenhagen defended his action: When the members of the State council placed the symbols of the monarchy on the altar, it became the office of the church and their servants to install the new King. Bugenhagen conceded that the unction might not be necessary. But he argued that the new monarch needed a sign for the necessary help from the Holy Spirit and had to remember his ecclesiastic duties. As the King was responsible for the salvation of his people and any negligence would cause God to seek vengeance against the King and his people, this symbolic action seemed appropriate.

The whole service took five hours and was delivered in the German language.[140] After the "Te Deum" the King had to unsheathe his sword and read from the Gospel. He finally had to swear to protect his realm with the Gospel and his sword. The community responded with the "Hallelujah".

137 Schwarz Lausten, "Kirchenordnungen in Dänemark-Norwegen," 287–288 for these particularities, which do not play an important role in this context.

138 Seegrün, "Schleswig-Holstein," 153.

139 Schwarz Lausten, "König und Kirche," 150.

140 Olesen, "Dänemark, Norwegen und Island," 57–58.

3.2.2 The Ordinance of 1537

The church ordinance of 1537 followed the directions of the 1536 bill and formally installed the new religion in all Danish provinces.[141] The ordinance was developed by Bugenhagen, negotiated at Haderslev and sent for approval to Luther and the Elector at Wittenberg. Six key components were announced:

- doctrine (*lerdommen*),
- the definition of the correct ceremonies and liturgies (*Ceremonier*),
- the regulation of schools (*Scholerne*) and of the common money box (*Almisse Kiiste*),
- of the clergy (*Superattendenter oc deris pruister*) and
- provisions on books (*Bøger*).

On the whole this clearly followed Bugenhagen's theology. Once again we find his four key elements, which complement each other: The establishment of the correct doctrine, the provisions for true services and liturgy, the establishment of education in a school-system[142] and the care of the poor.[143] But a closer look reveals that Bugenhagen also used texts from the recent past, such as the articles by Haderslev. The continued respect for penance as a sacrament is one example.[144] Obviously, Bugenhagen was flexible enough to respect local traditions, perhaps because he wanted to make his new order more agreeable to the public.[145] But it is pointless to try to determine the true form of the ordinance or to determine its more Danish or German character, as this was not an issue of the time.[146] A first translation in Latin was printed in 1539. In the same year, a new Danish version with small changes by Bugenhagen was enacted as the "Den rette Ordinans", the correct form of the ordinance.[147] A Latin translation

141 Cf. Martin Schwarz Lausten. "Kirkens nye ordninger." In *Reformationen i dansk kirke og kultur, Bind 1: 1517–1700*, eds. Niels Henrik Gregersen/Carsten Bach-Nielsen. Odense: Syddansk Universitetsforlag, 2017, 161–206.

142 Morten Fink-Jensen. "Kristendom, skole og pædagogik i Danmark før 1700." In *Reformationen i danks kirke og kultur, Bind 1: 1517–1700*, eds. Niels Henrik Gregersen/Carsten Bach-Nielsen. Odense: Syddansk Universitetsforlag, 2017, 369–389.

143 Cf. already Tarald Rasmussen, In *Norsk Kirkehistorie, 3rd ed.*, eds. Bernt T. Oftestad/Tarald Rasmussen/Jan Schumacher. Oslo: Universitetsforlaget, 2005, 97; Andreas Aarflot. *Kirke og stat i Norge, Fra reformatsjonen til våre dager.* Stavanger: Nomi, 1969, 68–69.

144 Göbell, "Das Vordringen der Reformation in Dänemark und in den Herzogtümern unter der Regierung Friedrichs I. 1523–1533," 61.

145 This has been used as an argument to detect the Danish aspects of the ordinance, cf. Martin Schwarz Lausten/Forord (ed.). *Kirkeordinansen 1537/39*. Denmark: deGruyter, 1989, 28.

146 In the same sense as Hoffmann, "Der Sieg der Reformation," 142–143.

147 Hoffmann, "Der Sieg der Reformation," 42. The text was edited in a contemporary Danish version by Olsen, *Den danske Kirkeordinants af 1539 og andre Aktstykker vedrørende den lutherske Kirkereformations Inaførelse i Danmark.*

followed soon again in 1542, when Ribe's articles on the election of pastors were added.

This complex of the Danish "Kirkeordinansen" forms an important document for the history of the Danish language. On the whole, the Danish ordinance kept close to the earlier church ordinances of Bugenhagen. From the beginning to the end, this text stressed the importance of producing the best possible text. The prologue is also known as the "royal letter", as the King greets his subjects in his kingdoms and duchies. It could have been drafted by Bugenhagen as well,[148] and refers to negotiations with doctors and preachers in order to introduce the correct form of Christianity that conformed to the new teachings of Martin Luther in "nouissimis temporibus nobis".[149] Thanks to the chancellor, with its wide range of goals, the new law claims to be the perfect ordinance (*perfectam ordinationem*). It aims to ensure the pure teaching of the Gospel, the use of the sacraments according to Christ's institution, the correct chants and lections, the right convention at the table of the Lord, the education of the youth in letters and arts, the defence of God's word, respectively the Holy Bible, and to look after the preachers, the schools, the poor and so on. The Catechism should be known not only by the nobility, but also by the poor, and therefore should be present in every home.[150] The norms of the faith, therefore, have to be taught to everybody.

The "royal letter" distinguished two parts of the ordinance.[151] The first part is "God's own ordinance", which is constituted by those norms which form part of Christ's own will: The correct education in the gospel and God's laws, the correct administration of the sacraments, the education of children, the alimony for the clergy and the poor. These provisions can never be changed. The second part, however, although divine in nature, is the King's own part of the ordinance. These norms can be changed in the course of time and are enacted by the King alone. Both parts have to be obeyed. This distinction has little to do with Luther's theory of the Two Regiments,[152] which of course legitimised the King's command in ecclesiastical matters. It rather mirrors the two tables of Moses' Ten Commandments. The first three commandments form

148 Schwarz Lausten, "König und Kirche," 156.

149 Ordinatio Ecclesiastica Regnorum Daniae et Norwegiae et Ducatuum Sleswicencis/ Holsatiae etc., o.O. 1537, Prologue, fol.2r.

150 Ordinatio Ecclesiastica, fol.3r.

151 Ordinatio Ecclesiastica, fol.3v and fol.5r.

152 This argument was brought forward by Jens Ulf Jørgensen. "Kirkeretten i Danske Lov." In *Danske og Norske Lov i 300 år: Festskirftet er udgivet i anledning af 300året for udstedelsen af Christian V's Danske Lov*, ed. D. Tamm. Viborg: Jurist – og Økonomsforbundet Forlag, 1983, 447–487, 453; Rasmussen, "Norske Kirkehistorie," 104.

God's ordinance, whereas the subsequent commandments can change in their range of coverage in the course of time. Martin Schwarz Lausten recalled Melanchthon's expression of the prince as the "custos duorum tabulae". This image undoubtedly shaped the Nordic monarchies. But the church ordinance of 1537 did not use this expression. The influence of Melanchthon in this instance is difficult to prove,[153] but became more notable and problematic in the following generation.

The institutional change brought about by this ordinance concerns the establishment of a uniform set of elementary schools and higher schools for Latin and other higher arts.[154] The schools were to have five different classes and the ordinance explained in each case what was to be taught. The local administrations had to give back to the poor what previously had been used by the public.[155] In this respect, the new Religion was installed in a bottom–up way in the realm from the parishes to the high magistracy.[156] It started with the pastors and the schools in the dioceses, where poor boxes were installed as a start to secular social care and where new state courts had to decide in marriage matters as well.[157] The higher level of Latin schools and of superattendents hinted already at a multi-layered form of administration, which in the end opened for efficient control by the central government, particularly due to the oath of fidelity prescribed for the superintendents.[158] The University of Copenhagen was reopened with a ceremony on 9 September 1537,[159] and Bugenhagen was asked to reorganise its structures and teaching. For this reason, the new structure has been claimed as proof of centralisation, the augmentation and professionalisation of bureaucracy, and a more scientific approach to settling state matters.[160]

The King's wish to change the habits of his subjects is effectively echoed throughout the ordinance. It contains not only the true doctrine, necessary for salvation, but it has to be divulged in the realm so that each Christian can

153 Against Schwarz Lausten, "Weltliche Obrigkeit und Kirche," 155; idem, Schwarz Lausten, "The early Reformation," 25.

154 Olesen, "Dänemark, Norwegen und Island," 62.

155 Ordinatio Ecclesiastica, fol.48v: *de hospitalibus*.

156 Schwarz Lausten, "Weltliche Obrigkeit und Kirche," 95, 91.

157 Olesen, "Dänemark, Norwegen und Island," 58, 62 for the schools, 67 for social care and marriage courts.

158 Schwarz Lausten, *Kirkeordinansen 1537/39*, 238.

159 Ditlev Tamm. *Retshistorie: Danmark – Europa – globale perspektiver*. Copenhagen: jurist – og Økonomsforbuddet Forlag, 2005, 155, 164; idem. "Law and Protestantism in Denmark." *Zeitschrift für Rechtsgeschichte: Kanonistische Abteilung* 102 (2016): 406–418.

160 Olesen, "Dänemark, Norwegen und Island," 68.

be reached.[161] To achieve this objective book printing comes into focus. The ordinance has to be printed so that each household could have a copy and in this way the faith was spread to all in a uniform way. A little later, Melanchthon would use this idea to ask for new laws that would contain all provisions written in the vernacular language and in a short, but complete form, so that the people could learn and obey the law.[162] It was not until around 1800 that the English philosopher Jeremy Bentham would label this new concept of law "codification". The ordinance was not yet concerned with laws in general. Its main objective was to ascertain the one and true faith.[163] A supplement to the church ordinance provided notes and text of the chants that were to be used in the services.[164] But print can be misused as well. The ordinance refers to bad books which could at the time be found in a large and growing quantity. They could infect the true faith of the subjects and, therefore, this danger had to be eradicated. Censorship and a list of prohibited books, therefore, was no exclusive invention of the Roman-Catholic Church.[165] It was the duty of the University of Copenhagen to decide whether new books were appropriate.[166]

It is hardly surprising, therefore, that the church ordinance not only remained in the books, but changed the country in such a major way. The King asked Bugenhagen to suggest the perfect candidate to lead Roskilde. Bugenhagen proposed Peder Palladius (1503–1560), who had studied at Wittenberg from 1531 to 1533, but had not yet obtained a doctoral degree. The King paid for this last step of Palladius' education, and Palladius was granted his doctorate at Wittenberg in 1537 by a jury composed of Luther, Melanchthon and Bugenhagen. He indeed became the leading, dogmatically settled Lutheran

---

161 Ordinatio Ecclesiastica, fol.5v: "per Typographum inuulagri".

162 For this Protestant ideal of spreading the knowledge of laws cf. Mathias Schmoeckel. "Leges et in carmina redigendae sunt. Die Erfindung der Kodifikation als Konzept durch Melanchthon und deren Rezeption in katholischen Staaten bis 1811." *Zeitschrift für Rechtsgeschichte: Kanonistische Abteilung* 126 (2009): 397–436.

163 Ordinatio Ecclesiastica, fol.A ij: "integra doctina euangelii omnibus ubique pura certa et uniformis sit".

164 Ordinatio Ecclesiastica, fol.94ss.

165 Cf. Martin Mulsow. "Johann Christoph Wolf (1683–1739) und die verbotenen Bücher." In *500 Jahre Theologie in Hamburg: Hamburg als Zentrum christlicher Theologie und Kultur zwischen Tradition und Zukunft: Arbeiten zur Kirchengeschichte No. 95*, ed. J. A. Steiger. Berlin/ New York: deGruyter, 2005, 1–112, 102–105.

166 Schwarz Lausten, *Kirkeordinansen 1537/39*, 136; Leif Grane. "Teaching the People – the Education of the Clergy and the Instruction of the People in the Danish Reformation Church." In *Die dänische Reformation vor ihrem internationalen Hintergrund. The Danish Reformation against its International Background*, ed. idem/K. Hørby. Göttingen: Vandenhoeck & Ruprecht, 1990, 164–184, 182.

the King had wanted.[167] His visitations ensured that the country respected the new faith and its order. Together with the university he particularly helped to spread Latin schools in Denmark.[168]

3.2.3 Later Developments

Due to the political success of Christian III, Denmark had effectively become a Lutheran territory. The Confessio Augustana from 1530, the confession of Augsburg, marked the contents of the true faith.[169] The defeat of the bishops empowered the King enormously. Now he controlled the church, not only by visitation for ecclesiastical and dogmatic questions, but also in economic issues. The former ecclesiastical properties were slowly secularized. Just as the clergy depended on their salaries, the church depended on royal subsidies.[170] His help for the church could even be seen as a special form of church service. Moreover, the education of the people, poor relief and censorship had become constituents of the royal administration. With his sword and the true understanding of the gospel, the Lutheran King had to ensure the salvation and the correct behaviour of his subjects.

But the Reformation itself had not come to an end. Particularly after the Peasants' War in 1525, Melanchthon tried to establish a new perspective on the function of good order, government and law. We have hardly any trace to show that he influenced Bugenhagen at this time. As Melanchthon's theory slowly developed, it became more distant from Luther's theology. This distanced him from Bugenhagen, whereas Jean Calvin was heavily influenced by Melanchthon. In the mid sixteenth century, therefore, there was a new debate on the correct faith. The followers of Melanchthon, Lutheran or Calvinistic "Philippists", also spread in Denmark.[171] Melanchthon's most arduous opponents were first the Antinomists, who tried to defend Luther's contempt for law and government in a religious perspective. Some theologians tried to use this discussion to divide Danish Lutheranism from Germany and to establish a Danish confession.[172] But Antinomism was not and could not be very attractive to the monarchy. Thus the Danish court remained loyal to Saxony, and the admonitions of the Elector and his wife continued to have considerable

---

167 Olesen, "Dänemark, Norwegen und Island," 59.

168 Olesen, "Dänemark, Norwegen und Island," 63.

169 Olesen, "Dänemark, Norwegen und Island," 77.

170 Schwarz Lausten, "Weltliche Obrigkeit und Kirche," 104–105.

171 Throkild Lyby/Ole Peter Grell. "The consolidation of Lutherism in Denmark and Norway." In *The Scandinavian Reformation*, ed. O. P. Grell. Cambridge: Cambridge University Press, 1995, 114–143, 115–118; Seegrün, "Schleswig-Holstein" (n. 110), 157–158.

172 Lyby/Grell, "The consolidation of Lutherism in Denmark and Norway," 117.

influence in Denmark. Only when "crypto-Calvinism" was prosecuted in 1574, was the King forced to react. This led, for example, to the condemnation of Denmark's most prominent theologian, Niels Hemmingsen, and the first Calvinists like Johannes à Lasco were not welcome in the country.[173]

This did not exclude Melanchthon's theology as long as it was accepted in the Lutheran mainstream, later in the formula of concord in 1577. His Apologia of the Augsburg Confession and his "Loci communes" were explicitly recognised by the 1537 ordinance as fundamental texts of the Lutheran faith.[174] Hence, Denmark was open to accepting Melanchthon's notion of the King as "custos utriusque tabulae" or "praecipuum membrum ecclesiae".[175] But the church ordinance of 1537 alone could not legitimise the King. Constantly the monarchy had to assure the one and only correct practice of the Lutheran faith.

Thus the King determined what the correct faith was and ascertained the confessional integrity and unity of his realm on the basis of the Confessio Augustana, which now had become the definition of the one and only faith according to the law. At least from this moment on, questions of faith and church were decided by the King. Vigorously the monarchy had to ensure Lutheranism throughout its realms. The Reformation therefore enhanced in the longer run a top-down form of government. The legitimation of the monarchy expressed by the 1537 ordinance became the foundation of the monarchy as well.

Later legislation in church matters reiterated or even enhanced these tendencies.[176] The last paragraph of the 1537 ordinance regulated possible amendments. On the King's initiative, the council and experts should participate to develop modernizations.[177] But this "revisjonsparaprapen" was never put into practice.[178] Instead, the ordinance remained the most important church law of Denmark and Norway.[179] For more than a century only minor changes occurred in ecclesiastical matters.

But secular laws even enhanced the effects of the church ordinance of 1537. The "Royal law" (*Lex Regia/ Konge Loven*) of 1665 started with the avowal of

173 Lyby/Grell, "The consolidation of Lutherism in Denmark and Norway," 18–20; Olesen, "Dänemark, Norwegen und Island," 79.

174 Göbell, "Das Vordringen der Reformation in Dänemark und in den Herzogtümern unter der Regierung Friedrichs I. 1523–1533," 164; Schwarz Lausten, *Kirkeordinansen 1537/39*, 136.

175 Schwarz Lausten, "The early Reformation," 25.

176 Cf. Holger Fr. Rørdam. *Danske kirkelove samt udvalg af andre Bestemmelser, Part 3: 1596–1683*. Copenhagen: Nabu Press, 1889.

177 Aarflot, *Kirke og stat i Norge*, 66–67; for the *revisjonsartikel* cf. Schwarz Lausten, *Kirkeordinansen 1537/39*, 243.

178 Aarflot, *Kirke og stat i Norge*, 84.

179 Aarflot, *Kirke og stat i Norge*, 67.

the correct faith: The best beginning of this law would be with God. Referring to the 1537 ordinance, the Kingdoms of Denmark and Norway were united in the faith as defined by the Augsburg Confession of 1530. The development of Danish absolutism obviously used the unity of the faith not only to unite the two kingdoms, but to underline the central power of the King. The exclusive power of the monarch, the *enevælde*, dominated Danish politics in the next centuries until 1848.[180]

Formally, the church ordinance of 1537 was abolished with the introduction of Denmark's grand codification, the Danske Lov of 1683. Its second book adopted most of its content.[181] It started with the definition of the correct form of religion and the office of clerics. With the authoritative texts of the Bible, the apostolic, Nicene and Athanasian creed as well as the Augsburg Confession of 1530, together with Luther's catechism, the law effectively defined the contents of the religion of the land. Most of the topics we already find in the ordinance of 1537, which were repeated in this most complete of all codifications. This law might have assumed an administrative character[182] as the regulations concerning pastors, churches and their properties, schools, hospitals, professors and even censorship are regulated in a very matter-of-fact way. The ecclesiastical questions now had become accustomed and could be regulated in a simple administrative style. In 1685, a new law restated the correct form of rituals and ceremonies, again in the tradition of the church ordinance of 1537.[183]

The 1537 ordinance did not last as long as in Schleswig–Holstein. But with the grand "Danske Lov" as its successor it becomes clear that the ordinance had a great influence on the creation of the Danish absolutism. The complete power of the Danish King, this Danish *enevælde*, started with the control over the church. A whole range of consequences can be distinguished here.[184]

- The administration of the newly acquired land and possession not only concentrated the administration in Copenhagen, but also required more representatives in the country. Concentrating mostly on Danish nobility, the territory was given as tenure (*len*), often clearly stating on the exact revenue,

180 Martin Schwarz Lausten. "Kongemagt og rigets vel." In *Reformationen i dansk kirke og kultur, Bind 1: 1517–1700*, ed. Niels Henrik Gregersen/Carsten Bach-Nielsen. Odense: Syddansk Universitetsforlag, 2017, 121–158.

181 Cf. V. A. Secher/Chr. Støchel (eds.). *Forarbejderne til kong Kristian V.s Danske Lov*. Copenhagen: 1891, 10 n. 7.

182 Jørgensen, "Kirkeretten i Danske Lov," 453.

183 Aarflot, *Kirke og stat i Norge*, 97.

184 This development has been identified only for the *envæld* regime, but is also valid for the period that led this way, cf. Birgit Bjerre Jensen. *Udnævnelses retten I enevældens magtpolitiske system 1660–1730*. Viborg: Jurist – og Økonomsforbundet Forlag, 1987, 16 and passim.

which had to be paid to the state (*genant*). Instead of the old powerful nobility (*stormaend*), these new *lenmaend* (tenants) were more bound to the crown.[185]

- For the administration of the royal policies over finances, the army and so on, more and more knowledge was required. This needed more offices in the centre and on lower levels (*overøvrigheden*). Public officials (*embedsmænd*) were installed for the financial administration (*Rentekammeret* – later the *Skatkammerkollegiet*), the customs (*toldvæsenet*) and the chancery.
- Besides the lawyers (*restbejente*) and judges (*landsdommere*), the administration required more and more magistrates.
- As bureaucracy spread in order to lead the country through administration and legislation, a growing professionalization and a scientific approach helped to shape matters along this way.[186] This slowly established a new order of civil servants in Copenhagen and required more and more university education for the new magistrates.

Henning Arnisaeus (approx. 1575–1636), the personal physician of King Christian IV since 1620, can help in understanding this role. Of course religion was still seen as necessary in this time. Religion would sustain all States, as it was the foundation of faith, oaths, and morality.[187] It was the highest duty of the monarch, therefore, to establish the foundations of religion and to ensure the obedience of the people in this matter just like his prerogative of legislation.[188] This was his own obligation. In 1610, Arnisaeus regarded the unity of religion as the "vinculum societatum" or even the "lightening and foundation of the Republic".[189] The "cura religionis", the legislation concerning the church, belonged exclusively to the King[190]. Arnisaeus cited a slightly pathetic text:[191]

> Tu es dux professionis fidei nostra, tu purgasti templum Dei haeretics & iis, qui caelestem doctrinam ibi vendebant.

---

185 Olesen, "Dänemark, Norwegen und Island," 27–106, 69–70.

186 For a similar development in the Lutheran county of Ostfriesland – as opposed to the conceptions of their Calvinist opponents – cf. Mathias Schmoeckel. "Zwischen Idealstaat und Realpolitik: Machiavellismus in Ostfriesland um 1600. Des Ostfriesischen Cantzelars Thomae Frantzij Getreuwer Rath." In *Jurisprudenz, Politische Theorie und Politische Theologie* (*Beiträge zur Politischen Wissenschaft, 131*), ed. F. S. Carney/H. Schilling/D. Wyduckel. Berlin: Duncker & Humboldt, 2004, 463–525.

187 Henning Arnisaeus. *De iure maiestatis libri tres.* Frankfurt, 1610, c.VI n. 1, 361 with n. 1 and 2.

188 Arnisaeus. *De iure maiestatis libri tres.* c. II n. 3, 236.

189 Arnisaeus. *De iure maiestatis libri tres.* c.VI n. 3, 369.

190 Arnisaeus. *De iure maiestatis libri tres.* c.VI n. 15, 420.

191 Arnisaeus. *De iure maiestatis libri tres.* c.VI n. 15, 420.

But the King essentially stood above the law. The King had the exclusive right to allow enclaves of different confessions. Friedrichstadt in Schleswig, Christiansfeld in Jutland and Christiansand in Norway are the most visible examples of this royal prerogative.[192] In the same way, some queens of a diverse confession obtained the privilege to practise their own religion in the court. This might appear as a contradiction to his obligation to install the true religion. In this matter, the idea of tolerance inspired by possible political advantages opened for a major exception to the rule of the one correct confession.

3.3 *Transfer to Norway*

3.3.1 The Introduction of the Reformation in Norway

Only in theory did the events in Denmark mark the development of Norway as well. In this electoral capitulation Christian emphasised that Norway, which had belonged to his predecessors as well, should permanently remain united with Denmark and become an inseparable part of the Danish realm.[193] In the "Recessen om reformationen" Christian denied again any independence for Norway.[194] Some historians used nineteenth century terms to separate the former "personal union" of the two kingdoms, which had now become a "real union" of territories.[195] Others suggested that only the name of the former kingdom remained[196] and even a complete dissolution of Norway has been proposed.[197]

Contrary even to Denmark, the Roman-Catholic confession still reigned in Norway after 1537. The vast distances in Norway and the small number of cities made communication more difficult.[198] It is true, therefore, that the Reformation had problems in reaching Norway completely. German

---

192 Rasmussen, "Norsk Kirkehistorie," 132; for Danish privileges for Roman-Catholics cf. Seegrün, "Schleswig-Holstein," 160–161.

193 For this famous "Norgesparagraf" and the relationship of these two nations cf. Sverre Steen. "Den Dansk-Norske Forbindelse 1536–1814." In *Omstridte Spørgsmaal I Nordens Historie, vol. 1*, ed. W. Carlgren et al. Copenhagen: Gads, 1940, 115–134; the debate can be found in Steinar Imsen/Steinar Supphellen (eds.). *Studier i norsk historie 1537– ca. 1800. (Norske Historikerei Utvalg, VII)*. Oslo: Universitetsforlaget 1981.

194 Schwarz Lausten, "The early Reformation," 31.

195 Ralph Tuchtenhagen. *Kleine Geschichte Norwegens.* Munich: C.H. Beck, 2009, 65.

196 Halvdan Koht. *Artikelen om Norge i den Danske handfest ninga fra 1536: (Norsk) Historisk tidsskrift 30.* Oslo: Universitetforlaget, 1936, 1–18.

197 Johan Schreiner. *Norges-artikkelen i Christian IIIs håndfestning, (Norsk) Historisk tidsskrift 30* (1934–1936), Oslo: Unviersitetsforlaget, 185–205.

198 Cf. Carl Fr. Wisløff. *Norsk Kirkehistorie*. Oslo: Universitetsforlaget, 1966, 393; Olesen, "Dänemark, Norwegen und Island," 38s.

merchants[199] and a Lutheran preacher first introduced Lutheranism in Bergen. A first Lutheran sermon was given in 1526. Two other preachers were granted royal privilege in 1529 by Frederick I, the German Herman Fresze and the Danish Jens Viborg (1552), who became the vicar of Holy Cross Church.[200] But most of the country remained faithful to the old confession. The archbishop of Trondheim, Olav Engelbrektsson (approx. 1480–1538, in office 1523–1537), even tried to collect profit from the "feud of the counts",[201] unite the opponents against Christian III and his command. However, his "coup d'état" failed, the archbishop had to leave the country and died at Liege.[202] But after his defeat, nobody else could represent the unity of the Norwegian realm.

With the downfall of the Norwegian Church, no other institution could prevent Norway's loss of independence.[203] The Norwegian State council was abolished as well. The extent to which Norway only remained a title of the Danish King has never been discussed.[204]

With the abolition of the bishops and archbishops, the supremacy of the Archbishop of Trondheim – who was succeeded by an ordinary superintendent – and the ecclesiastical identity of Norway were destroyed. The secularisation of the Norwegian Church property brought the King about 40% of the whole country. The church treasures were brought to Copenhagen with the exception of the shrine of St. Olaf, which was lost in this turmoil.[205] As in Denmark, these Church leaders had to swear their fidelity to the King. For some time not even a Norwegian chancery was installed, whereas the duchies were represented at the court by the "German chancery". All institutions were dissolved or transferred to Copenhagen, from where all administration emanated.

And yet the Danish control over Norway was not strong; it has been called a remote power.[206] Many laws had to be installed explicitly in Norway. The new Kings were proclaimed independently from the Danish ceremony. Even without an official autonomy, Norway succeeded in maintaining some administration of its own.[207] It has been argued, therefore, that the church ordinance

---

199 Poul Georg Lindhardt. *Kirchengeschichte Skandinaviens*. Göttingen: Evangelische Verlagsanstalt, 1983, 24; Schwarz Lausten, "The Early Reformation," 28.

200 Ralph Tuchtenhagen. *Kleine Geschichte Norwegens*, 60.

201 Lars Hamre. *Norsk politisk historie 1513–1537*. Oslo: Universitetforlaget, 1998, 37.

202 Hamre, *Norsk politisk historie*, 764; Thomas B. Wilsson. *History of the Church and State in Norway: From the Tenth to the Sixteenth Century*. Westminster: Bibliolife, 1903, 305, 341; Halvdan Koht. *Olav Engelbriktsson og Sjølvstende-Tapet 1537*. Oslo: Aschehoug, 1951.

203 Wilsson, *History of the Church and State in Norway*, 338.

204 Tuchtenhagen. *Kleine Geschichte Norwegens*, 65.

205 Rasmussen, "Norsk Kirkehistorie," 105, 112.

206 Schwarz Lausten, "The Early Reformation," 33.

207 Lindhardt, *Kirchengeschichte Skandinaviens*, 46.

of 1537, without precise regulations for Norway, could hardly introduce the Reformation in Norway. At least two reasons behind the difficulties in spreading the new faith into the distant parts of the realm were the absence of a Norwegian university and the lack of Norwegian printers. For these simple reasons, the Reformation, which was used to spreading from town to town, had considerable problems gaining hold in Norway.

In two cases even the old bishops were appointed as new Lutheran superattendents. As the denomination for this post was fluid – bishop, superattendent and superintendent were used simultaneously for this office almost like in Saxony[208] – this could hardly be regarded as a degradation of rank. One example is the Bishop of Bergen, Geble Pederssøn (approx. 1490–1557, in office: 1537–1550), who was more an Erasmian than a Lutheran. Hans Rev (Reff, approx. 1489–1545, in office 1541–1545) was his counterpart in Christiana, but he became a Lutheran.[209] The selection of Norwegian superattendents, therefore, led to a conservative attitude among the Norwegian clergy.[210] They did little to spread the new faith[211]. Only reluctantly, visitations were organised for the Norwegian church.[212] But in spite of the first visitations and synods the old faith survived for a long time.[213] Until the seventeenth century, condemnations of Catholics took place, and it is no surprise that even the Jesuits had some success in Norway,[214] which shocked the King.

In the second generation of superattendents, however, mostly Danes who had been educated in the Lutheran faith were chosen.[215] There can be no doubt that slowly Norway became a Lutheran country. In the long run, the King and his Copenhagen administration prevailed in Church matters. Representatives of Crypto-Calvinism and Jesuits were persecuted in Norway as vigorously as in

208 Andreas Aarflot. "Das bischöfliche Amt." *Zeitschrift für evangelisches Kirchenrecht* 51 (2006): 505–533, 517.

209 Olesen, "Dänemark, Norwegen und Island," 81s.

210 Cf. Lyby/ Grell, "The consolidation of Luthernism in Denmark and Norway," 123.

211 Olesen, "Dänemark, Norwegen und Island," 71.

212 Tore Nyberg. "Das religiöse Profil des Nordens – Die Entwicklung von Kirchlichkeit und Frömmigkeit in den skandinavischen Ländern vom Späten Mittelalter bis zum konfessionellen Zeitalter." In *Dänemark, Norwegen und Schweden im Zeitalter der Reformation und Konfessionalisierung: Nordische Königreiche und Konfession 1500 bis 1660* (*Katholisches Leben und Kirchenreform im Zeitalter der Glaubensspaltung, 62*), eds. M. Asche/A. Schindling. Münster: Aschendorff, 2003, 245–310, 291.

213 Rasmussen, "Norsk Kirkehistorie," 111, 108.

214 For the socalled *Kirchenlasse* cf. Rasmussen, "Norsk Kirkehistorie," 117; Georg Schwaiger. *Die Reformation in den nordischen Ländern*. Munich: Kösel, 1962, 83.

215 Lyby/Grell, "The consolidation of Luthernism in Denmark and Norway," 124.

Denmark during the second half of the sixteenth century.[216] But the process was much slower than in Denmark and developed different traits.

Even though the text was the same, the effect of the 1537 ordinance in Norway and Denmark differed. Whilst the ordinance had to solve doctrinal issues in Denmark, its primary objective in Norway was to provide for peace and unity under the new King[217]. It did not strengthen the cohesion of the territory but ensured the power of the Danish King, to whom all prelates had vowed their fidelity. Furthermore, the ordinance did not regulate matters effectively in Norway.[218] Particularly the establishment of schools was not put into practice. Additionally, the distance to Copenhagen opened a considerable gap between the official culture of the educated elite and the popular culture as it was practised at home.[219]

3.3.2 Norway and the Danish Absolutism

Initially, there was almost no consistent government over the Norwegian church after 1537,[220] as the ordinance garnered little respect in practice[221]. Most of all, it opened for new financial structures for the Norwegian church. But it might be too much to speak of autonomy for the Norwegian church[222] because this was rather caused by a lack of consistency on the King's side. There can be no doubt, however, that eventually Lutheranism was effectively installed in Norway. In Norway as well, the Danish court had to fight Philippism introduced to Norway through the influence of Niels Hemmingsen.[223] More and more, the situation in Norway resembled the administration in Denmark.[224] Particularly the new prosecution of crypto-Calvinists and Jesuits demanded that more attention be given to everybody obeying the ordinance of 1537.[225] During the reign of Christian IV it was the common conviction that this church ordinance had to be imposed.[226]

---

216 Lyby/Grell, "The consolidation of Luthernism in Denmark and Norway," 125, 133.

217 Ingun Montgomery/Svein Helge Birkeflet. "Norwegen." *Theologische Realenzyklopädie* 24 (1994): 643–659, 647.

218 Rasmussen, "Norsk kirkehistorie," 106.

219 Rasmussen, "Norsk kirkehistorie," 133.

220 Aarflot, *Kirke og stat i Norge*, 80.

221 Olesen, "Dänemark, Norwegen und Island," 71.

222 In this way Aarflot, *Kirke og stat i Norge*, 79.

223 Olesen, "Dänemark, Norwegen und Island," 76; Quam John Elliott/ Jørgen Ericssøn. *A Study in the Norwegian Reformation 1571–1604* (Ph.D. Thesis). Yale University, 1969, 229.

224 Olesen, "Dänemark, Norwegen und Island," 95.

225 Olesen, "Dänemark, Norwegen und Island," 79.

226 Aarflot, *Kirke og stat i Norge*, 87.

Towards the end of the sixteenth century and with the reforms of the Danish *enevælde* government, the people of Norway became Lutherans. The Kirke Ritual of 1685 reinforced the control of Copenhagen over the Norwegian church.[227] The situation in Norway has been compared to Saxony and researchers write of a "Lutheran Orthodoxy" in Norway which obliged its members to take part in the Sunday services. All private and family matters such as births, marriages and funerals had to be registered in the Church rolls. An ordinance for confirmation in 1736 ensured a minimum of religious education for every member of the parish. But this strong ecclesiastical administration was not primarily the expression of a strong hold of the religion over private matters such as in Saxony, but more of the Danish absolutism. Here, church and monarchy provided reciprocally for the strength of each other. But with respect to the authority of the clergy vis-à-vis their parish-members, this Norwegian situation resembled that of Germany.[228] In both cases there was a great distance between the reverend and his flock, which was quite the opposite of Luther's theory of the priesthood for everybody. This orthodoxy was also used as well for the evangelization of the Sami people who still practised their shamanic cults. This might resemble the prosecution of the witches in central Europe, but was more intended as a way of spreading royal power to the North. Here again, the official church was more closely linked to official politics, which in turn opened the gap between faith and piety.

In 1604, the Norwegian clergy benefitted from a plan to modernise the church ordinance of 1537. On the request of King Christian IV,[229] the four superintendents of Norway proposed a new version that aimed to be in accordance with the particularities of Norway.[230] As the old church ordinance contained hardly any guidelines for Norway, the new law should give more guidance. This proposal had two major objectives. The first was the definition of the correct *lærdom* (doctrine) for *Praediken, Sacramenterne, Børne lærdommen*, and *Præster* (for sermons, sacraments, teaching children and for pastors). It defined the correct ceremonies, the maintenance of churches and graveyards, schools, hospitals and contained the norms for superintendents and sinful books. The

227 Rasmussen, "Norsk kirkehistorie," 134.

228 In this sense Aarflot, *Kirke og stat i Norge*, 98.

229 Aarflot, *Kirke og stat i Norge*, 85.

230 Oluf Kolsrud. "*Den norske Kirkes Mindeskrift ved Reformationens 400-Aars-Jubilæum Aar 1917: Utkast til en norsk Kirkeordinants efter Kong Christian IVs Befaling forfattet av Norges Superintendenter i Aaret 1604*. Christiania: 1917; cf. Tarald Rasmussen. "Utkastet til en egen norsk kirke ordinans fra 1604." In *Reformationens konsolidering i de nordiska länderna 1540–1610*, ed. I. Brohed. Oslo: Universitetforlaget, 1990, 57–73, 57; Lindhardt. *Kirchengeschichte Skandinaviens*, 26.

second part was dedicated to the enforcement of the true doctrine, on church discipline (*kirketukt*) and prosecution (*kirkestraf*).[231] This approach might have been in accordance with the evolution of church ordinances in Germany.[232] It is less connected with Roman-Catholic teaching but with the stern and forbidding attitude of Lutheran Orthodoxy. The court, however, was not prepared to allow for deviations from the way determined by the 1537 ordinance. The new ordinance of 1607 has been called a compromise between the Norwegian proposals and the Danish tradition as well as a Danish dictate.[233] But basically, it reiterated the provisions of the church ordinance of 1537.[234] At least the new ordinance established an autonomous Norwegian church.

As in Denmark, the new ordinance was rather a copy of the ordinance of 1537.[235] The Norske Lov of 1687 restated the duty of all subjects to adhere to the Lutheran church[236] and mirrored once again the provisions of the Danske Lov. Danish absolutism ensured in the end that the church was governed by the state. As in the time before the Reformation, the church helped to preserve the sense of Norwegian autonomy.[237]

From the 1740s on, Norwegian bishops developed plans for a more effective school system,[238] as many citizens still did not receive any education at all. The State did not accept the "opportunity schools" and wanted to install a nationwide system of lower and higher schools. But this plan could not be carried out completely. This movement continued into the 1760s with a new Norwegian self-esteem and the urge to create literature of their own.[239] But it would take another century before these plans succeeded and the establishment of Norway's first university in 1811 was necessary before this could be realised.

The new dominance of Danish centralism led to some resistance. Several movements, inspired by Pietism, tried to shift the focus from the official

231 Rasmussen, "Utkastet til en egen norsk kirke ordinans fra 1604.", 63–65, 66.

232 As proposed by Rasmussen, "Utkastet til en egen norsk kirke ordinans fra 1604." 61, 68.

233 For the latter, cf Nyberg, "Das religiöse Profil des Nordens." 305.

234 Rasmussen, "Norsk kirkehistorie," 113.

235 En Kircke Ordinantz: Huor effter alle, Baade Geistlige oc Verdslige udi Norgis Rige, skulle sig rette oc forholde, Kiøbenhaffn 1607, 18–23 [via: http://www.nb.no/nbsok/nb/3fff7dd3a7fa03e9581bb2e174d4d303.nbdigital?lang]. Jørn Øyrenhagen Sunde kindly informed me about this internet resource.

236 *Kong Christian den Femtes Norske Lov af 15de April 1687*, ed. P. I. Paulsen. Kristiana: 1904, vol. 2, 60–63; cf. Arnd Heling. *Die Theologie Eivind Berggravs im norwegischen Kirchenkamp: Ein Beitrag zur politischen Theologie im Luthertum* (*Historisch-theologische Studien zum 19. und 20. Jahrhundert, 3*). Neukirchen-Vlyun: Neukirchener Verlagsgesellschaft, 1992, 22.

237 Heling, *Die Theologie Eivind Berggravs*, 24, 27.

238 Rasmussen, "Norsk kirkehistorie," 121.

239 Lindhardt, *Kirchengeschichte Skandinaviens*, 67.

religion and the offices of the State to the private practice of piety. They were connected with the aspiration to undermine the role of the State in theology as well as in religious practice.[240] This can be understood as resistance against absolutism.[241] Particularly Hans Nielsen Hauge (1771–1824) has been prominent in this context and may serve as an example of this broader movement.[242] The family home was considered to be a "private church".[243] But even the court decided in 1722 to sell Church property, including the churches,[244] so that the official church's importance was diminished. The followers of Hauge not only emphasised the importance of private piety, but also rejected the necessity of an ecclesiastical structure. Within the peace and stability of State order there was enough room for individual practice of devotion.[245] Perhaps we might add the opinion of the Bergen-born polyhistorian Ludvig Holberg (1684–1754) here: he emphasised the importance of the inner conviction for a Christian: "Børn maa gjøres til Mennesker, førend de blive Christne."[246] Children have to learn to doubt and to reason first, before they can be confronted with the principles of Christian faith. Everybody has to learn for himself what it takes to become an adult. Teaching Christian Theology too early would lead to uncritical followers ready to challenge other confessions. State authority in theological matters, therefore, is dangerous; religious convictions have to be left to the individual.

3.3.3 1814 and Beyond

Due to Danish centralisation, Norway had lost most of its own national administration during the union with Denmark. During the establishment of the constitution of 1814 at Eidsvoll, the state had to be re-invented under the modern concepts of constitution and human rights. Its famous art. 2 states[247]:

---

240 Rasmussen, "Norsk kirkehistorie," 145, 169.

241 Rasmussen, "Norsk kirkehistorie," 144.

242 Rasmussen, "Norsk kirkehistorie," 173.

243 Lindhardt, *Kirchengeschichte Skandinaviens*, 65.

244 Lindhardt, *Kirchengeschichte Skandinaviens*, 66.

245 Holze, Heinrich. Die Kirchen des Nordens in der Neuzeit (16. Bis 20. Jahrhundert), Kirchengeschichte in Einzeldarstellungen, III/11). Leipzig: Evangelische Verlagsanstalt, 2011, 142.

246 Holberg, Ludvig. Moralske Tanker. Book 1, epigram 5: Der er nødvendige, nyttige og skadelige studeringer [http://wayback-01.kb.dk/wayback/20101108104507/http://www2.kb.dk/elib/lit/dan/holberg/moralske.dkl/03.htm, last 17.10.2017] Aarhus: Aarhus Universitetsforlag, 1744. For the strong position of the house-father in Holbergs theory, cf. Søren Koch. "Holbergs naturreett i et funksjonelt perspektiv." In *Ludvig Holbergs Naturrett*, ed. Eiliv Vinje/J. M. Sejersted. Oslo: Tanum, 2012, 84.

247 https://www.stortinget.no/no/Stortinget-og-demokratiet/Lover-og-instrukser/Grunnloven-fra-1814, last visited 15 August 2017.

> §2. Den evangelisk-lutterske Religion forbliver Statens offentlige Religion. De Indvaanere, der bekjende sig til den, ere forpligtede til at opdrage sine Børn i samme. Jesuitter og Munkeordener maae ikke taales. Jøder ere fremdeles udelukkede fra Adgang til Riget. / The Evangelical Lutheran Religion shall remain the official religion of the State. Inhabitants who profess the same shall be required to educate their children therein. Jesuits and Monastic orders shall have no place in the realm.

According to this article, the Lutheran religion was the official religion of the State and children were to be raised in this confession. The same applied to all migrants who came to Norway. Jesuits and monks were not to be tolerated, nor were Jews allowed to enter the country. Furthermore, the King was obliged to be a member of the Lutheran church (art. 15). He had to convene all synods of the clergy (art.16).

For these reasons, many scholars saw a continuation of the old State church system of Danish absolutism.[248]. But the state itself had changed dramatically. The new Grundloven (Basic law/Constitution) established a constitutional state with the separation of powers, democracy, liberalism, fundamental rights and a constitutional monarch as fundamental principles.[249] Of course, religion was still seen as a necessary part of the state[250] as well as a precondition for individual piety, the possibility of making oaths and public morality. The unity of the people, as prescribed in the Gospel of St. John (17:21 "ut omnes unum sint"), was invoked in order to legitimise the constitution.[251] Indeed, in a time when nearly every Norwegian was a member of the Norwegian Lutheran Church, the Lutheran Church could be used to establish a key element that was common for all inhabitants. The confession helped to establish the unity of the modern Norwegian nation.

The original draft of the constitution included the fundamental right of religious liberty.[252] But this assertion was dropped in the final version. Was

---

248 Aarflot, *Kirke og stat i Norge*, 115; Bernt Torvild Oftestad, *Norsk Kirkehistorie*. Oslo: Universitetsforlaget, 2005, 181.

249 Brent Torvild Oftestad. "Religionen i Grunnloven – i kontekst og utvikling." In *Den Norske Grunnlovens Trosfundament – Grunnlovens §2 – Jødeparagrafen*, ed. Lorentz Stavrum/ Hans-Jørgen Wallin, Stavanger: Hertervig Akademisk, 2014, 22.

250 Oftestad, *Norsk Kirkehistorie* (n. 248), 181.

251 Mikael Hertzberg. "Die norwegische Kirche und die Einheit der Kirche." *Internationale kirchliche Zeitschrift* 11 (1921): 17–29, 28.

252 Frederick Hale. "The Norwegian Baptist Quest for Toleration." *Foundations* 22 (1979): 871, with a translation of this original draft of art.2, 1st sentence: "All citizens of the kingdom have freedom to practise their religion" [https://academic.oup.com/jcs/article-abstract/37/4/869/816670].

this just a slip in editing by the fathers of the constitution[253] or was this the consequence of the State Church and the banning of Jews and Catholics?[254] Or were the authors of the constitution even blind to the importance of this human right in the Danish tradition?[255]?Only recently, a more close reading of the article has revealed more convincing insights. The article refers to the "public religion" (*offentlig religion*) of Norway.[256] This invites an interpretation which separates public acts from private devotion. This is even more convincing if we consider this a special differentiation of the Norwegian tradition. This reading suggests that any private religious practice, as long as it did not touch on the public sphere, was unaffected by the constitution, which means that these other religions and confessions were neither threatened nor protected by the law.

The article lays down that religion remains ("forbliver") the same. But with the exception of the faith, almost everything changed at that time and hardly anything stayed as it was:[257] A new national State was attempting to establish a unity of its people and the principles for its legitimation. The focus was laid no longer on the preservation of the correct faith protected by an omnipotent monarch, but on fundamental rights and the possibility of religious plurality.[258] Indeed, the presence of Haugianism, Baptism, Quakers, and other groups that spread to the sea-faring nation constituted this plurality in practice.[259] It has been argued, therefore, that Norway had more religious freedom compared to other European countries, though the official recognition of the Roman-Catholic Church (1843), of other Christian communities (1845) and of Jews (1851) still took some time.[260] But this was rather the official recognition of what had previously been privately tolerated.[261]

---

253 Suggested by Lindhardt, *Kirchengeschichte Skandinaviens*, 97.

254 In this sense Hale, "The Norwegian Baptist Quest for Toleration", 871.

255 Dag Thorkildsen. "The Role of the Church in contemporary Norway: Changed Relations between State and Church." *Kirchliche Zeitgeschichte. Internationale Halbjahresschrift für Theologie und Geschichtswissenschaft* 25 (2012): 272–292.

256 Per Kristian Aschim. "Enige i tro til Dovre faller?" In *Den Norske Grunnlovens Trosfundament – Grunnlovens §2 – Jødeparagrafen*, ed. Lorentz Stavrum/Hans-Jørgen Wallin, Stavanger: Hertervig Akademisk, 2014, 51–71.

257 Oftestad, "Religionen i Grunnloven," 23.

258 Oftestad, "Religionen i Grunnloven," 26.

259 Lindhardt, *Kirchengeschichte Skandinaviens*, 102; Hertzberg, "Die norwegische Kirche und die Einheit der Kirche," 18.

260 Hale, "The Norwegian Baptist Quest for Toleration", 872.

261 Tuchtenhagen. *Kleine Geschichte Norwegens*, 128; Torkel Halvorsen Aschehough. *Norges nuværende Statsforfatning vol.* 2. Kristiania: P. T. Mallings Boghandels Forlag, 1885, 312, regarded Art.2 of the constitution as a basic guarantee of religious liberty with the exception of monk-orders and Jews.

In this tradition, in the 1814 constitution, the King of Norway had different duties compared to the traditional role of the Danish King. The King could only act together with the *statsraat* and the *Storthing* (Parliament) as the sovereign and he was bound by the law.[262] He represented the unity of his people in secular and ecclesiastical matters. This representation applied to public functions and the symbols for the unity of the country. But if our differentiation between public and private family practices is correct, the symbol of unity was never meant to prohibit particular practices of devotion in private. The traditional gap between the public sphere and private devotion suggests that the sphere of the inner conviction and practice within the families remained untouched by the new constitution.

The development of human rights over the last 200 years has been used to strengthen the rights of the individual. Reciprocally, it has become increasingly difficult for European societies to define what people have in common, what is necessary therefore for the maintenance of a national tradition, or how much new religions can ask for tolerance and acceptation. More than today it was felt necessary in the nineteenth century that people followed a common code of morals and conduct. Today we do not know if the proliferation in the number of laws can support such a union in beliefs and faiths.[263]

4. Summary

The Protestant Reformation was not only a movement of towns and merchants fostering their ambitions to obtain recognition as free imperial cities (*Freie Reichsstadt*), but also a movement aimed at strengthening all secular powers. Although the theology of Zwingli and Bugenhagen differed, the outcome of their teaching was not tremendously different in this respect. But the Reformation changed the power of the government dramatically for the political situation in the country. If we just look into the case of the church ordinance of Copenhagen in 1537 in isolation, we have to acknowledge the different paths opened by this law for its three territories, namely Denmark, Norway, and the duchies of Schleswig and Holstein:

---

262 Oftestad, "Religionen i Grunnloven," 23.

263 On this problem, cf. Tore Lindholm. "The Tenacity of Identity Politics in Norway. From Unabashed Lutheran Monopoly to Pseudo-Lutheran Semi-Hegemony?" In *Law and Religion in the 21st Century –Nordic Perspectives*, ed. Lisbet Christoffersen. Copenhagen: Norwegian Centre for Human Rights, 2010, 203–237.

1. In Schleswig and Holstein the establishment of a territorial Protestant church reinforced the administrative, religious and cultural cohesion of the two duchies, illustrated especially by the formation of new central authorities for the duchies. In Copenhagen, the duchies could defend their own *Tyske Kancelli*. The smooth introduction of the Reformation demonstrated that the respect for the local gentry and prelates strengthened the role of the estates (*Landtag*). Almost unified with his people, the Prince distanced the duchies more and more from Denmark. Moreover, Christian enhanced the political as well as cultural liaison with Saxony and the Empire. In the long run, the ordinance helped to install High German as the language of the administration. With its continued force until 1868, this church ordinance of 1542 helped to prepare the nineteenth century move away from Denmark.
2. In Denmark the abrupt and violent introduction of the Reformation not only helped to defeat the enemies of the King, but also to alter the constitution. The State Council had to yield to Christian III and the defeat of the Catholic bishops and their allies brought him the wealth and the power not only to introduce the Reformation, but to concentrate political power on himself. The King as protector of the correct faith became the authority to decide in ecclesiastical and secular matters. This clearly helped to install absolutism in Denmark in the following century.
3. The little practical effect of the 1537 ordinance in Norway in the first generation opened a gap between the State in theory and the people's faith. Even when the remaining pockets of Roman-Catholicism were slowly extinguished, there was still distance to the court at Copenhagen. The success of different Pietist groups illustrated the gap between private practice and the State Church. The Eidsvoll constitution in 1814 was not a continuance of Danish absolutism, but rather the expression of national characteristics. Of course a public religion was still seen as necessary for the maintenance of faith, oaths and public order. As almost all Norwegians were united in the Lutheran faith, the declaration of a State Church was meant more as the expression of a national identity. Within a constitutional system and fundamental rights, the difference between public life and private confessions could be maintained and protected by the new constitution.

As derived from ideas developed at Wittenberg, all three enactments can be regarded as legal transitions. The success in Denmark or in Schleswig–Holstein can hardly be explained, if we expect failures in legal transition as in Norway alone. And the "German" church ordinance hardly explains its success in Denmark.

Several historians have tried to establish patterns for the effects of the Protestant Reformation on states.[264] Mostly, case studies have to serve as examples.[265] Increasing precision in the description of individual protagonists of the Reformation and their changing ideas in the course of time cannot be wrong, of course, but it does not help to establish such general characteristics. The analysis presented here proves that we should be aware of the individuality of these developments. Each country received the Reformation in different ways; generalisations seem more and more unreliable or even impossible. Even one Reformer or a single church ordinance alone could have different, even contradictory effects. These developments responded more to the current political situation of the country when the Reformation was introduced.

The Reformations in Zurich and Hamburg are similar in their effects on the magistrature, even though we noted considerable discrepancies between the theologies of Zwingli and Bugenhagen. Although Hamburg could not claim to be a divine institution, it was rather more concerned with legislation. Does this mean that we should not overrate the significance of theological teaching? We cannot be certain, furthermore, that the effects on centralisation and administration, documented in the cases of Schleswig-Holstein, Denmark and even Hamburg, can be linked with Lutheranism, as it was proposed around 1600 by Calvinists at Emden,[266] as countries with a dominating Calvinist confession like the General States did not hesitate to introduce administrative innovations.

Certainly, in a very abstract way we can state that Protestant Reformation strengthened secular government, which took over the competence over matters, even in ecclesiastical matters. The concentration of power often led to the development of new administrations. Moreover, the competencies of the secular governments led to concern for financial matters and for effective ways to cope with the increasing obligations. Techniques of governance and the quest for educated personnel helped to establish a new class of civil servants and bureaucracy. But the closer we look, the more we discover how divergent the

264 Cf. Eike Wolfgast. "Formen landesfürstlicher Reformation in Deutschland. Kursachsen-Württemberg/Brandenburg-Kurpfalz." In: *Die dänische Reformation vor ihrem internationalen Hintergrund*, ed. L. Grane/K. Hørby. Göttingen: Vandenhoeck & Ruprecht, 1990, 57–90, without clarification of such patterns.

265 Recently, but a less academic and more popularized way, and leaving legal history out of focus cf. Volker Reinhardt. "Luther in Europa – Umrisse einer Wirkungsgeschichte" In *Der Luther Effekt. 500 Jahre Protestantismus in der Welt.* Munich: Manz, 2017, 22–29. In this exhibition and book, Sweden is selected as a model of a Nordic Protestant monarchy. Gustav Vasa himself rather tried to follow a "via media", cf. Nyberg, "Das religiöse Profil des Nordens," 292, this example might be ill chosen.

266 Schmoeckel, "Zwischen Idealstaat und Realismus," 186.

effects were: The Protestant Reformation could help to strengthen communities such as the towns, which on this point regarded themselves as democracies, it strengthened the aristocracy of the estates in Schleswig–Holstein, and helped to install absolutism in Denmark. With the common term of "Obrigkeit", many protagonist of the Reformation demonstrated their disregard for the specific and real form of government.

At least we find that the introduction of the Reformation had dramatic effects in each case and left nobody unaffected. Perhaps we should expect no more effects of the Reformation than a tendency to enhance local traditions. With regard to these particularities of the regions and countries of Europe, we should be open for a completely new understanding of the effects of Reformation in Europe, not looking for traits in common, but for the enriching multitude of religious and cultural pluralism.

Bibliography

Aarflot, Andreas. "Das bischöfliche Amt." *Zeitschrift für evangelisches Kirchenrecht* 51 (2006): 505–533.

Aarflot, Andreas. *Kirke og stat i Norge, Fra reformatsjonen til våre dager*. Stavanger: Nomi, 1969.

Andersen, J. Oskar. *Overfor kirkebruddet: den første Lutherske bevægelse og Christiern II's Forhold dertil*. Copenhagen: Universitetsbogtrykkeriet, 1917.

Arffman, Kaarlo. "The Lutheran Reform of Poor Relief: A Historical and Legal Viewpoint." In *Lutheran Reformation and the Law*, ed. V. Mäkinen. Leiden/ Boston: Brill, 2006.

Arnisaeus, Henning. *De iure maiestatis libri tres*. Frankfurt: Johann Thieme, 1610.

Aschehough, Torkel Halvorsen. *Norges nuværende Statsforfatning vol. 2*. Kristiania: P. T. Mallings Boghandels Forlag, 1885.

Aschim, Per Kristian. "Enige i tro til Dovre faller?" In *Den Norske Grunnlovens Trosfundament – Grunnlovens §2 – Jødeparagrafen*, ed. Lorentz Stavrum / Hans-Jørgen Wallin, Stavanger: Hertervig Akademisk, 2014.

Basse, Michael. "Luthers Kreuzestheologie und ihre Rezeption in der Evangelischen Theologie des 20. Jahrhunderts." In *Glaube und Lernen* 27 (2012): 33–44.

Beckey, Kurt. *Die Reformation in Hamburg*. Hamburg: Boysen Verlag, 1929.

Bieber, Anneliese. *Johannes Bugenhagen zwischen Reform und Reformation. Die Entwicklung seiner frühen Theologie anhand des Matthäuskommentars und der Passions- und Auferstehungsharmonie*. Göttingen: Vandenhoeck & Ruprecht, 1992.

Bugenhagen, Johannes. *Der ehrbaren Stadt Hamburg christliche Ordnung 1529*. reprint Hamburg: Wittig, 1976.

Bugenhagen, Johannes. *Johannes Bugenhagen, Pomeranus: Leben und ausgewählte Schriften*. Elberfeld: Friderichs, 1867.

Bugenhagen, Johannes. *Ungedruckte Predigten Johann Bugenhagens aus den Jahren 1524 bis 1529*. Leipzig: M. Heinsius, 1910.

Campi, Emidio / Wälchli, Philipp (eds.). *Zürcher Kirchenordnungen 1520–1675 vol. 1.* & 2. Zurich: Theologischer Verlag, 2011.

Elck, Paul Leemann-van. "Froschauer Christoph der Ältere." *Neue Deutsche Biographie* 5 (1961): 664–665.

Elliott, Quam John / Ericssøn, Jørgen. *A Study in the Norwegian Reformation 1571–1604* (Ph.D. Thesis). Yale University, 1969.

Fink-Jensen, Morten. "Kristendom, skole og pædagogik Danmark før 1700." In *Reformationen i danks kirke og kultur, Bind 1: 1517–1700*, eds. Niels Henrik Gregersen/ Carsten Bach-Nielsen. Odense: Syddansk Universitetsforlag, 2017.

Gäbler, Ulrich. *Huldrych Zwingli: Eine Einführung in sein Leben und sein Werk*. Munich: C.H. Beck, 1983.

Gøbel, Erik / Sprauten, Knut. *Kommenteret bibliografi til dansk-norsk historie 1536–1814 især vedrørende centraladministrationen*. Copenhagen/ Oslo: Rigsarkivet, 1997.

Göbell, Walter. "Das Vordringen der Reformation in Dänemark und in den Herzogtümern unter der Regierung Friedrichs I. 1523–1533." In *Schleswig-Holsteinische Kirchengeschichte, vol. 3: Reformation*. Neumünster: Wachholtz, 1982.

Göbell, Walter. "Die Anfänge der Reformation in Dänemark und in den Herzogtümern Schleswig und Holstein unter Herzog und König Friedrich I." In *Schleswig-Holsteinische Kirchengeschichte, vol. 3: Reformation*. Neumünster: Wachholtz, 1982.

Göbell, Walter (ed.). *Die Schleswig-Holsteinische Kirchenordnung von 1542*. Neumünster: Wachholtz Verlag, 1986.

Grane, Leif. "Teaching the People – the Education of the Clergy and the Instruction of the People in the Danish Reformation Church." In *Die dänische Reformation vor ihrem internationalen Hintergrund. The Danish Reformation against its International Background*, ed. idem/ K. Hørby. Göttingen: Vandenhoeck & Ruprecht, 1990.

Grell, Ole Peter. "The Emergence of Two Cities: The Reformation in Malmø and Cogenhagen." In *Die dänische Reformation vor ihrem internationalen Hintergrund*, eds. L. Grane/ K. Hørby. Göttingen: Vandenhoeck&Ruprecht, 1990.

Haas, Martin. *Huldrych Zwingli und seine Zeit, Leben und Werk des Zürcher Reformators*. Zurich: Theologischer Verlag, 1969.

Hale, Frederick. "The Norwegian Baptist Quest for Toleration." https://academic.oup.com/jcs/article-abstract/37/4/869/816670 (1979).

Hamm, Berndt. *Zwinglis Reformation der Freiheit*. Neukirchen-Vluyn: Neukirchener Verlag, 1988.

Hamre, Lars. *Norsk politisk historie 1513–1537*. Oslo: Universitetforlaget, 1998.

Hauschildt, Wolf-Dieter. "Die Reformation in Hamburg, Lübeck und Eutin." In *Schleswig-Holsteinische Kirchengeschichte, No. 3: Reformation.* Neumünster: Matthiesen, 1982.

Heckel, Johannes. *Lex charitatis. 2. Ed.* Cologne/ Vienna: Böhlau, 1973.

Heckel, Martin. *Martin Luthers Reformation und das Recht.* Tübingen: Mohr Siebeck, 2016.

Heling, Arnd. *Die Theologie Eivind Berggravs im norwegischen Kirchenkamp: Ein Beitrag zur politischen Theologie im Luthertum (Historisch-theologische Studien zum 19. und 20. Jahrhundert, 3).* Neukirchen-Vlyun: Neukirchener Verlagsgesellschaft, 1992.

Hertzberg, Mikael. "Die norwegische Kirche und die Einheit der Kirche." *Internationale kirchliche Zeitschrift* 11 (1921): 17–29.

Holze, Heinrich. Die Kirchen des Nordens in der Neuzeit (16. Bis 20. Jahrhundert), Kirchengeschichte in Einzeldarstellungen, III/11). Leipzig: Evangelische Verlagsanstalt, 2011.

Höpfl, Harro. "Luther and Calvin on Secular Authority." *Cambridge Texts in the History of Political Thought.* Cambridge: Cambridge University Press, 1991.

Hørby, Kai. "Humanist Profiles in the Danish Reform Movement." In *Teaching the People – The education of the Clergy and the Instruction of the People in the Danish Reformation Church: Die dänische Reformation vor ihrem internationalen Hintergrund,* eds. L. Grane/ K. Hørby: Göttingen: Vandenhoeck & Ruprecht, 1990.

Hoffmann, Erich. "Der Sieg der Reformation in den Herzogtümern Schleswig und Holstein." In *Schleswig-Holsteinische Kirchengeschichte, Volume 3: Reformation.* Neumünster: Wachholtz, 1982.

Holberg, Ludvig. Moralske Tanker. Book 1, epigram 5: Der er nødvendige, nyttige og skadelige studeringer [http://wayback-01.kb.dk/wayback/20101108104507/http://www2.kb.dk/elib/lit/dan/holberg/moralske.dkl/03.htm, last 17.10.2017] Aarhus: Aarhus Universitetsforlag, 1744.

Holfelder, Hans Hermann. *Solus Christus, Die Ausbildung von Bugenhagens Rechtfertigungslehre in der Paulusauslegung (1524/25) und ihre Bedeutung für die theologische Argumentation im Sendbrief "Von dem christlichen Glauben" (1526): Eine Untersuchung zur Genese von Bugenhagens Theologie.* Tübingen: Mohr Siebeck, 1981.

Jensen, Birgit Bjerre. *Udnævnelses retten I enevældens magtpolitiske system 1660–1730.* Viborg: Jurist – og Økonomsforbundet Forlag 1987.

Jørgensen, Jens Ulf. "Kirkeretten i Danske Lov." In *Danske og Norske Lov I 300 år: Festskirftet er udgivet I anledning af 300året for udstedelsen af Christian V's Danske Lov,* ed. D. Tamm. Viborg: Jurist – og Økonomsforbundet Forlag, 1983.

Kittelson, James M. "Learning and Education: Phase Two of the Reformation." In *Die dänische Reformation vor ihrem internationalen Hintergrund,* eds. L. Grane/ K. Hørby. Göttingen: Vandenhoeck & Ruprecht, 1990.

Koch, Søren. "Holbergs naturreett i et funksjonelt perspektiv." In *Ludvig Holbergs Naturrett*, ed. Eiliv Vinje / J. M. Sejersted. Oslo: Tanum, 2012.

Koch, Traugott. "'Der Ehrbaren Stadt Hamburg Christliche Ordnung' durch Johannes Bugenhagen (1529)." In *500 Jahre Theologie in Hamburg. Hamburg als Zentrum christlicher Theologie und Kultur zwischen Tradition und Zukunft: Arbeiten zur Kirchengeschichte, 95*), ed. J. A. Steiger. Berlin / New York: deGruyter, 2005.

Kötter, Ralf. *Johannes Bugenhagens Rechtfertigungslehre und der römische Katholizismus Studien zum Sendbrief an die Hamburger (1525)*. Göttingen: Vandenhoeck & Ruprecht, 1994.

Koht, Halvdan. *Artikelen om Norge i den Danske handfest ningafra 1536: (Norsk) Historisk tidsskrift 30*. Oslo: Universitetforlaget, 1936.

Koht, Halvdan. *Olav Engelbriktsson og Sjølvstende-Tapet 1537*. Oslo: Aschehoug, 1951.

Oluf Kolsrud. *"Den norske Kirkes Mindeskrift ved Reformationens 400-Aars-Jubilæum Aar 1917: Utkast til en norsk Kirkeordinants efter Kong Christian IVs Befaling forfattet av Norges Superintendenter i Aaret 1604*. Christiania: 1917

Lange, Ulrich. "Stände, Landesherr und Große Politik." In *Geschichte Schleswig-Holsteins: Von den Anfängen bis zur Gegenwart, 2nd ed.*, ed. idem. Neumünster: C.H. Beck, 2003.

Leder, Hans-Günter. *Johannes Bugenhagen Pomeranus – nachgelassene Studien zur Biographie*. Frankfurt am Main: Peter Lang, 2008.

Leder, Hans-Günter. *Johannes Bugenhagen Pomeranus – vom Reformer zum Reformator*. Frankfurt am Main: Peter Lang, 2002.

Lietzmann, Hans (ed.). *Die Wittenberger und Leisniger Kastenordnung: 1522, 1523*. Bonn: Nabu Press 1907.

Lindhardt, Poul Georg. *Kirchengeschichte Skandinaviens*. Göttingen: Evangelische Verlagsanstalt, 1983.

Lindholm, Tore. "The Tenacity of Identity Politics in Norway. From Unabashed Lutheran Monopoly to Pseudo-Lutheran Semi-Hegemony?" In *Law and Religion in the 21st Century –Nordic Perspectives*, ed. Lisbet Christoffersen. Copenhagen: Norwegian Centre for Human Rights, 2010.

Locher, Gottfried Wilhelm. *Die Zwinglische Reformation im Rahmen der europäischen Kirchengeschichte*. Göttingen: Vandenhoeck & Ruprecht, 1979.

Locher, Gottfried Wilhelm. "Huldrych Zwingli." In *Die Reformationszeit I.: Gestalten der Kirchengeschichte 5*, ed. Martin Greschat. Stuttgart: Kohlhammer, 1988.

Lohse, Bernhard. "Humanismus und Reformation in norddeutschen Städten in den 20er und frühen 30er Jahren des 16. Jahrhunderts." In *Die dänische Reformation vor ihrem internationalen Hintergrund*, eds. L. Grane / K. Hørby. Göttingen: Vandenhoeck & Ruprecht, 1990.

Lorentzen, Tim. *Johannes Bugenhagen als Reformator der öffentlichen Fürsorge.* Tübingen: Mohr Siebeck, 2008.

Ludolphy, Ingetraut. "Friedrich der Weise." *Theologische Realenzyklopädie* 11 (1983): 666–669.

Lück, Heiner. "Prudentia legislatorial: Regelungssystematik und Regelungstechnik in den Kirchenordnungen Johannes Bugenhagens." In *Johannes Bugenhagen (1485–1558): Der Bischof der Reformation*, eds. I. Garbe/H. Kröger. Leipzig: Evangelische Verlagsanstalt, 2007.

Luther, Martin. "Von weltlicher Uberkeytt wie weyt man yhr gehorsam schuldig sey (1523)." In *Martin Luthers Werke. Kritische Gesamtausgabe. vol. 11: Predigten und Schriften 1523*, ed. Heidelberger Akademie der Wissenschaften. Weimar: Universitätsverlag Winter, 1900.

Lyby, Throkild / Grell, Ole Peter. "The consolidation of Lutherism in Denmark and Norway." In *The Scandinavian Reformation*, ed. O. P. Grell. Cambridge: Cambridge University Press, 1995.

Mulsow, Martin. "Johann Christoph Wolf (1683–1739) und die verbotenen Bücher." In *500 Jahre Theologie in Hamburg: Hamburg als Zentrum christlicher Theologie und Kultur zwischen Tradition und Zukunft: Arbeiten zur Kirchengeschichte No. 95*, ed. J. A. Steiger. Berlin/ New York: deGruyter, 2005.

Montgomery, Ingun / Birkeflet, Svein Helge. "Norwegen." *Theologische Realenzyklopädie* 24 (1994): 643–659.

Nyberg, Tore. "Das religiöse Profil des Nordens – Die Entwicklung von Kirchlichkeit und Frömmigkeit in den skandinavischen Ländern vom Späten Mittelalter bis zum konfessionellen Zeitalter." In *Dänemark, Norwegen und Schweden im Zeitalter der Reformation und Konfessionalisierung: Nordische Königreiche und Konfession 1500 bis 1660 (Katholisches Leben und Kirchenreform im Zeitalter der Glaubensspaltung,* 62), eds. M. Asche/ A. Schindling. Münster: Aschendorff, 2003, 245–310.

Oftestad, Brent Torvild. "Religionen i Grunnloven – i kontekst og utvikling." In *Den Norske Grunnlovens Trosfundament – Grunnlovens §2 – Jødeparagrafen*, ed. Lorentz Stavrum / Hans-Jørgen Wallin, Stavanger: Hertervig Akademisk, 2014.

Olesen, Jens. "Staat und Stadt – über die Rolle der Landesväter und Behörden im Denken und Handeln Johannes Bugenhagens." In *Johannes Bugenhagen (1485–1558): Der Bischof der Reformation.* eds. I. Garbe/H. Kröger. Leipzig: 2007.

Olesen, Jens Ejnar. "Dänemark, Norwegen und Island." In *Dänemark, Norwegen und Schweden im Zeitalter der Reformation und Konfessionalisierung. Nordische Königreiche und Konfession 1500 bis 1660: Katholisches Leben und Kirchenreform im Zeitalter der Glaubensspaltung No. 62*, eds. Matthias Asche/ Anton Schindling. Münster: Aschendorff, 2003.

Olsen, Max W. *Den danske Kirkeordinants af 1539 og andre Aktstykker vedrørende den lutherske Kirkereformations Inaførelse i Danmark.* Copenhagen: Akademisk Forlag, 1936.

Park, Chang Soo. "Luthertum und Obrigkeit im Alten Reich in der Frühen Neuzeit: Dargestellt am Beispiel von Tilemann Heshusius (1527–1588)." *Historische Forschungen* 109 (2016): 15–29.

Rasmussen, Tarald, *Norsk Kirkehistorie, 3rd ed.*, eds. Bernt T. Oftestad/ Tarald Rasmussen/ Jan Schumacher. Oslo: Universitetsforlaget, 2005.

Rasmussen, Tarald. "Utkastet til en egen norsk kirke ordinans fra 1604." In *Reformationens konsolidering i de nordiska länderna 1540–1610*, ed. I. Brohed. Oslo: Universitetforlaget, 1990.

Reinhardt, Volker. "Luther in Europa – Umrisse einer Wirkungsgeschichte." In *Der Luther Effekt. 500 Jahre Protestantismus in der Welt.* Munich: Manz, 2017.

Repgen, Tilmann. "Art. Hamburg." In *Handwörterbuch zur Deutschen Rechtsgeschichte, vol. 2, 2nd ed.* ed. Albrecht Corded et al. Berlin: E. Schmidt, 2012.

Richter, Aemilius Ludwig. *Die evangelischen Kirchenordnungen des sechzehnten Jahrhunderts. Bd. 1: Vom Anfange der Reformation bis zur Begründung der Consistorial-Verfassung im Jahr 1542.* Weimar: Verlag des Landes-Industriecomptoirs, 1846.

Rørdam, Holger Fr. *Danske kirkelove samt udvalg af andre Bestemmelser, Part 3: 1596–1683.* Copenhagen: Nabu Press, 1889.

Schäfer, Dietrich. *Geschichte von Dänemark, vol. 4.* Gotha: F. Perthes, 1893.

Scheible, Heinz. *Melanchthon: Vermittler der Reformation: Eine Biographie.* Munich: C.H. Beck, 2016.

Schmoeckel, Mathias. *Das Recht der Reformation.* Tübingen: Mohr Siebeck, 2015.

Schmoeckel, Mathias. "Eine neue Konzeption des Rechts durch die Reformation." In *Reformation. Impulsgeber für die Moderne?*, eds. A. Lindemann/ Chr. Ammer. Leipzig: Evangelische Verlangsanstalt, 2017.

Schmoeckel, Mathias. "Leges et in carmina redigendae sunt: Die Erfindung der Kodifikation als Konzept durch Melanchthon und deren Rezeption in katholischen Staaten bis 1811." *Zeitschrift für Rechtsgeschichte: Kanonistische Abteilung* 126 (2009): 397–436.

Schmoeckel, Mathias. "Zwischen Idealstaat und Realpolitik: Machiavellismus in Ostfriesland um 1600. Des Ostfriesischen Cantzelars Thomae Frantzij Getreuwer Rath." In *Jurisprudenz, Politische Theorie und Politische Theologie (Beiträge zur Politischen Wissenschaft, 131)*, ed. F. S. Carney/ H. Schilling/ D. Wyduckel. Berlin: Duncker & Humboldt, 2004.

Schreiner, Johan. *Norges-artikkelen i Christian IIIs håndfestning, (Norsk) Historisk tidsskrift 30*, Oslo: Unviersitetsforlaget, 1934–1936.

Schwaiger, Georg. *Die Reformation in den nordischen Ländern*. Munich: Kösel, 1962.

Schwarz Lausten, Martin. "Kirchenordnungen in Dänemark-Norwegen in der Reformationszeit." In *Ordnungen für die Kirche – Wirkungen auf die Welt: Spätmittelalter, Humanismus, Reformation No. 84*, eds. S. Arend/ G. Dörner. Tübingen: Mohr Siebeck, 2015.

Schwarz Lausten, Martin. "Kirkens nye ordninger." In *Reformationen i dansk kirke og kultur, Bind 1: 1517–1700*, eds. Niels Henrik Gregersen/ Carsten Bach-Nielsen. Odense: Syddansk Universitetsforlag, 2017.

Schwarz Lausten, Martin/Forord (ed.). *Kirkeordinansen 1537/39*. Denmark: deGruyter, 1989.

Schwarz Lausten, Martin. "Kongemagt og rigets vel." In *Reformationen i dansk kirke og kultur, Bind 1: 1517–1700*, ed. Niels Henrik Gregersen/ Carsten Bach-Nielsen. Odense: Syddansk Universitetsforlag, 2017.

Schwarz Lausten, Martin. "König und Kirche. Über das Verhältnis der westlichen Obrigkeit zur Kirche bei Johannes Bugenhagen und König Christian III. von Dänemark." In *Johannes Bugenhagen – Gestalt und Wirkung*. Berlin: Evangelische Verlagsanstalt, 1984.

Schwarz Lausten, Martin. "The early Reformation in Denmark and Norway 1520–1559." In *The Scandinavian Reformation*, ed. O. P. Grell. Cambridge: Cambridge University Press, 1995.

Schwarz Lausten, Martin. "Weltliche Obrigkeit und Kirche bei König Christian III. von Dänemark (1536–1559). Hintergründe und Folgen." In *Die dänische Reformation vor ihrem internationalen Hintergrund. The Danish Reformation against its International Background*, eds. idem/ K. Hørby. Göttingen: Vandenhoeck & Ruprecht, 1990.

Schorn-Schütter, Luise. *Perspectum: Ausgewählte Aufsätze zur Frühen Neuzeit und Historiographiegeschichte anlässlich ihres 65. Geburtstages*. Munich: Oldenbourg Verlag, 2014.

Seegrün, Wolfgang. "Schleswig-Holstein." In *Die Territorien des Reichs im Zeitalter der Reformation und Konfessionalisierung. Land und Konfession 1500–1650, vol. 2: Der Nordosten – Katholisches Leben und Kirchenreform im Zeitalter der Glaubensspaltung No. 50*, eds. A. Schindling/ W. Ziegler. Münster: Aschendorff, 1990.

Sprengler-Ruppenthal, Anneliese. "Bugenhagen und das protestantische Kirchenrecht." In *Zeitschrift für Rechtsgeschichte: Kanonistische Abteilung* 57 (1971): 299–301.

Steen, Sverre. "Den Dansk-Norske Forbindelse 1536–1814." In *Omstridte Spørgsmaal I Nordens Historie, vol. 1*, ed. W. Carlgren et al. Copenhagen: Gads 1940.

Tamm, Ditlev. *Retshistorie: Danmark – Europa – globale perspektiver*. Copenhagen: jursit – og Økonomsforbuddet Forlag, 2005.

Tamm, Ditlev. "Law and Protestantism in Denmark." *Zeitschrift für Rechtsgeschichte: Kanonistische Abteilung* 102 (2016): 406–418.

Thorkildsen, Dag. "The Role of the Church in contemporary Norway: Changed Relations between State and Church." *Kirchliche Zeitgeschichte. Internationale Halbjahresschrift für Theologie und Geschichtswissenschaft* 25 (2012): 272–292.

Tuchtenhagen, Ralph. *Kleine Geschichte Norwegens*. Munich: C.H. Beck, 2009.

Vainio, Olli-Pekka. *Justification and Participation in Christ. The Development of the Lutheran Doctrine of Justification from Luther to the Formula of Concord (1580)*. Leiden/ Boston: Brill, 2008.

Vogt, Karl August Traugott. *Johannes Bugenhagen Pomeranus*. Elberfeld: Friderichs, 1867.

Vogt, Otto. *Dr. Johannes Bugenhagens Briefwechsel*, Hildesheim: Georg Olms, 1966.

von Friedeburg, Robert. "Das Gewissen in den Rechtslehren der protestantischen und katholischen Reformationen/ Conscience in the Legal Teachings of the Protestant and Catholic Reformations." In *Leucorea-Studien zur Geschichte der Reformation und der Lutherischen Orthodoxie, 31*, ed. W. Decock/ M. Germann. Leipzig: Evangelische Verlangsanstalt, 2017.

Weber, Sybille. *Die Stellung Hamburgs in der Verfassung des Alten Deutschen Reichs*. Diss.jur. Bonn/Munich: Hut, 2005/2007.

Weimer, Christoph. *Luther, Cranach und die Bilder, Gesetz und Evangelium – Schlüssel zum reformatorischen Bildgebrauch*, Stuttgart: Calwer, 1999.

Wenn, Hans. "Johannes Bugenhagens Hamburger Ordenige. Beiträge zu ihrer Entstehung und Überlieferung." In *Johannes Bugenhagen: Der Ehrbaren Stadt Hamburg Christliche Ordnung 1529*. Hamburg: Wittig, 1976.

Wilsson, Thomas B. *History of the Church and State in Norway: From the Tenth to the Sixteenth Century*. Westminster: Bibliolife, 1903.

Wisløff, Carl Fr. *Norsk Kirkehistorie*. Oslo: Universitetsforlaget, 1966.

Witte, John jr. *Law and Protestantism: The legal Teaching of Luther's Reformation*. Cambridge: Cambridge University Press, 2002.

Wolfgast, Eike. "Formen landesfürstlicher Reformation in Deutschland. Kursachsen-Württemberg/ Brandenburg-Kurpfalz." In: *Die dänische Reformation vor ihrem internationalen Hintergrund*, ed. L. Grane/ K. Hørby. Göttingen: Vandenhoeck & Ruprecht, 1990.

Ziegler, Walter. "Braunschweig-Lüneburg- Hildesheim." In *Die Territorien des Reichs im Zeitalter der Reformation und Konfessionalisierung: Land und Konfession 1500–1650, Volume 3: Der Nordwesten: Katholisches Leben und Kirchenreform im Zeitalter der Glaubensspaltung 51*, eds. A. Schindling/ W. Ziegler. Münster: Aschendorff, 1991.

Zwingli, Huldrych. "Aktenstücke zur ersten Zürcher Disputation: I, Die 67 Artikel Zwinglis." In *Huldreich Zwinglis sämtliche Werke. vol. 1: Corpus Reformatorum No. 88*, ed. Emil Egil. Berlin: Schwetschke, 1905.

Zwingli, Huldrych. "De vera et falsa religione commentarius, [März 1525]." *Huldreich Zwinglis sämtliche Werke vol. 3: Corpus Reformatorum No. 90*, ed. Emil Egil. Leipzig: Heinsius 1914, 628–911.

Zwingli, Huldrych. "Eine kurze christliche Einleitung [17.11.1523]." *Huldreich Zwinglis sämtliche Werke vol. 2: Corpus Reformatorum No. 89*, ed. Emil Egil. Leipzig: Heinsius, 1908.

Zwingli, Huldrych. "Von Erkiesen und Freiheit der Speisen." In *Huldreich Zwinglis sämtliche Werke vol. 1: Corpus Reformatorum No. 88*, ed. Emil Egil. Berlin: Schwetschke, 1905.

Zwingli, Huldrych. "Von götlicher und menschlicher gerechtigheit, wie die zemen schind und standind." In *Huldreich Zwinglis sämtliche Werke. vol. 1: Corpus Reformatorum No. 88*, ed. Emil Egil. Berlin: Schwetschke, 1905.

Church Law and Reformation

Comparing Denmark and Sweden

Tarald Rasmussen

New church law was introduced in Denmark and Sweden after the Reformation. This new legislation was part of the Reformation process in the two countries, both of which belonged to the "Lutheran North", and might be looked upon as Lutheran peripheries far away from the centres in Germany. At the same time, it could be argued that the political and cultural impact of the Lutheran Reformation was particularly strong precisely in these two countries. A comparison of early Reformation church law in Denmark and Sweden is therefore an interesting point of departure for identifying significant differences in their confessional profiles.

1. Denmark

The Danish Reformation took place in 1536, with the Lutheran Reformation in Wittenberg as its model. The new Lutheran King Christian III invited Johann Bugenhagen from Wittenberg to Copenhagen. Bugenhagen, who lived with his family for nearly two years in Copenhagen (1537–38), had a major influence not only on the new Danish church law, the Church ordinance of 1537–39, but also on questions relating to how to put new ideals of church legislation and church organization into practice.

Copenhagen emerged as a northern epicentre of the Lutheran Reformation.[1] The new Lutheran kingdom was characterized by a political and ecclesiastical elite educated in Wittenberg under Luther and even more under Melanchthon. Also from a German point of view the Danish Reformation kings were looked upon as exemplary Lutheran rulers. This is true not only of the Danish Reformation King Christian III, who ruled until 1559, but also of his

1 An overview of the cultural profiles and the religious centres of the Nordic Reformations is available in the chapter Tarald Rasmussen: "Reformasjonen i Norden", in: Tarald Rasmussen and Ola Tjørhom (Eds.): *Reformasjonen i nytt lys*, Oslo: Cappelen Damm akademisk, p. 111–138.

 | DOI:10.30965/9783657790746_005

son Frederik II (King 1559–1598) who was a devout Lutheran with close connections to the Lutheran elites in Saxony.[2]

In a legal perspective, Denmark is an interesting case due to its similarity to a number of Lutheran states in the German Empire, on the one hand, and its position as not being part of this empire, on the other. The similarity to Lutheran landscapes and cities in Germany was established by the new church legislation. Bugenhagen was a key figure in this respect, not only in Denmark, but also in Pomerania, Wittenberg, Lübeck and Braunschweig.[3] But Denmark was different from all these places since the Danish King had no obligation to pay heed to the legislation of the German Empire. Even though he held the position as a count of Haderslev in southern Jutland and therefore was entitled to take part in the Diet of the Empire, he was first of all the King of the independent double monarchy of Denmark and Norway. In this position, he was entitled to pass laws for his kingdom as he wanted. While since the late 1520s Lutheran princes and city councils in Germany always had to comply with the decisions of the empire Diets and their changing regulation of the relationship between the Catholic and the Lutheran territories, Christian III was free to enact laws from a Lutheran perspective as a key instrument for putting Lutheran ideals into social practice.

For these reasons, it is tempting to look upon early modern Denmark – with its unchallenged confessional profile, consequently supported by the King and successfully promoted in almost all parts of society – as a kind of ideal type of a Lutheran state.

2. Sweden

Seventeenth century Sweden (with Finland and the diocese of Åbo) was not a Lutheran model state like Denmark. In Sweden, the Reformation became a dominant political force when Gustav Vasa was confirmed as King in 1523. But he was not a committed and devout Lutheran like his colleague in Copenhagen. In Sweden, no early and consequential change in legislation took place, and no Lutheran church ordinance was passed until decades later. For Gustav Vasa, the most immediate Reformation change to be addressed was the confiscation

2 Frederik's sister Anna was married to August of Saxony, one of the political leaders of German Lutheranism, and resided as the wife of the elector in Dresden.

3 A recently updated analysis of Bugenhagen's work on the ordinances in Germany and in Denmark is Jens E. Olesen's: "Johannes Bugenhagens kirkeordnende virksomhed og syn på øvrigheden", in: *Religion som forklaring? Kirke og religion i stat og samfund, Festskrift til Per Ingesman*, Aarhus: Aarhus Universitetsforlag 2018, p. 179–194.

of church goods. Through the "reduction" of ecclesiastical property, the King expropriated the buildings and lands of the bishops and the monasteries.[4]

At the same time, this confiscation was not – like it was in Denmark – accompanied by a subsequent opposition to Catholic theology, Catholic Church law and traditional Catholic ways of thinking. Instead, the old and the new were allowed to co-exist for more than 70 years until a new Lutheran church law was finally passed. The main course was certainly defined as Lutheran, but concessions were regularly made to Catholic traditions and Catholic practices.

This was particularly the case during the reign of Johan III, the son of Gustav Vasa. He was married to the Polish princess Katarina Jagellonica in 1562. She was a Catholic, and in her wedding contract she was granted the right to practise her Catholic religion. When she became Queen of Sweden in 1568, she enjoyed several confessional privileges. These included the permanent presence of a Catholic confessor at the royal castle in Stockholm, maintaining contacts to Rome, the right to raise her son Stephan (later King of Poland) in the Catholic faith and the liberty to support the Birgittine Nuns in Vadstena as long as she lived. After her death, she was laid to rest in a separate Jagellonica chapel in Uppsala Cathedral, where regular masses were celebrated for her soul.

Not until the so-called Uppsala Meeting in 1593 did the ambivalent confessional course in Sweden come to an end. In Denmark, a Lutheran church law had been confirmed with the support of Bugenhagen immediately after the Reformation. In Sweden drafts of the new legislation had been discussed and revised for more than 20 years prior to 1593. Reforming the University of Uppsala in terms of the Reformation was also postponed until after 1593. Only after this late definitive turn to Lutheranism did Sweden transform into an important Lutheran power, as could be fully demonstrated by the thirty years' war.

This preliminary comparative overview first draws attention to the different confessional profiles of the two kingdoms during the seventeenth century. Moreover, another and perhaps even more interesting structural difference between the two kingdoms comes to our attention: the relationship between royal power and church hierarchy. In Denmark, from 1536 on, the church was redefined as an instrument of a King responsible for the political and religious

4 A brief presentation of the Reformation in Sweden is found in Tarald Rasmussen: "Stockholm. Gustav I Wasa und Olaus Petri", in Michael Welker, Michael Beintker and Albert de Lange: *Europa Reformata 1517–2017*, Leipzig: Evangelische Verlagsanstalt 2016, p. 385–394. The standard introduction is still Åke Andrén: "Reformationstid" (= *Sveriges kyrkohistoria* vol. 3), Stockholm: Verbum, 1999. A recent comprehensive reinterpretation of the Swedish Reformation is found in: Hannh M. Kress: *Reformation und Medialität* (= Beiträge zur historischen Theologie 200), Tübingen: Mohr Siebeck 2021.

changes known as the Reformation. In Sweden, on the other hand, a church with its own offices and conventions was from the outset in the 1520s and until the passing of the church ordinance in 1593 much more of an independent institution, with which the King had to find agreement and consensus. Indeed, after the politics of "reduction", on several occasions the church institution was able to stand up to the King. The church and its offices were not his instruments. Rather, the King had to seek solutions in agreement with the church and its leaders.

This structural difference between the two – otherwise quite similar – Nordic Reformation kingdoms is remarkable. Before investigating how these differences are expressed in early Lutheran church legislation in the two countries, a closer look at the political and cultural character of these two Nordic Reformations may contribute to a better understanding of the contexts relevant to their respective church legislation.

3. A Political and Ecclesiastical Re-Start in Denmark

Along with the Reformation, Copenhagen was radically reorganized and reinforced as a religious and ecclesiastical centre of Denmark and Norway.[5] The *political* importance of the city had already been growing during the sixteenth century. Legal rights of a city had been granted since 1422, the number of citizens had increased to almost 5000 during the century, the King had established one of his residences there, and since 1479, Copenhagen also had its own university.

But in spite of these developments, late medieval Copenhagen had never been a city of religious significance in Denmark. The bishop responsible for Copenhagen had his residence and his cathedral in Roskilde, 40 kilometres away. In addition to Roskilde, there was also Lund, where an archbishop had his residence and his cathedral. Located across the Øresund, Lund was nevertheless not very far away from Copenhagen, and it belonged to Denmark. However, during the late Middle Ages, the importance of Lund as a Nordic religious centre – in competition with Nidaros in Norway and Uppsala in Sweden – had decreased. For Danish ecclesiastical purposes, the location of Lund across the sea was surely also a drawback.

5 See Tarald Rasmussen: "Remembering the Past in the Nordic Reformations", in: Brian Cummings, Ceri Law, Karis Riley and Alexandra Walsham (Eds.): *Remembering the Reformation*, London and New York: Routledge 2020, p. 99–117.

From this point of departure, without central late medieval traditions to connect to, Copenhagen was established as a totally new Danish religious centre after the Reformation. In the first place, the residence of the bishop was moved from Roskilde to Copenhagen, and the bishop was no longer the bishop of Roskilde, but the superintendent of Seeland. As such, he was also the leading bishop of Denmark, and with his new residence in Copenhagen, he was closely linked to and ready at hand for the King, who had also appointed him as superintendent. Roskilde Cathedral was still used as the superintendent's church on special occasions, but another church: *Vor Frue kirke* (The Church of Our Lady) in the city centre of Copenhagen gradually replaced it as the main location for important celebrations.

As a church closely connected to Roskilde Cathedral, *Vor Frue* had also been important prior to the Reformation. Danish kings had been crowned here, and since 1479 the university used it as its official church. Nevertheless, the status of this church was radically enhanced after the Reformation, and *Vor Frue* was established as a kind of main church for the entire country. This status included closer ties to the consolidated Lutheran university as a location for disputations and university services. King Frederik II was crowned here in 1559, and a few years later he decided that the liturgical practice of *Vor Frue* was to be normative throughout the kingdom. The church also enjoyed increasing popularity as a burial place for Denmark's new Lutheran elite, not least for distinguished Lutheran university professors and superintendents.

Roskilde Cathedral had served as burial site for members of the Oldenburg dynasty, and this tradition was continued after the Reformation as well. Political considerations may have supported this choice: The dynastic context of Roskilde Cathedral demonstrated that the Reformation kings of Denmark were also part of the proud succession of Queen Margrete I, who ruled over the entire Nordic region.[6] Queen Margrete's sarcophagus in the quire of Roskilde Cathedral is particularly overwhelming, but the funeral monuments of the two Reformation Kings Christian III and Frederik II in the Chapel of the Holy Kings are also great works of art.[7]

6 On the legal aspects of the emerging Nordic dynasties, see Susan Richter: "Wissensaustausch und innerdynastische Verrechtlichung von Konfession in Schweden und Dänemark mittels deutscher Fürstentestamente", in: Irene Dingel/Ute Lotz-Heumann: *Entfaltung und zeitgenössische Wirkung der Reformation im europäischen Kontext* (= Schriften des Vereins für Reformationsgeschichte Nr. 216), Gütersloher Verlagshaus 2015, p. 15–32.

7 This is particularly true for the monument of Christian III and his queen Dorothea, sculpted around 1575 in Antwerp by Cornelis Floris. See Hugo Johannsen: "Christian III og Dorothea", in: Karin Kryger (Ed.): *Danske Kongegrave*, vol II, København: Museum Tusculanum forlag 2014, p. 267–296.

In Copenhagen, one of Christian III's first priorities as the new Lutheran King of Denmark and Norway was to reform the University of Copenhagen. This reform is closely linked to the reform Wittenberg University underwent during the 1520s. Wittenberg was the model for reform, and this model was applied as far as possible. For Christian III as well as for Frederik II, Wittenberg was the ideal to be imitated to bring about renewal, and the primary source or fount for this renewal was the university. In Copenhagen, Wittenberg was occasionally called a *Holy City* due to the rediscovery of the Gospel by Luther and his followers in this city.[8] This rediscovery had first of all been made at the university, and this knowledge was also passed on to broader audiences through the university. Consequently, the University of Copenhagen had to be reformed in the same way to also pave the way for true religion in Denmark. This could be achieved by maintaining close contact with Wittenberg, and by appointing men who were well acquainted with the teaching of Luther and Melanchthon after having spent time as students in Wittenberg to key positions in Copenhagen.

One of these men was Peder Palladius, who was installed by Johannes Bugenhagen in 1537 as the first Lutheran superintendent of Seeland in the Church of Our Lady in Copenhagen. The same year Palladius had been awarded the degree of Dr. theol. at the University of Wittenberg after a doctoral disputation in the Castle Church led by Luther himself – and in the presence of Melanchthon as well as Bugenhagen.[9] In this way, the theological quality of Palladius was solidified. He was a man to rely on, and could be entrusted with the most important position in the new Danish church.

Peder Palladius's younger brother, Niels, had spent several years as a student of Luther and Melanchthon in Wittenberg as well, and in 1552 he was elected as the new bishop in Lund (the previous see of the archbishop). He, too, was a man to be trusted, and a man who could promote the spirit of Wittenberg in order to bring about renewal in Denmark.

8 More on this from Martin Schwarz Lausten: *Die heilige Stadt Wittenberg. Die Beziehungen des dänischen Königshauses zu Wittenberg in der Reformationszeit* (= Schriften der Stiftung Luther-Gedenkstätten in Sachsen-Anhalt, Bd. 10), Leipzig: Evangelische Verlagsanstalt 2010.

9 A comprehensive presentation of Peder Palladius and his role in the Danish Reformation can be found in Martin Schwarz Lausten: *Biskop Peder Palladius og kirken 1537–1560* (= Studier i den danske reformationskirke 2), København: Akademisk forlag 1987.

4. The Medieval Heritage of the Reformation in Sweden

The late medieval church province of Sweden was led from Uppsala. Here, the archbishop was the head of six dioceses: Västerås, Strängnes, Skara, Linköping, Växsjö und Åbo. The archbishop of Uppsala was also the chancellor of the University of Uppsala, founded and approved by the pope in 1477.

Stockholm was not a bishopric, but nevertheless it was an important late medieval city. Due to close contacts to Lübeck and a profitable letter of trade privilege obtained from the National Council of Sweden in 1436, the city grew rapidly during the sixteenth century.[10] Around 1500 it was not only the wealthiest city in Sweden, but also the city with the most inhabitants (6000–7000), and well prepared for a role similar to that of Copenhagen: as the new religious centre of a Lutheran Sweden.

One important difference between Sweden and Denmark is related to the universities. In Sweden, the university was situated in Uppsala, about 40 miles north of Stockholm. And unlike what happened in Denmark, the Swedish Reformation could not rely on the support of its own strong university. The University of Uppsala was not re-established as a new centre of Lutheran learning until the early eighteenth century. In the meantime, Swedish students studied in Rostock or in Wittenberg.

But due to the archbishop and the cathedral, Uppsala remained a city of the highest importance, also after the Reformation. The title of archbishop was maintained, and continuity was also guaranteed by a Catholic bishop being responsible for installing the first post-Reformation archbishop. In this way, the apostolic succession was upheld, even though the consecration was never approved in Rome. This is significantly different from Denmark, where all Catholic bishops were dismissed after the Reformation and replaced by superintendents, installed by Johannes Bugenhagen, outside the ritual continuity of the apostolic succession.

How was this new Lutheran office of a superintendent included and defined in the new ecclesiastical legislation in Denmark and in Sweden? How were the superintendents elected, how were they introduced in their office and what was the competence of this new office in relation to the King?

---

10 On the development of the city in the sixteenth century, see Helena Friman and Göran Söderström: *Stockholm. En historia i kartor och bilder*, Stockholm: Bonnier 2008, p. 38–49.

5. Legitimizing the Ordinance in Pomerania and Denmark

During his almost two years' stay in Copenhagen from 1537 to 1539, Bugenhagen played a decisive role in preparing a church ordinance for Denmark. This new Lutheran church law was presented in Latin in 1537 and in a Danish version in 1539. Two and a half years before departing for Copenhagen in June 1537, Bugenhagen had completed his work on the Pomeranian ordinance. Before this, he had participated in developing new church law for a number of cities: Braunschweig, Hamburg, Wittenberg and Lübeck. His new challenge in Denmark could be seen as a continuation of the work in Pomerania, with another Lutheran prince or king asking for support in the process of developing new church law for his state.

The text of the Pomeranian church ordinance includes an interesting passage stating how the ordinance itself has been approved and what kind of authority it is based on as the ordinance articles were approved at the assembly ("Landtag") in Treptow on the day of St. Lucy[11] 1534: A) The initiative of the legislation ("auf Befehl und Fordern") came from the Pomeranian princes and cousins, Barnim and Philipp; B) The text of the ordinance had been put together and formulated ("gestellt und aufgerichtet") by Johannes Bugenhagen together with Pomeranian pastors[12]; and C) had finally been approved by the entire country ("von der ganzen Landschaft angenommen").[13]

The way of adopting and legitimizing the new Lutheran church law is here significantly different from what is the case in Denmark three years later. In the first place, in a much more radical and direct way the King is introduced as the supreme legislator. This may be observed in the way Christian III formulates himself in his extensive preface to the ordinance. He, too, explains how the

11 December 13th.

12 One week before the assembly in Treptow, the text of the ordinance had been discussed with representatives of the clergy in a separate meeting. See Karl Graebert: *Der Landtag zu Treptow an der Rega, Lucie (13. Dezember) 1534. Ein Beitrag zur Geschichte der Kirchenreformation im Herzogthum Pommern*, Berlin: G. Ebering, 1900, p. 13–22.

13 The full German text of this introductory statement is: "(Dies sind) Die Artikel der Ordnung, die im löblichen Fürstentum zu Pommern auf Befehl und Fordern der durchlauchten hochgebornen Fürsten und Herren, Herrn Barnim und Herrn Philipp, Vettern, Herzöge zu Stettin, Pommern usw. auf dem zu Treptow am Lucien-Tag 1534 gehaltenen Landtag von durch den hochgelehrten D(octor) Johannes Bugenhagen, gemeinsam mit den Predigern in Pommern von den Kirchendiensten, den Schulen und von der Versorgung der rechten Armen zu Gottes Ehre und der Menschen Seligkeit zu Friede und Einigkeit (zusammen) gestellt und aufgerichtet, und von der ganzen Landschaft angenommen ist." Translated into modern German by Sabine Pettke, in *Die pommersche Kirchenordnung von Johannes Bugenhagen 1535*, Ed.: Norbert Buske, Greifswald 1985, p. 160.

document has taken form: Several learned people have made their contributions, the most important being Johannes Bugenhagen. Luther has also read and approved the text. Similar to what was the case in Pomerania, the new law had also been presented to a representative assembly, the council of Denmark ("Riksrådet"), but not in Norway.[14]

The enforcement of the new law on Norway without any kind of representative confirmation there corresponds to a passage at the end of Christian III's preface: "We will also not let it go unpunished, if anyone dares to oppose this church law following his own will. For the power that God has entrusted to us has not been given us in vain."[15] Similarly, at the very end of the preface, the King states about the new Church law: "Enacted in Copenhagen at our castle Anno Domini 1537, on the 2nd of September, on the same day as the Superintendents of the dioceses were ordained in public."[16]

Where the Pomeranian church ordinance was enacted at the Treptow assembly in order to promote "peace and unity" and had been accepted by "the entire country" ("von der ganzen Landschaft"), the Danish ordinance was enacted at the royal castle in Copenhagen without similar support in the "entire country", and accompanied by explicit warnings against displaying disobedience to the King, since the power of legislation had been assigned to him by God himself.

6. Superintendents in Pomerania and Denmark

A significant difference between the two ordinances is also easy to recognize when looking a little closer into the way the office of the highest ecclesiastical order, the office of the superintendent, is regulated in the new Lutheran church law. This office is an interesting case for testing the relationship between royal and ecclesiastical power. Prior to the Reformation, the power of the bishops had to a great extent been defined through the regulations of Canon Law. Now, Canon Law had been put aside and the office of the superintendent (replacing the bishop) had to be regulated in a new way.

14 In Norway, where the new church law was also imposed, the corresponding council had been dissolved by the Danish takeover of political power. Consequently, a representative confirmation did not take place there.

15 Latin version 1537: "Neque etiam per nos impune fecerit quisquis his ordinationibus temere restiterit, id quos faciemus secundum potestatem nobis a Deo datam." (*Kirkeordinansen 1537/39*, Ed.: Martin Schwarz Lausten, Odense: Akademisk forlag, 1989, p. 96.)

16 "Datum Haffniae in Castro nostro Anno domini M.D.XXXVII secunda Septembris, qua die publice ordinati sunt dioecesium Superintendentes." (Ibid.)

Bugenhagen's ordinance for Pomerania includes a brief and simple article on the superintendent:

> *In every duchy and bailiwick one of the pastors should be entrusted with the office of a superintendent. Here, the other (pastors) belonging to the duchy or the bailiwick could find shelter and be advised. In case of outrage, resistance and danger to the doctrine, the superintendent should inform the bishop about this.*[17]

The superintendent here seems to be elected by the pastors in a specific region as a leader who deals with conflicts and protects the doctrine. When more severe challenges arise, the church ordinance instructs the superintendents to turn to a higher level of authority: the bishop. Since the bishops in Pomerania refused to accept the ordinance,[18] they were replaced by so called "Generalsuperintendents": officials appointed by the royal court.[19] However, this highest level of ecclesiastic authority was not further defined and regulated in the ordinance.

In the Danish church ordinance, there is only one level of superintendents (no "Generalsuperintendent"). Each diocese in Denmark as well as in Norway has a superintendent who replaces the former bishop. This office and its duties are carefully defined in part V of the Danish ordinance. Where the Pomeranian ordinance has one short paragraph on the superintendent, the Danish ordinance has more than ten pages. Moreover, a separate text at the end of the ordinance presents the oath that the superintendent has to swear to the King when entering his office, and also the ritual for installing the superintendent in his office. All in all, about 20% of the entire ordinance is dedicated to the regulations of the character, dignity and duties of this office.

The most striking part of these regulations is perhaps the way the obligations of the superintendent towards the King are formulated in the oath he has to swear.

17 *In einem jeden herzoglichen Amte oder Vogtei soll einem von den Pastoren das Superintendentenamt aufgetragen werden, zu dem die anderen Amts- oder Vogteiangehörigen ihre Zuflucht haben und guten Rat holen können…. Sollten aber Frevel oder Mutwillen und Gefahr für die Lehre vorliegen, sollte der Superintendent dies den Bischof wissen lassen.* (*Pommersche Kirchenordnung 1535*, p. 170–171)

18 The Bishops remained in their offices, and the Pomeranian Princes accepted that they were to be appointed by the cathedral chapters and not by the princes. Regulations on these matters were not included in the ordinance. See Graebert (Note 12), p. 16.

19 The office of the Generalsuperintendent is commented on in Buske (Ed.): *Pommersche Kirchenordnung 1535*, p. 226, note 32.

Most beloved, honourable Lord, I, NN, elected Superintendent of NN diocese, promise your Royal Majesty true faithfulness: that I to the utmost of my capability will promote what is to the best for the honour, benefit, peace, calm and obedience of your Royal Majesty and the Realm, in addition to other things that I owe to God in relation to your Royal Majesty. I will also oppose everything that can keep me away from this duty.

Furthermore, I promise that I, as long as I am in this office, will treat Scripture righteously, in accordance with the gift God has given to me, and that I will treat the Gospel and the sacraments righteously, in the way Christ himself has instituted them, (...)[20]

Here, the obligations to show obedience to the King seem to have priority over the duty of protecting the Gospel and the Sacraments. And even if a detailed procedure for recruiting a new superintendent is also foreseen in the ordinance,[21] the decisive part of the appointment is the testing of the loyalty to the King and the oath confirming this loyalty. The superintendents were first and foremost royal officials in service of the King.[22]

7. New Ordinance and the Power of the Bishops in Sweden

In Sweden, the first Lutheran ordinance was presented by the archbishop, Laurentius Petri, in 1571. Due to the complicated confessional situation in the country, it took 22 years until the national Church Council approved the ordinance in 1593. Sven Kjøllerstrøm, former professor of practical theology in Lund in Sweden, has presented several valuable studies on the background and profile of this Swedish ordinance, as well as of procedures for appointing bishops in post-Reformation Sweden. Most of his works were published in Swedish. The following observations concerning Sweden owe a lot to his research.

20 Translated from the Danish KO 1539: "Jeg N. wduald Superintendent til N. stict, loffuer eders Kongelig Maiestat sand troskab, at ieg det yderste meg mogeligt er vil forfremme det eders Kong: Maiestat oc Riiget kand wære til ære, gaffn, fred, rolighed oc lydighed, Oc andet, som ieg for Gud plictug er eders Kong: Maiestat, Oc wil wære emod alt, dette kand forhindre. Der nest loffuer jeg, At den stund ieg er wdy dette embede, da wil ieg forhandle den hellige schrifft retsindelig, effter den gaffue som Gud haffuer giffuet meg, retskaffelig tractere Euangelium oc Sacramenterne, ligesom Christus dennom sielff haffuer indskicket. (...)" (Lausten 1989, p. 238).

21 Lausten 1989, p. 228–229.

22 In *Superintendenten*, Oslo: Universitetsforlaget 1982, p. 120, the Norwegian historian Steinar Imsen has pointed out that this was the case not just in the legislation, but also in actual church politics.

In Sweden, the point of departure for presenting a church ordinance as well as for a legal regulation of the new office of a Lutheran bishop was quite different from what was the case in Denmark. True enough, the bishops had been stripped of much political power through the royal expropriation of ecclesiastical property (the so called "reduction" of Gustav Vasa), but the ecclesiastical office of the bishops was approached in a much more careful way than in Denmark, where the Roman bishops had been removed from their offices and replaced by superintendents. In Sweden, most of the bishops were allowed to remain in office, and the title of bishop was preserved. The significance of the office of the bishop was promoted by the consecration of Laurentius Petri as the first Lutheran archbishop of Sweden in Uppsala Cathedral in 1531. Here, the continuity back to Catholic traditions was signified by the fact that Laurentius Petri was installed in his new office by a Catholic bishop. The period of confessional ambiguity during the reign of Gustav Vasa's son, Johann III and his Catholic wife Catherina Jagellonica, also contributed to the political protection of bishops with more Catholic attitudes.

Not until 1593, when the ordinance from 1571 was finally accepted as official church law, was the confessional ambiguity laid to rest, and Sweden, too, was consolidated as a Lutheran country.

The questions are now: How was the new church law in Sweden legitimized? What was the relationship between royal and ecclesiastical power in legitimizing the new ordinance? And in particular: How was the office of the bishop defined and legitimized within this new legal context? In an attempt to answer these questions, Denmark will be used as a comparative context.

First, it is interesting to note that in Sweden, most of all, the archbishop, but also the bishops and pastors played a decisive role in putting together, presenting and promoting the new Lutheran church law. The archbishop took the initiative, and also in the final part of the process an ecclesiastical assembly confirmed the ordinance as official church law of Sweden. The role of the King was – quite different from what was the case in Denmark, and also different from Pomerania – reduced to confirming the new ordinance after the Uppsala Meeting in 1593.

In Sweden, this was the outcome of a long and quite complicated process. The King had also tried a harder line of confrontation in order to control the church. After an initial phase of religious toleration, Gustav Vasa instituted a new ecclesiastical office in 1539 and appointed a special superintendent with national responsibilities. This office should not replace the archbishop in Uppsala, but serve the King as his most important instrument in order to gain better political control over the Swedish church.

Toleration and room for local varieties in matters of religion were to be replaced by a much stricter confessional regulation in accordance with the Lutheran confession and Wittenberg ideals. The King recruited the Pomeranian nobleman Georg Norman from Rügen for this new office of a "royal superintendent".[23] He had studied at the universities of Rostock and Wittenberg, and was strongly influenced by Melanchthon. In Melanchthon's theology, suitable ideas in support of a more active ecclesiastical role for a Lutheran King were also ready at hand: A good Christian King is the ruler not only of secular matters, but also of the church: he is the *praecipuum membrum ecclesiae*, and it is his task to be a *custos utriusque tabulae*: responsible not only for civil, but also for ecclesiastical legislation. The office of the King is the highest office in the country, and the most important and most venerable duty of this office is "the defence and protection of the Christian religion".[24]

Gustav Vasa entrusted his new superintendent with the task of putting together a new church ordinance. The new church law was intended to be issued by the King and to regulate church life in the entire kingdom of Sweden, similar to what had been done in Denmark a few years earlier.

However, this royal initiative was not successful. Georg Norman's authorization as a royal superintendent was withdrawn in 1543, and his commission was left unfinished. The outcome of the King's initiative on this matter was the opposite of what he had intended: A critical attitude to the King and his church politics was growing within the ecclesiastical hierarchy, and the authority of their own traditional leader, the archbishop of Uppsala (who had been redefined and "protestantized" as a Lutheran church leader in 1531), was enhanced.[25]

Laurentius Petri, the archbishop, had started out on his own with the task of putting together a new church law parallel to the commission of Georg Norman. He had presented his first proposal in 1546, and a new version was finished in 1561. His most important sources of inspiration were German church ordinances, primarily the one from Württemberg from 1553. Laurentius Petri's 1561 version also rested heavily on pre-Reformation Swedish church law. In 1561, the ruling monarch (Erik XIV) was not satisfied with the proposal from his archbishop, and Laurentius Petri continued his work on revising the text

23 For an overview of Georg Norman's role in Swedish Reformation history, see Åke Andrén (1999), p. 96–107.

24 Kjøllerstrøm 1571, p. 206.

25 See Sven Kjøllerstrøm: *Svenska förarbeten till kyrkoordningen av år 1571* (= Acta Historico-ecclesiastica Suecana vol. 2), Stockholm: Svenska Diakonistyrelsens Bokförlag 1940, p. 9.

for another ten years. In 1571, the final version was ready.[26] After further political complications during the reign of Erik's successor, Johan III, the Uppsala Church Meeting approved this version (with some minor additions) in 1593.

8. Limits on the King's Power in the Danish and Swedish Ordinances

The preface is an interesting point of departure for a closer comparison between the Danish and the Swedish ordinances. Whereas the preface to the Swedish ordinance carries the signature of the archbishop, the Danish ordinance carries the signature of the King. Both prefaces refer to a fundamental distinction between two different areas of government, but their way of distinguishing between them is significantly different.

Moreover, in the Swedish preface the King has an important role. Laurentius Petri describes a number of examples from history where the political rulers have protected and supported true religion. From the Old Testament he mentions David, Ezechias, Iosias and Iosaphat, followed by rulers from the Roman Empire and early European history: Constantine, Valentinian, Theodosius and Carolus Magnus. But also Swedish history offers examples: Laurentius Petri mentions such medieval rulers as Bjørn (who brought the Christian missionary Ansgar to Sweden), Stenkill, Oluff and finally the most important of them all: Erik, the patron saint of Sweden, whose shrine had been brought to Uppsala Cathedral in 1273. The way all these regents had protected and supported the true religion was a result of "*vthaff theras retta kall och embete* ("their right vocation and office").[27]

> *Neither is it, on the other hand, the case that these two offices, that are – not without an important reason – so thoroughly distinguished from each other in Scripture: the office of (secular) authority and the service of the church, should be mixed together again, as it happened during the Papacy* (...)[28]

---

26 On the sources of the 1571 ordinance, see Sven Kjøllerstrøm: *Svenska förarbeten till kyrkoordningen av år 1571* (= Acta Historico-ecclesiastica Suecana vol. 2), Stockholm: Svenska Diakonistyrelsens Bokförlag 1940.

27 Sven Kjøllerstrøm: Den svenska kyrkoordningen 1571, jämte studier kring tillkomst, innehåll och användning, Lund: Håkan Ohlssons Förlag 1971, p. 18–19.

28 "Doch är thes heller icke thet meningen j sakenne, at thesse twenne embete, hwilken Scrifften icke vthan wigtigha orsaker så fliteligha åtskildt haffuer, nemliga Öffuerhetennes och Kyrkiotienarenars, skulle åter mengias tilsammans, såsom vnder Påwan skeedt är, ..." (Ibid. p. 19)

After a long passage characterizing the exemplary rule of King David, including the way he cared for and protected religion, the text of Laurentius Petri's preface continues:

> *And in order for all this to remain constant and unchanged, the secular authority confirms it in permanent ordinances and decisions, just as David did in his time, according to the arrangements he made with the priests and the liturgies in the Temple, recorded in the book of Chronicles. Assuredly, this is the kind of business that the holy King David cared for, and he promoted these kinds of useful regulations together with the Priests and the Levites; regulations aiming at the liturgy. Neither did he mix his royal office with the pastoral office that God wanted to single out and separate.*[29]

The archbishop here presents David as the role model of a King. The Old Testament can tell us how he cared for the church in the old days, before the Papacy emerged and disturbed the good old order. Part of David's exemplary status is also due to the fact that he respected and protected the fundamental distinction between the general political supremacy of the King and the power of the ecclesiastical hierarchy. Laurentius Petri here seems to present to the King a specific interpretation of this fundamental distinction between different kinds of supremacy in order to convince him that this distinction must be honoured if the King intends to be a good monarch according to the models presented in the Bible.[30]

---

29 "Och på thet alt slijkt må bliffua j lengdenne beståndigt oc warachtigt, författar och bekräfftigar Öffuerheten thet medh wissa ordningar och stadgar, sådna som Konung Dauid j sin tijdh, och effter then lägenheet, som tå war giord medh Presterskapet och Gudztiensten j Templet, såsom j Crönekebokenne scriffuit är. Ja, om slijkt lät sigh then helge Konung Dauid wårda, och sådana nyttigha ordningar genom Gudz Anda och befalning, giorde han medh Prester och Leuiter, som achta skulle på Gudz tiensten, och mengde thes heller icke sitt Konungzliga embete och Presternars embete tilhopa, thet Gudh wille haffua åtskildt, ..." (Ibid. p. 20)

30 The German historian of Church Law, Johannes Heckel, was also interested in Swedish Church Law. In a detailed discussion of one of the books of Kjøllerstrøm in the Zeitschrift der Savigny-Stiftung für Rechtsgeschichte, he writes: "Die schwedische Kirche (schuf) ihre Ordnung im Wege der autonomen Satzung. Diese (...) wurde vom Episkopat vorgeschlagen, von der Geistlichkeit angenommen und vom König bestätigt. (...) die Bestätigung durch den König sollte nur von Obrigkeits wegen die Beständigkeit der Kirchenordnung bekräftigen, also nicht ihre Verbindlichkeit begründen, sondern durch den Einsatz hoheitlicher Autorität verstärken. (...) Gemessen an der Rechtslage in Deutschland entspricht die selbständige Entwicklung des schwedischen Kirchenrechts im 16. Jahrhundert den Ansichten der Reformatoren besser als bei uns." (*Zeitschrift der Savigny-Stiftung für Rechtsgeschichte. Kanonistische Abteilung*, 01/1/1956, Vol. 42(1), S. 539)

A comparable distinction between two different kinds of order is also presented in the King's preface to the Danish/Norwegian church ordinance from 1537. The precise meaning of this distinction has been frequently discussed in Danish and Norwegian church historical research.[31] One striking difference compared to the Swedish text is found in the terminology: The Danish ordinance does not at all refer to two different kinds of supremacy, only to two different "Orders". There are, according to the King, two different kinds of Order ("Ordinanz"): God's and "ours". A distinction has to be drawn and upheld between the two of them.

On the first pages of the preface, Christian III has something to say about his own role in the process of formulating the ordinance. It is not only a product of Bugenhagen and Luther:

> *But in order to avoid the impression that we have only used the wisdom of other people in this matter, we will most gratefully confess that God in his mercy has also given us a certain understanding of the holy Gospel. Therefore, we now want to say what we think about this ordinance.*[32]

He then goes on to present his way of making fundamental distinctions:

> *Two different pieces are being treated in this ordinance. One of them belongs solely to God, and is that we want to have the word of God, which is the Law and the Gospel, properly preached, the sacraments rightly distributed, the children carefully fostered, in order for those who have been baptized into Christ also to remain in Christ. It is also that the servants of the church, the schools and the poor must be supplied with what they need.*
>
> *All of this is not our ordinance, but in all these matters we want to serve the ordinance of Our Lord Jesus Christ, who is our only teacher and master as well as our only saviour and true blessing (…)*[33]

---

31 A point of departure for a closer look is Oskar Skarsaune: "Duplex est hic ordinatio. En tolkning av Kirkeordinansens 'kongebrev' (1537/39/42)", i: *Kirkehistoriske Samlinger* 1991, p. 49–88.

32 Translated from the Danish text 1539: "Men at man ey skal mene oss at haffue aldielis her wdi brugt ander mands tycke, Da bekende wy med stoer tacknemmelighed, at Gud aff syn godhed haffuer end oc saa oss giffuet nogen forstand vdi det hellige Euangelio. Saa wille wy nu sige denne wor tycke om denne ordinantz." (Lausten 1989, p. 152)

33 Translated from the Danish text 1539: "To honde stycker forhandles her y denne ordinantz. Det ene hører Gud Alleeniste til, som er det at wy wille haffue Guds ord, som er Lougen oc Euangelium, retsindelige predickede, Sacramenterne ret wddelde, Børn wel oplerde, at de maa bliffue wdi Christo, som ind y Christum ere døbte, At kircketenerne, Scholerne, oc fattuge folck maa forsørges syn føde."

At the end of the quite elaborate description of God's ordinance that follows, the King summarizes his way of thinking:

> *This is what we have said so far about the parts that belong to God's Ordinance and order. All this should not be called ours. Neither should it be offended or violated by any human being. We also command that it has to be held in honour, in order for us to remain obedient to our Lord Jesus Christ, who has presented and ordered this very ordinance, to his own honour and to our blessing.*
>
> *But the other part of this ordinance has to be called ours, because there something (without God's anger) has to be changed, even if this also belongs to God. This is the case with regulations concerning persons, time, place, number, way, pastoral hours, singing and ceremonies* (...)[34]

In this presentation of the fundamental distinction concerning God's and the King's ordinance, the King is the authority who carries the responsibility for both sides, both ordinances. There is no sign of a special protection of the ecclesiastical order as a kind of authority distinguished from the royal power. Instead, the King is the authority with full responsibility, also for "God's ordinance". Moreover, the King is in command of his own ordinance, which mainly includes issues that in Sweden were left to the ecclesiastical hierarchy and the church council to decide.

9. The Oath and the Election of Bishops

Considering this comparative approach to the Danish and Swedish ordinances, it is hardly surprising that the oath of the bishop to the King – an essential theme in the Danish ordinance[35] – is not at all mentioned in the Swedish ordinance. This does not mean that no oath at all was to be sworn in Sweden. Since 1528 the bishops had to swear an *iuramentum episcopale* to the King. Gustav

---

Saadant er icke wor Ordinants, men dermed willy wy tiene wor Herris Jesu Christi Ordinants. Huilcken er wor eeniste lærer oc mester saa well som wor eeniste frelser oc wisse salighed (...)". (Ibid. p. 152)

34 "Dette haffue wy her till sagd om de stycker, som hører till Guds Ordinants oc skick. Huilcken icke skal kaldis wor. Icke heller skall aff nogen menniske krenckes oc offuertredis. Oc biude wy henne att holdes, paa det wy der med bliffue wor Herre Jesu Christo lydige, som samme Ordinants haffuer skicked oc befaled, seg till ære oc oss til salighed.

Men det andet stycke y denne Ordinants maa kaldes att være vortt, fordi der vdi maa vell sompt (foruden Guds fortørnelse) foruandles, endog det oc saa Gud tilhører, som er huad wy haffue skicked om personer, tid, sted, tall, maade, prestetider, sang oc Ceremonier (...)". (Ibid. p. 155)

35 See p. 145.

Vasa and his Son Erik XIV had also introduced oaths to be sworn by all new pastors in the Swedish church. Johann III had demanded that the archbishop would not consecrate pastors who had not sworn an oath to the King in advance.[36] The question of ecclesiastical oaths sworn to the King, then, was evidently also an important issue in Sweden. The fact that the church law from 1571 has nothing to say about this matter is interesting, and can be interpreted as confirmation of the ideological profile of the ordinance: Its intention is – without challenging the King too much – to confirm and reinforce the political independence of the clergy.

The Danish ordinance had a lot to say about the oath and the obligations of the superintendents, but hardly anything about how they were to be recruited and elected. There was no need for these kinds of regulations since the superintendents were mostly not only appointed, but also recruited by the King. This is quite different in the Swedish ordinance. Instead of dealing with the bishop's oath to the King, it offers a paragraph "Om Biscops wahl" ("On electing a bishop") with detailed regulations on how this should take place.[37] The process is legitimated from below. Firstly, the ordinance refers to tradition: In the old days, the entire congregation took part in electing a bishop.[38] Since the dioceses now are much bigger, and since most lay people are not well enough acquainted with relevant candidates, one has to appoint a representative group of people responsible for the election: Only competent persons – pastors and others – should take part in the process. Each of them had to be sworn in by oath and promise to suggest the person they "before God" found most suitable for the office. Subsequently, there was an election, and the *electus* (the candidate with the highest number of votes) was sent to the political authority *pro confirmatione.*

10. Conclusion

A closer comparative look at the early church law of the Lutheran kingdoms of Denmark and Sweden demonstrates several significant differences within a region otherwise often considered as dominated by the same kind of early modern confessional culture and very similar theological ideals. Here, the

36 See Sven Kjøllerstrøm: "Laurentius Petris Kyrkoordning 1571–1971. Tillkomst och användning", i: Kjøllerstrøm 1971, p. 201–277, on pastoral oaths: p. 222.

37 Kjøllerstrøm 1971, p. 168.

38 "I förtiden haffuer warit sedhwenia, at hela menigheten skulle wälia, så wel Biscopar som andra Kyrkiotienare." (Ibid.)

differences have been analysed by looking closely into two issues: the relationship of the King to the ecclesiastical hierarchy and the way of defining and regulating the office of the superintendent/bishop. The dissimilar ways of dealing with these issues are not just relevant for understanding the different profiles of the Nordic Reformations, but also for interpreting further developments in the Nordic region and further characteristic differences between the Danish and Norwegian churches, on the one hand, and the Swedish and Finnish churches on the other.

Bibliography

Andrén, Åke (1999): "Reformationstid" (= *Sveriges kyrkohistoria* vol. 3), Stockholm: Verbum.

Buske, Norbert, ed. (1985): *Die pommersche Kirchenordnung von Johannes Bugenhagen 1535*, Greifswald.

Friman, Helena and Göran Söderström (2008): *Stockholm. En historia i kartor och bilder*, Stockholm: Bonnier.

Graebert, Karl (1900): *Der Landtag zo Treptow an der Rega, Lucie (13. Dezember) 1534. Ein Beitrag zur Geschichte der Kirchenreformation im Herzogthum Pommern*, Berlin: G. Ebering.

Heckel, Johannes (1956): Review of Sven Kjølerstrøm: "Den kyrkliga lagstiftningen I Sverige", Sonderdruck aus Statens Offentlige utredningar 1955:47, 10–43, in: *Zeitschrift der Savigny-Stiftung für Rechtsgeschichte. Kanonistische Abteilung*, 42 (1956), 537–542.

Imsen, Steinar (1982): *Superintendenten*, Oslo: Universitetsforlaget.

Kjøllerstrøm, Sven (1940): *Svenska förarbeten till kyrkoordningen av år 1571* (= Acta Historico-ecclesiastica Suecana vol. 2), Stockholm: Svenska Diakonistyrelsens Bokförlag.

Kjøllerstrøm, Sven (1971a): Den svenska kyrkoordningen 1571, in: Kjøllerstrøm, Sven (ed.): Den svenska kyrkoordningen 1571, jämte studier kring tillkomst, innehåll och användning, Lund: Håkan Ohlssons Förlag, 1–200.

Kjøllerstrøm (1971b): "Laurentius Petris Kyrkoordning 1571–1971. Tillkomst och användning", in: Kjøllerstrøm, Sven (ed.): Den svenska kyrkoordningen 1571, jämte studier kring tillkomst, innehåll och användning, Lund: Håkan Ohlssons Förlag, 201–277.

Kress, Hannh M. (2021): *Reformation und Medialität* (= Beiträge zur historischen Theologie 200), Tübingen: Mohr Siebeck.

Lausten, Martin Schwarz (1987): *Biskop Peder Palladius og kirken 1537–1560* (= Studier i den danske reformationskirke 2), København: Akademisk forlag.

Lausten, Martin Schwarz (1989): *Kirkeordinansen 1537/39*, Odense: Akademisk forlag,

Lausten, Martin Schwarz (2010): *Die heilige Stadt Wittenberg. Die Beziehungen des dänischen Königshauses zu Wittenberg in der Reformationszeit* (= Schriften der Stiftung Luther-Gedenkstätten in Sachsen-Anhalt, Bd. 10), Leipzig: Evangelische Verlagsanstalt.

Olesen, Jens E. (2018): "Johannes Bugenhagens kirkeordnende virksomhed og syn på øvrigheden", i: *Religion som forklaring? Kirke og religion i stat og samfund, Festskrift til Per Ingesman*, Aarhus: Aarhus Universitetsforlag, 179–194.

Rasmussen, Tarald (2016): "*Stockholm. Gustav I Wasa und Olaus Petri*", in Michael Welker, Michael Beintker and Albert de Lange: *Europa Reformata 1517–2017*, Leipzig: Evangelische Verlagshaus, 385–394.

Rasmussen, Tarald (2017): "Reformasjonen i Norden", in: Tarald Rasmussen and Ola Tjørhom (ed.): *Reformasjonen i nytt lys*, Oslo: Cappelen Damm akademisk, 109–136.

Rasmussen, Tarald (2020): "Remembering the Past in the Nordic Reformations", in: Brian Cummings, Ceri Law, Karis Riley and Alexandra Walsham (ed.): *Remembering the Reformation*, London and New York: Routledge, 99–117.

Richter, Susan (2015): "Wissensaustausch und innerdynastische Verrechtlichung von Konfession in Schweden und Dänemark mittels deutscher Fürstentestamente", in: Irene Dingel/Ute Lotz-Heumann: *Entfaltung und zeitgenössische Wirkung der Reformation im europäischen Kontext* (= Schriften des Vereins für Reformationsgeschichte Nr. 216), Gütersloher Verlagshaus, 15–32.

Skarsaune. Oskar (1991): "Duplex est hic ordinatio. En tolkning av Kirkeordinansens "kongebrev" (1537/39/42)", i: *Kirkehistoriske Samlinger*, 49–88.

The Reformation and its Translation into Scandinavian Legal Culture

The Early Modern Legal Profession and its Relation to Religious Sources

Kjell Å Modéer

1. Prologue: Law and Religion as an Important Instrument of the Identification of the Scandinavian Legal Cultures

Current *post-secular* time confronts *law and religion* with totally unexpected dimensions of the legal culture. The 20th century was characterized with the Weberian metaphor the disenchantment of the world, in which secularization became a key-word for the modernity. Late-modern cognitive structures have reintroduced metaphysical perspectives as one parameter among others, and the late-modern legal paradigm is very keen to compare the current situation with that of the *early modern legal paradigm* from the end of the 15th century up to the period of German and French Enlightenment in the 18th century. This article will elaborate on that comparative legal culture-phenomenon.

In recent times jurists increasingly have expanded their legal dogmatic analysis into more bounder-less and transparent contexts. Critical perspectives in legal historical research have focused on different contexts, comparative and diversity studies. They play an important role in current legal scholarship.[1]

National legal and political conflicts and problems are identified as transnational with help of the concept of legal cultures and legal traditions. Critical perspectives on modern legal positivism are just taking care of the concepts of national legal cultures and local or transnational deep structures of law.[2] In a time of an increasingly identified legal globalization we can identify new professional networks and legal translations as well as a diversified and increasingly fragmented legal professionalization.[3]

---

1 Max Planck Institute for European Legal History, *Report 2015–2017*, Frankfurt/Main 2018.

2 Kaarlo Tuori, "Towards a Multi-layered view of Modern Law", in Aulis Aarnio et al. (eds.), *Aleksander Peczenik on the Occasion of his 60th Birthday on 16 November 1997*, Juristförtlaget i Lund: Lund 1997, 427–42.

3 Thomas Duve, "Von der Europäischen Rechtsgeschichte zu einer Rechtsgeschichte Europas in globalhistorischer Perspektive" ("From a European Legal History Towards a Legal History of Europe in a Global Historical Perspective"), in: *Max Planck Institute for European Legal History Research Paper Series* 2012:2 (2012), 1–80, http://ssrn.com/abstract=2139312.

 | DOI:10.30965/9783657790746_006

Those current perspectives are brought into legal history. Traditional history on institutions (*Institutionen-Geschichte*) has shifted to legal real history (*Juristische Realgeschichte*) due to new way of using the legal sources. Richard Helmholtz (Chicago) and Charles Donahue (Harvard) have both contributed to this new trend by going to the records, the legal sources when they investigated marriage litigation in medieval times.[4]

In this article the interest will be reduced to Swedish theologians and jurists and a try to make use of the theories and methods on how to get new information about the transformation of the legal culture in early modern Scandinavia.

2. Mapping Early Modern Legal Cultures – Europe and Scandinavia

Legal change is here a relevant keyword. A comparison in time of the cognitive structures of the Middle Ages with those in the Early Modern times demonstrates important divergences. The medieval renaissance law was constructed on the ancient heritage. Law and Theology were intertwined. Roman law and Roman Catholic thoughts were regarded as common universal entities.

The Early modern change became dramatic. Its legal culture was characterized by broken universalism in theology as well as in law. In northern Europe new cognitive structures were constructed. The *jus commune* became increasingly used as the important counterpart to the dominant national *jus patrium* or *jus proprium*, and canon law was substituted by protestant legal sources and of the Reformation.[5]

The doctrines within civil law were involved in ideological as well as theological discourses. In his important dissertation Wim Decock demonstrated how Jesuit and Scholastic thought resulted in quite new interpretations on how to implement and use contract law with help of moral theology.[6] Theologians and jurists interacted. Even if Decock uses continental European sources in his scholarly work the phenomenon is important also for the understanding of Scandinavian legal cultures. Especially the middle of the 17th century was

4 Richard Helmholz, *Marriage Litigation in Medieval England*, London 1974; Charles Donahue, *Law, Marriage and Society in the later Middle Ages*, Cambridge 2008.

5 Harold J. Berman, *Law and Revolution*: vol. 1. *The Formation of the Western Legal Tradition*, Harvard University Press: Cambridge/Mass. 1983, vol. 2. *The Impact of the Protestant Reformations on the Western Legal Tradition*: Harvard University Press: Cambridge/Mass. 2003.

6 Wim Decock, *Theologians and Contract Law, The Moral Transformation of the Ius Commune, (ca. 1500–1650)*, Brill 2012. Review in *Kyrkohistorisk Årsskrift* 2015 (Kjell Å Modéer) 227 ff.

characterized by an implementation of an extensive doctrine of European legal sources. They didn't only include religious Laws but also later Natural Law principles.[7]

3. The Creation and Identification of Sweden as an Early Modern Nation State

When the Nordic countries in 1523 broke up from the Nordic union into separate nation states with Western Scandinavia (Denmark and Norway) and Eastern Scandinavia (Sweden and Finland) Sweden created an increasingly powerful monarchic dynasty with Gustav Eriksson Wasa (1496–1560) as the king. He turned Sweden into a hereditary monarchy in 1544. Especially Gustav Wasa and his sons and grandson Gustavus II Adolphus had the ambition to create a Baltic Sea realm. An expanding and extensive foreign policy-created the presumptions for Sweden as a great power in the 17th century Europe.

The constitutional identity of this Great Power was its religion. Since the Diet of Västerås in 1527 Sweden was a protestant country. The Swedish Reformation, however, was less radical than the dramatic change in Germany and Denmark. Even if the ordinary communication with the Pope in Rome came to an end already in 1524, there were Catholic contra-forces during king John III (1537–1592) in the 1570s and of course the abdication of Queen Christina (1626–1689) in 1654 broke this Lutheran identity. However, on the whole during the Early modern times the Kingdom of Sweden on the European map was labeled as a protestant country.[8]

The Swedish protestant identity had of course legal consequences. It brought Sweden in conflict with Countries devoted to the Roman Catholic Church and its canon law. It had consequences for the training of the clergy as well as the judiciary, and this in a time when professionalization of the civil servants became an important instrument for creating the Great Power of Sweden.

7 Stig Jägerskiöld, *Studier rörande receptionen av främmande rätt i Sverige under den yngre landslagens tid*, Almqvist & Wiksell: Stockholm 1963. Sten Lindroth, *Svensk lärdomshistoria*, Del 1. *Medeltiden och reformationstiden*, Norstedt: Stockholm 1975, Del 2. *Stormaktstiden*, Norstedt: Stockholm 1975.

8 Lars Österlin, *Svenska kyrkan i profil: Ur engelskt och nordiskt perspektiv*, 2nd ed., Verbum: Stockholm 1997.

4. The Early Modern Judicial Revolution in Sweden

During the first decades of the 16th century we can observe a very important shift in European legal cultures. The transparent borders between politics and law, administrative and judicial power, the *judicialization of politics*[9] can be followed down to the delegation of royal judicial power to the creation of autonomous courts. The rulers of the nation-states reacted against private forms of conflict-solving, they prohibited the nobility to solve conflicts regarding honor with help of aristocratic duels and reacted against violent riots as the German Peasants' War in 1527. Conflicts should be solved in peace by courts. The parties had to be brought into sacralized court-rooms with well-educated judges. This transition was made possible by the construct of a well-educated and well-trained legal profession. The professional judiciary created and presumed the Early modern *judicial revolution*.[10]

One phenomenon of special importance for our topic was the use of consulting of the legal elite in the law faculties at the universities. In Germany this court-operation to ask for a decision or a *responsum* was called an *Aktenversendung*, as the laymen's court sent the records in a case to a learned law faculty or a so called *Spruchkollegium* to get an opinion, *responsum*, on how to decide in a case. This extra-ordinary way of decision-making besides the regular court-system had its parallels also in the Scandinavian countries by the King's creating of casual commissions with professionals to solve specific crimes.[11] The extensive witch-hunting trials of the 17th century were handled by for this task specially erected legal commissions. They became to a great extent decided by a mixed jurisdiction in which the clergy as well as the appellate judiciary were involved.[12]

Another phenomenon was the creation of professional high courts with appelate and corrective powers. In the late medieval times supreme courts such as the *Parlement de Paris*, created by Louis IX already around 1250, were empowered to hear appeals from parties dissatisfied with the justice they had

9 C. Neal Tate & Torbjörn Vallinder, *The Global Expansion of Judicial Power*, New York University; New York 1995.

10 Harold Berman, (2003). – Cfr V. A. C. Gatrell, Bruce Lenman, and Geoffrey Parker (eds.), *Crime and the Law: The Social History of Crime in Western Europé since 1500*, Europa: London 1980, 11–48. See also Kjell Å Modéer, "Suum Cuique Tribuere" [An Introduction], in: Kjell Å Modéer & Martin Sunnqvist (eds.), "Suum Cuique Tribuere: Legal Contexts and Deep Structures Regarding Courts of Appeal and Judiciaries from Early Modern to Late Modern Europe", *Rättshistoriska studier*, Vol. 27, Stockholm 2018, 14 ff.

11 See further below.

12 Bengt Ankarloo, "Trolldomsprocesserna i Sverige", *Rättshistoriskt bibliotek* 17, Lund 1971.

received in the courts of lower or ordinary jurisdiction. The continuous professionalization of the judiciaries in continental European Supreme Courts, started with the French *Parlement de Paris* in 1458 and continued with the Supreme Court of the German empire, *Reichskammergericht*, erected by the emperor Maximilian I. in 1495.[13] The new with this form of Supreme Courts was that the judicial power of the emperor/king was delegated to professional judges. This phenomenon appeared in the Scandinavian countries first in the beginning of the 17th century.[14] The high court in Sweden, the *Hovrätt*, with European archetypes was erected by Gustav II. Adolphus in 1614.

Despite the transnational character of the Early modern judicial revolution, it's focus became increasingly national with the Reformation. From a legal perspective the Lutheran reformation in Scandinavia not only meant a break of the monopolistic position of the Roman Catholic Church and its Canon Law. Also the universities as professional institutions were involved in this process. First in the 15th century the universities as European institutions met the countries around the Baltic Sea. The first university in this Baltic region was erected in Rostock (Mecklenburg) in 1419, the second in Greifswald in Pomerania in 1456. The two first universities in Scandinavia were those in Uppsala 1477 and Copenhagen 1479. At all those universities there was a faculty of theology and a faculty of law with curricula dominated by the common European law – not only in the profane civil law (*ius civile*) but also in canon law. The medieval universities didn't teach *ius proprium* or *ius patrium*. They were indeed true European institutions in which the learned European law was taught.

Lutheran Protestantism shifted the attitude regarding the national royal power to European legal knowledge and therefore also to the role of the universities. Scandinavian medieval jurists had got their education at European universities. From the 1530s Scandinavian students gave priority to protestant universities on their study tours, especially those in northern Europe, which started after the struggles related to the Reformation. As Uppsala University was closed throughout the 16th century the Swedish students had to take study tours to Protestant universities especially in northern Germany and the Netherlands.[15]

---

13 A. A.Wijffels & C. H.van Rhee (eds.), *European Supreme Courts: A Portrait through History*, Third Millenium Publishing London 2013, 66 ff, 90 ff.

14 Mia Korpiola (ed.), "The Svea Court of Appeal in the Early Modern Period. Historical Reinterpretations and New Perspectives", *Rättshistoriska studier* vol. 26, Jure: Stockholm 2014.

15 Åke Malmström, "Ur den juridiska fakultetens historia", *Acta Universitates Uppsaliensis*, Uppsala University 500 years: nr. 11. Uppsala 1976.

When the Scandinavian universities started their education after the Reformation, they also fostered a new academic legal culture.[16] The religion became a part of a stronger prince power and it had consequences for the tasks of the universities regarding the clergy as well as the jurists.[17] Also the curricula changed. The students were expected to serve as national civil servants after their studies at the university. So also the professors in the regional or national law were state employees. When e.g. the law faculty at Lund inaugurated in 1668, it had three law professors. One in Swedish and the regional Scanian Law, one in Roman law, and one in Natural Law and International Public Law to which Samuel Pufendorf was recruited from Heidelberg.[18]

The judicial revolution not only made judicial decision-making visible it also developed the issue of *jurisdiction*, judicial power. The ecclesiastical power was handled differently. In Scandinavia the ecclesiastical power in the medieval times had been handled by the Church and had its ultimate appellate judicial instance in the *Rota romana* in Rome.[19]

The situation changed with the Protestant Reformation. The establishing of a national church discipline was close related to the problems of *jurisdiction*. The royal jurisdiction and its delegation of judicial power to the nobility and to the clergy resulted in many and prolonged internal conflicts.[20] This became increasingly important when Sweden got provinces around the Baltic Sea, in Livonia, in the German Empire (Pommerania, Wismar and Bremen/Verden) and from 1658 the former Danish territories: Scanian provinces (Scania, Blekinge, Halland). From 1630 those territories were regarded as provinces and protected their domestic laws. During the absolutistic regime of Charles XI, however, from 1680 a more homogeneous legal culture was implemented with

16 Ditlev Tamm, *The Faculty of Law: The Teaching of Law at the University of Copenhagen since 1479*, Museum Tusculanum: Copenhagen 2011.

17 Lars Nihlén, "Peregrinatio academica. Det svenska samhället och de utrikes studieresorna under 1600-talet", *Bibliotheca historica Lundensis* 54, 1983, 123.

18 Kjell Å Modéer, *Det förpliktande minnet: Juridiska fakultetens i Lund 1656–2016*, Santérus Förlag: Stockholm 2017, 17 ff.

19 Kirsi Salonen, Jussi Hanska, *Entering a Clerical Career at the Roman Curia, 1458–1471* (Church, Faith and Culture in the Medieval West), Routledge: London 2013. – Kirsi Salonen, *The Penitentiary as a well of Grace in the Late Middle Ages: The Example of the Province of Uppsala 1449–1527*, Saarijärvi 2001. – Sara Risberg och Kirsi Salonen, "Auctoritate papae: The Church Province of Uppsala in the Apostolic Penitentiary 1410–1526" (*Diplomatarium Suecanum: Appendix: Acta pontificum Suecica II: Acta Poenitentiariae*), Riksarkivet: Stockholm 2008.

20 Mia Korpiola, "Kyrkotukt för hela folket: Hertig Gustafs av Saxen "horerei" och luthersk kyrkodisciplin i Sverige på 1500- och 1600-talen", in: Jukka Kekkonen et al. (eds.), *Norden, Rätten, Historia: Festskrift till Lars Björne*, Suomalainen Lakimiesyhdistys: Helsinki 2004, 65 ff.

Swedish laws. From this time also the Church Law and its own jurisdiction and judicial rules were established (1686).[21]

5. The Protestant Professionalization of the Clergy and the Judiciary From 1527

The university became the educator of the civil servants for the two regiments in the expanding Swedish realm. The successive decline of Uppsala University in the 1520s resulted in its abolition, and the king, Gustav I., had no ambition to restore it. First after the *Uppsala Meeting* in 1593, which established the constitutional role of the Protestant church in Sweden as a state church, this university was restored.

The responsibility for the education of the clergy had the Latin schools in the diocese' cities combined with theologian studies in the cathedrals. In Denmark- Norway university studies were compulsory for the clergy since 1569, in Sweden this claim came later. In 1604 the Swedish latin schools were provided with a theologian lecturer and the whole education took place in those institutions.[22]

Even if Uppsala university was restored by Gustav II. Adolphus in 1620 it took a long time until the university got a high status. All fields of education were involved in the reform plans of Gustavus Adolphus. The Dioceses were equipped with more lecturers, the quality of the education was raised and the education of the clergy got a higher esteem.

Around 1640 the theologian faculty at Uppsala was personally renewed. Queen Christina, who reigned between 1642–1654, wanted to strengthen Uppsala University and when it got its new constitution in 1655 the education of the clergy was taken over by the university. The university became the educator of the civil servants – the sacred and the profaned – for the two regiments.[23]

The law faculty at Uppsala from 1620 became a part of that education. Not only the professors but also their students saw possibilities to make a judicial career in the then newly erected High Court (1614) the law professors as Court of Appeal justices, and the students with training as auditors, *Auskultanten*. The Courts of Appeals (erected in Turku for Finland 1623, in Tartu for Livonia

21 Kjell Å Modéer, "Gerichtsbarkeiten der schwedischen Krone im deutschen Reichsterritorium", *Rättshistoriskt bibliotek* vol. 25, Lund 1975.
22 Nihlén, *Peregrinatio academica* (1983), 140.
23 Nihlén, *Peregrinatio academica* (1983), 142.

1630 and in Jönköping for southern Sweden 1634) became hubs for the mobility of jurists between jurisdictions in Early Modern Sweden.[24]

6. Ecclesiastic Law Constitutionally Founded

The national fundamental law/constitution with its embedded virtues, values and religious references gave a legal identity to the Protestant nation state. With Uppsala Meeting 1593 the Protestant religion became a part of this constitutionalization of the Early Modern Swedish state. The clergy made a *homagium* to the king to follow the Protestant texts. Luther pleaded for the *vocatio*, and all vocations are God-given. All members of the church, its clergy and laity as ordinary people were equally called to communicate Christ to each other, carpenters as well as bishops, housewives and teachers a like, as much as priests. The calling for the clergy to serve not only God, but also the king became important also for the legal civil servants, judges and other legal professionals. The *vocation, Beruf*, the calling became a sign of humble devotion for their important professional tasks. The priest promises (kyrkolöften) as well as the judge's oath (domareden) became the ritual *homagium* between the King and the professional priest or profane judge.[25] *The Rules for Judges* (Domarregler) from the 1540ies assigned to Olaus Petri is a perfect example of rules mixed and collected from canon law, *ius commune* and national traditional law.[26] These principles were confirmed with the Fundamental Law (*Regeringsformen*) 1634.

In this Fundamental Law the different ecclesiastical and profane jurisdictions were defined. The profane Supreme legal instance became the Hovrätt, in 1614. Even if it was kept as a Royal Court, already since 1615 the parties got a possibility to apply to the King and the Government with a brief for revision. The Court of Appeal became the protector of the *forum privilegiatum* for the

24 Kjell Å Modéer, "Karolinernas jurister: Det militära rättsväsendets aktörer under det karolinska enväldet", *Karolinska förbundets Årsskrift* 1992, 23 ff.; Rudolf Thunander: "Hovrätt i funktion: Göta hovrätt och brottmålen", *Rättshistoriskt bibliotek*, vol. 49, Stockhoölm 1993.

25 Martin Sunnqvist, "Domareden och dess religiösa inslag", in: Kjell Å Modéer (ed.), *Rätt, religion och politik. Ett rättshistoriskt seminarium tillägnat Magnus Sjöberg, Rättshistoriska skrifter* Band 9, Stockholm 2008, 85 ff.

26 Göran Inger, Olaus Petri i rättshistoriens ljus, in: Carl F Hallencreutz & Sven-Ola Lindeberg (eds.), *Olaus Petri – den mångsidige svenske reformatorn*, Svenska Kyrkohistoriska Föreningen, Uppsala, 1994. Heikki Pihlajamäki, "Gründer, Bewahrer oder Vermittler? Die nationalen und internationalen Elemente im Rechtsdenken des Olaus Petri", in: Jörn Eckert & Kjell Å Modéer, *Juristische Fakultäten und Juristenausbildung im Ostseeraum, Rättshistoriska skrifter*, Lund 2004, 29–38.

nobility for the profane sphere. As a parallel for the ecclesiastical jurisdiction a royal consistorium, *consistorium regni*, with the bishops, was established as a *forum privilegiatum* for the clergy. Throughout the 17th century there were frequent conflicts between the supremacy in the profane and ecclesiastical jurisdiction.[27] The ecclesiastical jurisdiction was defined in the Church Law 1686.[28]

Harald Gustafsson has argued that the early modern state was the *conglomerate state* – "composed of territories standing in different relations to their rulers, a state where the rulers found themselves in different relations to different parts of their domains. It was a political, judicial and administrative mosaic, rather than a modern unitary state. But it was a mosaic which was kept together more tightly than its medieval forerunner."[29] The conglomerate state was also a state for diversified privilegiated groups of the society.

The conglomerate state fostered jurists well oriented in comparative law. The early modern legal scholars as well as professional judges had to have an analogical analysis of the law. When the medieval and early-modern judge settled a dispute his cognitive views on the law presumed a comparative approach. "The plurality of normative orders of his world required a 'comparative' knowledge."[30]

The legal culture of the Swedish Reformation has to be studied with a long perspective. The latinists have observed that the latin of the 15th century belong to the most interesting periods of this language when it broke with the medieval latin to that of the standards of early renaissance generations.[31]

With the establishing of the nation state the *jus majestatis*-principles became central and upheld, regarding the *ius majestatis divinæ* as well as the *ius majestatis humanæ*.[32]

27 Sven Lindegård, *Consistorium regni och frågan om kyrklig överstyrelse: En studie i den svenska kyrkoförfattningens teori och praxis 1571–1686*, Gleerup: Lund, 1957.

28 Kyrkolagen 1686.

29 Harald Gustafsson, "The Conglomerate State: A Perspective on State Formation in Early Modern Europe", *Scandinavian Journal of History*, Volume 23, 1998 – Issue 3–4.

30 Adolfo Guiniani, "What is comparative legal history? Legal historiography and the revolt against fomalism, 1930–60", in: Aniceto Masferrer, Kjell Å Modéer, and Olivier Moréteau (eds), *Comparative legal history*, E. Elgar Publishing, Cheltenham, UK 2019, 52.

31 Egil Kraggerud, Review of Sara Risberg & Kirsi Salonen: "Auctoritate Papae. The Church Province of Uppsala and the Apostolic Penitentiary 1410–1526", Stockholm 2008., *Collegium Medievale* 2010, 240 ff.

32 Kerstin Malcus, "Maktpolitik och länsrättslig förvaltning: den regalrättsliga doktrinen i Sverige under 1560-talet", *Bibliotheca historica Lundensis* 25, Lund 1971.

7. Law and Gospel – The Two-Regiment Doctrine

In focus for Luther's Reformation was his complex theory of the Two Kingdoms, which he formulated in the later 1520s and 1530s. The two regiments- doctrine was legitimized in Matthew 22:21: "Render unto Caesar the things that are Caesar's, and unto God the things that are God's". This phrase has become a widely quoted summary of the relationship between Christianity, secular government, and society. The original message, coming in response to a question of whether it was lawful for Jews to pay taxes to Caesar, gives rise to multiple possible interpretations about the circumstances under which it is desirable for the Christian to submit to earthly authority.

The Catholic Church has a similar doctrine called the doctrine of the "two swords," in the papal bull *Unam Sanctam*, issued in 1302 by Pope Boniface VIII. Boniface teaches that there is only one Kingdom, the Church (here meaning the Catholic Church), and that the Church controls the *spiritual sword*, while the *temporal sword* is controlled by the State, although the temporal sword is hierarchically lower than the spiritual sword, allowing for Church influence in politics and society at large.[33]

Luther's two kingdoms doctrine was another form of the distinctive Lutheran teaching of Law and Gospel, and came to influence Swedish society with the adoption of a Lutheran identity.

"God has ordained two kingdoms or realms in which humanity is destined to live", Luther argued. The earthly kingdom is the realm of creation, of natural and civil life, where a person operates primarily by reason and law. The heavenly kingdom, on the other hand, is the realm of redemption, of spiritual and eternal life, where a person operates primarily by faith and love. These two kingdoms embrace parallel heavenly and earthly, spiritual and temporal forms of righteousness and justice, government and order, truth and knowledge. These two kingdoms interact and depend upon each other in a variety of ways, not least through biblical revelation and through the faithful discharge of Christian vocations in the earthly kingdom. But these two kingdoms ultimately remain distinct. The earthly kingdom is distorted by sin and governed by the Law. The heavenly kingdom is renewed by grace and guided by the Gospel. A Christian is a citizen of both kingdoms at once and invariably comes under the distinct government of each. As a heavenly citizen, the Christian remains free in his or her conscience, called to live fully by the light of the Word of God. But as an earthly citizen, the Christian is bound by law, and called to obey the

33 Brian Nelson, *The Making of the Modern State: A Theoretical Evolution*, Palgrave Macmillan US: 2006, 45.

natural orders and offices that God has ordained and maintained for the governance of this earthly kingdom."[34]

Luther rejected the medieval two-swords theory, the spiritual authority of the cleric and the canon were naturally superior to the temporal authority of the magistrate and the civil law. In Luther's view God has ordained three basic forms and forums of authority for governance of the earthly life: the domestic, ecclesiastical, and political authorities, or in modern terms, the family, the church, and the state. – – All three were needed to resist the power of sin and the Devil in the earthy kingdom.

The state was called to protect peace, to punish crime, to promote the common good, and to support the church, the family and other institutions, such as schools and charities, that were derived from them. Only the state, in Luther's view, held legal authority – the authority of the sword to pass and to enforce positive laws for the governance of the earthly kingdom. Contrary to medieval Catholic views, Luther emphasized that the Church was not a law-making authority. The Church had no sword, no jurisdiction. The formal legal authority lay with the state, not with the Church, with the magistrate, not with the cleric.[35]

The Protestant jurists implemented this doctrine. There was a whole coterie of sixteenth-century jurists and moralists who built on Luther's theories of law, politics and society. The three most important were Philip Melanchton, moral philosopher, systematic theologian and Roman Law Scholar at University of Wittenberg, further Johannes Eisenmann, a student of Melanchton and the founding law professor of the new Lutheran University of Marburg, and Johann Olderdorp, the most original and prolific jurist of the Lutheran Reformation. These three legal scholars brought many of Luther's cardinal theological teachings to direct and dramatic legal application.[36]

The Lutheran jurists emphasized, more than did Luther, that the Bible was an essential source of earthly law. They viewed the Bible as the highest source of law for life in the earthly kingdom. For them it was the full statement of the divine law. It contained the best summary of the natural law. It provided the surest guide for positive law.

The jurists laid special emphasis on the Ten Commandments. They provided the Lutheran jurists with a useful framework for organizing a good number of the new legal institutions of the Lutheran state. Interestingly enough,

34 John Witte, *Law and Protestantism: The Legal Teachings of the Lutheran Reformation*, Cambridge University Press: New York 2002, 5–6.

35 Witte, (2002), 7–8.

36 Witte, (2002), 9.

the Lutheran jurists adduced, more than Luther, Catholic Canon law as a valid source of Protestant civil law. Luther remained firmly opposed to the use of later medieval papal legislation. The Lutheran jurists were less reticent. They made ready use of the whole *Corpus iuris canonici* in their texts, courses, *consilia*, judicial opinions, and legislative drafting.[37]

In his book *Law and Protestantism* John Witte gives several examples of how the Lutheran jurists had a much more extensive interpretation of the Lutheran doctrines. In their application of Luther's doctrines they adjusted themselves to the legal contexts of its time. It was more of reforms than of revolutions. The reformers made ample use of scissors and paste in crafting the reformation laws. "They regularly duplicated their own formulations and those of their closest co-religionists in drafting new laws."[38] "Christ alone" and "faith alone" are Lutheran slogans that are reflected in this way.

8. Lutheran Doctrine in Swedish Law

Olaus Petri as well as his brother Laurentius Petri talked about *God's Laws* and *The ten commandments* and stated that the relationship between them and the positive law must coordinate. "All good and right law had to be conform with nature or God's described laws." Therefore all laws, the best and most righteous, follow God's commandments and the golden rule.[39]

Not only during the time for the Reformation but also in the 17th century the Mosaic law was regarded as an integrated part of Swedish positive law. The first example of the claims of the Reformers to include the ten commandments in the legislation come with the War Articles and the articles of the Court during the Reign of Gustav Wasa. This legislation was expanded and reorganized by Gustavus Adolphus 1621 and then later by king Charles XI in 1683 & 1685 but fulfilled the traditions regarding the religious laws.

Due to a failed attempt to reform the outdated medieval legislation King Charles IX 1608 confirmed and for the first time let print the Swedish National Law of Kristoffer from 1442. He included in the law an appendix with the Mosaic Laws. It was not a measure to substitute the obsolete church laws in the older editions of the laws but instead a realization of a reformatory claim

37 Witte, (2002), 10.

38 Witte, (2002), 190.

39 Sven Kjöllerström, *Guds och Sveriges lag under reformationstiden: en kyrkorättslig studie*, Gleerups: Lund 1957, 17.

to regard as the "Superior's protection of the two Tablets of the Law".[40] For the king it was also important to make clear, that it was the earthly jurisdiction and not the divine which had to apply the Mosaic Law. King Charles wanted to get rid of the jurisdiction of the bishops so the Laws of God were applied by the ordinary court.

The Appendix was valid law up to Sweden got a new national code in 1734 – even if it never was fully applied. The king made use of his right to give pardon, and also the Courts of Appeal had a nuanced position to the application of the strict Mosaic laws.[41]

With the entrance of the orthodox Lutheranism in Sweden during the latter part of the 17th century the witch-trials became very frequent and brought conflicts between the bishop's *consistorium* and the courts of appeal regarding the jurisdictions. Witch trials belonged to a group of trials, *causae mixti fori*, which could be applied in profane as well as in sacred courts. The principle said, that the instance which first handled the case, also should fulfil it. This type of cases had been frequent in the Middle ages, and now the *causae mixi fori* cases appeared again in witch-trials. It's a good example of the extensive application of continental foreign laws in Sweden in the 17th century. Even if it was the ordinary courts which had the jurisdiction in theses cases there was an interaction between the bishops in their *consistoria* and the Court of appeal. As in the German courts response were asked for in the law faculties, there is a version of that phenomenon in Sweden, when the Court of Appeal asks for a responsum in the Consistorium.[42] Interestingly enough the bishops argued for a strict application of the Mosaic Law, the judges, however argued for a more graceful decision.[43] So in the early modern times there were transparent borders between the two regiments doctrine in the Swedish conglomerate state. The mobility of the professional judiciary between the court systems also contributed to this translation of foreign elements into the Swedish legal culture.

9. Tolerance as the First Sign of a Modern Human Rights Discourse

The Westphalian Treaty 1648 became a European constitutional document introducing important new concepts. One of those was the concept of religious

40 Sven Kjöllerström, *Guds och Sveriges lag* (1957), 96.

41 Sven Kjöllerström, *Guds och Sveriges lag* (1957), 106.

42 Bengt Ankarloo, "Trolldomsprocesserna i Sverige", *Rättshistoriskt bibliotek* vol. 17, Nord. bokhandeln: Stockholm (1971), 90 ff.

43 Bengt Ankarloo, "Trolldomsprocesserna" (1971), 95.

tolerance, which became an important innovation in the religious divided Germany. as well as in international public law.[44]

Sweden, however, turned into an orthodox Lutheransim in the later part of the 17th century. It was a part of the nationalistic autocracy of the kings Charles XI and Charles XII. The 1680s became a period of royal initiatives regarding legal reforms not only regarding the secular code (adopted in 1734) and the Swedish Protestant church law, approved in 1686.

In 1726 it was regulated that religious meetings (conventicles) were prohibited outside the church. This regulation lasted up to the Tolerance edict in 1781. It also opened up for religious minorities like the Jews to settle in some places in Sweden.

10. Theologians and Jurists Collaborated in Creating the Protestant Swedish Law.

Family law is a good example of a field of law where the theologians and jurists interacted in creating a new Christian legal culture.

Marriage and divorce was regulated in a quite new way with help of Lutheran doctrines. The celibate was abolished and the clergy got a right to marry. A marriage could also be abolished. Divorce was accepted for married couples in two specific cases: Adultery and if one of the parties had abandoned the marriage.

One of the most important Lutheran principles was, however, that of ecclesiastical discipline, became one of the pillars on which the Church Law was published in 1686.

11. Law in Books and Law in Action

The innovative intellectual technology since the 15th century became the method of book-printing. It exploded within the book market from the early 16th century. It became an extremely important way to spread and increase legal thought and theological doctrine. Education became an important

44 Heinz Duchhardt (ed.) *Der Westfälische Friede. Diplomatie – politische Zäsur – kulturelles Umfeld – Rezeptionsgeschichte*. R. Oldenbourg Verlag: München 1998. – Winfried Schulze: *Pluralisierung als Bedrohung: Toleranz als Lösung*, (350 Jahre Westfälischer Friede – Entscheidungsprozesse, Weichenstellungen und Widerhall eines europäischen Ereignisse), Münster 1998. https://www.lwl.org/westfaelischegeschichte/portal/Internet/finde/langDatensatz.php?urlID=588&url_tabelle=tab_texte.

vehicle for the Protestants, and the legal as well as the theological sources were increasingly not only in Latin but also in the mother tongue.

Sweden is an as well important and useful example regarding the literacy of law and religion in a time of turbulent cognitive change. From people's court to royal state courts, from national profane law into European legal norms and from universal canon law into national religious laws and norms.

The Swedish King became the ruler in "The Two Kingdoms", the profane courts and their judiciary conquered their divine colleagues and counterpart. And the judges became the civil servants who with professional loyalty applied the virtues and duties they have learnt at the Lutheran universities in Germany.

A concrete artifact, demonstrating the intertwinement between law and religion, between profane and religious laws, is the collection of law-books for a well-educated clergyman in the beginning of the 17th century, probably assigned to Johannes Rudbeckius (1581–1646), bishop in the Diocese of Västerås,[45] and one of the main counselors of King Gustavus II. Adolphus.[46] He was also a strong supporter for the upholding of the privileges of the Clergy, a position that brought him in conflict with the King and his councellors. The Church law 1686, however, confirmed his threats. It subordinated the Church under the main administration in the way Rudbeckius regarded as wrong and dangerous.

This collection of law books in an impressive binding from 1629 is assigned to the bookbinder of king Gustavus II Adolphus, Marcus Sigfridsson (1607–1646). The volume has probably been Rudbeckius' personal collection of laws and statutes. It's a most interesting collection of laws, statutes and ordinances, some of them belong to the early law book printings from the early 17th century, some other are hand-written, so in a very concrete way it gives you information of the diverse and mixed legal culture representing two cultures, one older with hand-written legal sources and another modern with printed material. Within the handwritten material instructions for judges are included. The volume demonstrates the overlapping chronology regarding an earlier legal culture dominated by orality and hand-written legal material and another later based on printed material. The volume has initially belonged to a representative of the Swedish elite of civil servants, probably Rudbeckius. More research, however, has to be done regarding this material.

45 Erland Sellberg, [Art.] "Johannes Rudbeckius", *Svenskt Biografiskt Lexikon*, Bd. 30, Stockholm 1998–2000, 631 f.

46 The volume is in the possession of the author of this article.

12. Epilogue: The Transformation into a Protestant Legal Culture

Early modern Scandinavia experienced a transformation geopolitically in two entities: Western Scandinavia with Denmark, Norway and Iceland, and eastern Scandinavia with Sweden (and its provinces) and Finland. All the Scandinavian countries also experienced the creation of nationstates with their identities in their institutions and state religion. The professionalization of the Scandinavian judiciaries started earlier in Eastern Scandinavia. The intertwinement between law and theology was articulated not only in the legislation (crime and procedure) but also in interaction between the church and the courts. One example in the Swedish legal culture was the introduction in the Church law and confirmation in the 1734 code of the Court sermons to be held before the court-sessions begun. This very special religious ritual has been upheld up to modern times – also after the change of relation between Church and State 2000.

During the Early modern times Scandinavian jurists followed their European colleagues and used an historical argumentation in their professional work. Due to lack of legislative reforms the judiciary was urged to apply the medieval laws as supplementary legal sources. As late as 1726, when the Lund law professor David Nehrman in his published introduction to the Swedish civil law made an extensive evaluation to which extent those laws were obsolete and to which extent they should be applied.[47]

In Sweden Lutheran Protestatism wasn't introduced as in Denmark as a revolutionary change. Not until the Uppsala Meeting in 1593 Protestantism was accepted as the state religion. Until then there was a compromise with Catholic remains.

During the reign of Gustavus Adolphus (1610–1632) the Swedish Lawbooks for the first time were printed in 1608 and 1618 had a parallel in the publishing of the new translation of the Bible (that of Gustavus Adolphus) in 1542. The period was characterized by mixed jurisdictions, mixed cognitive structures, and an important intertwinement between their different contents.

During this period Sweden also geopolitically took the step towards a European great power in its ambition to control the Baltic Sea area. Consequently the jurists aimed to adopt a European legal culture. The judicial revolution in Sweden came with the new procedural reforms 1614–15, including a judicial reform with an ongoing professionalization of the Swedish

47 David Nehrman, *Inledning til then swenska jurisprudentiam civilem*, Lund 1726.

judiciary,[48] and study travels abroad resulted in the peak of those European influencies 1655–1680. The judges in the Swedish Courts of Appeal during this period extensively interpreted foreign legal sources, especially Roman Law and Natural Law. It also opened up for the professionalization of the Swedish judiciary, where in each lower court there had to be a professional judge, trained in law.

During the reign of Charles XI and Charles XII (from 1680–1718) the Swedish legal culture took a dramatically nationalistic turn, observed not only at the universities but also in the courts. The autocracy within politics also was reflected in the law. A parallel development was also to be observed within the religion with an orthodox monolithic Lutheranism and an autocratic society. There was no place for the Roman Catholic Church.[49] It was totally abolished up to the later part of the 19th century.[50]

Bibliography

Ankarloo, Bengt (1971), "Trolldomsprocesserna i Sverige", *Rättshistoriskt bibliotek* 17, Lund.

Berman, Harold J. (1983), *Law and Revolution*: Vol. 1. *The Formation of the Western Legal Tradition*, Harvard University Press: Cambridge/Mass. 1983,

Berman, Harold J.(2003), *Law and Revolution*, Vol. 2. *The Impact of the Protestant Reformations on the Western Legal Tradition*: Harvard University Press: Cambridge/Mass.

Decock, Wim (2012), *Theologians and Contract Law, The Moral Transformation of the Ius Commune, (ca. 1500–1650)*, Brill: Leiden.

Dahlman, Per (2009), "Kyrka och stat i 1860 års svenska religionslagstiftning", *Bibliotheca Theologiae Practicae* 87, Artos: Skellefteå.

Donahue, Charles (2008), *Law, Marriage and Society in the Later Middle Ages*, Cambridge University Press.

Duchhardt, Heinz (ed.) (1998), *Der Westfälische Friede. Diplomatie – politische Zäsur – kulturelles Umfeld – Rezeptionsgeschichte*. R. Oldenbourg Verlag: München.

48 David Gaunt, "Utbildning till statens tjänst: En kollektivbiografi av stormaktstidens hovrättsauskultanter", *Acta Universitatis Upsaliensis, Studia Historica Upsaliensia*, 63. Diss. Uppsala; Almqvist and Wiksell, Stockholm 1975.

49 Kjell Å Modéer, "Rättsfallet mot jesuitpatern Johan Ring 1735", *Kyrkohistorisk Årsskrift* 2002, 57 ff. – Arne Palmqvist, *Die Römisch-Katholische Kirche in Schweden nach 1781*, Almqvist & Wiksell: Uppsala 1954.

50 Per Dahlman, "Kyrka och stat i 1860 års svenska religionslagstiftning", [*Bibliotheca Theologiae Practicae* 87], Artos: Skellefteå 2009, 33 ff.

Gatrell, V. A. C., Lenman, Bruce and Parker, Geoffrey (eds.) (1980), *Crime and the Law: The Social History of Crime in Western Europé since 1500*, Europa: London, 11–48.

Gaunt, David (1975), "Utbildning till statens tjänst: En kollektivbiografi av stormaktstidens hovrättsauskultanter", *Acta Universitatis Upsaliensis, Studia Historica Upsaliensia*, number 63, Diss. Uppsala; Almqvist and Wiksell, Stockholm.

Giuliani, Adolfo (2019). "What is comparative legal history? Legal historiography and the revolt against formalism, 1930–60." in Aniceto Masferrer, Kjell Å Modéer, and Olivier Moréteau (eds), *Comparative Legal History*, E. Elgar Publishing, Cheltenham, UK, 30–77.

Gustafsson, Harald (1998), "The Conglomerate State: A Perspective on State Formation in Early Modern Europe", *Scandinavian Journal of History*, Vol. 23, Issue 3–4.

Helmholz, Richard (1974), *Marriage Litigation in Medieval England*, London.

Inger, Göran (1994), "Olaus Petri i rättshistoriens ljus", in: Carl F Hallencreutz & Sven-Ola Lindeberg (eds.), *Olaus Petri – den mångsidige svenske reformatorn*, Svenska Kyrkohistoriska Föreningen, Uppsala.

Jägerskiöld, Stig (1963), *Studier rörande receptionen av främmande rätt i Sverige under den yngre landslagens tid*, Almqvist & Wiksell: Stockholm.

Kjöllerström, Sven (1957), *Guds och Sveriges lag under reformationstiden: en kyrkorättslig studie*, Gleerups: Lund.

Kraggerud, Egil (2010), [Review] Sara Risberg & Kirsi Salonen: "Auctoritate Papae. The Church Province of Uppsala and the Apostolic Penitentiary 1410–1526", Stockholm 2008, in: *Collegium Medievale*, 240 ff.

Korpiola, Mia (2004), "Kyrkotukt för hela folket: Hertig Gustafs av Saxen "horerei" och luthersk kyrkodisciplin i Sverige på 1500- och 1600-talen", in: Jukka Kekkonen et al. (eds.), *Norden, Rätten, Historia: Festskrift till Lars Björne*, Suomalainen Lakimiesyhdistys: Helsinki, 65 ff.

Korpiola, Mia (ed.) (2014), "The Svea court of appeal in the early modern period. Historical reinterpretations and new perspectives", *Rättshistoriska studier* vol. 26, Jure: Stockholm.

Kyrkio-Lag och Ordning (1686) som then Stormächtigste Konung och Herre Herr Carl then Elofte, Sweriges, Göthes och Wändes Konung & Åhr 1686 hafwer låtit författa och Åhr 1687 af Trycket utgå och publicera … Johan Georg Eberdt, Stockholm.

Lindegård, Sven (1957), *Consistorium regni och frågan om kyrklig överstyrelse: En studie i den svenska kyrkoförfattningens teori och praxis 1571–1686*, Gleerup: Lund.

Lindroth, Sten (1975) *Svensk lärdomshistoria*, Vol. 1. *Medeltiden och reformationstiden*, Norstedt: Stockholm,

Lindroth, Sten (1975), *Svensk lärdomshistoria*. Vol. 2. *Stormaktstiden*, Norstedt: Stockholm.

Malmström, Åke (1976), "Ur den juridiska fakultetens historia", *Acta Universitates Uppsaliensis, Uppsala University 500 years*: nr. 11. Uppsala.

Malcus, Kerstin (1971), "Maktpolitik och länsrättslig förvaltning: den regalrättsliga doktrinen i Sverige under 1560-talet", *Bibliotheca historica Lundensis* 25, Lund.

Max Planck Institute for European Legal History, *Report 2015–2017*, Frankfurt/Main 2018.

Modéer, Kjell Å (2017), *Det förpliktande minnet: Juridiska fakultetens i Lund 1656–2016*, Santérus Förlag: Stockholm.

Modéer, Kjell Å (1975), "Gerichtsbarkeiten der schwedischen Krone im deutschen Reichsterritorium, I. Voraussetzungen und Aufbau 1630–1657", *Rättshistoriskt bibliotek* vol. 24, Lund.

Modéer, Kjell Å (1992), "Karolinernas jurister: Det militära rättsväsendets aktörer under det karolinska envåldet". *Karolinska förbundets Årsskrift*, 23 ff.

Modéer, Kjell Å (2015), [Review] Wim Decock, "Theologians and Contract Law, The Moral Transformation of the Ius Commune, (ca. 1500–1650)", Brill 2012, in: *Kyrkohistorisk Årsskrift*, 227 ff.

Modéer, Kjell Å (2002), "Rättsfallet mot jesuitpatern Johan Ring 1735", Kyrkohistorisk *Årsskrift*, 57 ff.

Modéer, Kjell Å (2018), "Suum Cuique Tribuere" [An Introduction], in: Modéer, Kjell Å & Sunnqvist, Martin (eds.), *Suum Cuique Tribuere: Legal Contexts and Deep Structures Regarding Courts of Appeal and Judiciaries from Early Modern to Late Modern Europe, Rättshistoriska studier*, Vol. 27, Stockholm 2018, 14 ff.

Nehrman, David (1726), *Inledning til then swenska jurisprudentiam civilem*, Lund.

Nelson, Brian (2006), *The Making of the Modern State: A Theoretical Evolution*, Palgrave Macmillan US.

Nihlén, Lars (1983), "Peregrinatio academica. Det svenska samhället och de utrikes studieresorna under 1600-talet", *Bibliotheca historica Lundensis* 54, 123.

Palmqvist, Arne (1954), *Die Römisch-Katholische Kirche in Schweden nach 1781*, Almqvist & Wiksell: Uppsala.

Pihlajamäki, Heikki (2004), Gründer, "Bewahrer oder Vermittler? Die nationalen und internationalen Elemente im Rechtsdenken des Olaus Petri", in: Jörn Eckert & Kjell Å Modéer, *Juristische Fakultäten und Juristenausbildung im Ostseeraum: Zweiter Rechtshistorikertag in Ostseeraum* (2002), *Rättshistoriska skrifter*, Lund, 29–38.

Risberg, Sara & Kirsi Salonen Kirsi (2008), "Auctoritate papae: The Church Province of Uppsala in the Apostolic Penitentiary 1410–1526" (*Diplomatarium Suecanum: Appendix: Acta pontificum Suecica, II: Acta Poenitentiariae*), Riksarkivet: Stockholm.

Salonen, Kirsi & Hanska, Jussi (2013, *Entering a Clerical Career at the Roman Curia, 1458–1471* (Church, Faith and Culture in the Medieval West), Routledge: London.

Salonen, Kirsi (2001), *The Penitentiary as a well of Grace in the late middle ages: The example of the province of Uppsala 1449–1527*, Saarijärvi.

Schulze, Winfried (1998), *Pluralisierung als Bedrohung: Toleranz als Lösung*, (350 Jahre Westfälischer Friede – Entscheidungsprozesse, Weichenstellungen und Widerhall eines europäischen Ereignisse), Münster.

Sellberg, Erland (2000),[Art.] "Johannes Rudbeckius", *Svenskt Biografiskt Lexikon*, Bd 30, Stockholm 1998–2000, 631 f.

Sunnqvist, Martin (2008), "Domareden och dess religiösa inslag", in: Kjell Å Modéer (ed.), *Rätt, religion och politik. Ett rättshistoriskt seminarium tillägnat Magnus Sjöberg, Rättshistoriska skrifter* Band 9, Stockholm, 85 ff.

Tamm, Ditlev (2011), *The Faculty of Law: The Teaching of Law at the University of Copenhagen since 1479*, Museum Tusculanum: Copenhagen.

Tate, C. Neal & Vallinder, Torbjörn (1995), *The Global Expansion of Judicial Power*, New York University; New York.

Thunander. Rudolf (1993), "Hovrätt i funktion: Göta hovrätt och brottmålen", *Rättshistoriskt bibliotek*, vol. 49, Stockholm.

Tuori, Kaarlo (1997), "Towards a Multi-layered view of Modern Law". in Aulis Aarnio et al(eds.), *Aleksander Peczenik on the Occasion of his 60th Birthday on 16 November 1997*, Juristförtlaget i Lund: Lund, 427–42.

Wijffels, A:A. & van Rhee, C. H. (eds.) 2013, *European Supreme Courts: A Portrait through History*, Third Millenium Publishing London, 66 ff, 90 ff.

Österlin, Lars (1997), *Svenska kyrkan i profil: Ur engelskt och nordiskt perspektiv*, 2nd ed., Verbum: Stockholm.

Witte, John (2002), *Law and Protestantism: The Legal Teachings of the Lutheran Reformation*, Cambridge University Press: New York.

Internet

Thomas Duve, *Von der Europäischen Rechtsgeschichte zu einer Rechtsgeschichte Europas in globalhistorischer Perspektive* (From a European Legal History Towards a Legal History of Europe in a Global Historical Perspective), in: Max Planck Institute for European Legal History Research Paper Series 2012:2 (2012), 1–80, http://ssrn.com/abstract=2139312. – Visited 2020-05-20.

Tolerance, Oppression, and Misapprehension

Bishop Petrus Bjugge's 1643 Report and the Swedish Legal, Religious, and Administrational Stance on the Orthodox in Ladogan Karelia

Johan Bastubacka

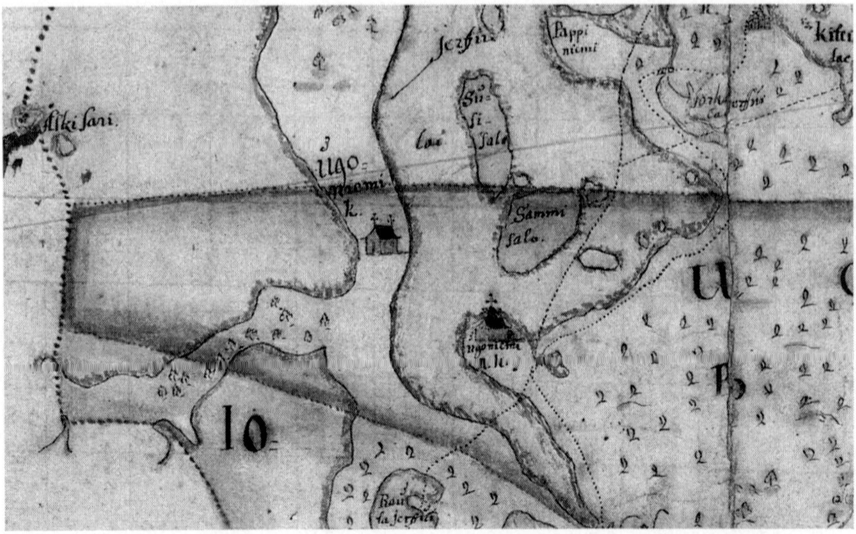

Picture 6.1 Excerpt from a seventeenth-century Swedish map depicting the core area of Uukuniemi parish in Southern Karelia northwest from Lake Ladoga. "Ugoniemi k.[yrka]" indicates the Lutheran parish church and "Ugoniemi R.[rysk] k.[kyrka]" the local Orthodox temple. Both are situated on respective sides of Lake Pyhäjärvi ("Sacred Lake"). Archeological excavations were made on the site of the former Orthodox church and near-by village in Papinniemi, Uukuniemi from 1995 to 2007.[1]

As the Kingdom of Sweden took over new eastern regions, it not only gained new land, but also generated a meeting of two different peoples, evolving different languages and writing systems, ecclesiastical structures, theological interpretations, laws, and administrative practices and structures. Expansion eastwards meant that the former Orthodox-Karelian majority gradually

1 See Laakso, Ville. *Papinniemi in Uukuniemi and related archaeological sites of the eastern Orthodox cultural area in Finland.* Diss. Turku: Suomen keskiajan arkeologian seura. Archaologia Medii Aevi Finlandiae XIX, 2014, esp. 18; Kexholm map, the digital archives of Riksarkivet, Stockholm, *Geographisch affrijtning upå Kiäxholms lähn.* 1649–1650.

 | DOI:10.30965/9783657790746_007

became a minority in its own territory. All the seventeenth-century events took place concurrently with difficult and even appalling weather conditions, in the worst years with a devastating famine. Within this framework, I want to study the practical impact of the emerging absolute monarch as the head of the Lutheran church and a divinely authorized administration on religious others in the kingdom. The ensuing conflict of cultures and worldviews will also be explored. The core of my study will be the relationship between the fundamental legal documents of the Lutheran Swedish realm, with a glance forward to the Church law of 1686, and the developments in Kexholm on the periphery of the Protestant Swedish realm, as can be seen from Bishop Bjugge's report of 1643 and the reply from the central government in 1644.

1. Karelian Kexholm Region In-Between East and West

The people who had lived in the area around Lake Ladoga since the Finno-Ugric tribes first inhabited the region had merged more or less into one population with its distinctive features in the Early Medieval Era. To the same cultural-geographical sphere belonged also the sparsely inhabited land of North Karelia. These people were gradually Christianized from the eleventh or twelfth centuries onwards, insofar as in the fourteenth century several monastic institutions were functional in the area with their distinctively Eastern Orthodox characteristics.[2]

Christianization began as a result of Varjag contacts with Byzantium and the Christianization of Kiev and Novgorod (Великий Новгород). Kiev, Novgorod, and Staraja Ladoga (on the eastern shore of Lake Ladoga) can be considered as settlements that had an effect on the area through cultural and commercial relationships.[3] Ladogan Karelia was to be regarded as part of the Novgorodian region in the Medieval Era, and Novgorodian ecclesiastical influences were prevalent in the area until the beginning of the eighteenth century.[4]

2 Kirkinen, Heikki. "Kalevalainen Karjala ja Kristinusko." In *Karjala 1. Portti Itään ja Länteen.* Hämeenlinna: Karisto, 1982, 259–260, 264–279; cf. Laitila, Teuvo. *Jumalat, haltijat ja pyhät – Eletty Ortodoksisuus Karjalassa 1000–1900.* Helsinki: Suomen kirkkohistoriallinen seura, 2017, 54–67.

3 Kirkinen, *Kalevalainen Karjala ja Kristinusko*, 1982, 264–279 (2); Korpela, Jukka. *Kiovan Rusj. Keskiajan eurooppalainen suurvalta.* Joensuu: Ortodoksisen kirjallisuuden julkaisuneuvosto, 1996, 65–98, 138–146.

4 Kirkinen, *Kalevalainen Karjala ja Kristinusko*, 1982, 275, 277–279 (2); Koukkunen, Heikki. "Ortodoksinen Karjala." In *Karjala 1. Portti Itään ja Länteen.* Hämeenlinna: Karisto, 1982, 281–289.

Picture 6.2 Valaam Monastery as the center of Christian influences ("mission" in Kirkinen, Kalevalainen Karjala ja Kristinusko, 1982, 274). The map is based on the year 1500 taxation catalogue of the (Kexholm) pogosts. Monasteries are marked with crosses and inhabited regions with dashes.

Picture 6.3 A map of Eastern border regions of Sweden in the first half of 17th century.[5]

Ever since the Medieval Era the ongoing tension and hostilities between first Sweden and Novgorod and then Sweden and Moscow had shadowed the history of the area. The list of hostilities is long. In the Nöteborg Peace in 1323 and in the treaties of Plussa in 1583, and Teusina in 1595, the border had constantly been drawn more and more eastwards and the Peace Treaty of Stolbova 1617 represented the culmination of that development. When the treaty was ratified, a new era dawned for the Orthodox population of Ladogan Karelia and Ingria.[6]

5 Karta över Finland, the digital archives of Riksarkivet, Stockholm, *Karta över Finland, sydöst om linjen Borgå-Padasjoki-Nyslott, området runt Ladoga och Ingermanland från 1600-talets förra hälft (Nyen skans angiven)*. 1600–1650.

6 Fredstraktat mellan Sverge och Ryssland, genom hvilken Ryssland och Sverge afträdde Keksholms län och Ingermanland mot det att Sverge återlämnade sina andra eröfringar. Stolbova, 1617, Februari 27. In *Sveriges Traktater med Främmande Magter jemte andra dit hörande handlingar.* Femte delens förra hälft 1572–1632. Stockholm: O. S. Rydbäck & C. Hallanderff, 1903, 242–267; Biafsked till traktaten i Stolbova. In *Sveriges Traktater med Främmande Magter jemte andra dit hörande handlingar.* Femte delens förra hälft 1572–1632.

Russia had, after the death of Ivan IV the Terrible, 1584, fallen into disarray and weakness. The "Time of Troubles" truly began when the last emperor of the Rurik Dynasty, Feodor Ivanovich, died in 1598. Russia seemed to collapse into turmoil, war, and famine. When the new Romanov dynasty began in 1613 with Tsar Michael Romanov (1596–1645) on the throne, Russia began to recreate itself in terms of regions, commerce, administration, and military forces. The division in Russian Orthodoxy at the synod of 1666–1667 is one example of this still turbulent era.[7]

When Russia floundered after the Rurik dynasty, Sweden was able to benefit from the situation. The military leadership of Gustaf II Adolf (1594–1632, regnant 1611–1632) propelled Sweden to become a significant and expanding power in Scandinavia, Finland, Karelia, and Ingria, the Baltic Region, and northern Germany. For a time, at the beginning of the seventeenth century, the Swedish regime planned to create the Swedish Vasa-family-led territory stretching into northern Russia with Novgorod as its center and the younger son of King Charles IX (1550–1611) Carl Filip as the Grand Duke. While these plans came to naught, Sweden still expanded considerably eastwards after the Stolbova Peace Treaty of 1617.[8] The reigns of Queen Christina (b. 1626, Queen 1632–1654, regnant 1644–1654, d. 1689), King Charles X (regnant 1654–1660), Hedvig Eleonora (served as regnant 1660–1672, 1697), King Charles XI (1660–1697), and King Charles XII (1697–1718) were marked by efforts to maintain and develop the "conglomerate kingdom" as a great power with evolving

---

Stockholm: O. S. Rydbäck & C. Hallanderff, 1903, 267–269; Villstrand, *Sveriges Historia 1600–1721*, Stockholm: Norstedts, 2011, 91–92; Isberg, Alvin. *Svensk segregations-och konversionspolitik i Ingermanland 1617–1704*. Uppsala: University of Uppsala, 1973, 9–12; Karonen, Petri. *Pohjoinen Suurvalta. Ruotsi ja Suomi 1521–1809*. Helsinki: WSOY, 1999, 25–33; Laasonen, Pentti. *Novgorodin imu. Miksi ortodoksit muuttivat Käkisalmen läänistä Venäjälle 1600-luvulla?* Helsinki: Suomalaisen kirjallisuuden seura, 2005, 11–16; Sivonen, Mika. *Me inkerikot, vatjalaiset ja karjalaiset. Uskonnollinen integrointi ja ortodoksisen vähemmistön identiteetin rakentuminen Ruotsin Inkerissä 1680–1702*. Bibliotheca Historica 111. Helsinki: Suomalaisen kirjallisuuden seura, 2007, 28–31. The Käkisalmi region had already been occupied by the Swedish in 1580–1995. The Peace Treaty of Teusina 1595 ended the occupation. Fagerlund, Rainer. "Vanhempi Vaasa-kausi 1523–1617." In *Kuninkaita ja alamaisia. Suomen historia 1523–1809*. Espoo: Schildts, 2000, 63–68.

7 Kuujo, Erkki. "Venäjä uuden ajan alussa." In *Venäjän Historia*. Ed. Heikki Kirkinen. Helsinki: Otava, 2002, 81–106, 98–106; Lappalainen, Jussi T. "Toipuva Moskovan valtakunta." In *Venäjän Historia*. Ed. Heikki Kirkinen. Helsinki: Otava, 2002, 107–131, 124; Fagerlund, *Vanhempi Vaasa-kausi 1523–1617*, 2000, 96.

8 Karonen, *Pohjoinen suurvalta*, 1999, 129–130 (6); Fagerlund, *Vanhempi Vaasa-kausi 1523–1617*, 2000, 98–100.

administration, unification efforts, and an emerging absolute monarchy. The Peace of Westphalia 1648 is one significant example of this position of Swedish power.[9]

As for Swedish Karelia, Count Axel Oxenstierna (in office 1612–1654) and Count Per Brahe the Younger (the General Governor of Finland 1637–1640 and 1648–1654) were prominent figures in the administration of the Great Duchy of Finland and the Kexholm province. Large parts of the region were also feudalized in the latter part of the seventeenth century.[10] The Academy of Åbo was founded in 1640 to consolidate learning and to produce officials for administration of the kingdom.[11]

2. Karelian Orthodox Population in the New Setting

For the first time in Ladogan-Karelian history, after 1617, the area was not only attacked or occupied by foreign forces for a brief period of time, but largely came under the umbrella of the realm of new Nordic military power, its administration, law and religion.[12] For the inhabitants of Ladogan Karelia, this meant uncertainty: they did not know whether the occupation, their home region made a province of Sweden, was to last for a few decades or for ages to come.

In the Uppsala Synod of 1593 it was decided to install Lutheranism as the sole confession of the kingdom, and this development was sealed by the 1611 declaration made by the new King Gustaf II Adolf.[13] The Örebro 1617 Charter sharpened the legislation in terms of religious otherness by specifically proclaiming that Catholics were outsiders who needed to be excluded – on the threat of the death penalty or deportation from the country.[14] This took place

---

9 Villstrand, "Suurvaltakausi 1617–1721". In Kuninkaita ja alamaisia. Suomen historia 1523–1809. Espoo: Schildts, 2000, 159–199, 210–217, 280–304.

10 Karonen, *Pohjoinen suurvalta*, 1999, esp. 212–243, 252–262, 271–273, 289–311 (6); Kuujo, "Venäjä uuden ajan alussa", 2002, 103.

11 Villstrand, *Suurvaltakausi 1617–1721*, 263–264.

12 This was not the first time the Kexholm area was under foreign occupation. It had been in the war-zone in 1570 when the 25-year war started, again after 1610, and the castle of Käkisalmi had been taken by Swedish troops in 1611. Fagerlund, *Vanhempi Vaasa-kausi 1523–1617*, 2000, 63–68, 96–99.

13 Knuutila Jyrki. "Kirkkolainsäädäntö – Kirkon vai Yhteiskunnan Asia? Kirkon ja Yhteiskunnan Väliset Suhteet ja Suomessa Käytetyt Säädökset Kanonisesta Oikeudesta Vuoden 1993 Kirkkolakiin." *Edilex 2012*, version 1.0, (2012): 18; Villstrand, *Sveriges Historia 1600–1721*, 2011, 324 (5); Fagerlund, *Vanhempi Vaasa-kausi 1523–1617*, 2000, 73–74.

14 *Svenska Riksdagsakter*. Andra handlingar. 1521–1718. Nils Ahnlund ed. Stockholm: P. A. Norstedt & Söner. 1957, II:2, 276/97, Örebro Stadga 27.2.1617, esp. 270–271; See also Villstrand, *Sveriges Historia 1600–1721*, 2011, 332 (6).

in the very same year that the Peace of Stolbova was reached with Russia.[15] The feared impact of the Counter-Reformation was the major factor behind this stipulation, and specifically the Polish Royal Vasa-family connection was regarded as politically dangerous.[16]

As the Kingdom of Sweden took over new eastern regions, it not only gained new land, but also ruled over the meeting of two different peoples with different languages and writing systems, ecclesiastical structures, theological interpretations, laws, and administrative practices and structures. Expansion eastwards meant that the former Orthodox-Karelian majority gradually became a minority in its own territory as a result of basically two major developments: Firstly, due to the influx of "Swedes", i.e. predominantly Finnish people from the Savolax and also Tavastland regions (of these the historical expansion of the Savolax people in all directions from the core Savilahti area was formative ever since the fifteenth century) and, secondly, due to the massive fleeing and emigration of the indigenous population, specifically to Tver Karelia in the Russian territory. The chief motivation of this emigration was the Nordic/Rupture 1656–1658 War, during which the greatest relocation of the population took place both in Ingria and Ladogan Karelia.[17]

The 1656–1658 war was anything but a Karelian-focused hostility. It began as a conflict between Ukrainian Cossacks and Poland, and soon flamed into a larger war when Russian military forces advanced (in support of the Cossacks) aiming to take over former Polish Baltic lands. The Swedish government did not want to let the Russians alone benefit from the weakened Polish position, hence Swedish forces advanced into both the Baltic region and Poland. Ingria, Ladogan Karelia, and Savolax were simply minor episodes far away from the hotspot of the conflict, and at the end of the hostilities their connection was made in the Roskilde Peace Treaty of 1658.[18]

In the end, the local hostilities included unsuccessful Russian attempts to regain the lost Karelian and Ingrian lands and to benefit from the local peoples' loyalty to the Russian Tsar and Orthodoxy. The Karelian Orthodox population

15 Fredstraktat mellan Sverge och Ryssland, genom hvilken Ryssland och Sverge afträdde Keksholms län och Ingermanland mot det att Sverge återlämnade sina andra eröfringar. Stolbova, 1617, Februari 27, 1903, 242–267; Villstrand, *Sveriges Historia 1600–1721*, 2011, 91–92 (6).

16 See Tham Wilhelm. *Den svenska utrikes politikens historia*. Stockholm: Norstedts, 1960: 102.

17 Pirinen Kauko & Jutikkala Eino. *A History of Finland*. Helsinki: WSOY, 2003, 153–154; Villstrand, *Suurvaltakausi 1617–1721*, 172–175 (11); Lappalainen Jussi T. *Kaarle X Kustaan Venäjän-sota v. 1656–1658 Suomen suunnalla*. Jyväskylä, Jyväskylän yliopisto, 1972, 264–265, 278–285.

18 Lappalainen. *Kaarle X Kustaan Venäjän-sota v. 1656–1658 Suomen suunnalla*, esp. 26–29, 42–45, 111–121, 226–229, 264–265 (17).

largely took part in the venture – that has in research even been characterized as a religious war – and as it proved unsuccessful, disappointment and fear of revenge were major catalysts for expatriation. In that setting, the Russian side also encouraged and even organized expatriation from Karelia.[19]

The division in the Russian Church at the 1666–1667 synod had its effect on both Swedish Ingria and Karelia, making the religious situation more complicated. These historical events started in the Russian realm in 1653 with Patriarch Nikon's renewals, but their impact only became evident in Karelia later, in the late seventeenth century. What effect the division had on Karelian Orthodoxy outside Russia is, however, an interesting question. Old Believer-based sects, e.g., the *Dukhobors*, the *Molokans*, the *Khlysty*, developed successively from the apocalyptic movement.[20]

All the seventeenth-century events took place concurrently with difficult and indeed appalling weather conditions (the "small ice age"), and during the worst years with the addition of a devastating famine. People were extremely dependent on the summer success in agriculture if they were to survive the harsh winters. Life was difficult as harvests were often poor. Hunger and illness were prevalent. The worst harvest disasters and years of hunger occurred at the very end of the century.[21]

3. Research Perspectives, Sources, and Research Questions

Within this context, it is important to ask what the practical impact was of having the emerging absolute monarch as the head of the Lutheran Church

---

19 Lappalainen. *Kaarle X Kustaan Venäjän-sota v. 1656–1658 Suomen suunnalla*, 111–121, 171–172, 264–265, 278–285. On the conflict in Karelia interpreted as a religious war, see the webpage of the South-Karelian museums, https://www.etelakarjalanmuseot.fi/etela-karjalan-historiaa/ 13 March 2019.

20 On the 1666–1667 Sobor, see Pospielovsky, Dimitry. *The Orthodox Church in the History of Russia*. Crestwood, New York: St Vladimir's Seminary Press, 1998, 71–77; Lappalainen Heikki. "Toipuva Moskovan Valtakunta". In *Venäjän historia* ed. Heikki Kirkinen. Helsinki: Otava, 2002, 109–110, 121–123. On the Old Believers in Karelia, see Katajala Kimmo. "Savuna taivasten valtakuntaan. Vanhauskoisten polttoitsemurhat Ruotsin-Karjalassa 1600-luvun lopulla." In *Manaajista Maalaisaateliin*, ed. Kimmo Katajala. Helsinki: Suomalaisen kirjallisuuden seura, 1995, 181–200.

21 See Fagerlund, *Vanhempi Vaasa-kausi 1523–1617*, 2000, 114; Muroma, Seppo. *Suurten kuolonvuosien (1696–1697) väestönmenetys Suomessa*. Helsinki: SHS, 1991, esp. 8–9. The culmination of this natural phenomena was the "great death years" 1696–1697, but the climate was remarkably harsh already in 1600–1601.

with a divinely authorized administration ruling over religious others in the kingdom. And what was the resulting conflict of cultures and worldviews like?

One specific, if even unique, document is a report by the eighth-in-line Lutheran Bishop Petrus Bjugge[22] of Wiborg, Finnish Karelia, dated in the summer of 1643.[23] In his research, Pentti Laasonen has characterized the report as "an unanalyzed list that gives an unrealistically horrific image of the intentions of the regime". But was the document so unrealistic and horrific?[24] While the research previously referred to comes to this conclusion,[25] a close reading of the text reveals numerous previously unexamined details that inform about the encounter between the two religious-cultural spheres: Swedish-Finnish Lutheranism and Russian-Karelian Orthodoxy.

This forced encounter took place as a result of the above-mentioned Stolbova 1617 Peace Treaty because the treaty obliged the peasants and their Orthodox priests to remain in the newly occupied provinces of Kexholm (Ladogan and North Karelia) and Ingria. They became subjects of the royal Swedish administration and legal regulations – but what that actually meant when it came to matters of religion is highly questionable.[26] I tend to find that Tarkiainen's position on this might emerge as the most reasonable one in terms of the focus in this study as well. He argued that the Swedish government and ecclesiastical administration did not want to give any guarantees that would allow the

22 On the biography of Bjugge, see Ch. 5.

23 The document is found in the university library of Uppsala, Nordinska samlingen 1920, document nr. 44. It consists of 22 paper sheets.

24 Laasonen, *Novgorodin Imu*, 44, footnote 96 (6).

25 See Isberg, *Svensk segregations- och konversionspolitik i Ingermanland 1617–1704*, 1973, 46 fn. 1, 54 (6); Laasonen, Pentti. *Suomen Kirkon Historia 2. Vuodet 1593–1808*. Porvoo, Helsinki, Juva: WSOY. 1991, 191–192; Laasonen, *Novgorodin imu*, 2005, esp. 72–73 (6); Tarkiainen Kari. *Moskoviten. Sverige och Ryssland 1478–1721*. Helsingfors: Svenska litteratursällskapet I Finland, 2017, 246–247. All these writers made references to certain aspects or sentences in Bjugge's 1643 report.

26 Fredstraktat mellan Sverge och Ryssland, genom hvilken Ryssland och Sverge afträdde Keksholms län och Ingermanland mot det att Sverge återlämnade sina andra eröfringar. Stolbova, 1617, Februari 27, 1903, 250; Villstrand, *Sveriges Historia 1600–1721*, 2011, 91–92 (6). Researchers have presented differing interpretations: cf. Tarkiainen, *Moskoviten. Sverige och Ryssland 1478–1721*, 2017, 234–242 (25); Laasonen, *Novgorodin imu*, 2005, esp. 16–103, 128–154 (6); Isberg, *Svensk segragations-och konversionspolitik I Ingemanland 1617–1704*, 1973, esp. 16–38, 79–120 (6). This discussion was opened already in 1900 in the following dissertation: Öhlander, Carl. *Om den Svenska Kyrkoreformationen uti Ingermanland. Ett Bidrag till Svenska Kyrkans Historia Åren 1617–1704*. Diss. Uppsala: Almqvist & Wiksells. 1900, 10–11. Öhlander believed that the guarantees given for Ivangorod merchants and King Charles the X's letter to the Polish Orthodox in 1656 were also to be applied to Ingria.

Orthodox population to continue. They could accept the status quo but did not want to safeguard this population's future.[27]

The 1643 report makes it possible to look more deeply into the concepts, instructions, control, rules, prohibitions, and punishments through which the royal ecclesiastical administration *wanted* to govern a significant cultural, linguistic, and religious minority. The text is not a singular, fragmentary document, but rather one preserved example of a sequence of documents framed by other, related, contemporary texts and by the development of seventeenth-century Swedish legislation and administration. Together, these texts illuminate Lutheranism's impact on law and religion in the kingdom.

Local, Karelian events were not isolated from European politics and interests. It is, moreover, worth considering whether the decades-long clash of faiths and life worlds – also within the context of the larger European conflict in the Thirty Years' War (1618–1648) – had an effect on the notions of divinely authorized laws and government. When divine rights and religious traditions clashed with no rational solution in sight, and dissenting faiths could not be completely rooted out, one may assume that certain reasonable grounds for coexistence and communality eventually needed to be found.[28]

Accordingly, even though it appears anachronistic to argue for the use of contemporary notions such as "religious tolerance" or "freedom of religion", and also "the secularity of law" in a mid-seventeenth century Swedish context, it is worth asking if certain local events at least in part influenced later Nordic ways of understanding the different relationships and configurations of religion and law. Potentially the elementary roots of the secularity of law could be discerned in the dysfunctional efforts to create and maintain religious uniformity.

Bearing these perspectives in mind, the document has been analyzed in the light of the following research questions.

Firstly, it was essential to know what the Orthodox population was subject to administratively and legislatively in Bjugge's realm. What were the Lutheran Bishop's and the Stockholm government's aspirations for them, and what was the goal of these policies? What was Bjugge's place in the administration? In other words, how did the regime "act out" the position of Her Royal Majesty as the head of the kingdom and its Lutheran church in this new eastern province?

27 Tarkiainen, *Moskoviten*, 2017, 240 (25).

28 See the "question on amnesty" regarding the Peace of Westfalen in Rosén, Jerker. "Westfaliska freden." In *Den Svenska Historien. Gustaf Adolfs och Christinas tid 1611–1654*, ed. Gunvor Grenholm. Stockholm: Bonniers, 1967, 125, 126–128.

What was actually achieved is another issue, but I will briefly refer to that as well.

Secondly, it is necessary to understand the "controlling gaze" of the (for the locals) alien bishop, and the religious-political grounds for the suspicion and misapprehension that seemed to govern his interpretation of the situation.

Presumably, all these aspects reflected the emerging Swedish seventeenth-century legal and theological understanding concerning a prominent religious minority that was never mentioned by name in the later 1686 Church Law.[29] Could Bjugge's text (through the writer's close contacts with the government) actually be regarded as a more or less influential element in the forging of the administration and even the law in constructing the nation in that era with respect to matters of religion?

The primary legal contexts for these questions were the two significant agreements that defined the country's confessional status: the 1593 Uppsala Treaty that made Lutheranism the religion of the country, and the 1617 Örebro Charter that defined Catholicism as forbidden with the penalty of capital punishment or expatriation. All the previous questions actually boil down to the question of how these legal documents were executed in practice. In a like manner, they are related to the question of the interpretation of the 1617 Stolbova Peace Treaty's few chapters on religious matters.[30]

4. Methodological Questions

Bearing in mind that the accessible data in this research was qualitatively rich, informative, and highly detailed, it primarily called for micro-historical

29 Kyrkio-Lag och Ordning / som then Stormächtigste Konung och Herre / Herr CARL then Elofte / Sweriges / Göthes och Wändes Konung / &c.Åhr 1686. hafwer låtit författa / ochÅhr 1687. af Trycket utgå och publicera. Jemte ther til hörige Stadgar. http://www.mlang.name/arkisto/kyrkio-lag-1686.html 21 June 2018.

30 Fredstraktat mellan Sverge och Ryssland, genom hvilken Ryssland och Sverge afträdde Keksholms län och Ingermanland mot det att Sverge återlämnade sina andra eröfringar. Stolbova, 1617, Februari 27, 1903, (on deportation of monks and the obligation to peasants and their priests to stay) 249–250, (on the religious rights of merchants) 255; Villstrand, *Sveriges Historia 1600–1721*, 2011, 91–92, 332 (6). See also Tarkiainen, who argues that even though the treaty itself said nothing about the religious rights of the peasants it, anyway, could be interpreted as safeguarding certain rights. Tarkiainen, *Moskoviten. Sverige och Ryssland 1478–1721*, 240: (25) "---Därmed antyddes det att de skulle få utöva sin egen religion och ha egna präster. Antaganet bekräftas av att det senare i Ivangorods privilegier står att stadsborna får 'niuta sin Grekesk Religions frijheet och Gudztienst efter de gamble.'" I strongly hesitate to draw a similar conclusion.

approaches[31] in the analysis of the sources. This in practice means undertaking a detailed close reading of historical documents, paying attention to the thinking and actions of the (common) people, and also seeing the significance of the phenomena that in a contemporary setting may appear as singular and exceptional. This means that it was important to avoid anachronistic conceptualizations and contemporary projections on the past, and instead look for the once-existent *emic* combinations of, for example, nature, faiths, habits, morals, and authorities.[32]

It is, certainly, far too one-dimensional to only talk about the meeting of two religions, or even two cultures when there is a mix of nature, language, culture, theology, morals, and economy that was clearly much subtler and complex. Sometimes, for the sake of clarity in the presentation, this may be expressed in terms of Lutheranism/Finnish, tribes/Sweden, and Orthodoxy/Karelian, people/Russia, but it is important to realize that even the historical setting was surprisingly complex. The very same actors could exemplify different life-worlds and dispositions in the Karelian reality.[33] the Orthodox religious contemporary understanding was also essentially one that preceded the later confessionalized notions.

In many instances the critical counter-readings of sources was absolutely necessary. In terms of this article, counter-reading also meant the methodological choice to analyze the sources and the post-Stolbova situation specifically from the viewpoint of the Karelian Orthodox population. These people

31 I am thinking here specifically of the considerations of Alapuro: "The focus on the (individual) processes that underlie the network of relations between people that implies another point shared by Barth and microhistory: a view of an *active* individual." Alapuro, Risto. "Revisiting Microhistory." In *Historical Knowledge: in Quest of Theory, Method and Evidence.* Eds. Susanna Fellman & Marjatta Rahikainen. Newcastle upon Tyne: Cambridge Scholars, 2012, 138.

32 The 1643 document was clearly designed for a purpose or actually several religious and political purposes – not to mention the writer's personal and career interests. So even if it can be regarded as an "unintentional" source, it must be read with the producers' interests in mind. See Rahikainen, Marjatta & Fellman, Susanna. "On Historical Writing and Evidence." In *Historical Knowledge: in Quest of Theory, Method and Evidence.* Eds. Susanna Fellman & Marjatta Rahikainen. Newcastle upon Tyne: Cambridge Scholars, 2012, 23, 25, 26; Ginzburg, Carlo. "Our Words, and Theirs." In *Historical Knowledge: in Quest of Theory, Method and Evidence.* Eds. Susanna Fellman & Marjatta Rahikainen. Newcastle upon Tyne: Cambridge Scholars, 2012, 107.

33 E.g., the story of the former Orthodox priest and later Lutheran pastor "Jaakkima Terentieff" in the seventeenth century. See Matikainen, Olli. "Kurkijoen manaajapappi." In Manaajista maalaisaateliin: Tulkintoja toisesta historian, antropologian ja maantieteen välimaastossa. Ed. Kimmo Katajala. Helsinki: Suomalaisen kirjallisuuden seura, 1995, 163–180.

regarded themselves as people of the "old Greek religion"[34] who suddenly found themselves as religious aliens in their own home areas. Close reading and counter-reading thus mean that many different critical objectives and procedures are used. Primarily, this is a question of employing "the hermeneutics of suspicion".[35]

In practice, when Queen Christina called the territory "heathen", or the bishop claimed that all Orthodox priests were drunkards and ignorant, it was important to interpret these expressions and undertones as intentionally derogative and as related to particular objectives of the writers and for the recipients. It is, in the end, fundamental to grasp that the voices of the Orthodox population appear in this data mainly as distorted echoes and in almost only in the written descriptions of their adversaries. This means that it was (with the help of other sources and literature) necessary to study the policies of rejection and oppression and delineate the reality that was opposed as meaningful for the subjugated.

An important aspect was to search for textual "counter-elements" that could undermine certain claims and could shine more light on the issues at hand. For example, if the ignorant or practically illiterate natives[36] were later told to obtain books from Novgorod,[37] the picture became certainly both complex and also more precise. A part of this analytical effort was also to critically examine sources in contexts that would reveal more: to determine larger networks of phenomena behind certain relatively one-dimensional notions of the writer. For example, when examining episcopal claims about declining sexual morality and desertion, it was meaningful to see the text from the viewpoint of the emerging state regulations on peoples' sex lives, and the public discipline that the state brought to Lutheran parishes in the seventeenth century – as contrasted with the more lenient local Orthodox ecclesiastical conduct.[38] In

34 Leinberg, K. G. *Handlingar Rörande Finska Kyrkan och Presterskapet. Andra Samlingen 1627–1651.* Helsingfors. 1893, 54, "grekiske gamble Religion och Christelige troon".

35 See the Latourian influenced interpretation in Felski, Rita. "Context Stinks!" In *New Literary History*, Volume 42, Number 4, (2011): 574.

36 "Desze kunna ellenast läsza Rydska, men förstå inthet huad the läsza. Äro olärde Åzsnar, brännevijns bulltar ---." Gummerus, Jaakko. "Viipurin piispa Petrus Bjugg'in kertomus hiippakuntansa tilasta 3. p. heinäk. 1643. Een kort och Sanferdigh Relation om Stifftzensz tillstånd uthj Vijborgh." In *Finska Kyrkohistoriska Samfundets Protokoll och Meddelanden II 1898–1902.* 1902. Helsingfors. V, 5., 107.

37 Gummerus, "Viipurin piispa Petrus Bjugg'in kertomus ---." V, 6., 107.

38 On the emerging Lutheran church discipline and the seventeenth century as the "golden era" ecclesiastical discipline, see Aalto, Seppo, *Kirkko ja kruunu siveellisyyden vartijoina. Seksuaalirikollisuus, esivalta ja yhteisö Porvoon kihlakunnassa 1621–1700.* Helsinki: Suomen Historiallinen Seura, 1996, 12–13, 19–20, 36–37. On the more lenient yet complicated

all this, it was necessary to not think of the "context" of historical phenomena as something given and constant.[39]

One significant aspect was the question of language and nationality. It is paramount to realize that in the sources the Orthodox were frequently called "Russians" – a concept that clearly did not denote nationality in the modern sense, but primarily ecclesiastical and religious Karelian orientation. This meant that a majority of "Russians" could be Karelian speaking, and the writer might for example be surprised by their unwillingness to use their own Karelian (close to Finnish) dialect in worship. "Russians" could not – according to the bishop – understand the Slavonic language.[40] The concept could therefore simply denote non-Swedish.

In a similar manner, "Swedes" or "Finns" could mean Lutheran or Swedish or Finnish speaking. The concepts were – from a modern viewpoint – blurred, referring to a reality prior to later nationalistic distinctions on language and country. They are also imprecise in the sense that the writers were ignorant of or disinterested in the differences between Finnish dialects, the Karelian dialect, Karelian Livvi language, Veps language, and probably even Church Slavonic, and Russian. All of these were in use by the "natives" in Ladogan Karelia.[41] Ethno-religious-linguistic identities existed, but they, too, were subject to misapprehension.

Within the scope of this article it was necessary to seriously limit perspectives and focus on certain selected aspects. Accordingly, the development of the position of the Orthodox in all eastern regions and provinces of the contemporary Sweden is not addressed. Neither is the whole development of the minority religious politics of the country in the seventeenth and early eighteenth centuries developed. Moreover, the question of the interpretation of all the peace treaties of the era concerning religion in Karelia (and even Ingria) is far too extensive to be dealt with here. This research opens a local in-depth perspective that can even challenge certain generalizing notions.

Slavonic sexual morals in the medieval era, see Levin, Eve. *Sex and Society in the World of the Orthodox Slavs, 900–1700*. Ithaca and London: Cornell University Press, 1989, e.g., 81–86, 105–111, 188–207. See also Pospielovsky, *The Orthodox Church in the History of Russia*, 1998, 49 (19).

39 Felski, "Context Stinks!", 574–578.

40 Gummerus, "Viipurin piispa Petrus Bjugg'in kertomus ---." V, 5., 107.

41 Tarkiainen, *Muskoviten*, 257–258 (25), mentions in the context of seventeenth-century ecclesiastical segregation politics the following language groups: Russians, Votes, Karelians, and Ingrians. See also Villstrand, *Sveriges historia 1617–1721*, 2011, 333 (6), who names Karelians, Ingrian, Votes, and immigrated Savolax people in Kexholm and Ingria.

5. The Context of Bishop Bjugge's 1643 Report: Writer's Biography, Previous Petition, and Royal Instructions

5.1 *Who Was Bjugge?*

After the passing away of Bishop Gabriel Melartopaeus (Bishop of Viborg 1633–1641) in 1641, in the bishopric of Viborg,[42] Ingria was made its own ecclesiastical region led by the superintendent of Narva.[43] Hence, when Per Jonae Bjugge[44] (1587–1656) was elected as Bishop of Viborg in 1642, his was a smaller but still in many respects a culturally and geographically demanding diocese.[45] Bjugge came from Söderköping, Östergötland, Sweden, and had studied both in Uppsala and Wittenberg.[46]

He became Duke Johan's[47] court preacher in 1613, pastor in Wårdsberg in 1618, and a lector in the upper secondary school at Linköping in 1628, where he first taught both "Physico-Medicus" and from 1636 Theology. He became the leading pastor of the parish of Söderköping in 1639, and finally bishop of Viborg in 1642. He was posthumously described as a learned agreeable, and cautious man.[48] He had no previous direct experience of Finnish or Karelian affairs, and did not know the Finnish or Karelian languages or dialects.[49] Bjugge

42 The Viborg Diocesis was founded by Gustaf Vasa in 1554, and re-established in 1618. See Fagerlund, *Vanhempi Vaasa-kausi 1523–1617*, 23; Villstrand, *Suurvaltakausi 1617–1721*, 269 (11).

43 Tigerstedt, K. K. *Bidrag till Kexholms läns historia under drottning Kristinas tid.* I–V. Åbo? 1850[–1900], 65.

44 In many sources also "Bjugg". The spelling of his first names could also be varying. I use here the manner he himself wrote his last name.

45 Tigerstedt, *Bidrag till Kexholms läns historia under drottning Kristinas tid*, 67 (42).

46 Boëthius B. "Petrus Jonæ Bjugg". urn:sbl:18268. *Svenskt biografiskt lexikon* used 2017-08-17.

47 Duke Johan of Östergötland, the younger brother of Sigismund, see Rosén Jerker. "Gustaf Adolf." In *Den Svenska Historien. Gustaf Adolfs och Christinas tid 1611–1654*, ed. Gunvor Grenholm. Stockholm: Bonniers, 1967, 21.

48 Rhyzelii, Andreae Ol. *Episcoposcopia Sviogothica.* 1752, section 9, p. 55; Leinberg K. G. *Handlingar Rörande Finska Kyrkan och Presterskapet. Andra Samlingen 1627–1651.* Helsingfors. 1893, 199, Carl Mörner's letter to Axel Oxenstrierna 8.12.1641. Mörner recommended both Bjugge [Biugh] and Christianus Farter. He also lamented the poor state of the seat. Rhyzelii, Andreae Ol. *Episcoposcopia Sviogothica.* 1752, section 9, p. 55; Leinberg K. G. *Handlingar Rörande Finska Kyrkan och Presterskapet. Andra Samlingen 1627–1651.* Helsingfors. 1893, 199, Carl Mörner's letter to Axel Oxenstrierna 8.12.1641. Mörner recommended both Bjugge [Biugh] and Christianus Farter. He also lamented the poor state of the seat.

49 Heininen, Simo. "Viipurin lukio lehtorit 1641–1710." In *Arki, kirkko, artefakti. Viipurin kulttuurihistoriaa Ruotsin ajalla (n. 1300–1710)*. Petri Karonen ed. Viipurin Suomalaisen Kirjallisuusseuran Toimitteita 19. Helsinki: Viipurin Suomalainen Kirjallisuusseura. 85–123. 2017. 2017, 100.

was, however, clearly intellectually and also politically active. He took part in the Swedish Diet several times, even before his election to bishop, supported reduction politics and was the delegate to present the wishes of the commoners to Queen Christina in 1650.[50]

Bjugge was called to meet the Queen after Easter in 1642.[51] Apparently the audience was successful, as the Queen's edict ordering the election to Bishop on "the coming Sunday" was sent to the Archbishop in May 16, 1642.[52] The post as Bishop of Viborg was not an attractive assignment, even if land was donated to support the bishop economically.[53] In his many letters to the government Bjugge complained about his difficult situation (also financially) and the huge demands of the post. As his first wife was ill, she could not follow him to Karelia, and meetings with the local people were difficult.[54]

On one return from the capital, Bjugge suffered a shipwreck apparently in 1654–1655 winter storms. He became seriously ill as a result of the ordeal[55] and died in 1656.[56] He was buried in Viborg Cathedral.[57] The Nordic/Rupture war began when the Russians attacked in June 1656.[58]

5.2 *The Petition of the Kexholm Commoners in 1633*

Bjugge did not come to a peaceful and well-governed diocese. Previously there had been less successful attempts to incorporate the region into the kingdom and to unify it religiously.

The local Swedish administrative policies relating to the Orthodox population had only ten years earlier, on June 8, 1633, resulted in the document

50 Heininen, "Viipurin lukio lehtorit 1641–1710," 101–102 (48).

51 Leinberg, *Handlingar Rörande Finska Kyrkan och Presterskapet. Andra Samlingen 1627–1651*, 209–210 (47), Letter of Queen Christina to Bjugge [Biugg] 26.March 1642.

52 Leinberg, *Handlingar Rörande Finska Kyrkan och Presterskapet. Andra Samlingen 1627–1651*. 210–211 (47), Edict of Queen Christina to Archbishop Lars[s] Paulinum 16 May 1642.

53 Leinberg, *Handlingar Rörande Finska Kyrkan och Presterskapet. Andra Samlingen 1627–1651*, 211 (47), Edict of Queen Christina 23 May 1642, donations of land to Bjugge.

54 Leinberg, *Handlingar Rörande Finska Kyrkan och Presterskapet. Andra Samlingen 1627–1651*, 247–248 (48), Bjugge to Oxenstierna 19 July 1643; 273–276 (48), Bjugge to Oxenstierna 22 Jan. 1646; 286–287 (48), Bjugge to Gyllenklo 2.10.1646; 331–333 (48), Bjugge to Oxenstierna 20.12.1648; Boëthius B. "Petrus Jonæ Bjugg" (46).

55 Leinberg, K. G. *Handlingar Rörande Finska Kyrkan och Presterskapet. Fjerde Samlingen 1652–1686*. Helsingfors. 1900, 49–50, Bjugge to Oxenstierna 10 Feb. 1655.

56 According to Rhyzelii in 1657, which is very obviously a mistake. See Rhyzelii *Episcoposcopia Sviogothica*, section 9, p. 55 (48); C.f. Leinberg, *Handlingar Rörande Finska Kyrkan och Presterskapet. Fjerde Samlingen 1652–1686*, 54–55 (55), the Government to the Chapter of Viborg 6 July 1656; 57 (55), The Chapter of Viborg to the Government 27 July 1656; Boëthius B. "Petrus Jonæ Bjugg" (46).

57 Boëthius B. "Petrus Jonæ Bjugg" (46).

58 Lappalainen, *Kaarle X Kustaan Venäjän-sota c 1656–1658 Suomen suunnalla*, 1972, 111.

"Translation vtaff Kexholmskes gemene Almogens supplication"[59], the petition of the Kexholm commoners to the Queen. Five Kexholm Orthodox men[60] asked for a royal audience claiming: "high and low royal officials are forcing us poor people away from our rightful and lawful Greek old religion and Christian faith to which we have been baptized". People were not allowed to have priests from Russia, and as a result many had fled to the east and "God's churches stood deserted."[61] The most provocative part of the petition is found in the plea to profess traditional religion without "harassment", and to have new priests of local origin ordained in Russia so that people need not "die without confessors and pastoral care".[62] The tone of the document was desperate.

The document, moreover, continued with specific complaints aimed at the official Johan Kaurain[63]. He was said to have forced "Swedish pastors" to marry Orthodox couples, against their consent, in the alien, Lutheran manner, even during the time of lent. This was a clear offence against Orthodox canonical understanding.[64] Kaurain had confiscated priests' headwear ("theris presterlige ståndz små myssor"), which they could only reclaim by paying for them. In a similar manner, he confiscated the keys of the churches, which could also be returned on payment. These complaints had already been submitted to Peder Sparre, president of the court of appeal in Dorpat 1631 and the Council of the State 1633,[65] nevertheless, Queen Christina was invoked to end the "tyranny" of Kaurain on the threat of the people abandoning their homes and disappearing to Russia.[66] This was the real currency the people had when facing oppression: they could threaten with their desertion. The peasants were not "bound to the turf" and were a valuable workforce and the economic foundation of the kingdom.[67]

---

59 Leinberg *Handlingar Rörande Finska Kyrkan och Presterskapet. Andra Samlingen 1627–1651*, 53–56 (48). Laasonen, in *Novgorodin imu*, 44–45 (6), has also briefly analyzed the petition and the offences of Juho Kauranen, the overseer of Tiurula mansion. In his interpretation the petition featured one isolated incident.

60 N. Simon Sinkoff, Lasarus Kuhnieff, Sergei Jvanoff, Stepan Stepanoff, and Muckei Pawloff. Leinberg *Handlingar --- Andra Samlingen 1627–1651*, 54 (48).

61 Leinberg *Handlingar --- Andra Samlingen 1627–1651*, 54 (48).

62 Leinberg, *Handlingar --- Andra Samlingen 1627–1651*, 55 (48).

63 Leinberg, *Handlingar --- Andra Samlingen 1627–1651*, 55 (48).

64 Leinberg, *Handlingar Rörande Finska Kyrkan och Presterskapet. Andra Samlingen 1627–1651*, 55 (48).

65 Sparre, släkt, https://sok.riksarkivet.se/sbl/artikel/6160, *Svenskt biografiskt lexikon* (Hans Gillingstam), read 2018-June-12.

66 Leinber, *Handlingar --- Andra Samlingen 1627–1651*, 55 (48).

67 Villstrand, *Suurvaltakausi 1617–1721*, 2000, 251 (11).

The royal answer to the petition came swiftly in September 23, 1633. It contained an initiative already presented to the Ingrian people to seek the Bishop's ordination from Constantinople[68] for a co-operator, Simon Wehme[69], and in this rather unorthodox way bypass ecclesiastical Novgorod and Russia. In this era there were several analogous phenomena, also in Russia: people who represented a bogus religion and conviction for their economic benefit. Greek petitioners and even imposters were common guests in Russia.[70]

One can, indeed, contemplate whether the bishop ordination issue was an effort to solve the ordination problem of the Karelian Orthodoxy in a manner that could also benefit primarily Swedish policies, or just a delay tactic, both dividing and appeasing the population.[71] Whatever the case, it is noteworthy that already in the 1580s Johan III had had plans to somehow merge together the Orthodox and Lutherans. This idea was encouraged by Swedish success on the eastern front.[72] However, what was certainly meaningful for the petitioners was that promises were made to bear Kaurain justice in mind.[73] More moderate means for unification were needed as the people were resistant. Bjugge's report has to be seen as documentation of this fact after 1633.

5.3 *Royal Instructions*

Bjugge's report can also be regarded (among other aspects) as an answer to Queen Christina's instructions that were addressed to the newly elected Bishop on October 10, 1642.[74] In that document the new Bishop was given altogether 25 different orders and instructions in relation to his office. As Heininen states, the clear mission of Bjugge was to accommodate the special features of the

68 Isberg, *Svensk segragations-och konversionspolitik I Ingemanland 1617–1704*, 1973, 34–35 (6). Also the Polish Belarus was presented as an option.

69 See Laasonen *Novgorodin imu*" 30, 50, 89 (6). Wäsme [here spelled with s], Simon Igumnov, was a learnèd originally Orthodox theologian who in 1643 created a Russian manuscript on the "errors" of the Orthodox. Per Brahe as General Governor organized the translation of the text into Swedish, but the work resulted in only an incomplete manuscript. See Tarkiainen on Igumnov, and analysis of the text in *Moskoviten*, 248–250 (25).

70 Pospielovsky, *The Orthodox Church in the History of Russia*, 1998, 72–73 (20).

71 Laasonen, *Novgorodin imu*, 28–33 (6) regards the initiatives as sincere efforts to solve the problem of the eastern provinces. In my opinion, Alvin Isberg's interpretation is more realistic. See Isberg, *Svensk segragations-och konversionspolitik I Ingemanland 1617–1704*, 1973, 35 (6). See also Tarkiainen's account on the issue in Tarkiainen, *Moskoviten*, 2017, 247–248 (25).

72 "The bishop of Finland was obliged to translate the Red [Book] Liturgy into Greek, and connections with the Patriarch of Constantinople were planned [1580–1581]." transl. J. B. Fagerlund, *Kuninkaita ja alamaisia*, 2000, 71. See also pp. 65–68.

73 Leinberg, *Handlingar --- Andra Samlingen 1627–1651*, 59 (48).

74 Tigerstedt, *Bidrag ---*, Appendix I (43).

eastern diocese to the religion of the country.[75] The 1643 report can thus also be regarded as Bjugge's effort to respond to the government's aspirations – a proof of his loyalty and capability in his office.

Several of the royal guidelines for the Bishop directly addressed the Orthodox worshipers in the diocese. The Kexholm region was defined as a heathen, unorganized area that needed to be brought to the true evangelical faith by following the apostles' example. Lutheranism needed to be strengthened. Those who had "fallen" from the "true religion" (apparently Lutheran converts to Orthodoxy) and those "still keeping the Greek religion" needed to be brought to the truth, but not by creating disturbance. The Queen's instruction was to use "saktmodighet", moderation, in instructing the locals, and the main goal was to lay the grounds for conformity and peace.[76]

Considering ecclesiastical discipline, the Queen needed to point out that Lutheran regulations could not be practiced over the Orthodox until they had opened to Lutheranism. After explanation, their ecclesiastical misconducts were to be punished by fees only – yet apparently in accordance with the Lutheran church order.[77] Heretics and false teachers were to be resisted,[78] yet, the Queen specifically emphasized that violence was not to be used in creating a "Reformation" for the Orthodox population. Instead, "suitable moderation" ("lämpa och saktmodighet") was to be used: friendly persuasion by the mercy of God.[79]

Acting in accordance with the law was a significant endeavor in even minor ecclesiastical matters,[80] and conformity was to be demanded in terms of annual catechism studies for the parish members: which were to be given twice a year in March and September – probably times suitably free from productive agricultural work – and by both Lutheran pastors and their Orthodox counterparts ("rysske prester eller diaker").[81] Orthodox priesthood was to be obliged to and involved in teaching Lutheran catechism. Together with Lutheran pastors, Orthodox priests were regarded primarily as teachers in accordance with the general intention of the instructions: faithful service for the Queen and the unity of the country.

---

75 Heininen, "Viipurin lukio lehtorit 1641–1710," 87 (49).

76 Tigerstedt, *Bidrag* ---, Appendix I, Chapter III (43). See also Laitila, *Coercion, Cooperation, Conflicts and Contempt – Orthodox-Lutheran Relations in Swedish-Occupied Kexholm County, Karelia, in the Seventeenth Century*, 2020, 40.

77 Tigerstedt, *Bidrag* ---, Appendix I, Chapter V (43).

78 Tigerstedt, *Bidrag* ---, Appendix I, Chapter XI (43).

79 Tigerstedt, *Bidrag* ---, Appendix I, Chapter XII (43).

80 Tigerstedt, *Bidrag* ---, Appendix I, Chapter XX (43).

81 Tigerstedt, *Bidrag* ---, Appendix I, Chapter XXI (43).

In his task, Bjugge could, according to the instructions, rely on his office to help the provincial governors and the Governor General of Kexholm. This statement interestingly reflects the situation of administering religious affairs in the province this time: it was complicated as different administrators interacted with religious matters.[82] Even the existence of the office of the Governor General is much telling: the civil administration needed strengthening and support.[83] A more detailed distinction concerning religious matters and the different branches of administration did not exist. In the coming years, moreover, large areas of the Wiborg diocese and Karelia were held in fealty by Count Carl Gustaf Wrangel and Count Per Brahe the Younger (the Governor General of Finland 1637–1640 and 1648–1654).[84]

6. Reporting on Dissenters: Administrational Concerns and Goals

6.1 *The General Content and Tone of Bjugge's Report*

Soon after arriving in his bishopric in 1642, Bjugge wrote a document "Een kort och Sannferdigh Relation om Stifftzensz tillstånd uthj Vijborgh, anteknad uthj näst håldne Visitation; och uhtj Vnderdånighet H. K. M. sampt dhen Kongl. Regeringen öffuerantvardatt I Stocholm den 13 Julij 1643". As the title indicates, the report was based on a recent visitation to certain anonymous parish(es), and addressed to Her Majesty and the government.[85]

It is safe to regard the report as a polemical and even manipulative text. It contains rhetorical, propagandic efforts to impress the readers by referring to the difficult situation of the bishop in his office, the nearly hopeless deviation of the population, and the lack of resources in a remote part of the country.[86] At any rate, the text can be seen as revealing the juxtaposition and competition between the two Christian forms of religion. Even if Orthodoxy was to

82 E.g., Tigerstedt, *Bidrag* ---, Appendix I, Chapter XXV (43); Leinberg, *Handlingar Rörande Finska Kyrkan och Presterskapet. Andra Samlingen 1627–1651*, 125–126 (48), Per Brahe to Bjugge, the Chapter in Viborg, and the Government.

83 Villstrand, *Suurvaltakausi 1617–1721*, 204 (11).

84 Villstrand, *Suurvaltakausi 1617–1721*, 186–188, 205–209 (11).

85 I use here the edited and published version of the report by Gummerus, 1902, however in comparison with the manuscript. Several different matters of the diocese were addressed in the 1643 Report. Yet, I analyzed the document specifically in view of the above-mentioned questions. This means that I leave primarily aside the lamentations and critical notes regarding the Bishop's "own people", Lutheran clergy and laity, and concentrate – as much as feasible – on the comprehension of Orthodoxy.

86 Gummerus, "Viipurin piispa Petrus Bjugg'in kertomus ---." See e.g. the beginning of the text, I–III, pp. 100–103 and the economic and other complaints.

be defeated by military means and was to be administratively subjugated, it appeared, however, to be viewed as a formidable opponent in this text.

Bjugge's text is, furthermore, illuminative in its precise detail when it comes to local Orthodox habits of the era. That Orthodoxy was so largely reflected is in fact not surprising as Bjugge was actively involved right in the middle of the initial conflict and encounter of the two populations just under 30 years after the 1617 peace treaty. As mentioned above, the report also contains information about the specifically Lutheran affairs of the diocese, for example the school of Wiborg.[87]

6.2 *Marriage and Desertion*

The first reference to the Orthodox population appears in the report when Bjugge laments the difficult situation regarding marriage and extramarital relationships in his diocese.[88]

People (according to the writer: men) from the Kexholm area fled to Ingria and Lithuania leaving their spouses to wait in vain.[89] Not only did people escape from Bjugge's jurisdiction, even worse, "many of them" also abandoned their Lutheran faith, turned to Orthodoxy, were baptized anew and took new names. What specifically worried the Bishop was how easily the religious conversion away from Lutheranism took place. "Many of them join their godless religion, which falls on them more easily than Lutheranism, in terms of which they have to provide proof of what they have learned ---."[90]

As a contrast to the emerging catechism learning and control over reading that Lutherans faced,[91] conversion to and life as an Orthodox worshiper seemed to be simpler and more tolerant: "The Russians do not care. When a person is christened, and has bowed to the idols that are on a shelf in home or at church, the practice of divinity is done ---."[92] However, in the same report the writer could also (probably rhetorically) claim that there was not even one Finn in his bishopric who could read the catechism properly.[93] The writer was

87 Gummerus, "Viipurin piispa Petrus Bjugg'in kertomus ---." II, 1.–4., 101–102.

88 Gummerus, "Viipurin piispa Petrus Bjugg'in kertomus ---." IIII, 1., 103–104.

89 Gummerus, "Viipurin piispa Petrus Bjugg'in kertomus ---." IIII, 1., 103.

90 Gummerus, "Viipurin piispa Petrus Bjugg'in kertomus ---." IIII, 1., 104.

91 Necessary, e.g., for participation in the Eucharist, becoming godparent, or entering into marriage. See Villstrand, *Suurvaltakausi*, 2000, 274–275. This was all foreign to the Orthodox.

92 Gummerus, "Viipurin piispa Petrus Bjugg'in kertomus hiippakuntansa tilasta 3. p. heinäk. 1643. Een kort och Sanferdigh Relation om Stifftzensz tillstånd uthj Vijborgh ---." IIII, 1., 104.

93 Gummerus, "Viipurin piispa Petrus Bjugg'in kertomus hiippakuntansa tilasta 3. p. heinäk. 1643. Een kort och Sanferdigh Relation om Stifftzensz tillstånd uthj Vijborgh ---." IIII, 6., 105–106.

worried about and blamed the fleeing deviators for God's punishment: the land becoming desolate. This reasoning might not have been merely political maneuvering in the harsh times. Probably, Bjugge was genuinely afraid that his unsuccessful efforts could result in the unleashing of God's wrath. The difficult political-religious situation and harsh climate of the era were thus connected to his thinking on the otherness of the godless and careless deserters and the "Russians" welcoming them: the Orthodox.

The chapter in the report is also very revealing. Several historical sources and previous research tell us that all during the post Stolbova era, even before the Nordic/Rupture War of 1656–1658, ordinary inhabitants, both Orthodox Karelian people and new settlers, Lutherans, were leaving Karelia. Fleeing was the peasants' rebellious resistance against taxation and the despised forced military recruitment. In the seventeenth century people fled in great numbers, for example, more than 6000 people left Savolax. The Russians were of course pleased to welcome this labor force to their estates, and in 1636 a huge number of Finns had also established themselves in Estonia and Livonia as their new home territories.[94]

That Bjugge connects this with issues of marriage and extramarital relationships can at least in part be seen as more than a rhetorical approach. As can be discerned from later Uukuniemi Visitation Reports, Lutheran clergy could skillfully use issues of marriage and sexual relationships to convert the Orthodox.[95] It is, moreover, feasible that the emerging Lutheran emphasis on control over sexual matters of the era and public humiliations of the "sinners" in churches[96] created anxiety in Karelia. Ecclesiastical overseeing and jurisprudence in sexual matters was shockingly different than the contemporary practice in Orthodox Eastern Europe, which was more lenient and basically pastoral in character.[97]

6.3 *Education and Books as Tools for Modification*

One chapter of the report also presents a clear program for creating publications both for the "Finnish" and the "Russians" to aid the Lutheranization of the region. Bjugge called for a useable Finnish catechesis (without "high and

94 Villstrand, *Suurvaltakausi 1617–1721*, 202 (11).

95 See Häkli 2015, 376, Casus 1. They also wanted to prohibit the use of "old Russian" (i.e., Orthodox) graveyards and to cut off men's (Russian style) beards. See Knuutila & Hiekkanen, *Viipurin kirkollinen elämä ja sen vaikutus kirkolliseen kulttuuriin 1200-luvun lopusta vuoteen 1710*, 2017, 61.

96 Villstrand, *Suurvaltakausi 1617–1721*, 278–279 (11).

97 Levin, *Sex and Society in the World of the Orthodox Slavs, 900–1700*, 1989, e.g., 81–86, 105–111, 188–207 (38); Pospielovsky, *The Orthodox Church in the History of Russia*, 1998, 49 (20).

unnecessary questions") an ABC-book for the Finnish and for the Russians, and a catechism in Finnish with Slavonic letters, and even a collection of sermons in the same manner for the Orthodox.[98] Of these, a catechism that he composed in Finnish was published in 1643, and it has since been lost. The catechesis with Slavonic letters that Bjugge called for – *the Selov Catechesis*, a Finnish-language Lutheran catechism printed in Slavonic letters, was published early the next year, 1644. It was, interestingly, based on the common Swedish catechism from the year 1608, thus obviously reflecting Bjugge's own tastes. In 1647, the local Lutheran pastors wanted an even more effective tool: a catechism in Swedish, Finnish, and Russian, but the crown did not have endless resources.[99]

It is, however, of significance, that the crown dedicated a certain amount of real resources for the conversion of the Orthodox. When bearing in mind the above-mentioned fear of divine punishment for dissenting beliefs, this has much to say about the motivation of the ruling class and the miscellany of contemporary religious and political ideas.

These books were necessary tools for the molding of the peoples' belief systems and were adapted to the circumstances of the region. Catechism was the major literature through which ordinary people could be in touch with the doctrinal aspects and practical applications of Christianity.[100] Literature needed to be produced for the locals to promote the Lutheran faith, to religiously unify the province, and thus to bind it more closely to the new homeland. Education of the common people was, in a proper Protestant Reformation manner, the main tool for convincing and winning over the others. Educated teachers and learning materials, books, were compulsory.

The economic situation of the Lutheran Parishes was lamented as poor in the diocese and, as a result, the recruiting of competent pastors seemed to be a difficult task. That was a problem for Bjugge because good pastors, who were well versed in the Bible, were needed in the encounter with and attempts to convince the Orthodox. They were supposed to be treated in a suitable and respectable manner in discussions, and with fairness, quite obviously with the aim of converting them.[101] Clearly, Bjugge could not (at least solely) rely on converts and those priests and deacons who wanted to cooperate.[102]

98 Gummerus, "Viipurin piispa Petrus Bjugg'in kertomus ---." IIII, 6., 106.

99 Purola, Aarne. *Selovin Katekismus*. Mikkeli: Mikkelin länin maakuntaliitto. 1984; Tigerstedt, *Bidrag till Kexholms läns historia under drottning Kristinas tid*, 76 (43); Tarkiainen, *Moskoviten*, 2017, 246–247 (25). On the translation work, see p. 247.

100 Villstrand, *Suurvaltakausi 1617–1721*, 274–275 (11).

101 Gummerus, "Viipurin piispa Petrus Bjugg'in kertomus ---." V, 2., 106.

102 Cf. Tarkiainen, *Moskoviten*, 2017, 247 (25).

One might think, bearing Bjugge's text in mind, that the locals would have been almost completely illiterate. However, it is important to see that the "Russian 'Pre-Renaissance'" – reanimation of education and writing – had influenced the northern Slavonic Orthodox realm prior to the time of troubles. The literary efforts made by Metropolitan Alexis and St Stephen, apostle of the Permian people, were significant.[103] Publications, such as the popular religious texts *Izborniki*, and the translation of some Old and New Testament books existed in the Slavonic literary realm. Significant libraries were found in certain monasteries, for example Beloozero-St Cyril and Holy Trinity-St Sergius.[104] Bjugge's 1643 report also hints at the presence of Slavonic books as he stated that the locals read not only passages from the Bible, but also other books that the Metropolitan of Novgorod had given to them.[105] Karelia was clearly not – at least entirely – cut off from the Slavonic literate realm, even under Swedish occupation.

6.4 *Places of Worship in Comparison*

In terms of ecclesiastical meeting places for worship, Bjugge claimed how poor the situation of the Lutheran parishes was. Pastors performed services in smoke-cottages ("wthan giöra Gudztiensten uthj sina egna ilaka och trånga Röökstugur"), which was one reason why the Orthodox ignored them. When worship was conducted without splendor and in great need ("uthan kiörkioskrudh I stor snöpligheet"), it could not impress them.[106]

Moreover, Bjugge's concern for Orthodox indifference due to the miserable places of worship[107] reveals the underlying theological aspect that reflects the fundamental Orthodox idea of the beauty of worship and everything that pertains to liturgy as a theological-esthetic concept of great significance.

For the Orthodox, church (the temple) and liturgy were traditionally thought to reflect and to be iconic when it came to the beauty of heavenly worship. The church building was regarded as "earthly heaven".[108] Lutheran worship in unimpressive ecclesiastical premises needed somehow to match up to that notion. Bjugge clearly saw a need for the impressive Lutheran church

103 Pospielovsky, *The Orthodox Church in the History of Russia*, 1998, 46 (20).

104 Pospielovsky, *The Orthodox Church in the History of Russia*, 1998, 48–49 (20).

105 Gummerus, "Viipurin piispa Petrus Bjugg'in kertomus ---." V, 6., 107.

106 Gummerus, "Viipurin piispa Petrus Bjugg'in kertomus ---." V, 1., 106.

107 Gummerus, "Viipurin piispa Petrus Bjugg'in kertomus ---." V, 1., 106. See also Laasonen, *Suomen Kirkon Historia 2*, 1991, 191.

108 See the famous notion in St. Germanus of Constantinople. *On the Divine Liturgy.* Crestwood, NY: St. Vladimir's Seminary Press. 1984, I:1. "The church is an earthly heaven in which the super-celestial God dwells and walks about."

art and architecture that was emerging elsewhere to be seen in his diocese as well. The baroque splendor of contemporary Lutheran churches in the kingdom was developing: expensive and impressive pulpits, donated reredoses with paintings, and funerary monuments.[109] The provincial Baroque style was just beginning to flourish, and Lutherans could experience impressive church interiors.[110]

These developments were featured in the interiors during this era – but apparently not in Ladogan Karelia.

Bjugge's account on the situation also refers to certain instructions[111] concerning the handling of Orthodox churches and their paraphernalia after the death of old Orthodox priests ("gambla Ryszprästernas död"). These orders had, according to Bjugge, not been effectively realized, and in cases where they were, the local people had already smoothly adjusted to Lutheranism.[112] These sentences very obviously referred to a plan to let the post-Stolbova situation evolve by waiting for the older Orthodox priests to pass away and then, freed from their influence, confiscate Orthodox temples and reform local communities into Lutheranism without any trouble.

However, Bjugge was clearly displeased to report that this scheme had only occasionally been realized. He rather informed about the complicated situation by describing the numerous Orthodox church buildings and chapels that were found in pogostas (погост) and villages. Not only was there one church in each pogost, but sometimes two, and several chapels in the larger villages. In these places people bowed and crossed themselves – performing thus in Bjugge's understanding godless actions, and thus angering the Divinity.[113] This fear (rhetoric within the presentation, but clearly also illustrative of the ideas of the era) characterizes the entire document. God was to be feared – and feared specifically with a view to collective punishments for wrongdoing. According to Villstrand, this severe spirit epitomized the spirituality of the era.[114]

6.5 *Friendly Persuasion, Restriction, and Subjugation*

Bjugge used the final pages of his text to report on particular problems in converting Orthodox worshipers and even more about his (and apparently his

109 Villstrand, *Suurvaltakausi 1617–1721*, 271–273 (11).

110 Hanka, Heikki. *Kuin Kuvastimessa. Suomalaisen kirkkomaalauksen yleispiirteitä uskonpuhdistuksen jälkeen.* Jyväskylä: Jyväskylän yliopisto. 1995, 7–8, 10–11.

111 They were from "Velb:te H. H:tt". See Gummerus, "Viipurin piispa Petrus Bjugg'in kertomus ---." V, 3., 106–107.

112 Gummerus, "Viipurin piispa Petrus Bjugg'in kertomus ---." V, 3., 106–107.

113 Gummerus, "Viipurin piispa Petrus Bjugg'in kertomus ---." V, 3., 4., 106–107.

114 Villstrand, *Suurvaltakausi 1617–1721*, 272–273 (11).

pastors', although no one is actually mentioned) success in the task. The following details were presented:

- Orthodox priests claimed to teach Lutheran catechism to their people, but they "in part" faked this, as they wanted to keep their offices and incomes. They were unlearned in terms of Lutheran teachings, but could be used in the work of the diocese and make progress in their learning.[115]
- Some priests had received goods from the government for teaching the catechism, but had not really actively done anything. Passive resistance had obviously prevailed, for example by finding excuses for holding meetings.[116]
- The Orthodox priests, deacons, and the priests' children could, in most cases, read chapters from the catechism, specifically in the parish of Kurkijoki (in the western corner of Lake Ladoga). This reading was successful both using Slavonic letters and in Finnish (Latin letters).[117]
- Three local merchants wanted to go to Novgorod for the ordination ("sättia möszan på sigh"), but Bjugge blocked their effort.[118] Instead, he planned a learning diary for them in Finnish, the Bible, the imminent (Selov) catechism in Slavonic letters, and an ABC-book. This plan was to be executed by local Lutheran pastors. Instead of old connections, new education was introduced. The whole vernacular Bible had been translated into Finnish only as late as 1642. It was printed in 1200 examples, of which some 800 were sent to Finland – mostly to churches, since the book was highly expensive.[119] This project clearly facilitated a Reformation campaign on the basis of the new book in Karelia. In the Orthodox (yet Polish-Lithuanian) circles, the Ostrog Bible was published for the first time in Slavonic in 1580 to counteract several East-European, Reformation, and antitrinitarian-influenced translations.[120] Yet, to what extent the Slavonic Bible was accessible in the Kexholm regions remains an open question.
- Bjugge presented similar demands to all Orthodox priests and deacons in his diocese in his effort to – even critically towards the careful policies of Her Royal Majesty and Her government – "to keep those who have learned the Finnish chapters". The Bishop's apparent eagerness to convert inhabitants clearly answered to the careful balancing of the government, whose predominant intention was to maintain the internal peace and stability of

115 Gummerus, "Viipurin piispa Petrus Bjugg'in kertomus ---." V, 10., 108.
116 Gummerus, "Viipurin piispa Petrus Bjugg'in kertomus ---." V, 11., 109.
117 Gummerus, "Viipurin piispa Petrus Bjugg'in kertomus ---." V, 11., 109;
118 Isberg, *Svensk segregations- och konversionspolitik i Ingermanland 1617–1704*, 1973, 54 (6).
119 Villstrand, *Suurvaltakausi 1617–1721*, 266 (11).
120 Florovski, Georges, *Venäläisen teologian tiet.* Heinävesi: Valamon luostari, 2008, 116–119.

the country.[121] Language as the reason for religious segregation was clearly emerging.[122]

The Orthodox worshipers were obliged to build Lutheran churches together with other local people and, accordingly, they should be given their own rows in churches. When arriving to listen to the preaching of the catechesis (which was obligatory) they should be greeted honorably and shown to first seats in the nave.[123] All ecclesiastical matters should be discussed and resolved within the Finnish (not Orthodox) congregation regardless of whether they actually affected this or that part of the population. Conversation should be friendly, and in Bjugge's plan, every parish council should be balanced an equal number of "Russian" and "Finnish" members.[124] An administrative incorporation of the locals into Lutheranism was also part of the strategy.

In the end, Bjugge presented himself as a voice speaking for the Orthodox by presenting a petition for the "Russians" to Her Majesty asking for a reduction in their taxes and duties in difficult situations to stop them from deserting their farms.[125]

One final surprise comes at the very end of the document: Bjugge also asked the government to support the building of "beautiful, spacious churches", to be completed "next summer", and to take (better) care of the incomes of the Lutheran pastors in his dioceses, so that pastors "need not to go the doors of the Russians and beg, and appreciate their lost ways for the sake of food".[126] Economic aid appeared to be extremely necessary and beneficial for the sake of the advancement of the work. Now was the time ("högh tijdh") to act – issues had been waiting for years to be addressed.[127]

Hence, after stories of advancement and plans for effectively Lutheranizing the locals by making their religion appear vulnerable to Reformation critiques

---

121 Gummerus, "Viipurin piispa Petrus Bjugg'in kertomus ---." V, 12., 109. The sentence describing Bjugge's efforts considering Her Majesty's politics is specifically difficult to interpret. It is also possible to read that Bjugge wanted to support Her Majesty's efforts to "with good consciousness" lead people out of their lost condition ("villfarellse"). Also that statement can be interpreted as careful criticism. Previous research has emphasized the eagerness of the pastors in contrast to the careful political reasoning of the government. See, e.g., Laasonen, *Novgorodin imu*, 2005, 20–23, 61 (6).

122 Laasonen, *Suomen Kirkon Historia* 2, 1991, 192 (106); Tarkiainen, *Moskoviten*, 2017, 258 (24).

123 Gummerus, "Viipurin piispa Petrus Bjugg'in kertomus ---." VI, 5., 110–111.

124 Gummerus, "Viipurin piispa Petrus Bjugg'in kertomus ---." VI, 6., 111; Laasonen, *Novgorodin imu*, 2005, 72–73.

125 Gummerus, "Viipurin piispa Petrus Bjugg'in kertomus ---." VI, 7., 111.

126 Gummerus, "Viipurin piispa Petrus Bjugg'in kertomus ---." VI, 111. "--- att dhe ickie skola gå för Ryssernes dörar och tiggia och gilla deras villfarelser för födan skuld ---".

127 Gummerus, "Viipurin piispa Petrus Bjugg'in kertomus ---." VI, 111–112.

(the significance of Sola Scriptura and the vernacular Bible) and by using friendly persuasion in the gradual and smooth inclusion of the Russians into Finnish-Lutheran parish life, finally the reality of the situation became apparent. There were few proper places for Lutheran worship, and at least some Lutheran pastors did not have decent incomes and were dependent on their wealthier Orthodox neighbors' good will. Economic resources were needed to advance and consolidate the results of the work.

7. The Controlling Gaze – Religious-Political Concerns

7.1 *Priesthood, Holy Services, Scripture, and Sacraments*

In the 1643 report, the basically sacramental problem of the ordination to the priesthood also turned into a political issue and tool: local "peasants and traders" (apparently mostly the same people in the Karelian economy[128]) were "running across [the border]" without permission to the Metropolitan of Novgorod for ordination into priesthood. Bjugge concentrated his account on powerfully discrediting local Orthodox priests. They were all drunkards, money-grubbing, and ignorant, and could not understand what they read in Slavonic. While unsuccessful in their farming and trade, they became false teachers who sold their services and specifically requiem masses ("Siälemäszor"). Bjugge even claims that the local Orthodox population believed in purgatory ("Skärszelden"), which made services for the deceased desireable.[129]

Bjugge's mention on "Siälemäszor" and purgatory reveals that he was both informed about certain aspects of Karelian Orthodoxy and also ignorant of many details and theological understandings. This was actually predictable as Bjugge had practically little if any previous knowledge of Orthodox theology, and at the same time there was little literature in Swedish on the issue. This at best resulted in varying judgements (basically Johannes Botvidi as the only more positive opinion) and dubious and even distorted ideas about the Orthodox faith.[130] Moreover, Bjugge's account is fundamentally not a

128 Already in 1627 Kexholm region received specific permission to realize trading in the countryside – outside of cities – and contrary to the mercantilist regulations of the era. See Villstrand, *Suurvaltakausi 1617–1721*, 233 (11).

129 Gummerus, "Viipurin piispa Petrus Bjugg'in kertomus ---." V, 5., 107.

130 He never refers to any known Swedish texts on the Orthodox (of the era) by name: Palma's and Rudbeckius' "Een kort Berättelse" (created earlier and printed 1640), Aschaneus' "Chronicon Russicum" (text lost), Petrus Petrejus' "Regni Muschovitici Sciographia 1614–1615 (on the basis of von Herberstain's "Rerum Muscoviticarum Commentarii", and the 1620 dissertation by Johannes Botvidi. See Tarkiainen's account and analysis on these in

theological analysis, but a rather one-sided judgement of the others' *habits*, and erroneous practices, as he saw them. What he meant by "requiem masses" probably referred to the many rites preceding, pertaining to, and following a funeral in Karelian Orthodoxy and, in particular, the *panihida* service (панихида) for the deceased.[131]

It is also possible that he was familiar with the Orthodox habit of commemorating the deceased in Divine Liturgies. In that meaning, a connection to the Eucharist really existed. However, it seems very unlikely that seventeenth-century the Karelian Orthodox population could have – despite Western influences of the era – adopted the principle of purgatory, a concept that was foreign to Orthodoxy. The issue was discussed several times in meetings of the Orthodox and Latins, also in Ferrara-Florence (1438–1445), but the idea never really merged into Orthodoxy. Orthodox worshipers generally believed in the *koinonia* of the church even in death, the spiritual progress of the departed souls, and the effectiveness of prayer and the Eucharistic "Bloodless Sacrifice" offered to everyone – even the saints and the Theotokos herself.[132]

Bjugge clearly utilized his understanding of Catholicism and applied it to Orthodoxy. It was, in many ways, meaningful to present the opponent as related to the old enemy. It was uncomplicated, comprehensible in the context, and potentially efficient in opening prospects for gaining the needed resources. It was, moreover, purposeful in terms of legislation since Catholicism was under special suspicion in the kingdom and was regarded as a specifically dangerous force with respect to the religion of the land. This conviction was legally embedded in the Stadga of Örebro in 1617.[133]

It seems, accordingly, that Bjugge presented these notions without fully understanding or even trying to understand the differences and nuances of the traditions. He was not really interested in comprehending Orthodoxy

---

Tarkiainen, *Moskoviten*, 2017, 235–239 (25). See also Mokroborodova, Larisa. *Quaestio nostro saeculo inusitata: русское православие в тезисах Йоханнеса Ботвиди "Христиане" ли Московиты? (1620)*. Åbo: Åbo Akademi University Press. 2013.

131 Melling, David, J. & Parry, Ken & Archmandrite Ephrem. "kollyba/kollyva". In *The Blackwell Dictionary of Eastern Christianity*. Ken Parry, David Melling, Dimitri Brady, Sidney Griffith & John F. Healey eds. Oxford: Blackwell. 1999, 285–286. It is tempting to think that Bjugge might have confused the use of *kollyva* to the Eucharist.

132 Meyendorff, John. *Bysantin theologia: opillisia kysymyksiä.* Heinävesi: Valamon luostari, 1987, 140–143.

133 *Svenska Riksdagsakter*, Andra handlingar. 1521–1718, 1957, II:2, 276/97, Örebro Stadga 27.2.1617, esp. 270–271. On the 1617 Stadga and the fates of revealed Swedish Catholics in Sweden in the early seventeenth century, see Nyman, Magnus. *Hävinneiden historia. Katolista elämää Ruotsi-Suomessa Kustaa Vaasasta kuningatar Kristiinaan.* Helsinki: Katolinen tiedotuskeskus. 2009, 205–235.

but rather wanted to eagerly point out its shortcomings in comparison to Lutheranism, and, what seemed to appear as somehow related to Catholicism was meaningful and useful to be interpreted as Catholicism.

Furthermore, in Bjugge's thoroughly critical account, certain specific details emerge concerning sacred scripture. Bjugge specified his claim regarding Orthodoxy in comparison to Catholicism: as in it, other texts, lies, were mixed with the Word of God. An Orthodox worshiper was thus "mostly papal" ("mest papistisk"). The Bible was read, but so were the books that came from "the Metropolitan", meaning most evidently the Metropolitan of Novgorod, the age-old ecclesiastical connection to Ladogan Karelia.[134] Hence, as Bjugge was lamenting the poor catechism reading capabilities of the people, he revealed that the Orthodox population had literature of their own available concerning issues of faith. Moreover, it is logical that Bjugge also wanted to denigrate the local populations' capabilities in understanding Slavonian ("Russian", as he wrote). Of about 80 listeners of Orthodox services, only some four people actually spoke "Russian", he claimed. And all spoke "Finnish".[135] What he had encountered (probably also in person) and described in the report is thus, undeniably, a local Karelian, Karelian-speaking, Orthodox community conducting their worship in Church Slavonian.

Bjugge was, moreover, clearly irritated to learn that people cherished this language of worship, and they wanted to continue with it as their ancestors had. The authority of Orthodox traditionalism and unwillingness to accept reforms was clearly surprising to the Lutheran bishop, and again the opponent was compared and associated with the better-known adversary, Catholicism.[136]

When it came to sacraments, Bjugge explained how the two sacraments (in his Lutheran regard Baptism and the Eucharist) were mixed together by the locals. Bread with wine and water was given to a newly baptized child orally, and a cross was put around the baby's neck to be kept for all days to come. This brief chapter gives a vivid but narrow image of a seventeenth-century Ladogan Karelian baptism with infants taking part in the Eucharist (though many elements and specifically the sacrament of the Anointing with Myrrh is absent), a conduct and understanding of Baptism and the Eucharist that differed radically from the contemporary Lutheran praxis. It was clearly unthinkable for Bjugge that the Eucharist and the Cross could be given to a baby,[137] *as infants*

134 Gummerus, "Viipurin piispa Petrus Bjugg'in kertomus ---." V, 6., 107. See above fn. 102 on the development of Russian medieval literary culture.

135 Gummerus, "Viipurin piispa Petrus Bjugg'in kertomus ---." V, 6., 107.

136 Gummerus, "Viipurin piispa Petrus Bjugg'in kertomus ---." V, 6., 107.

137 In Orthodox praxis babies could take part in four of the seven mysteries (i.e. baptism, myron anointing, the Eucharist and, also, in need, the anointing of the sick). On the mysteries, see Meyendorff, *Bysantin teologia*, 97–126 (132).

could not understand what was being done and benefit from it. "--- huru dhe små barnen kunna sigh pröfua till then måtijdhen, ställer man huariom och enom till att dömma." What was essential for him was (personal) preparation for the Eucharist, and the absence of that aspect seemed scandalous.[138]

Bjugge failed to realize, moreover, that the Orthodox notion of the original sin as mortality and weakness but not as inherited eternal damnation[139] was reflected in this conduct.

7.2 *The Question of Salvation and Folk Beliefs*

In his eagerness to find comprehensible similarities with Western theological movements and ideas Bjugge also made his own interpretations. Having heard the locals, he told them to represent features of Calvinism ("Släng af Calvinisterijt") concerning questions of personal salvation. When asked how people were going to be saved (from eternal damnation) when they did not have true faith in Christ and what he did, but believed in "idols" and signs of the cross, they claimed, according to Bjugge: if they were chosen to eternal life, they were going to be saved.[140]

For Bjugge this answer appeared to represent Protestant double predestination. Yet, in terms of this seventeenth-century discourse, it is apparent that both the question and the answer were misunderstood, and the above-mentioned political-economic prospective of the writer, also, has to be considered. Another question is whether Bjugge simply invented this discussion and if, or to what degree, the text is based on real encounters. It is possible, however, to interpret this part of the document as somehow mirroring real encounters and discussions of the Lutheran clergy with the Orthodox population. Both were living for the most part close to each other, and the Orthodox were subject to Lutheran efforts of instruction.[141] Human curiosity was a considerable factor, as well: people were inquisitive and made comparisons.[142]

Local Orthodox (peasant) clergy – without the destroyed and banned monastic institutions[143] – could probably not explain to the outsider bishop the doctrinal subtleties of Orthodox theology and its fundamental ideas of free

---

138 Gummerus, "Viipurin piispa Petrus Bjugg'in kertomus ---." V, 9., 108. See also Isberg, *Svensk segregations- och konversionspolitik i Ingermanland 1617–1704*, 1973, 54 (6).

139 On the sinless state of the newborn babies, see Meyendorff, *Bysantin teologia*, 31–36, 100–101 (132).

140 Gummerus, "Viipurin piispa Petrus Bjugg'in kertomus ---." V, 7., 108. "--- Suara dhe: om dhe äro till dhet evigha liffuet vthualde, bliffua dhe Salige." See also Isberg, *Svensk segregations- och konversionspolitik i Ingermanland 1617–1704*. 1973, 54 (6).

141 See above the chapter "Education and Books as Tools for Modification".

142 Gummerus, "Viipurin piispa Petrus Bjugg'in kertomus ---." V, 6., 107.

143 All the monasteries of Karelia were destroyed under Swedish rule. See Isä Ambrosius. Luostarilaitos Karjalassa. In *Karjala 1. Portti Itään ja Länteen.* Mäkinen, Yrjö-Pekka &

will and human and divine synergy in salvation.[144] Bearing in mind the highly significant role of monasteries in the structure and realization of Orthodoxy throughout time and also in Karelia, the destroying of the monastic superstructure inescapably meant that parishes and local communities were left without their spiritual and cultural support. Pilgrimages and visits to monasteries were made impossible, and the traditional religious web of contacts with believers was thus inescapably broken. Language barriers existed: from Finnish to Swedish and from Karelian dialect and Slavonian to Swedish. Moreover, in terms of Orthodox communality, the whole question of the salvation of a single person, the "I" seeking for personal salvation, probably appeared as alien, Protestant, and novel. People were saved together as members of the Church, with the aid of its holy prayers, and through the merciful judgment of Christ. Salvation was understood as a process of deification in the koinonia of the Church. The intercession of the Mother of God was understood as significant.[145]

It is also important to realize that the Swedish-Finnish and Karelian people of the era (and even long since) lived in multiple religious and cultural realities. People could be simultaneously Christian and practice magic and age-old beliefs. Christianity and shamanist paganism not only lived side-by-side – even in Karelian homes, in folk poetry (e.g., the versions of the poems that were later composed into the Kalevala folk poem compilation) and in spells for healing – but also merged more or less together. The Lutheran clergy had only begun to critically regard this medieval synthesis.[146] One epitome of the emerging rupture in belief systems could be seen in the seventeenth-century fear of witchcraft and the witch-trials that ensued in northern Europe as well.[147] In Karelia, however, at least the lay Orthodox were clearly not too eager to differentiate between native beliefs and Christian faith.[148]

Lehmusvaara, Ilmari & Sarrala, Hannu & Vihinen, Reino eds. Helsinki: Karisto. 1982, 322–324.

144 Meyendorff, *Bysantin teologia*, 61–62 (132).

145 Meyendorff, *Bysantin teologia*, 53–63, 77–81 (132). See also Timiadis, Emilianos. *Lebendige Orthodoxie. Eine Selbstdarstellung der Orthodoxie im Kreise der christlichen Kirchen.* Nürnberg und Eichstätt: Johan Michael Sailer Verlag. 1966, 163; and the medieval source: Eusebios Aleksandrialainen, *Johannes Edelläkävijän laskeutuminen tuonelaan.* Muinaisvenäjästä suom. Johannes Seppälä. Joensuu: Ortokirja. 1980.

146 Villstrand, *Suurvaltakausi 1617–1721*, 273 (11).

147 Villstrand, *Suurvaltakausi 1617–1721*, 276–277 (11).

148 Laitila, *Jumalat, haltijat ja pyhät – Eletty Ortodoksisuus Karjalassa 1000–1900*, 72–78, 181–183.

The Hesychast movement had already had significant impact, specifically in the north (trans-Volga) *startsy* and *sketes*,[149] but Bjugge's report does not reveal any contact with the movement. This is only predictable because monasteries, the strongholds, were destroyed and monks exiled. It is, however, possible that the resistance that Lutherans met was, at least to a degree, a result of the spiritual revival stimulated in the seventeenth century by the *Bogoliubtsy*, "lovers of God", the zealots. With their common preaching activities, they could also influence the border regions of Karelia.[150]

It is, moreover, possible that the passages in Bjugge's text highlighting the incomprehensibility of the language used by the locals can actually reflect the conduct of *Mnogoglasie*, polyvocality, that was part of the practices prevalent in the era in the Russian realm and also favored by the zealots. When long, originally monastic services were used in medieval Slavonic parishes, polyvocality was invented to enable the use of all liturgical texts within a shorter period of time: the priest, the deacon, reader, and the choir simply read and sang their parts simultaneously. This debatable conduct rendered services virtually incomprehensibile.[151]

7.3 *Holy or Unholy Icons?*

Consequently, when Bjugge claimed that some of the local people were ignorant about the real content of the Nikean Creed they used, and as they were told to believe in one great God and many small gods,[152] the icons ("dhe heliges beläten"), he was probably honestly describing a relatively Christianized part of a peasant belief system in remote pogostas far away from monasteries and ecclesiastical centers of learning. Some Orthodox writers actually wrote similar accounts about the same geographical area still in the late nineteenth century.[153] Russian bishops were in charge of generally hopelessly large dioceses in

149 Pospielovsky, *The Orthodox Church in the History of Russia*, 1998, 47–48 (20).

150 On the movement see Pospielovsky, *The Orthodox Church in the History of Russia*, 1998, 68–71 (20).

151 Pospielovsky, *The Orthodox Church in the History of Russia*, 1998, 70, 73 (19); Jopi, Harri. *Suomalainen kahdeksansävelmistö ja venäläinen traditio*. Turku: Turun yliopisto, 2001, 62–63. However, a certain degree of "polyvocality" or simultaneity has always been and still is a part of Karelian and Finnish Orthodox worship.

152 The use of the term "gods" was actually quite common in Karelia for a long time: it denoted the icons kept, e.g., in the corner of the main room of the farmhouse. See Keinänen, Marja-Liisa. "Everyday, Fast, and Feast: Household Work and the Production of Time in Pre-Modern Orthodox Karelia". In *Vernacular Religion in Everyday Life: Expressions of Belief*. Bowman, Marion & Valk, Ülo eds. London, New York: Routledge, 2014, 26.

153 Jopi, Harri, *Suomalainen kahdeksansävelmistö ja venäläinen traditio*. 2001, 38–43 (151).

the seventeenth century: almost 1500 parishes for one bishop in the Novgorod diocese, which Kexholm region was a part of.[154]

Regarding the fundamental question in Orthodoxy on the significance and use of icons, Bjugge's informants revealed theological knowledge. Icons (Bjugge's "idols"[155]) were found on a shelve in a Karelian Orthodox household – apparently the traditional icon corner on which the "gods" were located[156] – or in churches, and they were regarded as significant by the stranger.

The explanations of the Karelian people concerning this one example of Orthodoxy were not well-received by the Lutheran Bishop ("ynkeligitt och löijeligit"), and he wanted to discuss them in his report. Images were respected ("vyrdningh"[157]), they were significant in worship because people wanted to have a visual memory of Christ, which he had left to the world by printing his face on canvas, thus making his icon – in Bjugge's terms – a "portrait for commemoration" ("Conterfej till åminnelse"). Bjugge was told this was a Biblical story, a claim that he angrily denied on the basis of his understanding of the Biblical canon.[158] However, what the local Orthodox worshipers were presenting to him was actually the legend of the not-made-by-hands icon of Christ, the famous αχειροποίητα of Edessa. It is plausible that the previously popular *Izborniki* readings were behind this notion of the legend being seen as in a manner "biblical".[159]

Moreover, the Protestant idea of "sola scriptura" – understood in terms of the Bible as above or as against the tradition – was certainly alien to them. The burning debates of the previous centuries in Russian theology were connected in particular to the *Judaizers* (a movement that abandoned much of traditional

---

154 Pospielovsky, *The Orthodox Church in the History of Russia*, 1998, 71 (20).

155 Gummerus, "Viipurin piispa Petrus Bjugg'in kertomus ---." IIII, 1., 104. "--- och hafver buckatt för affguden på hyllan hemma eller I kyrckian står ---".

156 See Keinänen, "Everyday, Fast, and Feast: Household Work and the Production of Time in Pre-Modern Orthodox Karelia", 26.

157 Old Swedish: virdha/wyrda/wörda, meaning e.g. "to value", "to evaluate", "to hold to something", "to love", "to regard something as something", "to care about", "to respect", even "to praise". See Söderwall K. F., *Ordbok över Svenska Medeltids-Språket*, 1953–1973, 1073–1074.

158 Gummerus, "Viipurin piispa Petrus Bjugg'in kertomus ---." V, 8., 108. See also Laasonen, *Suomen Kirkon Historia* 2, 1991, 191 (107).

159 On the Izborniki, "popular collections of religious readings", in which historical, didactic, ethical, hagiographic, and theological materials coexisted with Biblical passages, see Pospielovsky, *The Orthodox Church in the History of Russia*, 1998, 48 (20). See also the interesting example of this Russian medieval tradition in Eusebios, *Johannes Edelläkävijän laskeutuminen tuonelaan*, 1980 (145). On the αχειροποίητα, see Ouspensky, Leonid & Lossky, Vladimir, *The Meaning of Icons.* Crestwood, New York: St Vladimir's Seminary Press. 1999, 69–70. "Better than any other sacred image, the *acheiropoietos* icon of Christ expresses the dogmatic principle of iconography." p. 72.

Christian theology, including the doctrine of the Trinity), and the ideological contradiction of the *Possessors* and *Non-Possessors* (a basically monastic disagreement that had a profound influence on the future unity of the church and church-state relationships in Russia).[160] For the Orthodox, the theological question on the veneration (not worship, "belätes vyrdhningh") of the holy icons was certainly neither an adiafora nor, as Bjugge claimed, misguided conduct, but an essential aspect of the dogma.[161]

It is surprising to realize that the defense of the local Orthodox people against the accusations of idolatry or ill-informed icon use was to present the story of the Not-made-by-hands, the miracle of the Incarnation, the invisible appearing in human form. This poetic Eastern understanding did, however, clearly not meet the demands of novel Lutheran Orthodoxy.

In the light of later Lutheran interpretations, Lutheran approaches on the image question, and even Martin Luther's opposition to the iconoclasm in his time, it is interesting how a seventeenth century Swedish Lutheran bishop vigorously attacked Orthodox notions and the use of icons.[162] But in doing so, he was in tune with Wäsme's text on "Om beläters tillbediande" that was under preparation with the protection of Per Brahe. Bjugge, however, could not have known the text as it was not translated until after 1643.[163]

None of the interlocutors in this odd discussion, moreover, ever mentioned the dogmatic teaching and authority of the Seventh Ecumenical Council in 787: the synod that discussed and, for the Orthodox (in concord with papal delegates), in a conclusive manner defined the meaning and use of icons.[164] Bjugge's report does not contain a hint of these perspectives. The viewpoints presented are exclusively local, "Evangelical" and "Biblical". Focus is on demonstrating the wrongness of the counterpart. Theology was not needed to build bridges but to point out lawless otherness. Bjugge's thinking was primarily politically theological.

---

160 Pospielovsky, *The Orthodox Church in the History of Russia*, 1998, 48, 57–63 (20).

161 Meyendorff, *Bysantin theologia: opillisia kysymyksiä*, 1987, 115–116 (132); Pospielovsky, *The Orthodox Church in the History of Russia*, 1998, 42 (20).

162 On Luther's position on religious images, see Malmisalo, Juha. *In Pursuit of the Genuine Christian Image: Erland Forsberg as a Lutheran Producer of Icons in the Fields of Culture and Religion.* Helsinki: Helsingin yliopisto. 2005, 48–49; Bjerg, Svend. *Synets Teologi.* Frederiksberg: Forlaget Anis. 1999, 91–92, see also pp. 93–96, and 232–235. See also Isberg, *Svensk segregations- och konversionspolitik i Ingermanland 1617–1704*. 1973, 54 (6).

163 See analysis of the text by Tarkiainen concerning its thoroughly anti-icon notions in Tarkiainen, *Moskoviten*, 2017, 248–250 (25). On the Lutheran convert Wäsme, Simon Igumnov, see fn. 69.

164 Gregory, Timothy E. *A History of Byzantium.* Malden, MA.: Blackwell 2005, 183–201.

7.4 *Conversions*

Bjugge saw great opportunities and expected clear success in the future, which was reasonable to expect, since even some of the most prominent of the Karelian people, specifically old deacons and merchants, had met the power of the Spirit and the word of God and had started to ponder and resolve "As if they were sunk into water ---." ("Som dhe hadhe varit quafde i Vatn ---").[165] Bjugge saw something similar happening in many places. People whom he encountered on a visitation initially seemed unattainable, but started to reconsider, and returned to talk with the bishop. They wanted to know about the Bible and their thoughts gave them sleepless nights.[166]

People were questioning their priests on issues of religion on the basis of Lutheran, vernacular Bible texts, and since they could not find the answer, they became irritated and, in several cases, acted violently towards their priests. They were also tired of paying the priest for every visit – and also their alleged thirst for spirits.[167] Under the watchful eye of the local priest, many had already wanted to convert, but were afraid, and those who came to Lutheran services had encountered the hatred and threats of their kinfolk.[168] Group pressure, the collective resistance of the local community, made conversion difficult.

8. Royal Response to the 1643 Report

Bjugge's report was not left without royal reaction. In the following year, 1644, the Queen answered with a resolution of 17 chapters in response to the propositions and problems that Bjugge had presented.[169] His lamentation had been carefully read and clearly also understood in Stockholm.

The emphasis in this answer at the beginning of the document was predominantly on the economic aspect. The government had clearly understood the economic difficulties that impeded Lutheran influence and parish building in the diocese. The problem concerning the dissolution of marriages in cases

165 Gummerus, "Viipurin piispa Petrus Bjugg'in kertomus ---." VI, 1., 109. The use of the old term qvaf/qwaff ("to suffocate") is dramatic.

166 Gummerus, "Viipurin piispa Petrus Bjugg'in kertomus ---." VI, 2., 110.

167 Gummerus, "Viipurin piispa Petrus Bjugg'in kertomus ---." VI, 3., 110.

168 Gummerus, "Viipurin piispa Petrus Bjugg'in kertomus ---." VI, 4., 110.

169 Tigerstedt, *Bidrag till Kexholms läns historia under drottning Kristinas tid*, Bilaga II (43). "K. M:ts vår Allernådigste Drottnings och Frökens nådige resolution och förklaring, gifven biskopen uti Wiborg, vyrdige och höglärde M. Petro Biugg uppå de af honom inlagde puncter och ärender. Actum Stockholm den 14 juli 1644. (Riksregistraturet för år 1644 s. 910–915 i Svenska riksarkivet).

of emigration or immigration should be dealt with by using fines,[170] and as for pastors' poor incomes, that problem should dealt with by forbidding the "skrifthållen", i.e., the priest travelling around his parish (specifically for catechesis teaching reasons), and by pointing out the significance of the compensations, payments, and taxes due the parish pastor, also in detail concerning different holy offices.[171] The idea of concentrating parish meetings within the local church was a general idea in the Rothovian era.[172] At the end of the resolution, new land ownership for the parish pastors was also stipulated as economic support.[173]

The awareness of people and their pastors living in smoke cottages was clearly disturbing for the government, and the resolution called for the pastors to build better houses equipped with chimneys.[174] The provincial governors of Viborg and Nyslott were to help in building houses for pastors in those newly divided parishes where proper dwellings did not exist.[175]

Regarding the Orthodox desire for ordination to priesthood in Novgorod ("Nougården"), the Government was adamant: this activity was strictly forbidden, and the Governor General was to use a "serious hand" in questioning the candidates and punishing them with a fee, incomes from which the Wiborg Cathedral and hospital were to benefit. The "brott och motvilja", "crime and opposition" of these people had to be dealt with.[176]

The latter part of the document demonstrates that Bjugge's lamentations about the Orthodox were heard in Stockholm. The last chapters of the resolution predominantly deal only with the religious minority.

Since most part of the local Orthodox people were Finnish-speaking, the Queen wanted the local Orthodox priests to preach for them in Finnish. The idea of Protestant vernacular teaching, catechesis, and worshipping in vernacular was prevalent. "Preaching" ("predika deras åhörare Guds ord") in this context obviously meant the entire liturgical service, an idea totally out of step with reality in the seventeenth-century Karelian realm, and can be deemed as an effort to alienate people from their liturgical worship in Church Slavonic (language). This goal was to be realized with the use of persuasion and without force.[177]

170 Tigerstedt, *Bidrag* ---, Bilaga II, VIII (43).
171 Tigerstedt, *Bidrag* ---, Bilaga II, IX (43).
172 Laasonen, *Suomen Kirkon Historia* 2., 173–174 (107).
173 Tigerstedt, *Bidrag* ---, Bilaga II, XVI (43).
174 Tigerstedt, *Bidrag* ---, Bilaga II, X (43).
175 Tigerstedt, *Bidrag* ---, Bilaga II, XI (43).
176 Tigerstedt, *Bidrag* ---, Bilaga II, XII (43).
177 Tigerstedt, *Bidrag* ---, Bilaga II, XIII (43).

A "small community" of six or eight Orthodox boys was to be created in Wiborg where they would be educated in "preaching" ("predikoembetet") to their own people – apparently in accordance with the religion of the land.[178] The Lutheran religion needed to be respected and admired by the Orthodox, and therefore the Queen ordered churches to be built in pogostas as they currently "did not exist", i.e., parishes without Lutheran places of worship. The Bishop was to look for convenient locations. Her Royal Majesty intended to supply bells and embellishments for the buildings.[179]

Finally, the resolution ended with the government's wish to remunerate those Orthodox priests who were willing to teach the Lutheran catechism with four, six, or eight casks of grain. The Bishop was expected to point out the cooperating priests to the Governor General for their reward.

Persuasion was to be applied and Lutheranism enhanced through economic and administrative means and, finally, cooperation was to be rewarded.[180]

9. Bjugge's Report as Implementation of the Law and Influencing the Law-Making Process – *"Oss och Gudz försambling"*[181]

Two orthodoxies met on unequal grounds, with two very different "right" ways of interpreting Christianity. One was recent, sharply doctrinal and had an ongoing doctrinal debate with and separation from its origins, Catholicism. It was actively involved in efforts to create doctrinal purity and Biblical "rightness", and unity of the kingdom. The other "Right Christianity" could be characterized as ancient, also doctrinal but in terms of a continuing tradition that had in its history merged together southern Greek components with local Slavonic and Karelian cultural elements. It pursued its doctrinal completeness in terms of continuity and regarded itself primarily as the true Christianity.[182]

As Dimitry Pospielovsky has stated, the military confrontations between Moscow, Sweden, and Poland were the "first large[-]scale encounters between Muscovite-Russia and Western Europe". They also affected the Russian culture

178 Tigerstedt, *Bidrag* ---, Bilaga II, XIV (43).

179 Tigerstedt, *Bidrag* ---, Bilaga II, XV (43).

180 See also Isberg, *Svensk segregations- och konversionspolitik i Ingermanland 1617–1704*, 1973, 54 (6).

181 Leinberg, *Handlingar --- Andra Samlingen 1627–1651*, 211 (48), Edict of Queen Christina 23.5.1642, donations of land to Bjugge.

182 E.g., in the Russian realm the significance of the medieval theologian Ilarion and his "Confession of Faith". See Maloney, George A., S. J. *A History of Orthodox Theology since 1453*. Belmont, Massachusetts: Nordland. 1976, 16–17.

by creating a duality in relation to everything Western. The conflict between the pro- and anti-Western sides, and the emergence of the *bogoliubtsy*, the zealots, shaped Russian Orthodoxy and the entire society.[183] The Swedish occupation may have prevented the Kexholm region from being influenced by the zealot movement, but certainly not entirely. The Russian Orthodoxy was, moreover, subject to and an actor in the fight for power and supremacy in the Russian realm. The establishment of the new Romanov dynasty also meant that the state wanted to renew its policies and administration, and also to gain a definitive supremacy over the church. The 1649 code of laws, and the disputes over the office and position of the Patriarch in the 1660s exemplified this development. In the end, and also as a result of the division, the church became "weak vis-à-vis the growing strength and secretarism of the autocratic state."[184] The office of the Patriarch lost influence and esteem, and the church was therefore incapable of resisting the growth of absolute monarchism.[185]

This battle over true orthodoxy is most apparent in the concluding chapters of the 1643 report. The administration did not only have governance duties but was also fighting for what was to be understood as the truth. Theological matters were essentially legal and political in nature – and law and politics were, also, inseparable from theological ideas and principles. All this was well-in-tune with the concurrent influence of the Åbo-Bishop Isaacus Rothovius (1627–1652), who molded and unified Finnish ecclesiastical life in close cooperation with the state officials.[186]

Language appeared as a demarcation sign: Bjugge clearly felt that the Finnish language or Karelian dialect acted as a sign of belonging to the domain of Lutheranism, whereas those few residents of the region with a genuinely Russian linguistic background could be regarded as belonging to the Russian religious sphere. This coupling of language and religion is interesting, and most likely had its roots in a thinking pattern generated by the Protestant Reformation; language of the people, the Bible for the people, and worship in vernacular language combined with the common religion of the country.

In the end Bjugge's plans can be regarded as ideal and but also – for the Orthodox worshipers – dangerously effective and well-coordinated.[187] Bjugge's own notion clearly was to appear as a reformer for his region. Administrative plans were based on theological-political convictions. What he was lacking

183 Pospielovsky, *The Orthodox Church in the History of Russia*, 1998, 68–71 (20).

184 Pospielovsky, *The Orthodox Church in the History of Russia*, 1998, 69, 75–76 (20).

185 Pospielovsky, *The Orthodox Church in the History of Russia*, 1998, 76 (20).

186 Villstrand, *Suurvaltakausi 1617–1721*, 269–270 (11).

187 Concerning the by Bjugge claimed success of his efforts, see 1648, see Laitila 2020, *Coercion, cooperation, conflicts, and contempt*, 47.

in his current situation was governmental and political support, economic resources, and adequate pastoral resources.

The Orthodox worshipers were invited, involved, instructed, and persuaded into Lutheranism, whereas Orthodoxy was disgraced, made practically difficult to attend to, and simply dismissed as something ignorant, corrupt, and not genuinely religious. Violence itself was, however, not recommended (even if it was potentially used by some locals). As Villstrand has stated, the Swedish administrative apparatus was instructed to be effective, and the Lutheran church was integrated into this venture. People, and also their thoughts, were subject to control, and the kingdom needed faithful subjects.[188]

If one is willing, it is possible to see here emerging a faint seed of tolerance and a fundamental principle somewhat dimly realized: people could not be forced to undergo a (genuine) conversion in matters of faith. However, in the light of these sources, the use of the expression "freedom of religion" to characterize the post-Stolbova era in Kexholm region seems very odd and illogical.[189] If freedom of religion means persuasion, impediments to practicing one's religion, and forced unification in terms of disregarding minority traditions, the concept becomes meaningless. Its anachronistic nature is evident.

Behind Laasonen's choice of concepts lies probably an overemphasized attempt to create an all-embracing image of the beginning of the post-Stolbova era. I think the reality was much more complicated and varying with different stakeholders and events in different regions; in its historical context, Bjugge's report is but one example of this. What was solemnly declared at the Dais of the Estates by Chancellor Axel Oxenstierna in 1640 did not necessarily characterize the actual, regional reality.[190]

188 Villstrand, *Suurvaltakausi 1617–1721*, 130 (11).

189 Laasonen, *Novgorodin imu*, 13 (6): "--- Sensijaan Käkisalmen läänin ja Inkerinmaan huomattavan suurelle valtakunnan uskonnosta poikkeavalle väestölle valtio antoi uskonnonvapauden." 18: "--- Pappien muuttokielto merkitsi siis, että voittomaan asukkaat saivat jatkaa uskonsa harjoittamista omien pappiensa johdolla." However, the Stolbova peace treaty dictates nothing on the religious rights of the peasants and parish priests. It, interestingly though, instead recognizes the religious rights of the commercial actors, who on both sides were guaranteed the right to worship in their own, traditional churches on foreign soil. See Fredstraktat mellan Sverge och Ryssland, genom hvilken Ryssland och Sverge afträdde Keksholms län och Ingermanland mot det att Sverge återlämnade sina andra eröfringar. Stolbova, 1617, Februari 27, 1903, (on deportation of monks and the obligation to peasants and their priests to stay) 249–250, (on the religious rights of merchants) 255.

190 See Oxenstierna's citation on the "Evangelical" stance of not using coercion on the dissenting Orthodox, in Laasonen, *Novgorodin imu*, 25 (6).

The religious-political and administrative considerations behind Bjugge's report also had serious legal dimensions. Swedish law permitted, forbade, and restricted certain forms of religiosity that, consequently, had to be theologically, even rudimentarily, defined. It is in this context that the reason for Bjugge's interest to define the doctrinal orientation of the native religion is found.

Bjugge not even once made explicit reference to the law of the land in his 1643 report. However, while emphasizing the sole and inescapable reality of the one religion of the kingdom, he effectively realized pertinent, still evolving seventeenth-century Swedish legislation, the Örebro Charter, in particular. Religious unity of the country was essential. For this he had both Queen Christina's clear instructions and carefully written and cautious political guidelines. People were not executed or expelled due to their nonconforming "Catholic-or-Calvinist-like" faith. It was more practicable to try to Lutheranize them, to eliminate – not the natives – but their catholic-like features.

But Bjugge's report must also be understood in the wider legal context of the era. When Johan III's ecclesiastical legislation, *Then Swenska Kyrkeordningen* 1571, was to be revised in the course of the seventeenth century, the process turned out to be a complicated and elongated power struggle. In Uppsala in 1593, this 1571 legal document had been accepted as binding together with the Books of Confession. Gustaf the II Adolf had, in terms of his sovereign pledges, given the 1571 ecclesiastical legislation constitutional status. From 1602 onwards, an over eighty-year process ensued during which the entire ecclesiastical legislation was revised.[191] Accordingly, Queen Christina pledged to create a new legal order for the church and, in a similar manner, the succeeding regents, Charles X and Charles XI, contributed to the work with their subsequent committees – the result of which was finally the 1686 Church Law. During the preparation period, the government published various charters and regulations that addressed several spheres in society, including religious matters.[192]

The Karelian experiment by Bjugge and the government can be seen as one of the building blocks in this process, together with other information concerning religious dissension in the country. The 1643 report and the documents framing it also demonstrate how the Queen exercised her position

191 Knuutila "Kirkkolainsäädäntö – Kirkon vai Yhteiskunnan Asia? Kirkon ja Yhteiskunnan Väliset Suhteet ja Suomessa Käytetyt Säädökset Kanonisesta Oikeudesta Vuoden 1993 Kirkkolakiin," 6–7.

192 Knuutila, "Kirkkolainsäädäntö – Kirkon vai Yhteiskunnan Asia? Kirkon ja Yhteiskunnan Väliset Suhteet ja Suomessa Käytetyt Säädökset Kanonisesta Oikeudesta Vuoden 1993 Kirkkolakiin," 7–8.

as the supreme leader of the church. The Queen and the government were informed about the religious situation of the province in detail, and then actively and deliberately developed tools for the religious assimilation of the population. The government – through its civil, military, and ecclesiastical branches – experimented in creating religious unity by stipulating guidelines and administering them accordingly. These efforts are in line with succeeding seventeenth-century royal regulations and legislation, which were by no means more lenient towards religious minorities. It seems, thus, that Bjugge's activity was one element of the legal development of the era, the culmination of which was the 1686 Church Law with its strict regulations on religious aliens – including the plan to merge them into the religious unity of the country through the conversion of the next generation.[193]

As a politically active player, Bjugge had close relationships with the highest echelons of society, and his report was not without legal-administrative consequences: the response it received in the Queen's 1644 Resolution in many ways addressed the Orthodox minority. Bjugge's ideas and the problems he raised were thus noticed at the top of the regime.

Within this frame Orthodox tradition (including canon law) meant nothing to the Lutheran Bishop, and he also failed to understand that all the reported non-legitimate religious activities were actually grounded and regulated by Eastern Canon Law.[194] It is likely that the administrators never realized this even existed and regulated more or less local Orthodox life. Accordingly, the Orthodox understanding on sacraments (including priesthood as sacrament) was totally unnoticed, as everything was judged in terms of Lutheranism or other Western theological ideas. The interpretation of the vernacular Bible was used to present Lutheran notions.

In this historical context, modern concepts such as "freedom of religion" or "the secularity of law" appear to be out of place. Were these terms used to denote elementary separations between religious and civil powers and the law, precepts grounded on nature or agreement instead of divine authority? It becomes clear that a seventeenth-century Swedish understanding emphasized what in a Protestant manner was understood as the authority of the Holy Scriptures. Law and administration were grounded religiously and entwined with state policies.[195] Using divine law as justification for the supremacy of the

193 See *Kyrkio-Lag och Ordning*, Church Law 1686, I §1–5, 8–10.

194 On the translation of the Eastern Canon Law sources to Slavonic in the medieval era, see Hauptmann, Peter & Stricker, Gerd. *Die Orthodoxe Kirche in Russland. Dokumente ihrer geschichte (680–1980)*. Göttingen: Vanderhoeck & Ruprecht. 1988, 163.

195 E.g., the war court articles and the war articles of the late seventeenth century that both began with religious stipulations. *Kongl. Stadgar / Förordningar / HREF och Resolutioner,*

ruler and state religion left practically little room to negotiate with religious others. However, the clash of faiths, in the end an unresolved conflict, in itself contained a seed from which toleration, moderation, and even secularization could grow as it became clear that the solution to the conflict laid beyond religious conversion and dogmatization. But this pattern of thought became apparent only later. The 1643 document was still saturated with belief in the vindication of the right of the winner.

If Karelian Orthodox worshipers were regarded as somehow protected by the Stolbovan Peace Treaty, that protection did not impede efforts to convert or demands for involuntary participation in Lutheran religious education. Bearing the documents used in this research in mind, the Swedish legal understanding of the situation of religious minorities was adamant in the 1640s. Religious dissension was to be kept strictly under control, and was not to be allowed to spread. Being in a religious minority meant practically being subject to restrictions and obligations. Life in a religious minority was made as difficult as possible, yet without physical violence or expatriation, since the government wanted to keep its peasant taxpayers to safeguard the equilibrium and basic societal functions. Thus, demands for religious unification were practically balanced by economic realities. Yet, the governmental view of the minority was one of suspicion, assimilation, and denigration. It was also one of Westernization – stating the otherness of Eastern religion, culture, and lifeworlds. After the powerful infusion of Lutheranism, Karelia was never the same again.

In the end Bjugge's intentions and efforts were dwarfed and largely erased by the 1656–1658 Nordic/Rupture War. In the aftermath, a majority of the Orthodox worshipers left the region disappointed in the feeble success of the Russian army that many of them had keenly and mutinously supported. The Russian forces took an active part in the evacuation of their supporters.[196] Toleration and friendly persuasion became less important.

It is very likely that the whole question relating to certain Karelian religious minorities was too trivial or peripheral to be further directly addressed in later ecclesiastical state legislation. It was already a solved problem, and needed no specific attention. The role of the minority was to fade away – to give way to

från åhr 1528 in til 1701. Kongl. May:ts hoff-articla, publicerade i Stockholm den 13 Junii 1655. Carl Gustaff. 300–310; Krigs-Artiklar som af then Stormächtigste konung och here / herr CARL the XI. Sweriges / Giötes och Wendes konung u. Åhr 1683. Förnyade och stadgade äre. 802–828.

196 Villstrand, *Suurvaltakausi 1617–1721*, 172–175, 251 (10); Lappalainen, *Kaarle X Kustaan Venäjän-sota v. 1656–1658 Suomen suunnalla*, 153, 171–172 (17).

the unity of the country. Religion was a continuation of state policies, such as warfare, and its utility grounded its meaningfulness.

These notions proved to be a total miscomprehension in terms of the Orthodox minority. Even though a major part of the Karelian Orthodox people left for Russia, many stayed. Orthodoxy in Karelia was not totally eradicated or merged into Lutheranism, and as the tide turned and a renewed, empowered Russia wanted retaliation and access to the Baltic sea in the early eighteenth century under the leadership of Tsar Peter the Great (Tsar 1682–1725), the situation of the Karelian population changed. The Lutherans in Ingria and Karelia now in turn found themselves as religious outsiders within the Russian Empire. The Great Northern War (1700–1721) meant that a major part of former Orthodox Karelia (with the exception of parts of northern Karelia) was once again Russian soil after the Treaty of Nystad in 1721. In terms of the Russian reorganization of religious life, the Lutherans in these territories were allowed to keep their faith and confession. Orthodox worshipers were protected under the State Religion, and the rebuilding of Karelia's monasteries and churches could slowly begin.[197]

Bibliography

Legal, Administrative, and Ecclesiastical Documents

Een kort och Sanferdigh Relation om Stifftzensz tillstånd uthj Vijborgh, antknad uthj näst håldne Visitation; och uthi Vnderdånigheet H. K. M:tt sampt dhen Kongl. Regeringen öffuerantvardatt i Stocholm den 3 Julij 1643. nr 1920, 44 i Nordiska samlingen, Uppsala universitetsbibliotek. A complete copy in the author's private collection, 22 digitalized sheets.

Gummerus, Jaakko. "Viipurin piispa Petrus Bjugg'in kertomus hiippakuntansa tilasta 3. p. heinäk. 1643. Een kort och Sanferdigh Relation om Stifftzensz tillstånd uthj Vijborgh ---." In *Finska Kyrkohistoriska Samfundets Protokoll och Meddelanden. Suomen Kirkkohistoriallisen Seuran Pöytäkirjat liitteineen. II 1898–1902.* Helsinki: Suomen kirkkohistoriallinen seura. 1902.

"Fredstraktat mellan Sverge och Ryssland, genom hvilken Ryssland och Sverge afträdde Keksholms län och Ingermanland mot det att Sverge återlämnade sina andra eröfringar. Stolbova, 1617, Februari 27." In *Sveriges Traktater med Främmande Magter*

197 Koukkunen, Heikki. Ortodoksinen Karjala. In *Karjala 1. Portti Itään ja Länteen.* Mäkinen, Yrjö-Pekka & Lehmusvaara, Ilmari & Sarrala, Hannu & Vihinen, Reino eds. Helsinki: Karisto. 1982, 286.

jemte andra dit hörande handlingar. Femte delens förra hälft 1572–1632. Stockholm: O.S. Rydbäck & C. Hallanderff, 1903, 242–267.

"Biafsked till traktaten i Stolbova." In *Sveriges Traktater med Främmande Magter jemte andra dit hörande handlingar. Femte delens förra hälft 1572–1632*. Stockholm: O.S. Rydbäck & C. Hallanderff, 1903, 267–269.

St Germanus of Constantinople. *On the Divine Liturgy*. Translation, introduction and commentary by Paul Meyendorff. Crestwood, NY: St. Vladimir's Seminary Press. 1984.

Karta över Finland, the digital archives of Riksarkivet, Stockholm, 1600–1650. *Karta över Finland, sydöst om linjen Borgå-Padasjoki-Nyslott, området runt Ladoga och Ingermanland från 1600-talets förra hälft* (*Nyen skans angiven*). Auss dieser Carthen ist zu sehen welchen gebrochen Land es ist und grosse Klipen bösse Wege mit Wagen das man kaum einer hinder dem andern reitten kan, derowegen hoch nottigh die Ladoga Sehe sich zu bemeistern, so kan der Feindt disser Örtter nocht thun, man kan kommen durch den Finum Sinnicum in die Ladoga gutte 6 Boijert auss Schweden geschigk mit Stücken und den gutte Scher-Bött darbeij ia besser will, reutter seindt hier wenigh Nutze; diss zum Nachricht E. Graff senden thue. Kan hierdurch defediret werden Kexholm, Nötteborch, Nieschloss, Wiborch etc. und dem Feinde zu Wasser einfallen nach Ladoga der Örtten wor man will. – N:o 15–16 – N:o 19. Code: SE/RA/81001/#/0003:00001.

Stadgar / Förordningar / HREF och Resolutioner, från åhr 1528 in til 1701. Angående Justitiae och Executions-Ährenden / med Förteckning på Stadgarne främst / och ett fulkommeligit Orda-Register efterst wid Werket öfver thes innehåld; Uppå Hans Kongl. May:ts allernådigste befalning och Privilegier, Tilt het almänne bästas tienst / och hwars och ens särskilte nytto / sålunda med flit samlade / och genom Trycket i dagsliuset befordrade. SEDERHOLM Tryckt med bekostnad af JOHANN HENRICH WERNER, kongl. May:ts få och Upsala Acad. Boktryckiare Åhr 1706.

Kongl. May:ts hoff-articla, publicerade i Stockholm den 13 Junii 1655. Carl Gustaff. 300–310.

Krigs-Artiklar som af then Stormächtigste konung och here / herr CARL the XI. Sweriges / Giötes och Wendes konung u. Åhr 1683. Förnyade och stadgade äre. 802–828.

Kexholm map, the digital archives of Riksarkivet, Stockholm, 1649–1650. *Geographisch affrijtning upå Kiäxholms lähn* /området Nurmes (Kuop.) – Suojärvi – Salmi – Kexholm (Vib.) – Libelits (Kuop.) / huru thet medh thes omliggiande provinsier, Nötheborgs, Wijborghs, Sawelax och Kaianeborgs läner sampt stoorförstendömedt Rysslands, grentzer ... Medh flijt observerat, mätit och rijtat anno 1649 och anno 1650 aff Erick Andersson Utter. [Papper, ritad, 125 x 72,5.] A. = [?] = 4. – /Reversal 1850 nr 158/ 91. Code: SE/RA/420571/02/1/0012:00001.

Kyrkio-Lag och Ordning / som then Stormächtigste Konung och Herre / Herr CARL then Elofte / Sweriges / Göthes och Wändes Konung / &c.Åhr 1686. hafwer låtit författa / ochÅhr 1687. af Trycket utgå och publicera. Jemte ther til hörige Stadgar. http://www.mlang.name/arkisto/kyrkio-lag-1686.html 21.6.2018.

Leinberg, K. G. *Handlingar Rörande Finska Kyrkan och Presterskapet. Andra Samlingen 1627–1651. Jämte tillägg till första samlingen*. Helsingfors. 1893.

Leinberg, K. G. *Handlingar Rörande Finska Kyrkan och Presterskapet. Fjerde Samlingen. Med Understöd af Allmänna Medel i Tryck Utgifna*. 1652–1686. Helsingfors. 1900.

Rhyzelii, Andreae Ol. *Episcoposcopia Sviogothica, Elelr En SweaGöthift Sticht- och Biskops-Chrönika, Om alla Swea- och GöthaRikets Sticht och Biskopar, ifrå början, in til närwarande tid; Bestående af twå delar. Med några anmerkningar Och fullkomligt Register*. Linköpings Läns och Stichts Boktryckare Gabriel Biörckegren. 1752.

Svenska Riksdagsakter. Andra handlingar. 1521–1718. Nils Ahnlund ed. Stockholm: P.A. Norstedt & Söner. 1957, II:2, 276/97, Örebro Stadga 27.2.1617.

Suomalainen katekismus kyrillisin kirjaimin (1644) eli ns. van Selowin katekismus. – Suomen kirkkohistoriallisen seuran Vuosikirja 1985, 37–71.

Tigerstedt, K. K. *Bidrag till Kexholms läns historia under drottning Kristinas tid*. I–V. 1850[–1900] [Åbo?]. 1850.

Webpages

The webpage of the South-Karelian museums, https://www.etelakarjalanmuseot.fi/etela-karjalan-historiaa/ 13 March 2019.

Literature

Aalto, Seppo. *Kirkko ja kruunu siveellisyyden vartijoina. Seksuaalirikollisuus, esivalta ja yhteisö Porvoon kihlakunnassa 1621–1700*. Helsinki: Suomen Historiallinen Seura, 1996.

Alapuro, Risto. "Revisiting Microhistory." In *Historical Knowledge: in Quest of Theory, Method and Evidence*. Eds. Susanna Fellman & Marjatta Rahikainen. Newcastle upon Tyne: Cambridge Scholars, 2012.

Boëthius B. "Petrus Jonæ Bjugg". urn:sbl:18268. *Svenskt biografiskt lexikon*. Used 2017-08-17. https://sok.riksarkivet.se/Sbl/Presentation.aspx?id=18268.

Isä Ambrosius. "Luostarilaitos Karjalassa." In *Karjala 1. Portti Itään ja Länteen*. Mäkinen, Yrjö-Pekka & Lehmusvaara, Ilmari & Sarrala, Hannu & Vihinen, Reino eds. Helsinki: Karisto, 1982.

Bjerg, Svend. *Synets Teologi*. Frederiksberg: Forlaget Anis, 1999.

Fagerlund, Rainer. "Vanhempi Vaasa-kausi 1523–1617". In *Kunikaita ja alamaisia. Suomen historia 1523–1809*. Espoo: Schildts, 2000.

Florovski, Georges. *Venäläisen teologian tiet*. Heinävesi: Valamon luostari, 2008.

Eusebios Aleksandrialainen. *Johannes Edelläkävijän laskeutuminen tuonelaan*. Muinaisvenäjästä suom. Johannes Seppälä. Joensuu: Ortokirja, 1980.

Felski, Rita. "Context Stinks!" In *New Literary History*, Volume 42, Number 4, Autumn 2011, pp. 573–591.

Ginzburg, Carlo. "Our Words, and Theirs." In *Historical Knowledge: in Quest of Theory, Method and Evidence*. Eds. Susanna Fellman & Marjatta Rahikainen. Newcastle upon Tyne: Cambridge Scholars, 2012.

Gregory, Timothy E. *A History of Byzantium*. Malden, MA.: Blackwell, 2005.

Hanka, Heikki. *Kuin Kuvastimessa. Suomalaisen kirkkomaalauksen yleispiirteitä uskonpuhdistuksen jälkeen*. University of Jyväskylä. Studies in Art History 5. Jyväskylä: Jyväskylän yliopisto, 1995.

Hauptmann, Peter & Stricker, Gerd. Die Orthodoxe Kirche in Russland. Dokumente ihrer Geschichte (680–1980). Göttingen: Vanderhoeck & Ruprecht, 1988.

Heininen, Simo. "Viipurin lukio lehtorit 1641–1710." In *Arki, kirkko, artefakti. Viipurin kulttuurihistoriaa Ruotsin ajalla (n. 1300–1710)*. Petri Karonen ed. Viipurin Suomalaisen Kirjallisuusseuran Toimitteita 19. Helsinki: Viipurin Suomalainen Kirjallisuusseura. 85–123. 2017.

Jopi, Harri. *Suomalainen kahdeksansävelmistö ja venäläinen traditio*. Turku: Turun yliopisto, 2001.

Karonen, Petri. *Pohjoinen Suurvalta. Ruotsi ja Suomi 1521–1809*. Helsinki: WSOY, 1999.

Keinänen, Marja-Liisa. "Everyday, Fast, and Feast: Household Work and the Production of Time in Pre-Modern Orthodox Karelia." In *Vernacular Religion in Everyday Life: Expressions of Belief*. Bowman, Marion & Valk, Ülo eds. London, New York: Routledge, 2014.

Kirkinen, Heikki. "Kalevalainen Karjala ja kristinusko." In *Karjala 1. Portti Itään ja Länteen*. Mäkinen, Yrjö-Pekka & Lehmusvaara, Ilmari toim. Hämeenlinna: Karisto. 259–279. 1982.

Knuutila, Jyrki. "Kirkkolainsäädäntö – Kirkon vai Yhteiskunnan Asia? Kirkon ja Yhteiskunnan Väliset Suhteet ja Suomessa Käytetyt Säädökset Kanonisesta Oikeudesta Vuoden 1993 Kirkkolakiin." *Edilex 2012* article, version 1.0 published 8 October 2012. www.edilex.fi/artikkelit/9105 https://www.edilex.fi/artikkelit/9105.pdf.

Knuutila, Jyrki & Hiekkanen, Markus. "Viipurin kirkollinen elämä ja sen vaikutus kirkolliseen kulttuuriin 1200-luvun lopusta vuoteen 1710." In *Arki, kirkko, artefakti. Viipurin kulttuurihistoriaa Ruotsin vallan ajalla (n. 1300–1710)*. Petri Karonen ed. Helsinki: Viipurin suomalainen kirjallisuusseura. 26–84. 2017.

Korpela, Jukka. *Kiovan Rusj. Keskiajan eurooppalainen suurvalta*. Joensuu: Ortodoksisen kirjallisuuden julkaisuneuvosto. 1996.

Koukkunen, Heikki. "Ortodoksinen Karjala." In *Karjala 1. Portti Itään ja Länteen.* Mäkinen, Yrjö-Pekka & Lehmusvaara, Ilmari & Sarrala, Hannu & Vihinen, Reino eds. Helsinki: Karisto, 1982.

Kuujo, Erkki. "Venäjä uuden ajan alussa." In *Venäjän Historia.* Päätoimittaja Heikki Kirkinen. Uudistettu laitos. Helsinki: Otava. 81–106. 2002.

Laakso, Ville. *Papinniemi in Uukuniemi and related archaeological sites of the eastern Orthodox cultural area in Finland.* Diss. Turku: Suomen keskiajan arkeologian seura. Archaologia Medii Aevi Finlandiae XIX, 2014.

Laasonen, Pentti. *Suomen Kirkon Historia 2. Vuodet 1593–1808.* Porvoo, Helsinki, Juva: WSOY, 1991.

Laasonen, Pentti. *Novgorodin imu. Miksi ortodoksit muuttivat Venäjälle Käkisalmen läänistä 1600-luvulla?* Helsinki: Suomalaisen kirjallisuuden seura. 2005.

Laitila, Teuvo. "Coercion, Cooperation, Conflicts and Contempt – Orthodox-Lutheran Relations in Swedish-Occupied Kexholm County, Karelia, in the Seventeenth Century." In *Entangled Religions* 11.1 (2020).

Lappalainen, Jussi T. "Toipuva Moskovan valtakunta." In *Venäjän Historia.* Päätoimittaja Heikki Kirkinen. Uudistettu laitos. Helsinki: Otava. 107–131. 2002.

Levin, Eve. *Sex and Society in the World of the Orthodox Slavs, 900–1700.* Ithaca and London: Cornell University Press, 1989.

Malmisalo, Juha. *In Pursuit of the Genuine Christian Image: Erland Forsberg as a Lutheran Producer of Icons in the Fields of Culture and Religion.* Helsinki: Helsingin yliopisto, 2005.

Maloney, George A., S. J. *A History of Orthodox Theology since 1453.* Belmont, Massachusetts: Nordland, 1976.

Matikainen, Olli. "Kurkijoen manaajapappi." In *Manaajista maalaisaateliin: Tulkintoja toisesta historian, antropologian ja maantieteen välimaastossa.* Ed. Kimmo Katajala. Helsinki: Suomalaisen kirjallisuuden seura, 1995.

Melling, David, J. & Parry, Ken & Archmandrite Ephrem. "kollyba/kollyva". In *The Blackwell Dictionary of Eastern Christianity.* Ken Parry, David Melling, Dimitri Brady, Sidney Griffith & John F. Healey eds. Oxford: Blackwell. 1999, 285–286.

Mokroborodova, Larisa. Quaestio nostro saeculo inusitata: русское православие в тезисах Йоханнеса Ботвиди "Христиане" ли Московиты? (1620). Åbo: Åbo Akademi University Press, 2013.

Muroma, Seppo. *Suurten kuolonvuosien (1696–1697) väestönmenetys Suomessa.* Helsinki: SHS, 1991.

Nyman, Magnus. *Hävinneiden historia. Katolista elämää Ruotsi-Suomessa Kustaa Vaasasta kuningatar Kristiinaan.* Helsinki: Katolinen tiedotuskeskus. 2009.

Ouspensky, Leonid & Lossky, Vladimir. *The Meaning of Icons.* Crestwood, New York: St Vladimir's Seminary Press, 1999.

Parvio, Martti. "Den svenska kyrkorätten under 1600-talet." In *Den svenska juridikens uppblomstring i 1600-talets politiska, kulturella och religiösa stormaktssamhälle. Skrifter utgivna av Institutet för rättshistorisk forskning grundat av Gustav och Carin Olin*. Rättshistoriska studier. Serien 2:9. Stockholm. 247–259. 1984.

Pospielovsky, Dimitry. *The Orthodox Church in the History of Russia*. Crestwood, New York: St Vladimir's Seminary Press, 1998.

Rahikainen, Marjatta & Fellman, Susanna. "On Historical Writing and Evidence." *In Historical Knowledge: in Quest of Theory, Method and Evidence*. Eds. Susanna Fellman & Marjatta Rahikainen. Newcastle upon Tyne: Cambridge Scholars, 2012.

Rosén Jerker. "Gustaf Adolf." In *Den Svenska Historien. Gustaf Adolfs och Christinas tid 1611–1654*, ed. Gunvor Grenholm. Stockholm: Bonniers, 1967.

Rosén Jerker. "Westfaliska freden." In *Den Svenska Historien. Gustaf Adolfs och Christinas tid 1611–1654*, ed. Gunvor Grenholm. Stockholm: Bonniers, 1967.

Sivonen, Mika. *Me inkerikot, vatjalaiset ja karjalaiset. Uskonnollinen integrointi ja ortodoksisen vähemmistön identiteetin rakentuminen Ruotsin Inkerissä 1680–1702*. Bibliotheca Historica 111. Helsinki: Suomalaisen kirjallisuuden seura, 2007.

Söderwall, K. F. *Ordbok över Svenska Medeltids-Srpåket*. Av Gustav Ljunggren och Elias Wessén. Lund: Berlingska Boktryckeriet, 1953–1973.

Tarkiainen, Kari. Moskoviten. Sverige och Ryssland 1478–1721. Helsingfors: Svenska litteratursällskapet i Finland, 2017.

Timiadis, Emilianos. *Lebendige Orthodoxie. Eine Selbstdarstellung der Orthodoxie im Kreise der christlichen Kirchen*. Nürnberg und Eichstätt: Johan Michael Sailer Verlag, 1966.

Villstrand, Nils Erik. "Suurvaltakausi 1617–1721". In *Kuninkaita ja alamaisia. Suomen historia 1523–1809*. Espoo: Schildts, 2000.

Villstrand, Nils Erik. *Sveriges Historia 1600–1721*. Stockholm: Norstedts, 2011.

Öhlander, Carl. *Om den Svenska Kyrkoreformationen uti Ingermanland. Ett Bidrag till Svenska Kyrkans Historia Åren 1617–1704*. Diss. Uppsala: Almqvist & Wiksells, 1900.

Law and Piety in the 1736 Reforms in Denmark-Norway

Kristian Mejrup

Religious sentiment, piety, and modernizing concepts of natural law might seem a contradictory blend or a strange combination. There is, however, something in the way reforms in the first part of the eighteenth century were brought about in order to shape and promote education, civility, social obligations and religious feelings, that reveals strong collaborative traits and concord rather than conflict.[1] In this essay I shall pursue two central events initiated in 1736. That year the king of Denmark and Norway had the bicentennial of the Lutheran reformation celebrated.[2] To mark the occasion reforms were enacted: a) on January 13 new standards for the religious rite of confirmation were introduced, and b) on February 10 examination at the Faculty of Law was instituted and thereafter required of all students of law or administrators holding juridical positions. But what are the notions and concepts that link confirmation and the study of law together; and how were they respectively vehicles for piety and law?

The 1736 reforms were both a means to sustain the Reformation and to renew its impact on society.[3] They generated a shift in power that placed authority in religious and juridical matters in new hands. The 1732 reform of the University of Copenhagen had already signalled that the university comprised other faculties and intellectual disciplines and no longer revolved around the Faculty of Theology.[4] The legal documents and manuals related to the 1736 reforms continued that process of differentiation. They professionalized and modernized

1 Martin Gierl has written insightfully on the relation between pietism, modernism and enlightenment thinking. Gierl Martin. "Pietism, Enlightenment, and Modernity". In *A Companion to German Pietism 1660–1800*, ed. Douglas Shantz. Leiden: Brill, 2014, 348–392.

2 The celebratory events and reforms in the north were translated into German and published in *Dänische Bibliothec oder Sammlung von alten und neuen gelehrten Sachen aus Dännemarck*. Vol. 1. Copenhagen and Leipzig, 1738, 256–392.

3 A jubilee is a way of using the past to actualize religious, political, cultural, and denominational identity. See Howard, Thomas Albert. *Remembering the Reformation: An Inquiry into the Meanings of Protestantism*. Oxford: Oxford University Press, 2016. Bach-Nielsen, Carsten. *Fra jubelfest til kulturår Danske reformationsfejringer gennem 400 år*. Aarhus: Aarhus Universitetsforlag, 2015.

4 Glebe-Møller Jens. "Det teologiske Fakultet 1597–1732." In *Københavns Universitet 1479–1979. Vol. 5*. Ed. Leif Grane. G. E. C Gads Forlag, København 1980, 93–211.

 | DOI:10.30965/9783657790746_008

educational standards, and introduced a concept of law that it was expected would apply to all modern Christian citizens.

In the first part of the essay I make inquiries into a) the royal decree that instituted confirmation, and b) notions of law in Pontoppidan's catechetical manual that resulted from the decree. In the second part, I examine a) the statute that brought in standardized examinations at the Faculty of Law, and b) Andreas Hojer's manual that resulted from it.

1. Turning a Private Practice Public

The decree of 13 January 1736 introduced new standards for the religious rite of confirmation in the Danish and Norwegian kingdoms. It was authorized by king Christian VI (1699–1746), allegedly based on an initiative formulated by two of the king's trusted executives.[5] In continuation of the initiative, the king appointed his court preacher, Erik Pontoppidan (1698–1764), to write a manual with instructions on how to teach and train aspiring candidates. Pontoppidan's book was published in 1737 under the title "Truth to Godliness – a Short, Simple and Sufficient Explanation of Martin Luther's Small Catechism".[6] Short, simple and small, however, correspond little with the actual curriculum, consisting as it does of 759 questions intended for youngsters between the ages of 14 and 19. For decades, however, this book was the only one in use in the kingdoms. In Denmark it kept its official monopoly until 1794, when it was replaced with bishop Nicolai Balle's manual of 1791. But long into the nineteenth century, Pontoppidan's book was cherished. Some even considered it as almost holy writ, and placed the name of the author on a level with biblical authorities.[7]

---

5 Neiiendam Michael. *Erik Pontoppidan II (1735–1764) Studier og Bidrag til Pietismens Historie*. Copenhagen, Gad, 1933, 77–81.

6 Pontoppidan Erik. *Sandhed til Gudfrygtighed udi en eenfoldig og efter Muelighed kort, dog tilstrekkelig Forklaring over Sal. Doct. Mort. Luthers Liden Catechismo*. Copenhagen. Wäysenhuses Forlag, 1770 [first edition 1737]. In Schleswig and Holstein, where the Danish king was duke, a German translation was issued in 1741. *Anweisung zum Erkentniss der Wahrheit zur Gottseligkeit*, Altona, 1752 [first edition 1741]. Pontoppidan's manual was furthermore translated into Icelandic, Swedish, Finnish, Greenlandic and Sami. See Neiiendam, *Pontoppidan II*, 263.

7 Brøndsted Mogens. "Historien om Pontoppidans 'Forklaring' i Danmark og Norge". In *Fund og forskning*, No. 12 (1965): 48–66 (52–63). For the reception of the book among Norwegian immigrants in America, see Olson James B. "Erik Ludvigsen Pontoppidan and the American Influence of His Catechism". In *The Lutheran Historical Conference, Essays and Reports 1990*. Vol. 14. *Lutheranism and Pietism*. Minneapolis, 1992, 20–39. For recent theological accounts on Pontoppidan's manual see Stopa Sasja Emilie Mathiasen "A communion of saints?

On its impact at the end of the eighteenth century, Henrik Horstbøll states: "The same book which had previously been diffused by way of royal decrees could not be eliminated by law, nor by any sort of verdict in the parishes ...".[8] The manual thus became an integral part of the religious mindset of the Nordic peoples. It contained religious instruction and ideas of early enlightenment; it facilitated new reading standards, and gave rise to educational reforms and the building of new schools.[9] It promoted the idea that good Christian citizenship would be an honour to God and of benefit to society.

Still, the religious rite of confirmation was much older than the new standards instituted in 1736. Indeed, the focus on catechesis and confirmation dated back to the sixteenth and seventeenth centuries, which in turn looked back to even earlier medieval, patristic and biblical texts and practices.[10] What was new in the Danish realm in the eighteenth century, however, was the standardized format – that confirmation was mandated by law, which eventually brought catechetical instruction into the ambit of the state. What once was a private church affair, was now turned into a public event with examination and due ceremony. An immediate effect of the reform was that the title of catechetical instructor ("Kateketembedet") became official and a chair in catechism was established in 1736 at the University of Copenhagen.[11] The first

---

Reincorporating sinners into the created order of eighteenth-century Denmark through catechetical practice" and Larsen Kurt E. "Pontoppidan versus Spener: No 'better times' but more personal piety within the national Church". In *Pietismus und Neuzeit* 45, 2021, 84–116 and 117–142.

8 Henrik Horstbøll argues that Pontoppidan's manual merges religious and enlightenment ideas, and that the book is more than a redaction of Spener's manual. "Pietism and the Politics of Catechisms. The Case of Denmark and Norway in the Eighteenth and Nineteenth Centuries". *Scandinavian Journal of History* 29, No 2 (2004): 143–160 (150). See also Horstbøll Henrik. "Læsning til salighed, oplysning og velfærd: Om Pontoppidan, pietisme og lærebøger i Danmark og Norge i 17- og 1800-tallet." *Fortid og Nutid* (2003): 83–108 (100).

9 Horstbøll, "Catechisms", 144, 151–153. See also Markussen Ingrid. *Til Skaberens Ære, Statens Tjeneste og Vor Egen Nytte: Pietistiske og kameralistiske idéer bag fremvæksten af en offentlig skole i landdistrikterne i 1700-tallet*. Odense: Odense Universitetsforlag 1995.

10 Grethlein Christian, Germann Michael. "Confirmation (Protestant)". In *Religion Past and Present*. Online version of 2011. Consulted August 2018: http://dx.doi.org.ep.fjernadgang.kb.dk/10.1163/1877-5888_rpp_COM_12065. For the Danish context, see Lindhardt Poul Georg. *Konfirmationens historie i Danmark*. Copenhagen: Lohse, 1936, 11–26. Haarberg Jon. "Earways to Heaven: Singing the Catechism in Denmark-Norway, 1569–1756". In *Religious Reading in the Lutheran North: Studies in Early Modern Scandinavian Book Culture*. Eds. Charlotte Appel, Morten Fink-Jensen. Cambridge Scholars Publishing 2011, 48–69.

11 Pedersen Johannes. "Pietismens Tid 1699–1746. In *Den Danske Kirkes Historie*. Eds. Hal Koch, Bjørn Kornerup. Copenhagen, 1951, 11–227 (164). See also the Royal Decree of 28 April 1736, published in *Dänische Bibliothec*, Vol. 1, 372–385.

professor of catechism was Christian Langemach Leth (1701–1764). He was the one who provided the official *imprimatur* for Pontoppidan's *Truth to Godliness*. In order to have access to the confirmation ceremony, which was held twice a year in rural churches and thrice a year in the capital, children had to receive educational and religious instruction from either an ordained minister or a state cleric / catechetical instructor. The confirmation reform and the new office and education of the instructor thus went hand in hand. Although the instructors were to assist and unburden the workload of ministers, some felt their presence to be an encroachment on pastoral turf.[12]

From the outset, the confirmation reform relied on other developments and in its turn contributed to further reforms of the educational system. Basic training in reading was required for the religious instruction that was necessary for confirmation, and for that purpose capable teachers were needed. If in the 1736 reform of confirmation we see the dawn of public schooling, we should add that it augmented the need for professional teachers. In fact, the evident connection between the instruction of children and competent teachers, makes a comparison with Halle Pietism worthwhile. That reform movement, initiated in 1695 – and from 1706 collaborating with the Danish authorities on the Christian mission to East India – combined schooling, education, erudition and piety with pastoral instruction and catechesis. Indeed, its leading figures often enough emphasized how catechesis was the means for ensuring and nurturing both scholarly and religious standards.[13] At Halle, school books and manuals, as well as the way social life was organized – students and teachers living and dining together – demonstrated and idealized the benefit of the mutual obligation between student and teacher.[14]

The international literature on catechesis that flourished in the seventeenth and eighteenth centuries offers another relevant context for the confirmation reform of 1736. This literary genre, at times conventional, at times stylistically enhanced, consists of narratives, manuals, expositions and explanations of authorized compilations, dialogues and instructions – often complete with Latin, Greek and Hebrew scripture references.[15] One worth attention is a manual of 1722, written by one of the influential Pietist theologians, the

12 Neiendam, *Pontoppidan II*, 78, 262.

13 Mejrup Kristian. "Grand Prospects of Halle Pietism: The Acrobat, the Project-maker and the Shepherd". PhD-dissertation. Copenhagen: *Publikationer fra Det Teologiske Fakultet 64*, 2016, 104–109.

14 Mejrup, "Grand Prospects", 97–104.

15 See the substantial list of titles in *Biblioteca Danica Systematisk fortegnelse over den danske litteratur fra 1482–1830*. Ed. Bruun Christian. Copenhagen: Rosenkilde og Bagger 1961–1965. Vol. 1, 256–280.

hymn-writer and professor of theology, Johann Jakob Rambach (1693–1735) – and entitled "The well-instructed catechetical instructor". It was translated into Danish in 1728.[16] Rambach, who in 1731 was offered a position as court preacher and professor of theology at the University of Copenhagen[17], explains the meaning of the word *catechesis* with reference to the Greek ἦχος. The noun, he explains, means *sound* ("Schall"), the verb to *reverberate* ("Wiederschallen"). This is taken as illustrative of what catechesis should achieve, namely to generate resonance in each candidate.[18] A similar idea would recur in the royal decree that introduced standardized confirmation.

2. Instituted by Law

Both in content and as a legal document, the royal decree of 13 January 1736 is a text worth attention.[19] It regulates religious matters – both the *ius sacrorum* and the *ius circa sacra* – and demonstrates the sovereign power of the Protestant ruler of Denmark and Norway in the age of absolutism.[20] It defines confirmation as "public confirmation of the divine grace offered in baptism to those who now are about to attend the Lord's Table." It offers a repetition

16 Rambach Johann Jakob. *Der wohlunterrichtete Catechet, das ist deutlicher Unterricht wie man der Jugend auf die allerleichteste Art den Grund der christlichen Lehre beybringen könne, darinnen die wichtigsten Vortheile, die bey dem Catechisiren in acht zu nehmen sind, treulich entdecket werden*. Jena, 1722. Rambach Johann Jakob. *Monita catechetica, eller Catechetiske Betænkninger, hvilke meddeele os I. M. Johan Jac. Rambachs Vel underrettet Catechet* (…). Copenhagen, 1728 (second edition 1731, third edition 1744).

17 Döring Heinrich. "Rambach. In *Die gelehrten Theologen Deutschlands im achtzehnten und neunzehnten Jahrhundert*. Neustadt a. d. Orla: Wagner, 1833, 437–446 (439). For more on Rambach's biblical hermeneutics see: Mejrup Kristian og Nørgaard Cyril Lars. "Den pietistiske bibellæser og de helliges hermeneutik. Eksegese og formaning i Halleteologen Rambachs forelæsninger". In *Bibelske konfiguratoner i kunst og kultur*. Eds. Gitte Buch-Hansen and Jesper Tang Nielsen. København: Eksistensen Akademisk, 2021, 117–138.

18 Rambach, *Catechet*, §1. Rambach evokes Acts 2:2 as an example of where the word is applied in Scripture; a passage recounting the gathering of Apostles at Pentecost and the coming of the holy spirit: "And suddenly from heaven there came a sound [ἦχος] like the rush of a violent wind, and it filled the entire house where they were sitting". Acts 2:2. All Bible quotations are from the New Revised Standard Version of 1989.

19 "Forordning Angaaende den tilvoxende Ungdoms Confirmation og Bekræftelse udi deres Daabes Naade af 13. januar 1736." A transcribed version is accessible online and hosted by the School of Culture and Society, Aarhus University: http://danmarkshistorien.dk/ (consulted August 2018).

20 The point of view is discussed and defended in Peder Hersleb's *Epistola Pastoralis* of 1737, in which Hersleb defends the right of the king, to whom he alludes as a Josiah, to enact the rite of confirmation. Hersleb Peder. *Epistola Pastoralis*. Copenhagen 1737, 5, 53–60.

of the words once spoken to and confirmed by godparents, and it encourages the candidates to be seized by the grace once given to them ("med Eftertryk opvække dem til bestandig Troeskab i den Naade, som de have annammet i Daaben ..."). The old baptismal act is thus accentuated to incite new action.

The text consists of twelve points, of which the eleventh – full of instructions as to how the ritual is to be conducted, including the prayers to be spoken quoted at full length – is the longest. In the first paragraph, confirmation is stated to be "an ordinary rule and a mandatory duty" ("en almindelig Regel og en skyldig Pligt", §1). Schooling is a prerequisite for confirmation, and candidates must be given preparatory instruction in basic Christian doctrines. If no school building is at hand, the church or vicarage is to be used. The task of the catechetical instructor is to guide and to test the candidates. He must ensure that everyone attends school and receives instruction (§§2–3). The fourth paragraph spells out that teaching is to take the form of questions and answers, but also that the instructor should invite the candidates to his house and guide them in how to grasp the literal sense of the articles of faith ("At fatte den Bogstavelige Meening af de fornødenste Troens Artikler") and to seize the living knowledge and have their life transformed by it (§4).[21]

The liturgical dates set for the ceremony allegedly follow the example of the primitive church ("efter den første Kirkes Exempel"). It is held either the first Sunday after Easter, *Qvasimodogeniti* or – in larger churches – in the Autumn on the first Sunday after Michaelmas or the first Sunday after the New Year (§5).[22] Three months in advance, parents must inform the instructor of aspiring candidates. Conversely, the instructor must ensure that the children are sufficiently informed (§6). He must teach with distinction and kindness ("Tydelighed og Venlighed") and mix instruction with encouragement. He must pay close attention to how each child is affected, whether one soul is strongly moved by lessons in godliness, while another, if for instance inclined

21 "Forordning", §4: "Skal Læreren selv (...) lade dem komme til sig i sit Huus, for at underviise dem i deres Christendom, og det saaledes, at de ikke alleene blive anførte til at fatte den Bogstavelige Meening af de fornødenste Troes Artickler, men end og blive opmuntrede til at faae fat paa den levende Kundskab deraf, og at føre dem i Øvelse, paa det at Ungdommen kand ved det GUds Sandheder blive dem ret opvækkelig og alvorlig forestillede og indskærpede, opvækkes til at give Sandheden Rum, og de maae derved bringes til en ret Smag og Aandelig Erfaring til at efterfølge den i deres Liv og Levnet, og saa med et Ord, bringes til en sand Hiertens og Sinds Forandring."

22 The *Qvasimodogeniti* is a Latin adaptation of the first words of 1 Peter 2:2: "Like newborn infants (long for the pure, spiritual milk, so that by it you may grow into salvation)" which thematically relates well to notions of confirmation and rebirth. See for instance my analysis of August Hermann's sermon of 1697 on the subject of rebirth: "Die Lehre unsers HErrn JESU CHristi von der Wiedergeburt". Mejrup, "Prospects", 36–40.

to sinful actions, requires admonishment (§7).[23] Those who do not pass the preparation are to be informed that they need further instruction. Should they refuse to accept the offer, care must be taken to expel them (§8).[24]

Eight days before confirmation, the instructor advertises the event to the congregation, and on the day, it is thematically emphasized in the liturgy [§9]. When the sermon is over, the congregation sings one of two traditional Lutheran hymns: "I Jesu Navn skal ald vor Gierning skee" or "Kom Gud Skaber o Hellig Aand". Then the candidates approach the altar: boys on one side, girls on the other. After a short prayer and an edifying speech, the examination begins (§10). If a child does not know how to answer the instructor's questions, he must turn to another without embarrassing the former in front of the congregation (§10). The detail indicates that the decree is not without pedagogical intent.

> If a child does not know how to answer a question, the instructor must let it pass and ask the next one in line making sure not to embarrass the former with any word in front of the congregation. In general, the instructor conducting this holy work, must by no means show any partiality or be opinionated. If he notices that the children do not answer clearly or comprehensibly, then he must patiently encourage them to speak up boldly, so that people may understand.[25]

When the public examination is ended, the act of confirmation proceeds (§11). This is by far the most detailed part of the text. Here the candidates must confirm the words once warranted by their godparents, proclaim their Christian faith, and renounce the devil. The instructor then places his hand on their heads and seals the act with a prayer. The act is then prolonged with another speech, in which the instructor reminds the candidates of their oath to God

---

23 "Forordning", §7: "Og ligesom han dem alle tilsammen underviiser, saa bør han nu og da, tage et andet Barn for sig i sær, og spørge det om sin Siæles Tilstand, hvad det merker hos sig af Omvendelse og Troe, og i Fald han veed om et eller andet Barn, hvad Synder det i Sær kand være tilbøyeligst til, og hvad særdeles Omstændigheder det kand staae udi, saa maae han af forbarmende Kiærlighed foreholde samme Barn sin Siæls elendige Tilstand, og enten give det Anledning til en sand Omvendelse, eller og stadfæste det udi det Gode."

24 "Forordning", §8: "… og saafremme de ikke vil lade sig bevæge med det Gode, da viise dem bort, dog med den Forsigtighed, at hvad han udi dette Fald giør, han altiid er viis paa, det at kunde forsvare …"

25 "Forordning", §10: "Er der et Barn, som ikke kand svare til et eller andet Spørgsmaal, da gaaer han det forbi, og spørger det andet derom, som staaer næst ved, og det uden at beskiæmme det andet Barn med noget Ord for Meenigheden, saasom Læreren ved dette hellig Verk, over alt maae entholde sig fra ald Parthiskhed og Persons Anseelse; Og formerker han, at Børnene ikke svare tydelig og forstaaelig nok, saa opmuntrer han dem med Sagtmodighed til at tale frit, høyt og saa Folk kand forstaae det."

("en Formel Eed for HErren"), and that the world must know that they now are part of a divine union ("Guds Bunds Forvante"). Hereafter the confirmed believers are called to the altar for communion.

The ceremony is completed with a prayer that proclaims loyalty to the *Confessio Augustana* and declares that the believers from now on are fellow citizens and peers in God's household ("Medborgere og Huus-Egne", §11). The main events of the day and their liturgical meaning are recapitulated in the prayer, and an exclamation to God is voiced, that he dress the young believers in wedding gowns ("Ifør dem Selv de rette Bryllups=Klæder", §11).[26] The description of the new life in God's household is of interest. It mimics a scripture verse from Titus 2:11, that chimes well with the tenor of the pietistic reform movement at Halle. In August Hermann Francke's Titus Lectures of 1703, published in 1726, this one verse allegedly 'comprises all essential features of education'. And it shows divine grace in her role as universal schoolmistress teaching humankind to renounce impiety and worldly passions, and to live lives that are self-controlled, upright, and godly.[27] Similar to Francke's exposition of the verse, the allusive modification of Titus 2:11 in the decree blends education with religious salvation. Moreover, it links efforts in the present age to a hope for heavenly bliss rather than the threat of doom.

In the extensive prayer a passage is devoted to the king. Indeed, confirmation is presented as an effort of benefit to the king, because it makes for good, obedient and Christian subjects.[28] Such a statement – vocalized as prayer –

---

26 "Forordning", §11: "Ifør dem Selv de rette Bryllups-Klæder, danne dem saaledes, som Du vil have dem, og lad dem saa imodtage Dit Huses Gode og Din Tempels Hellige Ting, som de, der agte at leve og døe forsikkrede om at lodtages i Din Himmel og Herlighed, i Din Ære og Saglighed; Giør at de ikke nogensinde glemme, hvorledes Du har givet dem et Rum i Dit Huus, et Navn bedre end Sønners og Døttres; Hielp dem hver Gang, de betræde Dine Forgaarde, at findes i Dit Huus som Dine Huus-Egne, samt, inden og uden for det, at kunde kiendes for Dine Sønner og Døttre; Din sagliggiørende Naade tugte og oplære dem at forsage U-gudelighed, og de verdslige Begierligheder, at leve tugteligen, retfærdeligen og Gudfrygteligen i denne Verden, som de, der vente og ere forvissede at lide evigligen vel i den anden; Thi naar de tænke paa Dig deres Skabere, i deres Ungdom, da vil Du tænke paa dem til det Beste her og hisset, i Tiden og i Evigheden."

27 "Es fasset aber das Wort *παιδεύειν* in sich *totam educationem, & quaecumque ad eam pertinent …*". Francke August Hermann. *Lectiones Paræneticæ*, vol. 1. Halle: Waysenhaus, 1726, 90–113 (103). See also Mejrup, " Prospects", 172–179.

28 "Forordning", §11: "Din Salvede Vor Allernaadigste Arve-Herre og KONGE, KONNING CHRISTIAN den Siette, være og blive velsignet af Dig nu og herefter, i denne og den tilkommende Verden; Lad Ham høste Frugten, end og af denne Dags Forretning, saa at Han i alle dem, der have fornyet deres Daabes Løfte, maa finde gode og lydige Undersaatter, som viide at enhver, der frygter GUD, skal ære Kongen."

shows the affinities between the king as a religious and a secular ruler. The outlined ceremony ends with *Our Father*, the *Lord's Blessing* and a last hymn.[29]

The royal decree testifies to a remarkable intervention. In the preamble, the king is cast in the role of a bishop regulating the life of his flock. Basic educational training and religious insight are facilitated through instruction, public examination and church ceremony. The preamble informs us that the king has sought the advice of "certain bishops", but no reservation or protests are referred to. One would, however, expect that the church authorities only reluctantly accepted the state intervention that eventually turned a wholly ecclesiastical practice into a public event.[30] The reform had far-reaching consequences for the religious formation of youth, and most spheres of everyday life. Having passed the rite of confirmation, one obtained Christian citizenship and thus the right to marry and obtain land.[31] By turning a private practice into a public and mandatory event, the confirmation reform eventually took power from the religious authorities and placed it in new hands, thus combining pious and secularizing initiative.

3. Catechetical Manual

Erik Pontoppidan's catechetical manual is arranged as an explanation of Martin Luther's small catechism, one that elaborates on and expands the original.[32] The small catechism was part of the collection of authoritative texts listed in the Danish Law code of 1683.[33] Thus, by latching on to a rock-solid authority and adopting its genre, Pontoppidan could play by conventional rules. He

29 "Forordning", §11: "OG derpaa Fader Vor! Og HErrens Velsignelse; og efter at samme Hellige Forretning saaledes er til Ende, siunges: Mit Barn frygt Den sande GUD! Eller: GUd Fader udi Himmerig Sin Villie Han os kiende; Derpaa læses af Degnen den sædvanlige Bøn i Chors-Døren, hvormed den heele GUdstieneste for den Gang bliver besluttet og skal være til Ende."

30 Neiendam, *Pontoppidan II*, 78, 259. The supportive texts of bishop Peder Hersleb and bishop Christian Worm are paraphrased in German in *Dänische Bibliothec*, Vol. 1, 201–241.

31 Neiiendam, *Pontoppidan II*, 78.

32 Pontoppidan's manual consists of the following parts: (a) Extract of the royal privilege that appoints the Royal Orphanage as the sole publisher; (b) Exordium dated Copenhagen October 9, 1737 [1–5]; (c) Admonition to the schoolmasters [1]; (d) Introduction (1–9); and (e) Four parts (9–194).

33 Danske Lov 1683 2-1-1: "Den Religion skal i Kongens Riger og Lande alleene tilstædis, som overeens kommer med den Hellige Bibelske Skrift, det Apostoliske, Nicæniske og Athanasii Symbolis, og den Uforandrede Aar et tusind fem hundrede og tredive overgiven Augsburgiske Bekiendelse, og Lutheri liden Catechismo." Kong Christian den Femtis Danske Lov. Copenhagen, 1929, 204–205. See also Kolderup-Rosenvinge Janus Lauritz

also drew inspiration from Philipp Jacob Spener's catechetical exposition of 1677 – from 1728 available in Danish translation – that equally actualized and reworked the Lutheran heritage.[34]

The ponderous title "Truth to godliness" (*Sandhed til Gudfrygtighed*), calls for clarification. It is a quotation from the Letter to Titus: one of the New Testament Pastoral Letters (the First and Second to Timothy and the Letter to Titus), ascribed to the apostle Paul. In the initial words of Titus 1:1 we read: "Paul, a servant of God and an apostle of Jesus Christ, for the sake of the faith of God's elect and the knowledge of the truth that is in accordance with godliness."[35] It is to the last part of this verse that Pontoppidan alludes in the title of his manual: "truth that is in accordance with godliness" (ἀληθεια κατ' εὐσέβειαν). Unfortunately, the Danish word for godliness, "Gudfrygtighed" literally meaning 'fear of god', is a misleading translation of the Greek *eusebeia*, which in Latin is translated with *pietas*, in German with *Gottseligkeit* or *Frömmigkeit*, and in English with *piety* or *godliness*. From the outset, the book concerns 'truth that accords with piety', and bearing in mind the words of Titus 1:1, *truth* implies *knowledge*.[36] Pontoppidan's title thus hints at both intellectual and religious capacities: full knowledge of the truth that conforms with piety [ἐπίγνωσιν ἀληθείας τῆς κατ' εὐσέβειαν].[37] This combination of epistemo-

Andreas. *Grundrids af den danske Kirkeret.* Copenhagen, 1851 [first edition 1834], §24: "Om den danske evangelisk=lutherske Kirkes Forhold til Staten efter Aaret 1660".

34 Spener Philipp Jacob. *Einfältige Erklärung Der Christlichen Lehre Nach der Ordnung Des kleinen Catechismi Des theuren Mannes Gottes Lutheri.* Halle: Waysenhaus, 1717 [First edition Frankfurt 1677]. The book was translated into Danish in 1728 (second edition 1730, third edition 1740). *Den christelige Lærdoms eenfoldige Udleggelse efter D. M. Lutheri liden Catechismi Orden.* Copenhagen: Missionskollegiet.

35 All Bible quotations in Greek are from the Nestle Aland edition 28.

36 Rather *full* knowledge of the truth, due to the emphasis of the Greek ἐπίγνωσις. Von Lips Herman. *Glaube – Gemeinde – Amt, zum Verständnis der Ordination in den Pastoralbriefen.* Göttingen: Vandenhoeck & Ruprecht, 1979, 38.

37 The Pastoral Letters provided the Halle Pietists with plenty of material for giving nuances to the Lutheran Protestant tradition to which they adhered. See Krumbiegel Friedemann. *Erziehung in den Pastoralbriefen. Ein Konzept zur Konsolidierung der Gemeinden. Arbeiten zur Bibel und ihrer Geschichte.* Leipzig: Evangelische Verlagsanstalt, 2013, 13–14; 24–29. Von Lips Hermann. "Der Gedanke des Vorbilds im Neuen Testament". In *Evangelische Theologie* 58. No 4 (1998), 295–309; Von Lips Hermann. "Von den 'Pastoralbriefen' zum 'Corpus Pastorale': Eine Hallische Sprachschöpfung und ihr modernes Pendant als Funktionsbestimmungdreier neutestamentlicher Briefe." In *Reformation und Neuzeit 300 Jahre Theologie in Halle*, ed. Udo Schnelle. Berlin / New York: De Gruyter, 1994, 49–71. See also Mejrup Kristian. "Instruktioner i frelse: Det pietistiske skoleprojekt og Pastoralbrevene" In *Forum for Bibelsk Eksegese 20: Bibelen og reformationen.* Eds. Gitte Buch-Hansen et al. Copenhagen: Eksistensen, 2017 (open acces: http://teol.ku.dk/abe/publikationer/forum_for_bibelsk_eksegese/bibelen-og-reformationen/12_Mejrup_FBE_20_1_.pdf).

logical and moral notions chimes in with the pietistic reform programmes of Spener and Francke that heavily influenced Denmark and Norway in the first half of the eighteenth century.[38] Like the title of his book, Pontoppidan's introduction vocalizes words and ideas from the Titus letter of universal salvation advanced through instruction:

> God, who wants humankind to be saved, also wants everyone to obtain truth to godliness. Indeed, to grow and to advance in piety on all occasions and by all the means they are offered in this era more than in any other.[39]

Pontoppidan distinguishes present from former time. The present era offers a great number of truths and insights available to a degree which would be fathomless to our forefathers. Today it seems, he claims, that no one is content to be partly informed, except when it comes to matters of religion, although such matters ought to be the highest aim of all our endeavours.[40] While our forefathers were more engaged and less thoughtful; we today are more attuned to reflection than action. Our forefathers resemble, Pontoppidan points out, a productive Lea with weak eyes, while we bring to mind an unproductive Rachel of dazzling beauty.[41] Still, the present time has this advantage, that it has access to an ever-increasing amount of information and knowledge. Therefore Pontoppidan encourages his reader to combine the different qualities of Lea and Rachel and to turn full knowledge of truth ("Sandheds Kundskab") into the prerequisite for Christian life.

4. Rules for Christian Believers

Of the four parts that take up the bulk of the book and its 759 questions, we shall focus on the first and see how Pontoppidan conceptualizes notions of law. Part one begins with reflections on Scripture and Bible reading (questions

---

38 Pedersen, "Pietismens Tid", 11–226.

39 Pontoppidan, *Truth*, preface: "Den Gud, som vil, at alle Mennisker skulle blive salige, vil ogsaa, at de alle skulle komme til Sanheds Kundskab, ja voxe og gaae frem i den same efter de Leyligheder og Hielpe=Midler, som dem tilbydes i een Verdens Alder, mere end i den anden."

40 Pontoppidan, *Truth*, preface.

41 Pontoppidan, *Truth*, preface: "Seer jeg paa vore Forfædre, da synes mig, de gjorde mere, end de vidste, men vi vide mere, end vi giore. De lignede en frugtbar Lea med svage Øyne, vi en ufrugtbar Rachel med skion Anseelse." There is a pun in the Danish between looking with 'weak eyes' ("svage Øyne") and looking with regard for one's appearance ("skion Anseelse").

1–28). Since the Bible is too vast a complex of texts, the catechism restricts itself to a survey of the Christian Gospel (questions 28–38). Pontoppidan follows the traditional form of the catechism structured in five sections covering a) the ten commandments, b) the articles of faith, c) the Lord's prayer, d) baptism and e) communion. A short version of the catechism can be outlined with the distinction between Law and Gospel. Law concerns the ten commandments, Gospel the remaining parts (questions 37–38). As we see, the first notion of law in Pontoppidan's manual equates Law with the ten commandments. Building on this starting point, clarifications and explanations are added in the following pages and series of questions (Questions 39–328). For instance, in the Old Testament, Pontoppidan explains, God granted three types of law: the ceremonial church law, the secular law of governance and the moral law. Only the third of these is still valid. He defines this moral law as a law of love and life ("Den Moralske eller almindelige Kierligheds og Levneds Lov"). It is universal, it is inscribed in the hearts of humankind – citing Romans 2:15 –, and it comprises love of God, love of oneself and love of others. This moral law is also referred to as natural law.[42]

> [Question 42] Is the moral law or the universal law of love ("almindelig Kierligheds Lov") no longer valid?
>
> [Answer] By all means. This law is founded on God's splendid and just nature, and it therefore implies God's firm and constant will for mankind at all times, that is love of God, oneself, and the other.
>
> [Question 43]: How has God revealed this law and his constant will?
>
> [Answer] He has inscribed it in humankind at creation, it therefore is called the natural law. Romans 2:15.[43]

We would expect this definition of law to correspond with the distinction of Law from Gospel just mentioned: *law* concerning human restrictions and obligations towards the divine, *gospel* pertaining to God's gracious act towards creation (questions 34, 35). But Pontoppidan complicates matters by adding a series of notions to specify the validity moral law. This law is rooted in God's *nature* and it captures God's *will*. It is furthermore presented as "love for God,

42 Pontoppidan, *Truth*, 9–10.

43 Pontoppidan, *Truth*, 9–10: "(42.) Staaer da den Moralske eller almindelige Kierligheds Lov ey heller længere ved Magt? – Jo visselig, thi denne Lov grunder sig paa Guds herlige og retfærdige Natur, og altsaa indeholder Guds uforanderlige og bestandige Villie til alle Mennisker i alle Tider, som er Kierlighed imod Gud, sig selv og Næsten. (43.) Hvorledes har Gud aabenbaret denne sin Lov og bestandige Villie? – Hand har ved Skabelsen indskrevet den i alle Menniskers, og allsaa kaldes den Naturens Lov. Rom. 2,15."

oneself and others" and altogether summarized as natural law. Natural law, moreover, is accessible in two ways. It is inscribed in the hearts of all creation (Romans 2:15) and explicated in the ten commandments revealed to Moses on Mount Sinai and recorded on two tablets. Pontoppidan applies the two tablets to explain the definition of law as love of God, oneself and others. While the first tablet (commandments 1–3) informs us of man's duty to God, the second (commandments 4–10) captures our social obligation towards ourselves and others.[44] This is a remarkable combination of traditional and modern principles. It merges the metaphor of divine law cut in stone on two tablets with the concept, drawn from natural law, of social duty towards oneself, the other and God – as famously plotted by Samuel Pufendorf in his *De officio hominis et civis juxta legem naturalem* (1673).[45]

From the first part of the manual, it is clear that only one of three types of law in the Old Testament is still valid. What remains clouded is whether the valid moral law is natural law (ius naturale), divine law (ius divinum), a divine law revealed (ius divinum positivum) or a bit of everything put together. The one law valid to all Christian believers is thus full of facets. It is divinely mandated, inscribed in nature, sustained by revelation, morally valid and explicable in terms of social duties owed to God, oneself and others. Yet this conception surpasses the strict limitation of the traditional Lutheran idea of law and gospel. It obligates the Christian believer to follow the law, not by force or threat, but compelled by the love of God, and thus made fit for social duties toward oneself, others and God. The bewilderment voiced in question 51 is well placed: "How, then, should I understand this which seems strange to me?"

> [Answer to question 51] You should notice two things: a Christian believer is free from the curse and the constraint of the law, but not from obedience to it. That is, he must fulfil what the law requires of him, not out of compulsion or fear of the curse, but because the love of Christ compels him. And when he against his will and out of fragility fails, the curse of the law shall not be inflicted upon him, because he is in Christ (Romans 8:1).
>
> Question 53: Is the law content with mere deeds?
>
> [Answer] No, the law is spiritual, and requires the entire body, soul, mind, desire and vigour of man.[46]

---

44 Pontoppidan, *Truth*, 11–13, 33–79.

45 The book was translated into Danish in 1742 and according to the translator with the support of Andreas Hojer. See Pufendorf Samuel. *Et Menniskes og en Borgers Pligter efter Naturens Lov, beskrevne i det latinske Sprog*. Translated by Christian Homfred Bugman. Copenhagen: Det Kongelige Vajsenhus, 1742.

46 Pontoppidan, *Truth*, 12: "(51.) Hvorledes skal jeg forstaae dette, som synes mig underligt? – Merk da disse to Ting. En troende Christen er fri fra Lovens Forbandelse og Lovens

This concept of moral law remains central to and is elucidated in the remaining exposition of the ten commandments. The concept is difficult to translate or to put into juridical terms, which of course, is not a concern within the context of catechism and religious instruction, but becomes relevant when it enters other intellectual discourses.

We find a strong example of such translation from legal thinking and theological concepts in the debate on Andreas Hojer's juridical treatise on incestuous marriage of 1718.[47] Hojer set forth the argument that the prohibition of consanguine marriages should be sought in honesty and Christian precepts and morals. That is to say, at least theoretically, it is not the law, but the love of Christ that prevents and prohibits incestuous marriage. Such a statement is both pious and radical; *pious* because it places responsibility on individual Christian and moral standards; *radical* because it undermines all other legal concepts on which prohibition of marriages between relatives are traditionally based.[48] In a letter of 1726, Hojer accounts for the intention behind the treatise:

> Indeed, in the main part of the work, I believe that I have firmly proved that neither natural law (*jus naturæ stricte sic dictum*) strictly speaking has anything to do with this; nor has the concept of universal positive law (*lex positiva universalis*) in its true sense. The question rather hinges on honesty and virtue (*doctrina honesti*), Christian precepts (*præceptis christianismi hypotheticis*), and public and private good sense (*doctrina prudentiæ publicæ et privatæ*).[49]

Tvang, men ey fra Lovens Lydighed, det er, hand giør, just hvad Loven kræver, dog ey af Lovens Tvang og Forbandelses Frygt, men fordi Christi Kierlighed tvinger ham dertil, og naar hand, imod sin Villie, af Skrøbelighed forseer sig, da rammer Lovens Forbandelse ham aldeles ey, fordi hand er i Christo. Rom 8,1. (52.) Er Loven tilfreds med udvortes Gierninger? – Ney, Loven er aandelig, og kræver det gandske Menniske med Legem, Siel, Sind, Begierlighed og al Kraft."

47 Hojer Andreas. *Diagramma de nuptiis propinquorum iure divino non prohibitis*. Lemgow, 1718. The text is available online via The Royal Library, http://www.kb.dk/e-mat/dod/130021919951_color.pdf (consulted August 2018). The work consists of seven short chapters: 1: "Gradus Prohibiti Jure naturae nulli sunt", 2: "Nullum datur Jus diuinum positivum vniversale", 3: "Institutio Coniugii Genes[is] I. vtrum Legis instar sit?", 4: "Legem Levit[icus] XVIII non esse vniversalem", 5: "Rationes Legis XVIII. cap. Leviti exponit", 6: "Consensus doctorum, Theologorum, & Jure consultorum", and 7: "Finis vsusque dictorum".

48 Mejrup Kristian. "Andreas Hojer (1690–1739) – The Standard-Bearer of Danish-Norwegian Pietism" In *Law and the Christian Tradition in Scandinavia. The Writings of Great Nordic Jurists*. Eds Kjell Åke Modeer and Helle Vogt. Routledges Law and Religion Series. New York, 2021, 180–195.

49 "Allein im Hauptwerk meine ich unwidertreiblich erwiesen zu haben, dass das Jus naturæ stricte sic dictum, so wenig als lex positiva universalis in sensu proprio hierin etwas disponiren, sondern die Gründe dieser Frage allein aus der doctrina honesti oder virtutis, den præceptis christianismi hypotheticis und der doctrina prudentiae publicæ et privatæ herzuleiten seyn." Hojer's letter to Johannes Fabricius of 1726 is published by Rørdam

Hojer's juridical treatise and Pontoppidan's catechetical manual are two very different texts. But each in its way emphasizes the role of the law for Christian believers. Divine law is not an external matter but a social obligation. The seeming lack of juridical precision in Pontoppidan's manual could be seen as compensated for in Hojer's treatise. Equally, the exposition of the ten commandments as a guideline for Christian morals, well accounted for by Pontoppidan, adds relevant detail to Hojer's claim. Furthermore, in Pontoppidan, we find a restructuring of the exposition of the ten commandments. The two tablets are of course retained, but they are explained by means of a tripartite Pufendorfian structure of social duties. The attempt to derive principles from the two tablets as duties towards oneself, the other and God is evident in Pontoppidan's manual. This is also the case in Nicolai Balle's manual of 1791 that was to replace Pontoppidan's, but here the tripartite structure is highlighted and the two tablets played down.[50]

5. Reforming Jurisprudence

The same year that Pontoppidan's manual was published, a Danish translation of a Latin disputation was issued. The Latin text originated in lectures given by Andreas Hojer (1690–1739), professor of law at the University of Copenhagen, outlining the standards and requirements for future lawyers. The guidelines were published in a manual entitled *Idea Icti Danici* (1736) and the following year issued in a Danish translation supplemented with a synoptic outline of the Danish and the Norwegian law codes: *Forestilling paa en Dansk Jurist.*[51] This *Spiegel* for Nordic lawyers was the first of its kind and it latched onto the statute of 10 February 1736 that instituted standardized examinations at the Faculty of Law.

Andreas Hojer was a versatile scholar, who had frequented the universities of Halle, Copenhagen and Helmstedt. He excelled in disciplines such as medicine, history, law, economy and politics. He is known for his role in reforming

Holger. *Historiske Samlinger og Studier vedrørende danske forhold og personligheder især i det 17. Århundrede.* Vol. 1, Copenhagen, 1891, 403.

50 Balle Nicolai Edinger. *Lærebog i den evangelisk christelige Religion.* Copenhagen, 1791, 57–58–94. I should like to thank Nina Javette Kofoed for this reference.

51 Hojer Andreas. *Idea ICti Danici, partem I: Disputatione Anniversaria Expositam Publico Eruditorum Examini.* Copenhagen 1736. Hojer Andreas. *Forestilling paa en Dansk Jurist.* Translated by Peder Sommer. Copenhagen 1737 and 1744. The Latin version (1–43) is slightly shorter than the Danish translation (1–59) which includes a synoptic outline of the Danish and Norwegian law codes (1–53). References are made to the Latin edition in order to make technical terms and concepts more transparent.

the study of law at the University of Copenhagen, and in general for his tireless effort as a state executive. Indeed, Hojer was involved in several of the reforms instigated in the years 1734–1739.[52] The statute of 10 February 1736 was no exception. It was based on – and almost in full accordance with – a suggestion sent to the king, written and signed 21 December 1735 by Hojer.[53] Both the statute and his manual for Nordic lawyers testify to Hojer's conception of and impact on the study of law.[54]

The procedure and standards of the statute of 10 February 1736 were not devised in a vacuum, but followed those in force at the Faculty of Theology from 1707. Instead of a probationary theological sermon, however, the aspiring lawyer now had to deliberate on how to process a lawsuit.[55] The Faculty of Law was obliged to offer public examination once a month for up to eight candidates. Three grades could be obtained: the *haud contemnendus*, the *haud illaudabilis* and the *laudabilis*. To obtain the mark *haud contemnendus* (literarily: by no means contemptible) one had to demonstrate knowledge of natural law, the Danish and Norwegian law codes of 1683 and 1687, and an awareness of juridical procedure and terminology. The second mark, *haud illaudabilis*, required additional knowledge of international public law (*ius gentium*), and German-Roman law (*jurisprudentia romano-germanica*). The third degree, *laudabilis*, furthermore implied insight into universal law (*ius universale*); differences between the Danish, Norwegian and German law codes; and military

52 For excellent accounts in English on the life and work on Hojer see: Jensen Mads Langballe. "Serving Danish Foreign Policy. Andreas Hojer's De eo quod iure belli licet in minores (1735)" In *The Law of Nations and Natural Law 1625–1800*. Brill 2019, https://doi.org/10.1163/9789004384200_004 (accessed February 2023). Jensen Mads Langballe. "Contests about Natural Law in Early Enlightenment Copenhagen", *History of European Ideas 42:8*, 2016, 1027–1041. http://dx.doi.org/10.1080/01916599.2016.1182045 (accessed February 2023)

53 This proposition, including remarks on amendments made by J. L. Holstein, is printed in Rørdam Holger. *Historiske Samlinger og Studier vedrørende danske forhold og personligheder især i det 17. Århundrede*. Vol. 4, Copenhagen, 1902, 151–160.

54 Mejrup Kristian. "Andreas Hojer (1690–1739) – The Standard-Bearer of Danish-Norwegian Pietism" In *Law and the Christian Tradition in Scandinavia. The Writings of Great Nordic Jurists*. Eds Kjell Åke Modeer and Helle Vogt. Routledges Law and Religion Series. New York, 2021, 180–195.

55 The following paraphrase of the statute is based on the edition published by Henric Schou Jacob. *Chronologisk Register over de kongelige Forordninger og aabne Breve, samt andre trykte Anordninger, som fra Aar 1670 ere udkomne* (...). Part 3: 1730–1746. Copenhagen, 1795, 191–197. A German version of the statute was published in 1738 in *Dänische Bibliothec oder Sammlung von alten und neuen gelehrten Sachen aus Dännemarck*. Vol. 1. Copenhagen and Leipzig, 1738, 360–372.

law (*ius militare*).[56] Prior to the examination, candidates had to render account of their name, age, place of birth, graduation, parents' position, level of ambition, and which part of jurisprudence they expected to engage with. They were also to disclose which courses they had attended, and provide the Faculty with letters of recommendation from their preceptors. Conversely, the Faculty was required to take note of those candidates who demonstrated extracurricular knowledge. The juridical examination was ended with a pledge, by which the candidate with a raised hand (*stipulata manu*) swore never to deviate from law and justice, nor to incite anyone to file needless lawsuits. The final test was to present a case and give suggestions on how to proceed with it.[57]

Not only students but everyone in juridical positions had to take the exam. Doctors of law and licentiates, however, were excused. In fact, they were privileged. Doctors of law now had the right to be addressed as noble and erudite ("*Velædle og Høilærd*"), and to wear velvet and scarlet ("*Frihed at bære Fløiel samt Skarlagen*") and only licentiates and doctors were permitted to teach law. A new professional hierarchy was thus established. Licentiates were more likely to be hired as judges, and only candidates with the highest degree (*laudabilis*) could become judges of the supreme court.[58] Since not everyone had the resources or the intellectual capacity to clear so high a hurdle, an inferior Danish examination – supposedly impossible to fail – was established the following year. This became the more frequented of the two. Despite the fact that Hojer took the first step towards a modernization of the study of law, the road to the establishment of high standards was long.[59]

6. Idea of a Danish Lawyer

Hojer's *Idea of a Danish Lawyer* was designed to match and elucidate the requirements set forth in the statute, to which it alluded. In the preliminary chapter, Hojer claims that the scope of Nordic jurisprudence is to promote

56 Schou, *Register*, 192. According to Poul Johannes Jørgensen the universal law mentioned (*ius universale*) should be understood as the universal impact of divine law (*ius divinum positivum*). Jørgensen Poul Johannes. "Retsundervisningen og Retsvidenskaben ved Københavns Universitet 1537–1736: Forordningen af 10. Februar 1736." In *Festskrift i anledning af tohundrede Aars Dagen for Indførelsen af Juridisk Eksamen ved Københavns Universitet*. Eds. Erik Reitzel-Nielsen and Carl Popp-Madsen. Copenhagen, 1936, 11–114 (101).

57 Schou, *Register* (1795) 191–197.

58 Schou, *Register* (1795) 191–197.

59 Hammerich Kai Frederik. "Juristerne og Embedslivet". In *Festskrift*, 259–307 (289).

both the human and the divine quality of the law (*ad promouendam Iuris & prudentiam & sanctitatem*). The discipline is not only for judges, lawyers and advocates, but for all who desire to engage in public affairs.[60] Therefore it is required of doctors of law that they be role models lighting the way for others.

> Doctors of law must carry the torch for those who vigorously will run through this course that is of the utmost necessity for the commonwealth, civil society and the church. They must show the royal road, so that those who run it become not only good citizens in themselves, but also citizens capable and worthy of usefully leading others.[61]

That the study of law is of general benefit to society, only makes the responsibility of doctors and professors of law the greater. They are like the professional catechists expected to help and instruct both students and ordinary citizens. Scholars and students, however, are the main addressees in the *Idea*, which embraces a surprisingly broad definition of juridical objects. It encourages students to master all disciplines in order to be good lawyers, and since jurisprudence is a discipline that operates with divine, natural and mortal laws, the study itself is essentially an infinite endeavour. The premises for studying law are thus presented in a paradox: no one has ever or will ever fully master jurisprudence. But everyone who fulfils his duties skilfully and rightly earns the title.[62] The idea calls to mind the Christian believer in Pontoppidan's manual, who at once is under the law and only capable of fulfilling it if compelled by the love of Christ.

As if to demonstrate the infinity of the study of law, Hojer presents a list of relevant and desired qualifications. Character and sharp wits, a good education or a bright mind are important preconditions for students of law. Mere finances do not suffice and linguistic skills are also preferable. A lawyer must master his mother tongue, German, Latin and French. Moreover, aspiring lawyers should be acquainted with a) the Old Norse and Danish (*Antiquissima lingua Septentrionalis*) in which the old laws are written; b) Swedish,

60 Hojer, *Idea*, preface: "… non futuri modo Iudices & Aduocati aut Procuratores ad legitimam scientiam rite sint formandi, sed cuius (…) qui recte & cum fructu in publicis regnorum negotiis cupiunt olim versari" ("Not only the future judges, advocates or procurators, who will be formed by legitimate knowledge, but everyone (…) who at any time desires to be rightly and usefully versed in public affairs.")

61 Hojer, *Idea*, preface: "[Iuris Doctoribus … mandatum est] in hoc stadio reipublicæ & Ciuili & Ecclesiasticæ summopere necessario decursuris facem pro virili præferre, viamque regiam ita monstrare, vt non ipsi modo boni ciues, sed & digni habilesque euadant, qui aliis ciuibus cum fructu præesse (…) possint."

62 Hojer, *Idea*, introduction, §§1–5.

c) English – 'relevant in regard to our laws and mores'; not to mention d) Greek and Hebrew – needed when consulting Scripture, 'the source of all divine law and religion', and 'for settling religious disputes'.[63] The series of demands continues. Relevant skills include decent handwriting, knowledge of geography, (church) history, genealogy, heraldry, moral philosophy, metaphysics, medicine, economics and theology.[64] The long list surely feeds back on the image of Hojer as an erudite and versatile scholar.[65] But the *Idea* remained a torso without limbs. Of the thirteen chapters listed in the index, only the first three were realized (7–59). They elaborated on the topic of 'Nordic jurisprudence' advertised in the preliminary introduction (1–7). The following ten chapters never followed, but the titles do give us an idea of what Hojer had in mind.[66] Although the work was not completed, posthumous editions, based on manuscripts and notes from Hojer's lectures, give an impression of the full account. The editions of the *Juridical Lectures on Procedural Law* (1742, 1764, 1769) and *Public Law* (1783) are thus important testimony of Hojer's juridical work and his impact.[67]

---

63 Hojer, *Idea*, chapter 1, §§1–5.

64 Hojer, *Idea*, the remaining part of chapter one, §§6–16.

65 As with other writings stemming from Hojer's pen, the manual provoked his contemporary rival Ludvig Holberg's ridicule. With an allusion to the *Idea of a Nordic Lawyer*, Holberg published his deliberation on the *Idea of a Shoemaker*, in which he exhibited an endless list of lofty requirements necessary for this trade. Holberg Ludvig. *Epistola 293*. Copenhagen, 1750. See Müller Theodor Alfred. *Den unge Ludvig Holberg 1684–1722*. Copenhagen, 1943, 270.

66 The index of the *Idea* presents both the work Hojer realized, and the one he imagined. The expounded chapters concern: (1) prerequisites for Danish and Norwegian jurisprudence; (2) divine law, natural law and revealed law ("*de iure universali diuino, naturali et revelato*"); (3) present day jurisprudence in Denmark and Norway ("*de iurisprudentia Dano-Norwagica moderna*"). The planned chapters were devoted to: (4) the origin and history of the Danish and Norwegian Laws – and differences between old and present laws; (5) the related old Germanic laws, especially Saxon, Salic, British and Swedish law; (6) the modern laws ("*de moderna iuribus*") in the Duchy of Schleswig, especially in regard to the *ius Iutico*; (7) the present day laws in the Duchy of Holstein, especially in regard to the *ius Lubecense*; (8) the county law in Oldenburg and Delmenhorst; (9) the Roman law and its use in the king's countries; (10) Canon law and its use in the king's countries; (11) ecclesiastical law; (12) public law (*ius publicum*) in Denmark, Norway and Schleswig; and (13) German public law and its application in the Danish provinces.

67 Andreas Hojer's *Juridisk Collegium over Processen* was first edited by Hans Hagerup in 1742, followed by the enlarged edition of Christian Ditlev Hedegaard from 1764 and 1769. The *Jus Publicum* was translated and published by Peder Mortensen Bredsdorff in 1783. These editions are all available online at the Royal Library.

7. The Institutional Hub

Both Pontoppidan and Hojer's manuals were in stock at the Royal Orphanage. This institution functioned as a publishing house and a book store responsible for distributing edifying and useful books at a low price. Its collection included Bibles, Bible translations, psalm books, and books by such authors as Thomas à Kempis, Philipp Jacob Spener, August Hermann Francke, Samuel Pufendorf, Johan Franz Buddeus and Jeremias Friedrich Reuss.[68] Inspired by the model at Halle, the Royal Orphanage was inaugurated in 1727 by Frederik IV. It was a multifunctional enterprise that housed public schools, a printing press, a bookstore and an apothecary shop. It was open to visits, donations, support and advice, and it was intended to be a model for society. It had its own staff and jurisdiction, and it enjoyed royal privileges, and exemption from taxes. In return, it took care of the social welfare and education, not only of the residing orphans, but also of children of the gentry and university students.[69] Large parts of the building complex were destroyed by the fire of 1728, but the fabric was restored – a process completed in 1734. That year Andreas Hojer moved into the building, where he resided until his death in 1739. The Department for Promoting the Gospel of 1714 (*Collegium de cursu Evangelii promovendo*) and the Department for Church Supervision of 1737 (*Generalkirkeinspektionskollegiet*) were both housed in and administered from the Royal Orphanage. Not only was Hojer a member of both committees, he was soon in charge of them as well as being appointed co-director of the Orphanage.[70]

The Royal Orphanage is an important context for grasping the link between Pontoppidan and Hojer's manuals, as well as in general, the interrelationship between religious instruction, devotion, edification and the dawn of modern, secularized enlightenment thinking. This institution was a vehicle for the reforms of 1736 as well as the subsequent ones. While the Department for Promoting the Gospel (1714) was in charge of missionary activities and foreign affairs, including translation of the Bible and edifying literature, the Orphanage

---

68 See the book list advertised in Erik Pontoppidan's Collegium Pastorale. Pontoppidan Erik. "Fortegnelse Paa en Deel af det Kongelige Wäysenhuses Forlags=Bøger". In *Collegium pastorale practicum*. Copenhagen 1757.

69 No substantial account of the Royal Orphanage at Copenhagen exists in the English language. The main documents concerning the founding of the Royal Orphanage (the rescript 8 April 1720, the open letter of 21 July 1727, the constitution of the orphanage of 21 July 1727, the instruction, the regulation of 21 July 1727, and the regulation of 22 July 1727) are in Danish and published in: *Kong Frederik d. Fjerdes Anordninger, Instruks og Fundats m.m. af 21. Juli 1727*. Copenhagen, 1914, 1–33.

70 Rørdam Holger. "Blade af Waisenhusets ældste Historie". In *Kirkehistoriske Samlinger*. Vol. 4, No. 3. ed. Holger Rørdam. Copenhagen, 1893, 533–535.

Administration and from 1737 the Department for Church Supervision were focused on internal affairs. The latter was Hojer's initiative, and it was discreetly developed behind the backs of the bishops. It was designed to monitor religious affairs and oversee book censorship in order to sustain social order, which in those years was challenged by the competing forms of Pietism entering the country.[71] It was also in charge of improving educational standards, and supplying churches and schools with affordable Bibles and edifying literature. To a large degree, the new department handled assignments that already were an integral part of the Royal Orphanage administration. But the need for it increased after the 1736 reforms. The legal charter, written by Hojer, spelled out that the new office should 'unburden the religious authorities of their duties'. This inevitably meant that bishops and professors of theology were deprived of power that traditionally had belonged to them. The Department for Church Supervision was furthermore granted the authority to overrule the censorship of the press imposed by theological professors and bishops.[72] As a whole, the Royal Orphanage was an institutional hub that combined state administration, juridical competence and a will to reform and inculcate religious standards. From this centre, a variety of religious and secular interests were managed; interests that during the century were progressively disentangled and specialized into separate units.

We find an echo of the interests that were united at the Royal Orphanage in a manual for law students of 1752 published by the successor of Andreas Hojer, the professor of natural law at the University of Copenhagen Peter Kofod Ancher (1710–1788). In his first chapter, discussing whether the ground of law is based on (a) human actions or b) the will of a legislator, Ancher steers the middle course by claiming that both principles are reasonable and thus not mutually exclusive. If natural law alone is understood as the will of God, then it is reduced to strict and despotic precepts. Conversely, to reduce natural law to human action alone, is to deprive our duty of its due weight and to ignore the impact of the almighty legislator. Ancher equally points out that it takes a

---

71 The negotiations concerning the new office were kept discreet in order to avoid the episcopal interference. Hojer's decisive part as an initiator is described by Rørdam, "Studier", vol. 4, 220, 222. See also Engelhardt Juliane. "Pietisme og krise. Den Halleske og Radikale Pietisme i den danske Helstat under Christian 6." In *Historisk Tidsskrift*, 116, No. 2. Copenhagen 2016, 281–308.

72 "Patent XXI of 1 October 1737 ("Anlangende at Hans Kongl. Majestæt Allernaadigst har funden for got [sic] at anordne en General Kirke=Inspektion, som bestandig skal have Opsigt med Kirken og Geistligheden"). In *Kong Christian Den Siettes allernaadigste Forordninger og Aabne Breve* (...) Vol. 2 (1730–1746). Copenhagen, 1746, 100–105. Rørdam, Studier, vol. 4, 222–234.

Christian subject to swear an oath. If the oath taker is not a Christian believer, the oath is not valid.[73] Such statements bear witness to the impact of the 1736 reforms and the attempt to combine piety, religious education, natural law and enlightenment thinking.

8. In Conclusion

The 1736 reforms actualized the past by reforming the present, and by latching on to existing patterns, they launched new standards and norms. We have seen examples of this in two central documents pertaining to the reform of confirmation. The royal decree cast the king in the role of bishop, entering the religious domain and turning a private into a public practice. It prescribes a church ceremony and emphasizes the importance of professional catechetical instruction. The new standards for confirmation were furthermore presented as an honor to God and of benefit to the king, ensuring him loyal citizens. Pontoppidan's catechetical manual offers a view of the curriculum. The manual combines ideas of piety and early enlightenment, both in its wide-ranging concept of moral law that surpasses the traditional distinction of law and gospel; and by structuring the exposition of the ten commandments around the triptych of duties towards ourselves, others and God.

The two main texts that instituted and defined new standards for the study of law equally reflect combined religious and secular interests. Already in 1718 the thought-provoking idea was published that the prohibition of contested marriages hinged *only* on individual Christian morality. That idea was at once pious and radical; pious in its high esteem of honesty and Christian virtue; radical in disavowing all other legal support for prohibition. The statute enforced 18 years later was preoccupied with students and administrators holding juridical positions, but also aimed at promoting piety and the benefit of both state and church. It staged doctors of law as role models for students of law and for all citizens. Finally, the essay describes the Royal Orphanage as an important context for the 1736 reforms. This was where texts of religion, education and edification, enlightenment and thinking on natural law were disseminated. It was also the headquarters of the variety of interests and disciplines that were central to the modernizing efforts of the 1736 reforms.

73 Ancher Peter Kofod. *Anviisning for en Dansk Jurist, angaaende Lovkyndigheds adskillige Deele, Nytte og Hielpemidler*. Copenhagen, 1777 [first edition 1752], chapter 1, §3–§4.

Bibliography

Ancher, Peter Kofod. *Anviisning for en Dansk Jurist, angaaende Lovkyndigheds adskillige Deele, Nytte og Hielpemidler*. Copenhagen, 1777 [first edition 1752].

Bach-Nielsen, Carsten. *Fra jubelfest til kulturår Danske reformationsfejringer gennem 400 år*. Aarhus: Aarhus Universitetsforlag, 2015.

Balle, Nicolai Edinger. Lærebog i den evangelisk christelige Religion. Copenhagen, 1791.

Biblioteca Danica Systematisk fortegnelse over den danske litteratur fra 1482–1830, ed. Bruun, Christian. Copenhagen: Rosenkilde og Bagger, 1961–1965. Vol. 1. Brøndsted, Mogens. "Historien om Pontoppidans 'Forklaring' i Danmark og Norge". In *Fund og forskning*, No. 12 (1965): 48–66 (52–63).

Dänische Bibliothec oder Sammlung von alten und neuen gelehrten Sachen aus Dännemarck. Vol. 1. Copenhagen and Leipzig, 1738.

Döring, Heinrich. "Rambach. In *Die gelehrten Theologen Deutschlands im achtzehnten und neunzehnten Jahrhundert*. Neustadt a. d. Orla: Wagner, 1833, 437–446 (439).

Engelhardt, Juliane. "Pietisme og krise. Den Halleske og Radikale Pietisme i den danske Helstat under Christian 6." In *Historisk Tidsskrift*, 116, No. 2 (2016), 281–308.

Festskrift i anledning af tohundrede Aars Dagen for Indførelsen af Juridisk Eksamen ved Københavns Universitet. Eds. Erik Reitzel-Nielsen and Carl Popp-Madsen. Copenhagen, 1936.

"Forordning Angaaende den tilvoxende Ungdoms Confirmation og Bekræftelse udi deres Daabes Naade af 13. januar 1736." A transcribed version is online accessible and hosted by School of Culture and Society, Aarhus University: http://danmarksh-istorien.dk/ (consulted August 2018).

Francke, August Hermann. *Lectiones Parœneticœ*, vol. 1. Halle: Waysenhaus, 1726.

Gierl, Martin. "Pietism, Enlightenment, and Modernity". In *A Companion to German Pietism 1660–1800*, ed. Douglas Shantz. Leiden: Brill, 2014.

Glebe-Møller, Jens. "Det teologiske Fakultet 1597–1732." In *Københavns Universitet 1479–1979. Vol. 5*, ed. Leif Grane. G. E. C Gads Forlag, København, 1980, 93–211.

Grethlein, Christian, Germann, Michael. "Confirmation (Protestant)". In *Religion Past and Present*. Online version of 2011. Consulted August 2018: http://dx.doi.org.ep.fjernadgang.kb.dk/10.1163/1877-5888_rpp_COM_12065.

Haarberg, Jon. "Earways to Heaven: Singing the Catechism in Denmark-Norway, 1569–1756". In *Religious Reading in the Lutheran North: Studies in Early Modern Scandinavian Book Culture*, eds. Charlotte Appel, Morten Fink-Jensen. Cambridge Scholars Publishing, 2011.

Hersleb, Peder. *Epistola Pastoralis eller En venlig og velmeent Erindrings- og Opmuntrings Skrivelse til det vel-ærværdige, hæderlige og vel-lærte Præsteskab udi Aggerhuus Biskops=Dømme, efter Kongel. allernaadigste Befalning*. Copenhagen, Wäysenhuses Bogtrykkerie, 1737.

Hojer, Andreas. *Diagramma de nuptiis propinquorum iure divino non prohibitis.* Lemgow, 1718.

Hojer Andreas. *Ideae ICti Danici, partem I: Disputatione Anniversaria Expositam Publico Eruditorum Examini.* Copenhagen 1736.

Hojer Andreas. *Forestilling paa en Dansk Jurist.* Translated by Peder Sommer. Copenhagen 1737 and 1744.

Horstbøll, Henrik. "Pietism and the Politics of Catechisms. The Case of Denmark and Norway in the Eighteenth and Nineteenth Centuries". *Scandinavian Journal of History* 29, No 2 (2004): 143–160.

Horstbøll, Henrik. "Læsning til salighed, oplysning og velfærd: Om Pontoppidan, pietisme og lærebøger i Danmark og Norge i 17- og 1800-tallet." *Fortid og Nutid* (2003): 83–108.

Howard, Thomas Albert. *Remembering the Reformation: An Inquiry into the Meanings of Protestantism.* Oxford: Oxford University Press, 2016.

Jensen, Mads Langballe. "Serving Danish Foreign Policy. Andreas Hojer's De eo quod iure belli licet in minores (1735)" In *The Law of Nations and Natural Law 1625–1800.* Brill 2019, https://doi.org/10.1163/9789004384200_004 (accessed February 2023).

Jensen Mads Langballe. "Contests about Natural Law in Early Enlightenment Copenhagen", *History of European Ideas 42:8,* 2016, 1027–1041. http://dx.doi.org/10.1080/01916599.2016.1182045 (accessed February 2023).

Kong Christian den Femtis Danske Lov. Copenhagen, 1929.

Kong Frederik d. Fjerdes Anordninger, Instruks og Fundats m.m. af 21. Juli 1727. Copenhagen, 1914, 1–33.

Kolderup-Rosenvinge Janus Lauritz Andreas. *Grundrids af den danske Kirkeret.* Copenhagen, 1851 [first edition 1834], §24: "Om den danske evangelisk=lutherske Kirkes Forhold til Staten efter Aaret 1660".

Krumbiegel, Friedemann. *Erziehung in den Pastoralbriefen. Ein Konzept zur Konsolidierung der Gemeinden. Arbeiten zur Bibel und ihrer Geschichte.* Leipzig: Evangelische Verlagsanstalt, 2013, 13–4; 24–9.

Larsen Kurt E. "Pontoppidan versus Spener: No 'better times' but more personal piety within the national Church". In *Pietismus und Neuzeit 45,* 2021, 117–142.

Lindhardt, Poul Georg. *Konfirmationens historie i Danmark.* Copenhagen: Lohse, 1936,

Markussen, Ingrid. *Til Skaberens Ære, Statens Tjeneste og Vor Egen Nytte: Pietistiske og kameralistiske idéer bag fremvæksten af en offentlig skole i landdistrikterne i 1700-tallet.* Odense: Odense Universitetsforlag, 1995.

Mejrup, Kristian. "Grand Prospects of Halle Pietism: The Acrobat, the Project-maker and the Shepherd". PhD-dissertation. Copenhagen: *Publikationer fra Det Teologiske Fakultet 64,* 2016.

Mejrup, Kristian. "Instruktioner i frelse: Det pietistiske skoleprojekt og Pastoralbrevene" In *Forum for Bibelsk Eksegese 20: Bibelen og reformationen.* Eds. Gitte Buch-Hansen et al. Copenhagen: Eksistensen, 2017 (open acces: http://teol.ku.dk/abe/publikationer/forum_for_bibelsk_eksegese/bibelen-og-reformationen/12_Mejrup_FBE_20_1_.pdf).

Mejrup Kristian. "Andreas Hojer (1690–1739) – The Standard-Bearer of Danish-Norwegian Pietism" In *Law and the Christian Tradition in Scandinavia. The Writings of Great Nordic Jurists*. Eds Kjell Åke Modeer and Helle Vogt. Routledges Law and Religion Series. New York, 2021, 180–195.

Mejrup Kristian og Nørgaard Cyril Lars. "Den pietistiske bibellæser og de helliges hermeneutik. Eksegese og formaning i Halle-teologen Rambachs forelæsninger". In *Bibelske konfiguratoner i kunst og kultur*. Eds. Gitte Buch-Hansen and Jesper Tang Nielsen. København: Eksistensen Akademisk, 2021, 117–138.

Müller, Theodor Alfred. *Den unge Ludvig Holberg 1684–1722*. Copenhagen, 1943.

Neiiendam, Michael. *Erik Pontoppidan II (1735–1764) Studier og Bidrag til Pietismens Historie*. Copenhagen, Gad, 1933, 77–81.

Olson, James B. "Erik Ludvigsen Pontoppidan and the American Influence of His Catechism". In *The Lutheran Historical Conference, Essays and Reports 1990*. Vol. 14. *Lutheranism and Pietism*. Minneapolis, 1992, 20–39.

"Patent XXI of 1 October 1737 ("Anlangende at Hans Kongl. Majestæt Allernaadigst har funden for got [sic] at anordne en General Kirke=Inspektion, som bestandig skal have Opsigt med Kirken og Geistligheden"). In *Kong Christian Den Siettes allernaadigste Forordninger og Aabne Breve* (…) Vol. 2 (1730–1746)

Pedersen, Johannes. "Pietismens Tid 1699–1746. In *Den Danske Kirkes Historie*, eds. Hal Koch, Bjørn Kornerup. Copenhagen, 1951, 11–227.

Pontoppidan, Erik. *Sandhed til Gudfrygtighed udi en eenfoldig og efter Muelighed kort, dog tilstrekkelig Forklaring over Sal. Doct. Mort. Luthers Liden Catechismo*. Copenhagen. Wäysenhuses Forlag, 1770 [first edition 1737].

Pontoppidan, Erik. *Collegium pastorale practicum*. Copenhagen, 1757.

Pufendorf, Samuel. *Et Menniskes og en Borgers Pligter efter Naturens Lov, beskrevne i det latinske Sprog*. Translated by Christian Homfred bugman. Copenhagen: Det Kongelige Vajsenhus, 1742.

Rambach, Johann Jakob. *Der wohlunterrichtete Catechet, das ist deutlicher Unterricht wie man der Jugend auf die ellerleichteste Art den Grund der christlichen Lehre beybringen könne, darinnen die wichtigsten Vortheile, die bey dem Catechisiren in acht zu nehmen sind, treulich entdecket werden*. Jena, 1722.

Rambach, Johann Jakob. *Monita catechetica, eller Catechetiske Betænkninger, hvilke meddeele os I. M. Johan Jac. Rambachs Vel underrettet Catechet, hvor udi den allerletteste Maade og de vigtigste Fordeele, som ere at tage i agt hos Catechisationen troligen vises. II. Doct. Phil. Jac. Speners Tanker om Catechismus-Information, af den sal. Mands Skrifter, og særdeles af hans Theologiske Betænkninger sammensøgte, og i en Samtale forestillede*. Copenhagen, 1728 (second edition 1731, third edition 1744).

Rørdam, Holger. "Blade af Waisenhusets ældste Historie". In *Kirkehistoriske Samlinger*. Vol. 4, No. 3, ed. Holger Rørdam. Copenhagen, 1893, 533–535.

Rørdam, Holger. *Historiske Samlinger og Studier vedrørende danske forhold og personligheder især i det 17. Århundrede*. Vol. 1, Copenhagen, 1891, 403.

Rørdam, Holger. *Historiske Samlinger og Studier vedrørende danske forhold og personligheder især i det 17. Århundrede*. Vol. 4, Copenhagen, 1902, 151–160.

Schou, Jacob Henric. *Chronologisk Register over de kongelige Forordninger og aabne Breve, samt andre trykte Anordninger, som fra Aar 1670 ere udkomne* (…). Part 3: 1730–1746. Copenhagen, 1795.

Spener, Philipp Jakob. *Einfältige Erklärung Der Christlichen Lehre Nach der Ordnung Des kleinen Catechismi Des theuren Mannes Gottes Lutheri*. Halle: Waysenhaus, 1717 [First edition Frankfurt 1677].

Spener, Philipp Jakob. *Den christelige Lærdoms eenfoldige Udleggelse efter D. M. Lutheri liden Catechismi Orden*. Copenhagen: Missionskollegiet 1728 (second edition 1730, third edition 1740).

Stopa, Sasja Emilie Mathiasen "A communion of saints? Reincorporating sinners into the created order of eighteenth-century Denmark through catechetical practice". In *Pietismus und Neuzeit 45*, 2021, 84-116.

Von Lips Herman. *Glaube – Gemeinde – Amt, zum Verständnis der Ordination in den Pastoralbriefen*. Göttingen: Vandenhoeck & Ruprecht, 1979, 38.

Von Lips Hermann. "Der Gedanke des Vorbilds im Neuen Testament". In *Evangelische Theologie* 58. No 4 (1998), 295–309.

Von Lips Hermann. "Von den 'Pastoralbriefen' zum 'Corpus Pastorale': Eine Hallische Sprachschöpfung und ihr modernes Pendant als Funktionsbestimmungdreier neutestamentlicher Briefe." In *Reformation und Neuzeit 300 Jahre Theologie in Halle*, ed. Udo Schnelle. Berlin / New York: De Gruyter, 1994, 49–71.

Contributors

Bastubacka, Johan
Adjunct Professor of Practical Theology, University of Helsinki, Finland

Bühmann, Henning
Dr. phil., Wissenschaftlicher Mitarbeiter, Chair of Church History, University of Göttingen, Germany

Decock, Wim
Professor of Roman Law, Legal History and Comparative Law, UCLouvain and ULiège, Belgium

Mejrup, Kristian
PhD. in Church History, University of Copenhagen, Denmark

Modéer, Kjell Åke
Professor emeritus in Legal History, Lund University, Sweden

Rasmussen, Tarald
Professor emeritus in Church History, University of Oslo, Norway

Schmoeckel, Mathias
Executive Director of the Institute of German and Rhenish Legal History and Civil Law, University of Bonn, Germany

Sunde, Jørn Øyrehagen
Professor of Legal History, University of Oslo, Norway

Index of Names